W9-CMA-950

"With this revised edition of *Cut by Cut*, Chandler has written a book which will become a bible to all those interested in film and video editing. There was no book I could rely on in my days as a film editor. *Cut by Cut, 2nd Ed.*, would have squared that away."
— Jim Clark, Academy Award-winner for editing *The Killing Fields*, nominee for *The Mission*, and author of *Dream Repairman: Adventures in Film Editing*

"Masterful, concise, and illuminating.... *Cut by Cut, 2nd Ed.*, covers all aspects of film editing, right up to the latest digital breakthroughs, and Chandler manages to make it all immensely readable and entertaining...the mark of a great film editor! A must for every student and lover of film."
— Joan Sobel, A.C.E., *A Single Man* and *Being Flynn*

"An invaluable resource, filled with concise step-by-step explanations that do a fantastic job of demystifying the editing process. While I especially recommend *Cut By Cut, 2nd Ed.*, for aspiring editors, it deserves a place on the bookshelf of working editors as well, where it is sure to become a trusted resource."
— Rob Goubeaux, A.C.E., supervising editor/producer, *Beyond Scared Straight*

"What most impresses me about this invaluable text is the way the author embraces new technology and wrestles it down to the very basic concept of storytelling. With insightful comments from today's top editors, *Cut by Cut, 2nd Ed.*, is both an important primer for aspiring editors looking to improve their craft and an articulate resource to keep editors at the top of their game."
— Michael Ruscio, A.C.E., director/editor, *True Blood*, HBO

"Those interested in film editing or wanting to expand their knowledge to advance beyond the button-pusher role should read this book, which illustrates the foundation of editing. Chandler balances the importance of both advanced technique along with a strong grasp of day-to-day cutting room activities."
— Gordon Burkell, founder, Art of the Guillotine, www.aotg.com

"The second edition of Chandler's book is a quantum leap forward. *Cut by Cut, 2nd Ed.*, is the most comprehensive and understandable text available for both students and professionals on the art and craft of editing in the 21st century. It should be the required text for every class on editing."
— Jack Tucker, A.C.E., editor and teacher, CSULB, CSUN, and UCLA. First winner of the Robert Wise Award for Promoting the Art and Craft of Film Editing.

"Chandler's *Cut by Cut, 2nd Ed.*, is a practical masterpiece. By thoroughly detailing the editing process, both historically and technically, it empowers new filmmakers with the skills and knowledge they need to realize their visual dreams."
— Ken Roth, award-winning documentary producer and professor, Digital Media Arts, California State University, Dominguez Hills

"*Cut by Cut, 2nd Ed.*, is an excellent and comprehensive introduction and exploration of the craft and art of film and digital editing. Chandler demystifies editing technology and reveals the creative work flows and storytelling secrets of professional editors. I highly recommended the book for aspiring editors, assistants, and anyone who is interested in how motion pictures are made."
— Mark Goldblatt, A.C.E., *Rise of the Planet of the Apes, Terminator 1* and *2, Starship Troopers,* and *Armageddon*

"This encyclopedic gem deftly defines complicated terminology, so that the art and science of cutting is readily accessible to a wide range of practitioners and students alike. It is mandatory reading for anyone interested in fully grasping the technical and aesthetic foundations of storytelling in moving pictures and sound."
— Paris Poirier, associate professor, Film Studies & Entertainment Technology, Santa Monica College

"*Cut by Cut, 2nd Ed.*, is an essential guide for aspiring and professional editors and *should be required reading for anyone who really wants to direct.* Chandler gives us a bird's-eye view of what it takes to create our invisible art while proving that we are not invisible artists. This truly amazing book has the info that new filmmakers need to embark on their projects."
— Briana London, A.C.E., *Army Wives, Necessary Roughness, Grey's Anatomy, Crossing Jordan, Northern Exposure,* and A.C.E. Eddie winner

"*Cut by Cut, 2nd Ed.*, demystifies the art of film editing. Chandler breaks down the editorial process both technically and creatively. She lets the reader experience the choices and decisions editors confront on a daily basis. You are taken into the heart and mind of the editor wherever or whatever they're cutting: on a feature, TV, YouTube or off an iPhone."
— Bruce Cannon, film editor, *Boyz n the Hood, Higher Learning, Baby Boy, 2 Fast 2 Furious, Four Brothers, Abduction*

"*Cut by Cut, 2nd Ed.*, provides a wealth of valuable information for novices and industry professionals alike. Chandler's extensive post production knowledge and editing experience are evident throughout the text and a solid foundation for the book. Detailed, practical information is clearly and simply presented, making this a valuable reference for anyone interested in post production and editing."
— Jill Mittan, operations manager, Warner Brothers Advanced Media Services

"Gael Chandler, noted picture editor and author, has completely reworked her seminal book *Cut by Cut,* updating it from the ground up to reflect the ever-changing technical landscape of the filmmaking process. All serious editors will want this guide to always be within arm's reach."
— Woody Woodhall, CAS; president, Allied Post; founder, The Los Angeles Post Production Group; author, *Audio Production and Postproduction*

"Chandler's informative book illustrates how the editor's job and tools are rapidly changing. Now a fellow artistic filmmaker, the Editor, partnered with the Director and the Cinematographer, form a trio that defines the film from Pre-Production through Post. The Story. The Look. The Pace. The Magic."
— Kelley Dixon, editor, *Breaking Bad*

"Chandler's love of editing — the craft, the process, and the results — makes *Cut By Cut, 2nd Ed.*, an excellent resource and friend, whether you are getting a project started or in the middle of a mess because you didn't plan ahead. Editing requires practice, training, and experience; without them, you can waste a lot of resources. Read *Cut by Cut* and be way ahead."
— Patrick Gregston, two-time Emmy editing nominee, past Editors' Guild Board member, producer

# GAEL**CHANDLER**

# **CUT**BY**CUT**

## **Editing Your Film or Video 2nd EDITION**

MICHAEL WIESE PRODUCTIONS

Published by Michael Wiese Productions
12400 Ventura Blvd. #1111
Studio City, CA 91604
(818) 379-8799, (818) 986-3408 (FAX)
mw@mwp.com
www.mwp.com

Cover design by MWP
Interior design by William Morosi
Edited by David Wright
Printed by McNaughton & Gunn

Manufactured in the United States of America

Copyright © 2012 by Gael Chandler
All rights reserved. No part of this book may be reproduced in any form or by any means without permission
in writing from the author, except for the inclusion of brief quotations in a review.

Library of Congress Cataloging-in-Publication Data

Chandler, Gael
 Cut by cut : editing your film or video / by Gael Chandler. -- 2nd ed.
     p. cm.
 Includes bibliographical references and index.
 ISBN 978-1-61593-090-6
 1. Motion pictures--Editing. 2. Video tapes--Editing. I. Title. II. Title: Editing your film or video.
 TR899.C45 2012
 777'.55--dc23
                              2012003410


Printed on Recycled Stock

To Mary Beth Denny Chandler and Robert W. Chandler,
who showed me the value of reading and continuous learning,
with ever-loving gratitude.

# Contents

List of Tables . . . . . . . . . . . . . . . . . . . . . . . . . . . . . . . . . . . . . . . x

2nd Edition Foreword . . . . . . . . . . . . . . . . . . . . . . . . . . . . . . . . xi

1st Edition Foreword . . . . . . . . . . . . . . . . . . . . . . . . . . . . . . . . . xiv

Preface: The Practical Alchemy of Editing . . . . . . . . . . . . . . . . . . xvii

Acknowledgments . . . . . . . . . . . . . . . . . . . . . . . . . . . . . . . . . . xix

Permissions . . . . . . . . . . . . . . . . . . . . . . . . . . . . . . . . . . . . . . . xx

Introduction: Stepping Aboard and Navigating the Book . . . . . . . . . . xxiii

## STAGE I
## SETTING UP AND ORGANIZING YOUR PROJECT

Introduction . . . . . . . . . . . . . . . . . . . . . . . . . . . . . . . . . . . . . . . 1

## Part One
## Starting Your Project

Introduction . . . . . . . . . . . . . . . . . . . . . . . . . . . . . . . . . . . . . . . 2

**1.** Decisions, Decisions: Getting Started on the Right Path
through Postproduction . . . . . . . . . . . . . . . . . . . . . . . . . . . . . . . 3

Appendix A   Project Checklist . . . . . . . . . . . . . . . . . . . . . . . . . . 26

**2.** Video, Digital, and Film Basics: Terms, Concepts, and Practices . . . . 28

## Part Two
## Organizing for Editing

Introduction . . . . . . . . . . . . . . . . . . . . . . . . . . . . . . . . . . . . . . . 64

**3.** Setting Up the Cutting Room: Workflows, Labeling Shots,
and Other Common Cutting Room Tasks . . . . . . . . . . . . . . . . . . . . 65

Appendix B   DIY Postproduction Schedule . . . . . . . . . . . . . . . . . . . . . 100
**4.** Preparing Dailies
Appendix C   Stage One: Budget Form for Dailies . . . . . . . . . . . . . . . . 101

## STAGE II
## EDITING

Introduction. . . . . . . . . . . . . . . . . . . . . . . . . . . . . . . . . . . . . . . . . . 139

## Part One
## How to Approach the Footage

Introduction. . . . . . . . . . . . . . . . . . . . . . . . . . . . . . . . . . . . . . . . . 140
**5.** To Cut or Not to Cut: Where to Cut and Why . . . . . . . . . . . . . . . 141
**6.** Everyday Editing Challenges. . . . . . . . . . . . . . . . . . . . . . . . . . . . 172
**7.** From Animation to Reality: Editing Different Genres. . . . . . . . . . . 193

## Part Two
## Getting from First Cut to Final Cut

Introduction. . . . . . . . . . . . . . . . . . . . . . . . . . . . . . . . . . . . . . . . . 222
**8.** Making the Cuts: Editing on a Digital System . . . . . . . . . . . . . . . 223
**9.** The Process: Getting from First Cut to Locked Cut . . . . . . . . . . . . 252
Appendix D   Tape and Tapeless Show Continuity Form . . . . . . . . . . 276
Appendix E   Film Show Continuity Form . . . . . . . . . . . . . . . . . . . . . 277
Appendix F   Stage Two: Budget Form for Editing. . . . . . . . . . . . . . . 278

## STAGE III
## COMPLETING YOUR PROJECT

Introduction. . . . . . . . . . . . . . . . . . . . . . . . . . . . . . . . . . . . . . . . . 279

## Part One
## Sound, Music, and the Mix

Introduction. . . . . . . . . . . . . . . . . . . . . . . . . . . . . . . . . . . . . . . . . 280
**10.** Designing Sound and Music . . . . . . . . . . . . . . . . . . . . . . . . . . . 281
**11.** Editing and Mixing Sound and Music . . . . . . . . . . . . . . . . . . . . 311
Appendix G   ADR Cue Sheet
Appendix H   Stage Three: Budget Form for Sound, Music,
and the Mix . . . . . . . . . . . . . . . . . . . . . . . . . . . . . . . . . . . . . . . . . . 338

# Part Two
# Finishing and Delivering

Introduction. . . . . . . . . . . . . . . . . . . . . . . . . . . . . . . . . . . . . . . . 342

**12.** Finishing on Tape, File, or the Web. . . . . . . . . . . . . . . . . . . 343

**13.** Finishing on Film and via Digital Intermediary. . . . . . . . . . . . . 385

Final Wrap-Up . . . . . . . . . . . . . . . . . . . . . . . . . . . . . . . . . . . . 407

Appendix I   Stage Three: Budget Form for Finishing. . . . . . . . . . . . 408

How to Find an Editing Job . . . . . . . . . . . . . . . . . . . . . . . . . . . . 410

Resources . . . . . . . . . . . . . . . . . . . . . . . . . . . . . . . . . . . . . . . 418

Glossary . . . . . . . . . . . . . . . . . . . . . . . . . . . . . . . . . . . . . . . . 425

Bibliography . . . . . . . . . . . . . . . . . . . . . . . . . . . . . . . . . . . . . 463

Index. . . . . . . . . . . . . . . . . . . . . . . . . . . . . . . . . . . . . . . . . . 469

About the Author . . . . . . . . . . . . . . . . . . . . . . . . . . . . . . . . . . 477

# List Of Tables

**1.1.** Coding and Measuring

**1.2.** Determine Your Finishing Format

**1.3.** Film and Video Formats: How Shows are Shot, Input, and Finished

**2.1.** Digital vs. Analog Video

**2.2.** Worldwide Tape and Television Signal Standards

**2.3.** Drop and Non-Drop Time Code

**2.4.** NTSC Frame Size, fps, and Scanning Types

**2.5.** Retrofitting a 16:9 to a 4:3 Aspect Ratio

**3.1.** Typical Postproduction Schedules

**4.1.** Reel Labeling Methods

**4.2.** TV Series and Multi-cam Show Labeling Methods

**4.3.** Daily Database from Telecine

**4.4.** Database File for Telecined Negative

**4.5.** How Data Typically Enters the Editing System

**4.6.** Telecined Negative Database File Entry

**5.1.** Smooth Cutting Angles

**5.2.** Mismatched Shots and How to Fix Them

**5.3.** Editing Styles: Classic vs. Modern

**6.1.** Parallel Action and Cross Cutting

**6.2.** Examples of Montage Types

**6.3.** Scenarios for Cutting Pictures and Music

**8.1.** Insert and Overwrite Edits

**8.2.** Types of VFX

**9.1.** Three Methods to Play Out to Tape

**9.2.** Sample Change List

**10.1.** Translating Story to Sound and Music

**10.2.** Scene Beats, Sound, and the Wizard of Oz

**10.3.** Types of SFX and Viewer Perception

**11.1.** ADR Cue Sheet

**11.2.** Sound Effects Mix Cue Sheet

**12.1.** Disk Sides and Layers

**12.2.** EDL vs. Project Files

**13.1.** Fixes for Cutback Frames and Frame Re-use

**13.2.** Sample Cutlist with Key Codes

# 2nd Edition Foreword

Filmmaking is a complicated, collaborative art form. We tend to think that the director is always at the helm. He or she is, ultimately. But the film editor has a definite seat of power. One thing I've learned from writing, directing, and editing my own films over the last 20 years, is that it's really *not* a good idea to edit your own films! It's a wonderful feeling to put the material you've nurtured by writing and shooting it into the hands of the puzzle-master — the editor. The editor — who wasn't there on the set to witness how long it took to set up the shot — can see your footage for what it is and simply consider, "Does the shot move the story forward in the best way possible?" The editor pieces together the story, often coming up with something completely unique and different from the words of the script and surprising the director who wonders, "Did I really shoot that?"

Anyone with a computer and a video camera can shoot and edit a film today. So what makes the difference between a good film and "Cousin-Bobby-shot-a-movie-and-wants-us-to-come-over–and-watch-it" type of film? It's the choices/decisions that are made when the film is written, shot, and edited. Editing choices determine point-of-view, giving the audience that glorious, vicarious feeling of being the hero. Mark Rydell, the director of *On Golden Pond* and *The Rose*, equates editing to creating a sculpture: You chisel and cut away the pieces to reveal the art, keeping only what you need and nothing that you don't.

With newer computer editing systems coming out every day, editing choices are practically endless. Add to that all the cool fades, dissolves, transitions, and colors and you've got an almost professional level of editing system at your fingertips. There are many books that will tell you *how* to work the machines to make edits. Although *Cut by Cut: Editing*

*Your Film or Video* isn't tied to any one software, it thoroughly covers software and how to operate a digital system from dailies through delivery.

However, machines don't make edits. Editors make edits. This book will give you a place to explore the *why*. Why choose this shot and not that one? Why go from this angle to a closer angle? Editing is making tons of little decisions so that, in the end, it looks like no editing at all and lets the story shine through.

This second edition of Gael Chandler's book shares the years of her wisdom in the cutting room, where she interfaced with all types of personalities and deadlines. With up-to-date info on editing digital media, Web content, reality shows, and 3-D, she propels her wisdom into the ever-updating future. This book is a tried and true compass that can help the student filmmaker as well as a seasoned professional navigate the ever-changing waters of the editing world. It stands on its own and its *how-to* and *why* will always outlast any new editing work systems that will inevitably come out tomorrow.

Though I write, direct, and edit my own short films and commercials, I'm primarily known in the industry for being a supervising sound editor — specifically, supervising and editing production dialogue and ADR on feature films. (If you don't know what ADR is, you can look it up in this book!) Sound editors must interface with picture editors as well as directors: No job in the filmmaking process is done in a vacuum. We must coordinate and talk to each other. Gael's book helps people in and out of postproduction communicate to make the process as smooth as possible, saving time, money, and headache.

I have known Gael as a friend and colleague for over 30 years — from 35mm film to digital images — and her passion for editing has never waned. A good writer — like a good teacher — doesn't just impart knowledge and experience, but offers a way for readers to think of solutions for themselves. This is Gael's gift to editors, students, indie filmmakers, and professionals. Her guidebook will put you at the helm of the editing process from production to final delivery. While editing tools and media change — and this book thoroughly covers them — the way we *think* about telling a story with images doesn't. Use it to help tell your story the best way possible.

**Victoria Rose Sampson**
Born in a trim bin (look *that* up) to a director and film editor father, Sherman Rose, and the first woman sound editor to win an Oscar, Kay

Rose. For over 30 years, she has supervised and/or edited the sound on such films as *Ironweed, Ordinary People, On Golden Pond, The Rose, The River, Romancing the Stone, Return of the Jedi, Clan of the Cave Bear, Donnie Darko, Speed, Sex and the City 1* and 2, and *Scream 4*. She's also written and directed award-winning short films *Click Three Times,* starring Isabel Sanford, and the grand prize–winning Harley Davidson advertisement *Her Need for Speed.* She belongs to the Academy of Motion Picture Arts and Sciences and serves on the board of directors for The Alliance of Women Directors.

# 1st Edition Foreword

I'm often asked what is my favorite part of directing a movie and my standard reply is that I'm still waiting to find a part of it that I enjoy — and there is a great deal of truth to that statement. Making a film is both the greatest job in the world and also one of the worst. I find there is little singular enjoyment in what is basically a primitive manufacturing job (little has really changed in filmmaking since the advent of sound some 80 years ago). This challenges you to inspire 150 some-odd people to help complete far too much work each day for four to five months… during which you seem to subsist on nothing but donuts, coffee, and meals which make you long for your Jr. High cafeteria, and sleep as little as a child molester on his first night in San Quentin.

But in fact there is a part of filmmaking that I do cherish and that is the editing process. Finally relieved of the pressures of production and far removed from the hectic scouting, casting, and endless rewriting, you can finally sit in a quiet room for weeks on end and take the hundreds and hundreds of thousands of feet of tiny individual frames and study them, and arrange, and then re-arrange them until (hopefully) you've told a story capable of moving an audience to laugh, or cry, or think.

Film is an illusion; in fact "moving pictures" don't move, it's our persistence of vision that turns twenty-four still pictures a second into motion pictures. We create the illusion that a man can fly by no more than hanging him on piano wires in front of a stretched sheet of blue cloth and give the appearance of velocity simply by blowing his hair with a fan and making an occasional burst of smoke.

Filmmakers are experienced magicians and nowhere are these black arts practiced with more skill than in the editing room. There are no secrets to success in this field; the tools necessary to succeed are common sense and the ability to open yourself up to the endless possibilities available in assembling the pieces to a puzzle in which you create the means by which they fit together.

It is a process that requires patience, vision, and, above all, imagination; for rarely does the finished product come together as you originally envisioned it. It is a process governed by many "rules" (for example, matching positions with people and objects, though breaking these rules is often unimportant). For instance, in a key scene in *Scent of a Woman*, the ash of Al Pacino's cigarette varies widely from cut to cut, but one is so absorbed in his masterful performance, you don't notice or care.

And breaking the "rules" can sometimes produce exhilarating results. Witness Jean Luc Goddard's jump cuts in *Breathless;* or consider Academy Award-winning editor Sheldon Kahn's solution to director Sydney Pollack's anguish over the fact that Robert Redford and Meryl Streep's single kiss in *Out of Africa* was too brief; Kahn printed twelve additional copies of the kiss and strung them one after another and made the moment unforgettable.

Nor do you have to be a Hollywood professional to practice this visual sleight of hand. Thanks to home video cameras and affordable editing software, you have access to everything we have at the studio, except maybe the kid who picks up lunch. I must confess that some of the most satisfying work I've ever done has been by marking special family occasions; by making short films composed of nothing but stills, home movies, and a piece of music. Simply by editing, by choosing which image follows each previous image and building the life stories of the people, it's possible to illuminate the poetry and beauty of everyday life.

Although some directors edit their own work (James Cameron, John Sayles, and Robert Rodriguez), and others (Robert Wise, Hal Ashby, and Raja Gosnell) began their careers as editors, I have always enjoyed the company and collaboration of a film editor. In my experience, editors are the most skilled, calmest, and happiest people I've ever known.

Gael Chandler and I have sat side-by-side for months on end working in television and features creating our illusions, and I've enjoyed every minute of it. Gael is a pioneer in electronic editing and all of her work reflects her vision, skills, and kind spirit.

This book is the sum of her knowledge derived from years in the trenches holding the hands of anxious directors, meeting producers' impossible deadlines, and making writers' dreams realities.

Gael cannot make your creative decisions for you, but she can assist you by sharing her substantive knowledge on every phase of this complex, creative process... and I hope you enjoy her assisting you in reaching your goals as much as I have. Good Luck.

**Brian Levant**

Director of *Vanilla Gorilla, The Spy Next Door, The Flintstones* (both movies), *Jingle All the Way, Problem Child 2* and *3*, and *Beethoven.*

Producer on *Scooby Doo (*TV movies)*, The New Leave it to Beaver, Happy Days, Mork & Mindy*, and *The Bad New Bears* and other series.

# Preface

*The Landscape of Editing Today*

In the introduction to the 2004 (first) edition of *Cut by Cut* I stated, "We're in the midst of a digital technological revolution that annually changes the editorial landscape." This statement has proved true in the intervening years: In 2005 YouTube emerged on the scene, in 2007 Final Cut Pro outsold Avid 2:1, and in 2009 broadcast TV went digital. In the course of writing this second edition, Apple launched Final Cut Pro X, a three-camera app for shooting on cell phones appeared, and the Streamys, the Web series awards show, failed to revive itself after its 2010 debacle. So the revolution — more like a hyper evolution — rages on with no sign of let-up.

## What's new

Today's editors are more focused on what codec to use than what Kodak's up to. With that in mind, I have gone through each section of the book, word by word, and brought all material up to date. I've created workflows for film, tape, and file-based shows and updated music and sound editing workflows as well as the disk authoring workflow. I have placed the two chapters about editing directly on film work print online at my website www.joyoffilmediting.com where you can download them from the Free tab. I have retained and updated all the information necessary for shooting, finishing, and delivering on film including creating cutlists and understanding the negative cutting process. I have expanded the section on the Digital Intermediary (DI) with a new workflow and added HD and 3-D practices throughout the book.

To prepare this new edition, I interviewed fifteen editors working in all film genres from comedy to news to music videos to reality shows.

I've included their experiences and advice along with that of esteemed feature editors and other postproduction personnel. You'll hear from them extensively in an expanded Stage II, Part Two which is all about how to approach and edit the footage to create dynamic, engaging stories. It features a new section that takes a thorough look at the modern MTV editing style, contrasting it with the traditional cutting style.

## Last words before we begin

While the landscape continues to morph faster than you can key in virtual trees, and the sky's the limit with video effects, the solid ground of editing principles and practices holds firm: You still have to log and view dailies, you still need to tell a story well, and you still must deliver a show that connects with your audience. And so *Cut by Cut*, 2nd Edition, sets out to traverse the current terrain of postproduction. The book will illuminate the new practices and devices as well as the tried and true methods, all with the aim of guiding you and your project through the territory from start to finish.

Editing, like the rest of filmmaking, fluctuates between the magical and mundane. It demands organization and inspiration, listening to the director's intent and melding it with the reality of the footage, and the ability to shift from the intimacy of one scene to the broad view of the entire show and back in an instant. And so, once again, I invite you into the cutting room with all its rhythms and routines, both profound and practical. Onward and forward!

# Acknowledgments

Like an awardee accepting an Oscar, I know that none of this would be possible without a posse of generous experts behind me. Boundless thanks to:

Lori Motyer for always believing and Bruce Motyer for the extensive tour of Technicolor.

Jayne Weber for her illustrious drawings and Chris Senchack for his unmatchable photos.

Rachelle Dang and Les Perkins for taking the time to be interviewed and providing much follow-up information.

Herb Dow for the lunch salon of bountiful connections and good food.

All the interviewees: David Abramson, Ryan Byrne, Barry Cohen, Adam Coleite, Dean Gonzalez, Sue Odjakjian, Liz McHale, Carol Mike, Fred Peterson, Lugh Powers, Steve Rasch, Victoria Rose Sampson, Joan Sobel, and Tim Tobin.

Marcia Bauman, Suhail Kafity, Jane MacNett, Mickey McGovern, Jenee Muyeaux, and Sharon Holley Smith for invaluable help along the way.

Ken Lee and Michael Wiese for making it all possible once again.

David Wright and Bill Morosi for their painstaking professionalism in copyediting and laying out the manuscript.

Sherry Green, who dreamed up the rewrite idea and aided and abetted the effort the entire way.

# Permissions

All illustrations are by Jayne Weber. All charts and photos (unless credited) are by the author. All quotes, unless spoken in the author's presence, are credited in the bibliography.

The author is grateful to the following virtual friends and brief acquaintances for their time and effort in providing photo material: Sean Williams, Paul de Cham, and Terence Curren of AlphaDogs; Noreen Lovoi, consultant to Adobe; DIT Tom Turley; Celia Donnoli of ARRI; Nicole Figuccio from Panasonic; Heather Mayer and Suzanne Lezotte of Panavision; Gabriel Whyel of Fostex; Kimberley Fuller, partner at Delamere Marketing for DFT Spirit Datacine; Ed Meyers of Canon; Rich Montez of The Whipping Post; Nick Shilling of Avid; Tony Schmitz of Voice Over There; Kim Bova, Andika Dungan, David Mallory, F. Hudson Miller, and Dan Weeks.

The author acknowledges the copyright owners of the following motion pictures from which single frames have been used in this book for purposes of commentary, criticism, and scholarship under the Fair Use Doctrine.

*127 Hours* ©2010 Twentieth Century Fox, All Rights Reserved.

*Avatar* ©2010 Twentieth Century Fox, All Rights Reserved.

*Bored to Death,* "The Case of the Missing Screenplay" ©2009 Home Box Office, Inc, All Rights Reserved.

*Brick City,* "Summer Is Ours" ©2009 Brick City TV and Sundance Channel, All Rights Reserved.

*Burn Notice,* "Devil You Know" ©2010 USA Today, All Rights Reserved.

*Bury My Heart at Wounded Knee* ©2007 Home Box Office, Inc, All Rights Reserved.

*Dexter*, Ep. 305 ©2008 Showtime Networks Inc, All Rights Reserved.

*Fahrenheit 9/11* ©2006 Lions Gate Films, All Rights Reserved.

*Friday Night Lights,* Season 4, Ep. 1, "East of Dillon" and Ep. 3, "In the Skin of a Lion" ©2010 Universal Media Studios, Imagine Television, and FILM 44, All Rights Reserved.

*Glee,* "The Power of Madonna" ©2010 Twentieth Century Fox, All Rights Reserved.

*Hot Fuzz* ©2007 Rogue Pictures/Universal Pictures, All Rights Reserved.

*How I Met Your Mother,* "The Playbook" ©2010 Twentieth Century Fox, All Rights Reserved.

*Import Export* trailer ©2009 Palisades Tartan, All Rights Reserved.

*Modern Family* Pilot ©2010 Twentieth Century Fox, All Rights Reserved.

*Nurse Jackie,* Season 2, Ep. 212 ©2010 Showtime and Lion's Gate, All Rights Reserved.

*Paprika* ©2006 Madhouse/Paprika Film Partners/Sony Pictures Entertainment, All Rights Reserved.

*Parks and Recreation,* "Hunting Trip" ©2009 Universal Pictures, All Rights Reserved.

*Spider-Man 2* ©2004 Marvel/Columbia Pictures, All Rights Reserved.

*The Aviator* ©2004 Miramax, All Rights Reserved.

*The Constant Gardener* ©2005 Focus Features/Universal Pictures, All Rights Reserved.

*The Office,* "Niagara" ©2009 Universal, All Rights Reserved.

*United 93* ©2006 Universal Pictures, All Rights Reserved.

*When the Levees Broke: A Requiem in Four Acts* ©2007 HBO, All Rights Reserved.

# Introduction

Just as every film has a beginning, middle, and end, so does the process of making a film. You start the journey in preproduction when you write a script or compose a nonfiction video outline. You continue the journey in production when you film the actors or follow your documentary subject. You complete the journey in postproduction by taking the raw (shot) material and making it into a finished project. Postproduction, commonly called editing, determines how your project will turn out, despite or because of what you've planned. Editing writes the end of the story.

## What *Cut by Cut, 2nd Ed.,* Covers

Your project can be a drama, documentary, comedy, music video, Web short, commercial; anything of any length destined for viewing in a theater or on TV, the Web, a home entertainment system, or mobile device. This book guides you through the editing process from dailies to destination. It defines a myriad of cutting room terms and practices — film, video, digital, music, sound, and more — and explains how to:

- Log dailies, set up a cutting room, make a post schedule, and prepare dailies.
- Edit dialogue, action, and montage scenes and add music and narration.
- Cheat shots, add reactions, make overlaps, and deal with mismatches, pace, and many other common editing challenges.
- Work on a digital editing system and take a show from dailies to locked cut.
- Design sound and prepare for sound and music editing and the mix.

- Finish your show on a digital editing system, or by onlining or using the Digital Intermediate (DI) process.

*Cut by Cut, 2nd Edition*, contains editing exercises and over 150 tables, charts, photos, and illustrations. It also includes budgeting, logging, and other blank forms to use on your film or video. Additionally, you can download these forms by going to my website, www.joyoffilmediting. com and searching under the Free tab. For teachers, there are syllabi for editing courses. The site's blog, which *MovieMaker Magazine* judged one of the 50 best filmmaker blogs in 2009 (they haven't issued the award since), supplements the book with regular articles on a wide array of editing topics.

## Navigating the Book — The Three Stages of Postproduction

The postproduction process breaks into three distinct stages. Accordingly, *Cut by Cut, 2nd Ed.*, is divided into three stages of two parts each:

### Stage I *Setting Up and Organizing*
**Part One** Starting Your Project
**Part Two** Organizing for Editing

### Stage II *Editing*
**Part One** How to Approach the Footage
**Part Two** Getting from First Cut to Final Cut

### Stage III *Finishing*
**Part One** Sound, Music, and the Mix
**Part Two** Finishing and Delivering

After Stage III the book concludes with a section on how to find that elusive editing job and a list of resources to aid your quest. Following this is an extensive glossary for quick lookups which also includes some terms and concepts that I couldn't squeeze into the main contents of the book.

# STAGE I

# Setting Up and Organizing Your Project

*"The buck stops in the cutting room."*
— DEDE Allen, A.C.E.[1], *Bonnie & Clyde*, *Dog Day Afternoon*, and *Reds*

## Introduction

Stage I lays the foundation for every project. It is the critical stage where you set up and organize your show so it moves smoothly through the cutting room and emerges as a well-edited film or video. Part One informs you about the important editorial decisions you must make at the start of every project and helps you make them. In Part Two dailies arrive in the cutting room and you learn how to organize them and the cutting room for the next stage in the postproduction process: editing.

Stage I, as well as Stages II and III, contains a number of appendices which consist of charts and forms. You can photocopy them and use them on your projects or download them from www.joyoffilmediting. com by clicking on the Free tab.

---

1. A.C.E., American Cinema Editors, is an honorary society of editors who are voted into membership based on their professional achievements, dedication to the education of others, and commitment to the craft of editing. A.C.E. always follows their names on screen. A.C.E. hosts its own annual editing awards ceremony for which winners receive a Golden Eddie award. It also runs an editing internship program.

# PART ONE
# Starting Your Project

## Introduction

In Part One you will find out how to make the critical decisions necessary to set up your project properly for editing. Chapter 1 provides a thorough overview of the editorial process so that you're clear on how to get started and can plan your project's path through postproduction. Its appendix supplies you with a checklist for setting down your decisions, which you can also download at www.joyoffilmediting.com by clicking on the Free tab.

Chapter 2 of Part One introduces you to the world of video and its terms and practices. It then concentrates on the features and components of popular digital editing systems to help you choose the right system for your project. After Part One you'll be ready to step into the cutting room and learn how to prepare it for the task of editing in Part Two.

## CHAPTER 1

# Decisions, Decisions

*Getting Started on the Right Path*
*through Postproduction*

*"A film is like a boat; it's just waiting to be sunk."*
—Francois Truffaut, director

## Overview

In order to stay afloat and on course, you must put your project on a proper path through postproduction. To do this, you need to make critical decisions right at the start. It's best to know where you're going before you set out! Consequently, this chapter begins by summarizing the six phases of film and video projects. Next, a substantial section advises you on shooting correctly to achieve an efficient postproduction process and create the best footage possible for editing. The chapter then lays down some key cutting room terms and acquaints you with how and why shows are measured and coded. This leads to the last part of the chapter which details the formats that projects shoot, edit and finish on. You'll then be ready to determine your project's format(s) in Appendix A, which follows the chapter.

Let's begin!

# Be clear on what happens before and after editing

*"Ten years ago postproduction was at the end of the food chain. Now we are in production meetings."*
—ALICIA HIRSCH, VP of postproduction, Fox Television Studios

There are six phases to any film or video project. Understanding what goes on before and after editing will give you more insight into the filmmaking process and make you a better participant in the process. It will help you communicate more effectively with those whose work overlaps yours, primarily the script supervisor and cinematographer (from the production phase) and promo producer and publicist (from the distribution phase). More importantly, current workflows are converging postproduction with production and even preproduction, especially in animated shows and those with lots of VFX (visual effects). The lines between filmmaking phases are less distinct today and will get even fuzzier in the future. The following list describes each phase.

## Six Phases of Every Project

**1. GREENLIGHT:** Project is formally approved and acquires its financing. Once green-lit, a.k.a. greenlighted, it moves into the development phase.

**2. DEVELOPMENT:** Script is set and director, producers, casting director, and principal talent (actors) are hired.

**3. PREPRODUCTION:** Preparatory phase during which script and money are finalized, the rest of talent and crew hired, locations and schedules locked, and sets, wardrobe, props, etc. created. On animated and VFX-driven films, previsualization (previz) takes place in the cutting room or VFX house to plan and prepare for the shoot.

**4. PRODUCTION:** Primary filming takes place on set and/or location and VFX are created at the lab or VFX house during this phase, which is also referred to as "the shoot" or "principal photography."

**5. POSTPRODUCTION:** Also referred to as editorial, editing, or simply post, this is the final creative phase during which all picture and sound editing takes place. Music is composed and sound mixed, VFX are finalized, and all other finishing work completed. Post produces the final show for viewing on tape, file, disk, and/or film.

**6. DISTRIBUTION:** Time when completed project goes to market (with a little or a lot of marketing!) and is viewed by its audience.

# Shoot Right for Postproduction

Too many projects show up in the cutting room sadly compromised due to poor audio, lighting, or planning in general. Don't let this happen to your show. If you're an independent or student filmmaker, you'll probably be participating in all phases of your project and production will be a most critical phase. So when you're on location or on the set, remember that after the wrap someone — you, most likely — will have to put the footage together. You serve the editor/yourself and the show by getting the critical shots, recording the important sounds, and keeping accurate logs and records during production. Shooting correctly also saves time, stress, and money in postproduction. Here's how:

## Maintain an Organized Shoot

A well-organized shoot sets the stage for a well-organized editing room. During the shoot be sure to:

- Keep accurate records, notes, camera logs, and sound logs.
  This gives the editor important information about the shots and assists the editing crew immensely in keeping track of the footage.
- Maintain good communication with the crew
  Good communication, particularly between director, script supervisor, camera, and sound recordist, means that the right shots are filmed and printed and editorial does not have to chase down the crew or the lab to get the anticipated shots.
- Stick to the shooting schedule as much as possible.
  This makes it easier to coordinate and schedule work in the cutting room.

## Shoot Good Slates on Every Take

Mark the slate clearly with:

- ▶ Scene and take
- ▶ Date and location
- ▶ Camera designation (A, B, C, etc.)
- ▶ Camera roll and sound roll
- ▶ Director and production name
- ▶ MOS (if shot has no recorded sound)

Hold the slate squarely in frame and voice slate the take, e.g., "Scene 57, Take 5" on a scripted show or "McDonald's farm, 12/15" on a documentary piece. Then clap it if you're shooting double system (capturing sound and picture on separate mediums) before whisking it out of frame. Clearly slating each take consumes but a few seconds in the field and saves valuable time and temperaments in the cutting room.

Voice slating is essential because dialogue editors will need to find the original takes for the audio tracks used in the show. "We can't see the slate," explains dialogue editor Victoria Rose Sampson. "We locate takes by the voice slate."

## Cut in the Camera

**NOT!** Don't dictate where the editor should cut by ending shots or pointing the camera away from the action too early. Always remember: *The camera sets the pace of the shot, the editor sets the pace of the show.* An inexperienced camera operator, believing static shots are boring, may push the zoom button as if playing a trombone. This frustrates audience and editor alike. The editor can set a fine rhythm with a lovely series of static shots and should not be limited by a hyperactive camera that zooms and pans without purpose and gathers no usable shots.

## Get Coverage

To "cover" a scene means to shoot angles in addition to the master shot such as close-ups and two-shots. Directors usually plan coverage for every scene. Why? Because most scenes — when edited — don't work when played all the way through in a master shot. Coverage adds needed pace and points of view and gives editors options for how to cut the show. Additionally, coverage serves as insurance in case the planned shot doesn't work, e.g., a master shot drags or is repetitive in the middle. By cutting to coverage, the editor can skip over the slow spot and cut back at a more vital point. Directors who don't cover themselves usually regret it.

## Hold and Repeat Action at the Start and End of Takes

When shooting a new take, don't just continue from where the last take left off; repeat dialogue and actions from take to take. To clarify, let's say you've filmed a master shot of a dining room scene where nutty

Uncle Ed sits down and tells a weird joke. When you film the medium shot of Uncle Ed, don't start with his joking. Rather, have him sit down and begin joking, repeating the action of the master. When you repeat action at the tail (end) of one angle and the head (beginning) of the next angle, the editor has the latitude to cut to any take at the best possible frame.

## Hold the Camera

Before starting and after ending every shot, be it a static shot, a zoom, pan, or dolly, hold the camera still for five seconds. As with repeated action, these static seconds can make all the difference in the editor being able to cut to shots at the best moment. Additionally, these action handles allow for dissolves, wipes, and other effects that an editor may apply to transition between shots. Occasionally, holding the camera even solves an editing problem: For example, editors sometimes use the footage from when the camera was rolling before the director yelled "Action!" or after he or she called "Cut!"

## Shoot Good Continuity

A good script supervisor, who keeps an eagle eye on continuity, is always an MVP on a film set. Make every effort to match pacing, actions, lighting, wardrobe, placement of props, hair, makeup, etc., from take to take. It's a shame to force the editor to cut earlier or later than optimal due to a lack of continuity. We've all noticed the laughable mismatch between an interior and exterior shot of a traveling car moving at different speeds and with different scenery in each shot. This mismatch underscores why continuity is so important: Mismatches can take viewers out of your film, risking their distrust and disengagement, and lead to bad word-of-mouth. Here are four vital components of good continuity:

### 1) SHOOT CUTTABLE ANGLES

Shots that are similar in angle and focal length jar the audience when cut together. If jarring is what you want, shoot this way. Otherwise stick to the 30° rule: Vary the new camera angle at least 30° from the last and your angles should cut together "like butter." (For more on cuttable angles, see the sections on smooth cutting angles and mismatches in Chapter 5.)

**1.a** Example of an eyeline match. Notice that in the boy's close-up, he maintains the correct eyeline.

## 2) MATCH EYELINES

When a scene calls for cutting back and forth between shots of interacting characters, they need to be looking at each other, i.e., their eyelines must match. If shot incorrectly, their eyelines won't match and the characters will not be looking in the right direction. This may confuse the audience and cause them to take an unintended meaning from the characters' interaction.

## POV and eyeline

A common eyeline error occurs when making the Point of View (POV) shot. Example: You're shooting a close-up of someone and their eyes (and possibly head) move left to right as they look at something. When you cut to that something, you're cutting to their POV. To match their eye and head movement, the POV shot must move the same direction, from left to right.

## 3) MATCH SCREEN DIRECTION

**1.b** Follow the floating balloon as it matches screen direction.

If a character or object moves right out of the frame, they need to enter the next shot from the left of the frame so they look like they're moving normally, from left to right. If exits and entrances don't match, your audience wastes time keeping up with the action instead of immersing themselves in your movie.

## 4) DON'T CROSS THE LINE: OBSERVE THE 180° RULE

Crossing the line (a.k.a. crossing the axis), is an extension of screen direction.

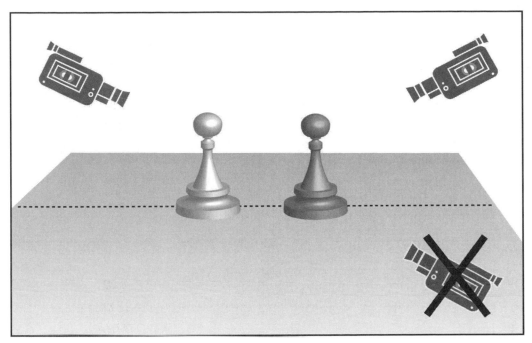

**1.c** Crossing the line. Shoot the pawns from the correct cameras or they will appear to jump sides.

## EXAMPLE

A car is going down a street and you shoot two angles, one from each side of the street. Perfectly valid angles but if cut together, the car appears to be traveling in the opposite direction.

## REASON

There is an invisible line in every camera set-up that bisects the scene horizontally at 180°.

## *The 180° Rule: How to observe it*

### SCENARIO

If two people face each other, the 180° line runs across their heads. When editing, if you cut to the angle behind them, the person on the left now appears to jump to the right. Jumping the line disturbs the audience, especially in 3-D movies, which, by their nature, immerse viewers more deeply than 2-D movies.

### THE RULE

When shooting, keep Person A on the left and Person B on the right by not moving the camera across the 180° line. When editing, don't cut angles together that cause actors to unintentionally jump sides in a scene.

**EXAMPLE**

Cinematographers and their crews observe this rule daily when they shoot football games from one side of the field only. This way there is no chance to cut to the other side of the field and make the players appear to be running toward the wrong goal.

## Get the angles you need without crossing the line

Of course there are many times when you want to shoot a lot of angles that cover both sides of the action. Here are several methods:

> *"Robert Wise would always plan his axis change…there was always one key shot. When you don't get those shots, and you just have somebody coming in without any reason, then you have a scene where nobody relates to anyone. Nobody is looking anybody else in the eye, and it's totally disorienting. The audience might get thrown out of the scene because it's non-connective. Film is connective; that's what film is."*
>
> — DEDE ALLEN

1.  Establish a new 180° line

    Have the characters move within the shot or move the camera within the shot to break the line and create a new one. As Dede Allen notes, director Robert Wise always anticipated his axis changes.

2.  Shoot cutaways

    Cutaways diminish the disorientation, allowing the editor to cut away before cutting to the line-breaking angle. An overhead angle keeps the audience oriented and enables the editor to freely cut to any angle.

3.  Break the 180° rule deliberately

    More and more frequently, filmmakers flout the 180° line. If you choose to ignore the rule, be aware that you are breaking it and be smart: Shoot some cutaways for insurance in case you don't like the resulting cut. (More about this in Chapter 5, "To Cut or Not to Cut: Where to Cut and Why," during the discussion of traditional editing style vs. modern style.)

# Getting the "Film Look" with a Digital Camera

"We want the film look," says the client or producer. Many budget-conscious filmmakers, notably students, independents, documentarians, and television networks, use low cost digital video cameras but desire the film look. We've all seen the scratchy, old timey film look applied after the shoot and many of us have used software to produce a supposed film look. But what exactly is the film look and what's the best way to get it when you shoot digitally? As an editor, how do you advise clients and producers?

As production and post overlap more and more in the area of perfecting a show's images, these questions continue to crop up. The topic has been coming up in Final Cut Pro and other digital system users groups for awhile and here's the common wisdom: To get the film look, shoot for it — surprise — during the shoot! Below are tips on how to do this, preceded by a little background.

**1.d** Millennium film camera. *Photo courtesy of Panavision.*

Film and digital cameras capture images in two distinct ways. Film capture is a photochemical process which creates the grain (texture, fullness) and highlights we're accustomed to seeing on screen. Digital capture relies on electronic signals to produce non-grainy images that are cool, clean, and crisp and often described as harsh.

**1.e** HVX200 digital camera. *Photo courtesy of Panasonic.*

The digi-cam's ability to capture film-like shots is continually improving. So get the best digi-cam you can afford; either video

**1.f** EOS 7D HDSLR camera. *Photo courtesy of Canon.*

camera or the new DSLR still cameras that can shoot videos. As of this writing, however, the best HD camera does not approach the look of 16mm film, let alone 35mm. So, to achieve a film look, address the differences between the two mediums using these specific methods:

1. Shoot 24p as this format has the most film-like motion characteristics.

2. Be conscious of how you block the camera: Leave enough room for zooming and separate the camera from the set. If space is lacking, direct the talent to move forward; this is preferable to having them move sideways.

3. Choose a camera that allows you to adjust the depth of field (DOF). Since video has an infinite DOF and film has a shallow DOF, you need to narrow the DOF to approach film. Do this by using film-style lenses, zooming, adding a digital adapter, and changing the F-stop to widen the aperture.

4. Light film-style to avoid the cold video look. Go beyond "room lighting" and use key, fill, and backlighting in different scenes.

5. Adjust the white balance to mimic film's photochemical color timing.

6. Pay attention to where the audience's focal point will be with every setup. What will they notice first? Catch in their peripheral vision? Gravitate to next?

7. Finally, because sound is vital to viewers' acceptance of visual images, record high quality audio to bolster your film-image look. Which neatly brings us to the last subject in this section.

## Record Location Sound

*"One misconception that many people in the film business have…is that if you want great sound in your movie you don't really need to think about sound early on."*

—RANDY THOM, C.A.S.[1], sound designer and mixer, *How to Train Your Dragon, The Incredibles, The Right Stuff,* and *Return of the Jedi.*

To create the best-sounding film or video, start during preproduction. Anticipate how your show will sound, budget for sound, and record your desired audio during the shoot. This way you'll capture the sound you want for when your show comes together audio-wise during postproduction.

---

1. Cinema Audio Society. U.S. sound honorary society equivalent to A.C.E. for sound mixers and their associates: sound editors, recordists, and technicians.

## Record clean tracks

Be the sound editor's best friend. Record clean tracks: no helicopters whirring overhead, no doors banging, no dolly squeaking, etc. Make sure all dialogue is crisp and clear so your audience won't miss a word. Poor sound can

**1.g** Fostex digital sound recorder, *Photo courtesy of American Music & Sound.*

only be corrected so much in postproduction — and usually at a cost — so do it right during production!

## Get RT and WT on every location and set

### RT, A.K.A. ROOM TONE, AMBIENCE, OR PRESENCE

Record a minute of RT — wordless, noise free background sound — for every scene. Sound editors need RT to smooth out scenes, especially dialogue scenes.

### WT, A.K.A. WILD TRACK OR WILD SOUND

Record WT — non-sync, non-dialogue sound — on every outdoor location. Get the forest sound, the traffic sound…all the natural sounds. Record specific sounds that are crucial to how you want your project to sound. The sound editor can access thousands of sound effects but won't have the mating sound of the ring-tailed lemur your show's documenting. Picking up such sounds later could be costly. Make a list beforehand of WT you need to record and add to the list when you're on location.

## Create a sound vision

Part of realizing the vision of your film is conceiving what the viewer will hear. Think about the different scenes or parts of your show and how you want them to sound: light and sprightly, cheery with a sinister threat in the air, painful but upbeat, etc. You might start by imagining each character or subject as an instrument or a theme: What would they sound like? What tune would they play? Next, envision how scenes or sections will sound as purely musical themes. The goal is to get an idea of the subtle and grand tones of your film and consider how sonics can support them.

## Last word

There's a belief in the film industry that you "pay it up front during production or pay it downstream during post." So, save yourself time and money by getting picture and sound right, right from the start. Shoot your footage correctly so that shots cut together the way you want and are logged and slated properly for maximum editorial efficiency.

## Cutting Room Terms
## Overview

Cutty, hissy, tubby; editing has a language of its own. This section lays down the basic editing, audio, and film terms in this section and adds more as we go along. But first, some background: It's helpful to know when and how the terms originated in the history of film editing so they make sense and are easier to remember.

## A 10-frame History of Editing Tools or the Genesis of Cutting Room Terms

In the beginning — the 1900s — there was a light well for viewing film frames, a razor blade for cutting the film, and a cement splicer for gluing the cut frames together. Cutters, as editors were promptly called, propelled the film with their hands in order to see the footage move. In 1924 Iwan Serrurier invented a mechanical editing device. The Moviola featured a hand crank for moving the footage and an electric light. Before long it ran reels of picture and sound via electrified foot pedals and a magnetic sound head picked up the sound and amplified it through a built-in speaker.

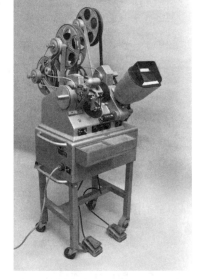

**1.h** Moviola. *Photo courtesy of Chris Senchack.*

Flash forward to the late 1960s and behold! The upright Moviola, with its two vertical reels, evolved into the flatbed, a table top machine with three or four reels running horizontally. And the flatbed became known as the KEM, the Steenbeck, or the flatbed Moviola according to its brand name.

The 1970s begat more for editors: viable videotape editing machines. Since tape was faster and cheaper, news shows and documentary filmmakers migrated to it. In the 1980s many independent filmmakers, corporate, and commercial editors followed as did low budget TV shows. And thus was born the term linear. By the end of the '80s a majority of TV shows cut on tape and the term nonlinear editor (NLE) arose.

Now all this time feature film editors, with a few exceptions, remained on film. They held out until the digital age dawned, bringing film and tape together in one machine in the early 1990s. By the decade's end, news editors, TV editors, commercial editors, independent filmmakers, and feature editors were cutting on digital editing systems as were college students, prosumers (professional/consumer), and home moviemakers.

And thus it came to pass with the millennium that the computer has made digital technology available to all editors and almost all use it. Digital systems,

**1.i** Marking the cut point on a KEM. *Photo courtesy of Chris Senchack.*

**1.j** Ediflex, nonlinear tape editing system, which harnessed 12 VHS decks to view and review cuts. *Photo courtesy of Tony Schmitz.*

**1.k** Making the cut on a digital editing system. *Photo courtesy of Les Perkins.*

along with the new editing terms they've brought forth, are ever changing with each new version, plug-in, add-on, download, and capability.

*Moral*: Change will prevail and ever yield to more change. And that is the state of the firmament in which we all dwelleth until kingdom come. Or the next evolution.

# Editors' Lingo: How Editors Call It and Do It

*"The cliché about sculpture, that the sculptor finds the statue which is waiting in the stone, applies equally to editing; the editor finds the film which is waiting hidden in the material."*
—Tom Priestly, editor and cinematographer, *The Thomas Crown Affair, Deliverance,* and *Return of the Pink Panther.*

## General Cutting Room Terms

As editing has moved from being performed on film to being performed on video tape and then digital editing systems, new terms have been added and old terms have lived on. For instance, picture and sound — film terms — are freely mingled with video and audio (tape terms) in today's digital domain. Also, while the days when editors used scissors to cut film are scores of years behind us, editing is still referred to as cutting and the editing room is still called the cutting room. As more and more movies are shot, edited, and projected digitally, perhaps in the future we'll go to the theater to see not a film but a "digi." But for now, film, video, and digital terms are freely intermixed in the cutting room and everywhere else. Here are the current general terms:

### Picture editor, a.k.a. the editor
Editor who puts the show together.

### Sound editor
Editor who perfects the show's sound. Sound editors finesse the dialogue, ambience, wild track, and narration and add sound effects among other duties.

### Dailies
Footage, usually shot the previous day by the production crew, that arrives daily in the cutting room.

### Shot
Camera start to camera stop.

### Take
A slated shot.

### Edit (noun)
A portion of a take or shot put into a show.

## Cut (noun)

A series of edits.

Cut and edit are used interchangeably: An edit can be made up of cuts, a cut can be made up of edits. Compounding the confusion, the words are both nouns and verbs. For consistency's sake, this book will use *cut* to stand for a series of edits except for a few instances where its meaning will be clear within the context.

## Locked cut

The final edited version of the cut created by the editor in the cutting room. Locking a show means that there should be no more editing changes. The editing is finished, finalized, complete, done. Now it's time for the next part of post — sound editing and mixing and more — which depends on and utilizes the locked cut.

## Cutting room

Room where editor puts the show together.

## Post house

Postproduction facility that offers a myriad of services to the production company including film scanning (telecine), offline and online editing, editing rooms and system rental, screening rooms, etc. Big post houses usually affiliate with a film lab and offer VFX, color grading, and graphics design services as well.

**1.1** Post house rental suite of editing workstations. *Photo courtesy of AlphaDogs.*

## Sync (shortened from synchronize)

Align the recorded picture and sound so they play together as originally shot and can be edited.

## Single and double system

These two production terms are crucial to fathom because they help determine in what form your dailies will arrive. Single system means audio and video are shot on the same format; tape ordinarily. Double system means the picture is shot on one format — film or card most commonly — and the sound is recorded on another format such as a card, disk, or hard drive. With double system the audio and video will need to be synced by you or the post house.

## Source tape

Original footage — recently shot or archival — used for editing or to make dubs for editing. Sometimes referred to as the original tape or raw tape.

## Field tape

Source tape shot on location or on the stage.

## Dub

Copy or re-record video and/or audio from one tape to another tape.

## Transfer

Copy or re-record video and/or audio from tape to tape or film or film to tape.

## Telecine (noun or verb)

Scan film to tape or file.

## Colorist, a.k.a. telecine operator

Person who performs telecine and color grading.

## Color grade, a.k.a. color correct or color time

Change or improve the color or lighting of an image to be consistent with the desired look of a scene or show.

## Master

High-quality tape, file, or film source employed to finish the show. Master is often used as a verb, e.g., "We're shooting on film but mastering on HDV (high definition video)."

## Show master

Final tape or file of a show complete with audio mix and color grading from which the deliverable(s) — broadcast tape, film print, file, or disk — will be made.

## Edit master

Master created from the locked cut's data of the final edited show on file, film, or tape before sound mix is laid back and color grading performed.

# Sound and Audio Terms

### Laydown
Noun or verb meaning to record or transfer audio, video, time code, etc. from one tape or other format to another tape or format.

### The mix, a.k.a. the dub
The blending of a show's sound to produce a temp (temporary) or final soundtrack. The work is performed by mixers on a mix stage or room via digital recorders.

### Mixer
Person or equipment that does the mixing. Mixers are often credited as "re-recording mixers" to differentiate them from the original recording mixer (sound recordist) who records the sound during the shoot.

### Sweetening
Improving and finalizing the audio on the edit master.

### Layback
Transfer of the completed audio tape mix onto the edit master.

# Film Terms

### Negative, a.k.a. original camera negative (OCN) or camera roll
Film shot in the camera where the colors are opposite their true (positive film) hues. A camera assistant loads negative camera rolls of up to 1000 feet (10 minutes with 35mm film stock) into camera magazine and labels them, e.g. A201 for Camera A, Roll 201. After the film is shot (exposed), the lab develops the OCN and uses it to make film dailies for shows cutting on film and then vaults (stores) it. For shows cutting digitally, the OCN is telecined to file, tape, or hard drive, then vaulted. (Stay tuned: The OCN plays a significant role later in creating a film master for theatrical release in Chapter 13, *Finishing on Film and via Digital Intermediary*.)

## Work print

Positive print developed and printed in the lab from the negative camera rolls. Used on shows that cut directly on film for screening and conforming as well as editing.

## Mag

Magnetic-coated film stock which contains the sound transferred from the shoot. Commonly called *the mag* or referred to as *mag film*. Used on shows that cut on film.

## Key code, a.k.a. key number or latent edge numbers

Sequential numbers embedded on the edge of the film stock at regular intervals during manufacturing that are visible on the negative and work print. Key code numbers are crucial reference data that the negative cutter and digital intermediate process rely on to reproduce the locked cut. Keykode, a bar code version of key code, is added on Kodak film.

## Ink code, a.k.a. edge code, Acmade code, or rubber numbers

Code stamped on the edge of the work print and its corresponding mag sound reel after dailies are synced up and screened to keep a picture and sound reel in sync.

**1.m** Work print reel. *Photo courtesy of Chris Senchack.*

**1.n** Reel of mag sound. *Photo courtesy of Chris Senchack.*

**1.o** Key code, starting with KV, on an enlarged edge of 35mm film. *Photo courtesy of Chris Senchack.*

**1.p** Ink code, starting with 008, on a piece of 35mm film. *Photo courtesy of Chris Senchack.*

### Negative cutting, a.k.a. negative conforming, a.k.a. negative matching

Conforming (matching) the negative film (OCN) to the final locked cut to make the film print master. The DI (digital intermediate) process creates the print master differently (full explanation in Chapter 13). Both processes create positive prints for projection in theaters. The DI process can also create a file for digital projection.

### Negative cutter

Person who cuts the negative from the stored OCN.

### Cutlist

List of key codes and camera rolls for each edit in the final, locked cut. Created by the picture editor or assistant and used by the negative cutter to matchcut the negative to the locked cut or in the DI process to create the print master.

### An ode to editing on film now that's it's fading out

All editing systems are merely tools. There is a rhythm — a sense of timing and control — which one grows accustomed to on any system whether it's stomping the pedal and brake on the Moviola, toggling the lever to run a KEM, manipulating the jog shuttle on a tape editor, or pressing key or mouse on a digital editing system.

There is something about touching the film — the very frames that were shot and will be projected — that is philosophically and spiritually satisfying. Walter Murch wrote poetically about this connection in his book *In the Blink of an Eye*: "There is a wonderful alchemy in this: that hydrocarbons and silver and iron and various colored dyes, plus intangible time, can transmute themselves into the stuff of dreams."

Now dreams are transmuted using digital systems — and Murch was an early adapter — but we all owe much to the editing practices and editors that preceded us.

## Coding and measuring

Coding means putting a number reference on a reel of film or tape or a file. The purpose of coding is twofold: 1) to locate footage and 2) to measure a shot, scene, or entire show. Coding is an absolute necessity in most editing situations. More about why, when, and how you code in the next chapter. For now, see Table 1.1 to familiarize yourself with how shows are coded and measured, depending on whether you're measuring film, tape, or a digital cut.

**TABLE 1.1**
**CODING AND MEASURING**

| MEASURING ON | | CODING | MEASURE IN | |
|---|---|---|---|---|
| FILM | | Key code (negative) Ink code (workprint) | Length | Feet + frames |
| TAPE | | Time code | Time | Hours, minutes, seconds, and frames |
| DIGITAL SYSTEM | | Time code and/or key code or ink code | Time and/or length, depending on the finishing format | |

# Choose Your Show's Finishing Format

When you determine your show's finishing format, you establish a clear path for your project from shooting to completion. There are four types of formats to select from: file, film, tape, or disk (DVD, Blu-ray, or other optical disk).

## *The Question*

To start figuring out which format your project will finish on, ask yourself: Where will the audience view my show? To answer this question, look at Table 1.2. It outlines the five scenarios for where an audience could view your show. Read the scenarios to find out which one fits your project and note the finishing format(s). You may pick more than one scenario; for instance, your audience may see your show in a movie theater and then on TV. This means your project could have three finishing formats: file, film, and tape.

TABLE 1.2
DETERMINE YOUR FINISHING FORMAT

| WHERE AUDIENCE WILL VIEW YOUR SHOW | FINISHING FORMATS | | BEHIND THE SCENES: HOW YOUR SHOW WILL BE SCREENED |
|---|---|---|---|
| MOVIE THEATER | FILM FILM | | Your show will consist of reels run through a film projector or, increasingly, a digital file downloaded and run through a digital projector. |
| TELEVISION | TAPE FILE | | Your show will be broadcast on tape or from a file uploaded from the network's disk server. |
| HOME ENTERTAINMENT SYSTEM | TAPE DISK FILE | | Viewers will pop a tape into a deck or more likely a disk into a drive to see your show. Or they may download it from Netflix (or another company) or stream it live from the Internet. |
| COMPUTER | FILE DISK | | Viewers will watch your show on a file streamed or downloaded from their corporate intranet (example: a QuickTime file) or from the Internet (examples: a YouTube video, webisode, or Hulu show). Alternatively, they may insert a disk to see it. |
| FILM FESTIVAL | TAPE, DISK, FILE, FILM | | |
| | Initially, you'll send a tape, file, or disk. If you're accepted into the final round, some festivals will require a film print. If your show, like most today, didn't originate on film see Chapter 13 for how to make a film print. Bottom line: be prepared. Check out festival requirements beforehand and know your path through postproduction so you can put your best show forward. | | |

Now that you've read the five scenarios and know your show's general finishing format(s) — film, tape, file, or disk — it's time to get acquainted with the specific formats you'll encounter in the cutting room.

## Shooting formats — picture

The format you shoot on may not be the format you finish on. For example, you may shoot on a file on a card but deliver on tape or shoot on film and deliver on tape. Also, you may shoot on all different formats: film, tape, drive, and card. News editors routinely receive source footage on a variety of formats. Documentary filmmakers often dig up source footage from past decades on outmoded formats such as 8mm film or ¾" tape. Luckily all formats can meet up and be edited together on the digital editing system. More about how this happens in Chapter 4, Preparing Dailies for Editing. But for now, just be aware of these different formats.

## Shooting formats — sound

Sound is often recorded on tape along with picture — single system. An equally common choice is to go double system and use a digital recorder which records the sound to DAT (digital audio tape) or a reusable media: memory card or stick, optical disk, and hard drive.

## Finishing format and delivery requirements

Usually your finishing format is specified by your show's delivery requirements which you'll find in the film festival submission guidelines, the TV network's contract, or your agreement with the distribution company. When you're hired as an editor, you'll be told the finishing format along with show length, etc. by the post supervisor or AP (associate producer). If you're an independent filmmaker, you may decide your show's exact shooting and finishing format(s). You'll weigh the aesthetics, delivery requirements, and your budget to make your decision.

## Last word

Whether or not you're the decision maker, you should be familiar with the many possible formats as you will be dealing with them in the editing room. Table 1.3 lists the film, tape, disk, and file formats most used for shooting and finishing projects. It also shows how your dailies — no matter what they're shot on — will be ingested (input) into your digital editing system (DES). Use this table to identify your project's specific finishing format(s) and understand your show's basic path from start to finish.

TABLE 1.3
FILM AND VIDEO FORMATS:
HOW SHOWS ARE SHOT, INPUT, AND FINISHED

| FORMAT | SHOOT PICTURE ON | INGEST TO DES | FINISH |
|---|---|---|---|
| FILM | 16mm, super 16mm, 35mm (3- and 4-perf), super 35mm, 70mm (rare). | Transferred to tape and digitized. | 16mm, super 16mm, 35mm (4-perf), super 35mm, 70mm, IMAX (a special type of 70mm). |
| TAPE | DV* (DVCAM, DVCPRO, DVPRO50, DVCPRO P, DVCPRO-HD), HDV, 24p** SD*** or HD, 60i, 60p SD & HD, BetaSX, BetaSP, DigiBeta, MPEG IMX, HDCAM, or HDCAM SR, Hi8, Video8, Digital8. | Captured (digital tapes) or digitized (analog tapes). | D1-D9, 24p SD or HD, DV HD, DVPRO, DVPRO50, DVCAM, DigiBeta, VHS, Hi8, Video8, Digital8. |
| DISC, FILE, TAPE | XDCAM. | Imported. | Disk (DVD or Blu-ray), file, film, tape. *(See film and tape finish formats in rows above for all possible formats.)* |
| FILE | Computer card, referred to as a flash card or a memory card, such as P2 or SxS. | Imported. | |

* Digital video. There are many DV formats; the most popular are listed above.
** 24 progressive. This DV format runs at the normal film speed (frame rate) of 24 frames per second (fps) instead of 30 fps, the normal video frame rate. (More details on frame rates in Chapter 2.) There are three types: 24p, 24pN (native), and 24pA (advanced).
*** Standard definition as opposed to HD (high definition).

With your new knowledge of film and tape formats and how to determine them, mark down your important decisions using the checklist in Appendix A. You can also download this form at www.joyoffilmediting .com by selecting the Free tab. We'll build on this table, adding vital tape and digital information and describing different types of workflows in the next two chapters.

## CHAPTER WRAP-UP

Now that you're familiar with basic cutting room terms and know what format your show is shooting and finishing on, it's time to enter the world of video tape and digital editing. Chapter 2 focuses on key tape, film, and digital practices and gives you an overview of digital editing systems.

# Appendix A

## Project Checklist

Check all that apply to your project. Be as specific as you can. You can also download this checklist by going to www.joyoffilmediting.com and clicking on the Free tab.

1) **My project is a/an:**

   _____ Animated show

       _____ *Episode* _____ *Feature*

   _____ Comedy

       _____ *Single camera* _____ *Multiple camera*

   _____ Commercial

   _____ Corporate video

   _____ Docudrama

   _____ Documentary

   _____ Dramatic short

   _____ Educational or training video

   _____ Event video

   _____ Feature movie

   _____ Infomercial

   _____ Interview

   _____ MOW (TV movie of the week)

   _____ Music video

   _____ News story

   _____ Promo

   _____ PSA (public service announcement)

   _____ Reality show

       _____ *Segment of a reality show*

   _____ Rock or music concert

   _____ Stage play

   _____ Television dramatic episode

   _____ Training piece

   _____ Web video

       _____ *Webisode* _____ *Web series*

   Other_____

2) **Where the audience will see my show:**
   Awards show _____
   Film festival _____
   Home entertainment center: DVD ____ Blu-ray ____
   Movie theater _____
   TV _____
   Web _____
   Kiosk _____
   Video game _____
   Other _____

3) **My project will be this long:**
   _____hours _____minutes _____ Exactly_____ Approximately _____

4) **My shooting format is:**
   Digital tape:     24p ____ DVCPRO ____ DVCPRO50 ____
           DVCPRO-HD ____ DVCAM ____ MiniDV ____ Other _____
   Drive:     Hard disk ____ Other _____
   File:   Memory card ____ Disk____ Other _____
   Film:   35mm ____16mm ____ Super 16mm ____ 70mm ____
           Other _____

5) **I will also receive stock, library, and other footage on these formats:**
   _____

6) **The format I need to finish on is:**
   Disc: DVD ____ Blu-ray_____
   File _____
   Film _____
   Tape: SD _____ HD _____ 3-D_____

CHAPTER 2

# Video, Digital, and Film Basics: Terms, Concepts, and Practices

*"Film editing is now something almost everyone can do at a simple level and enjoy it, but to take it to a higher level requires the same dedication and persistence that any art form does."*
—WALTER MURCH, A.C.E., picture and sound editor, *Cold Mountain, The English Patient,* and *Apocalypse Now* (co-editor)

## Overview

This chapter begins by explaining essential video terms so that you're ready to take in crucial videotape concepts such as time code, frame rate, and HD. Then it describes aspect ratios so that you can set up your project appropriately. For those finishing and/or shooting on film, the next section introduces you to telecine, the first step after production. Moving on, the chapter covers digital editing systems, identifying their basic features and components. This last section includes a rundown of the current popular systems and an expansive list of criteria to enable you to choose the right system for your project. Time to shove off.

## Videotape Terms

### Linear and nonlinear editing

Linear and nonlinear are the two ways that editing systems make edits and impact the way editors edit.

### LINEAR EDITING

With linear editing you make (record) each edit sequentially, one after another, from the beginning of the show to the end of the show, normally on videotape. You can't add a shot two minutes in without starting over again. The one advantage to linear editing is that when you're finished editing you've got a completed tape to show; no need to export it to your finishing format, which is necessary on a nonlinear system. While nonlinear digital systems have vanquished most linear, tape-based editing systems, there are still quite a few around, mostly in online editing bays.

### NONLINEAR EDITING

Nonlinear editing means you can edit non-sequentially — in any order that you desire, e.g., Scene 34, 1, 17, 119. Because you're working on a computer, you have random access to footage and scenes: You can add or remove a shot or shots at any time in any place. Since digital editing systems are nonlinear, they are often referred to as NLEs (nonlinear editing systems).

## Playback

You run (playback) a tape or file from a deck, camera, or other device in order to review the footage or record it to another device. Editors routinely playback material in the cutting room and at the post house during postproduction. Playback also occurs on the set during production from time to time. Raw or edited footage is played back as a reference for actors or other performers so they can perform and be filmed in sync with music or an action or a character they can't see, e.g., an animated character or green screen action such as a tiger attacking them.

## Offline and online — the two major phases of editing

Born in the age of videotape editing, these two terms are hanging on to their original meaning but the distinctions are blurring. Read on to learn why.

### OFFLINE

Offline editing is the trial and error phase during which the editor (with input from the director, producer, or client) structures the story and makes the majority of the creative decisions. Once the show is locked, the offline editor makes a file for the online editor.

### ONLINE

During online editing, the online editor remakes each offline edit from the best quality source media available — film, tape, or file — to produce the edit master.

### WHEN OFFLINE BECOMES ONLINE

In the digital age, there may be no online: Finishing may be a matter of a simple upres[1] after a sound mixdown and color grading on the offline system. Conversely, the finishing process may be complex and costly, employing a Digital Intermediary (more on the DI later in the chapter). However it goes down — finish by DI or online, or on offline system — the editor will have some responsibilities. (Chapters 12 and 13 — which are all about the finishing stages of postproduction — will detail these thoroughly.)

## Videotape Essentials

Although editing on tape has long been supplanted by editing on digital systems and tapeless workflows are on the increase, videotape still plays a major role in the digital cutting room and has at least a supporting role in the film cutting room. Therefore, videotape essentials are injected throughout the book whenever they're relevant, primarily in this chapter and the next. This section covers useful tape terms and practices so that you will be ready for your overview tour of the digital cutting room.

### *Analog and digital*

It's important to understand digital and analog videotape because we still live in a world of both. Nowadays all shows that shoot on tape use digital tape. However, sooner or later you will work on a show that uses archival source footage. Then you will encounter analog tape. So what exactly do the terms mean? Analog and digital refer to three standards:

**2.a** Analog VTR. *Photo courtesy of Chris Senchack.*

**2.b** HD digital VTR, *Photo courtesy of Panasonic.*

---

1. Convert from a lower resolution to a higher resolution, e.g., from SD to HD.

1. **Tape signal.** Analog and digital signals record and convert video and audio information and store data. There are A-D converters to change analog signals to digital, and D-A converters which do the opposite.

2. **Tape device.** Devices include digital and analog cameras, decks, and editing systems. Analog devices are now referred to as "legacy" equipment: Post houses keep them around for analog jobs that crop up from time to time. For instance, the three major boxing matches in the 2010 movie *The Fighter* were shot on Betacam-SP to match HBO's original broadcast style from the mid-1990s.

3. **Tape format.** Digital video formats are higher quality than analog, with a few standard definition (SD) exceptions. Unlike analog, digital video incurs no generation loss so it can be duplicated thousands of times and stay pristine. DV sports superior video and audio quality, speed, and compatibility with other equipment. It also converts from one nation's video standards to another's more easily.

Both tape formats incur video and audio imperfections. Table 2.1 explains and compares the two standards in further detail.

**TABLE 2.1**
**DIGITAL VS. ANALOG VIDEO**

| | TECHNICAL EXPLANATION | EXAMPLES | DISADVANTAGES |
|---|---|---|---|
| **ANALOG** | An electrical signal that varies continuously in amplitude (strength) of video (brightness) and audio (loudness) as it records.<br><br>**RECORDING PROCESS**<br>Takes the original data and converts the video and audio information into a varying voltage or magnetic field. | **VIDEO**<br>¾", Beta, Betamax, BetaSP, Hi 8, SVHS, VHS.<br><br>**AUDIO**<br>¼" tape, cassettes. | *1. Drop outs and glitches*<br>Loss (drop out) or distortion (glitch) of video or audio during playback.<br><br>*2. Generation loss*<br>Analog audio and video degrades with each succeeding dub to analog tape.<br><br>*3. Age deterioration*<br>Over time, stored analog tape degrades due to noise, distortion and other electronic phenomena. |
| **DIGITAL** | A *digital* signal that has limited variation within a small set of numerical variables.<br><br>**RECORDING PROCESS**<br>Records audio, video, and data as files composed of binary numbers (zeroes and ones) for reading by a computer. | **VIDEO**<br>24P, Digital tape, e.g., HDCAM, miniDV, DVCAM, DigiBeta.<br><br>**VIDEO FILES**<br>JPEG, MPEG.<br><br>**AUDIO**<br>CD, DAT, DA-88, DA-98.<br><br>**AUDIO FILES**<br>aiff, bwf, wav, mp3, au, ogg, Quick Time, Real Audio, Windows Media | *1. Artifacts*<br>Unwanted effects or distortions on a digital tape, file, or disk not found in the original (digital or analog) video or audio caused by technical problems. Just as annoying as analog glitches, artifacts at least are predictable — the same problem in the same place — on every tape, disk, or file.<br><br>*2. Aliasing*<br>Artifact that occurs while reproducing digital video or audio. Examples: flashing, moiré, pixilation (blurred pixels*), staircasing, sticking, strobing (animation only), and vignetting. |

\* A pixel — <u>pix</u> element — is the smallest unit or sample of a digital image on a screen. It holds data such as black-and-white, color, and gray scale information.

# Time code

Created by engineers during the videotape era, time code continues to be a critical component of the digital age. Today time code arrives on a digital tape or a memory card and remains a reliable reference in the digital system.

## *What exactly is time code?*

Time code is a set of numbers embedded on each frame of a videotape or in the digital file's metadata[2].

It groups eight numbers into four pairs based on 24-hour clock time: hours:minutes:seconds:frames.

2.c Time code display on a VTR.

Since videotape runs at 30 frames per second the last set of pairs — the frames — runs from 00 to 29. So **01:01:13:14** (see figure 2.c) is 1 hour, 1 minute, 13 seconds, and 14 frames.

The lowest time code is **00:00:00:00**.

The highest time code is **23:59:59:29**. One frame after that, time code starts again at **00:00:00:00**.

## *Why does time code matter?*

Time code is important because it provides an accurate, numerical reference for many editing, dubbing, and duplicative postproduction processes. Specifically, editors rely on time code to:

- *Locate frames*

  Time code allows you to locate frames quickly and accurately on a tape, file, or sequence. To search, just type in the time code and the deck or digital editing system will go to it.

- *Edit and measure shows frame accurately*

  Time code lets you edit on the exact frame you wish and helps you measure the duration of clips, scenes, sequences, and show.

- *Assure frame-accurate dubs*

  If you're making a dub for viewing only, time code is not required. However, if you're dubbing material that needs to be timed, such as a tape for a music composer, time code is essential.

---

2. Summarized as the "data about data," metadata is the background information that identifies the condition, content, and other qualities of data. In film and video, metadata includes time code, key code, blanking, frame rate, aspect ratio, and color burst information as well as descriptive data such as the type of VFX in the sequence.

- *Reproduce media precisely*
  Any media that needs to be reproduced exactly — whether original source tapes or edited footage — must have time code. So it must be machine-readable, i.e., recognizable by all devices.
- *Replace lost media*
  If you wish to recapture or re-link clips that have lost their media due to data corruption, earthquake, power surge, or other disaster, time code (along with other data like reel numbers) is the super action hero that comes to your rescue. It helps you rebuild your cut footage and restore all ingested media without having to re-edit.
- *Make online editing possible*
  Time code plays a key role in the online edit by allowing each edit made offline to be reproduced exactly from the source tapes or files.

## How does the time code get there?

- *Source tapes and files*
  Normally, the camera crew records time code during the shoot. If a tape arrives with no time code or unusable time code, you should dub it to a pre-striped tape. Pre-striping means recording time code to a new tape before recording video and/or audio. A pre-striped tape can also be used in the camera to capture the footage.
- *Digital system*
  When you create a sequence, the system automatically gives it a time code of 1:00:00:00. You can change this number at any time with a few mouse clicks. The digital system also automatically gives all clips and any non-time coded source tapes a time code — usually 00:00:00:00 — a default setting which you can change.

## Breaks in time code

Time code should increment continuously, one frame at a time. When a frame — a number — is skipped, you have what is called a break in time code. From the break point on, accuracy is lost.

DV cameras will reset to a 00:00:00:00 time code with each camera restart, causing not only breaks in time codes but repeated time codes, if the shooter does not know how to manipulate the camera so it records continuous time code. Consumer tape-based cameras can make it more difficult to record continuous time code. The best solution? Dub the problematic tape to a pre-striped tape for ingesting. Digital systems have other effective ways for dealing with time code breaks which save you the price of the tape but involve more data entry and record keeping.

### Visible time code, a.k.a. vizee, BITC, window burn, or a window dub

Visible time code matches the tape's time code and is added to dubs in postproduction. Visible time code is superimposed — burnt in — over video so that you can see both the image and the time code. Burnt-in time code (BITC — pronounced bit-see) can be positioned any-where on a tape or sequence. Other numbers — video reel number, camera roll, film codes, etc. — can also be burnt in.

Visible time code (see fig-ure 2.d) can't be separated from the video — the picture image — nor can it be read by decks or devices. Visible time code is solely for the human eye. Why

**2.d** Visible time code is burned into the picture. *Photo courtesy of Chris Senchack.*

bother? Because window dubs are good for viewing, logging, and refer-encing shots and information. We'll talk more about this as we progress through postproduction.

### Time code reader (TCR)

Device or software that deciphers (reads) time code.

### Time code generator

Device or software within a digital editing system that creates, syncs, or records time code to a tape or sequence.

### SMPTE time code

SMPTE (pronounced simp-tee) time code is found on analog and all other non-digital media. SMPTE (Society of Motion Picture and Television Engineers) is an international technological society which invented time code in 1967. SMPTE recommends and often effectively sets the stan-dards that manufacturers worldwide use for time code as well as a host of other tape, film, and telecommunication applications. For more infor-mation about SMPTE time code and where it's placed on analog tapes, please click on the Free tab at www.joyoffilmediting.com

### Digital time code

DV time code looks and works exactly like SMPTE time code but is placed with other metadata on a different part of the tape.

### SMPTE time code and DV time code

Just think "time code." For most editorial purposes, that's enough. No need to get hung up about whether the time code is SMPTE or DV. It's time code. Period.

## What doesn't have time code?

Graphic files (GVX), CDs, photos, some consumer digital cameras.

## When does time code not matter?

Most of the time, to be safe, fuggeddabout it: You want time code. However, if you are editing and completing your project directly on a digital editing system and NEVER plan to input and re-edit the material or re-make the show off the system, you can live without time code. Examples: a corporate video that will be uploaded to the company's network or a family video.

## Bottom line

One of postproduction's major responsibilities — at the post house as well as in the cutting room — is to ensure that all source media have good, machine-readable time code without breaks. In the editing room, this means checking to be certain that the footage entering and exiting the digital system has correct, accurate time codes. We'll give more details as to how you do this in subsequent chapters. But for now, consider yourself introduced to time code!

# TIME CODE STANDARDS
# The Nitty-Gritty of NTSC, PAL, and SECAM, DF and NDF, Scan lines and SD, HD, and 3-D

This last section of tape essentials zeroes in on the technical standards of time code that you need to know if you are to survive and thrive in the land of postproduction. First let's start with a definition: frames-per-second (fps) is the rate at which frames move. Film runs at 24 fps and tape at 30 fps in the United States. These frame rates were originated to sustain persistence of vision (the frame rate at which the human eye perceives motion as continuous). If video plays at 24 fps, there's a noticeable judder but wait, it gets more complicated...

### 30 fps is really 29.97 fps and 24 fps is really 23.976 fps

Huh? At first, all U.S. (NTSC) videotape ran at 30 fps. The change from black-and-white to color in 1953 slowed video down 0.1% to 29.97 fps. Commonly, filmmakers refer to a 30 fps format when they really mean 29.97 fps. It's just easier to say. Likewise, they say 24 fps when 23.976 is intended and 60i when 59.94 is the true rate due to the 0.1% slow down. This book will do the same, unless the distinction is critical.

Professional digital cameras can and do shoot at all these frame rates and the footage shows up in the cutting room. To add to the complexity, digital editing systems have different settings and may actually let you export a project or create a project, sequence, or clips that run at 30 fps, 29.97 fps, 24 fps, and 23.976. Apple's much-used Final Cut Pro editing system rounds 29.97 fps to 29.98 fps when the real rate is 29.97 fps, and 23.976 fps to 23.98 fps when 23.976 fps is the true rate. Other systems make different choices with frame rates. One last consideration is audio: When shooting double system, the audio rate must be recorded at a rate that can sync with the video.

## NTSC, PAL, and SECAM

There are three primary videotape standards worldwide: NTSC[3], PAL[4], and SECAM[5] (pronounced see-cam). They all have upsides and downsides, and none is compatible with the other. For instance, an NTSC tape will not play properly on a PAL deck. Table 2.2 illustrates how the three standards vary in frame rate and Hertz-per-AC power cycle.

---

3. National Television Standards Committee. The U.S. system that pundits tag "Never Twice the Same Color" due to the inconsistent color it delivers.

4. Phase Alternating Line. The British system alternatively described as "Pay A Lot," referring to the price of its huge, complex circuitry.

5. Sequential Color and Memory. The French system nicknamed "System Essentially Contrary to American Method" alluding to the political motivations behind its creation. SECAM is similar to PAL but (quelle surprise!) incompatible with it.

TABLE 2.2
WORLDWIDE TAPE AND TELEVISION SIGNAL STANDARDS

| STANDARD | COUNTRIES | FRAME RATE | HERTZ |
|---|---|---|---|
| NTSC | U.S., all of North and Central America, Japan & environs, South Korea, the Netherlands, and parts of South America. | 30 fps | 60 Hz |
| PAL | U.K., China, most of Europe, parts of Africa and of South America. | 25 fps | 50 Hz |
| SECAM | France, Poland, Russia, most of Asia, and parts of Africa. | 25 fps | 50 Hz |

## How these standards affect editors

If all your media is shot in a PAL format, you will set up a PAL project and most likely live outside the Americas or work at a post house. In the United States, like most editors, you will probably deal exclusively with NTSC formats and never see a PAL project in your career. You will always set up NTSC projects. For this reason, the rest of this book will stick with NTSC.

What happens if you need to cut in some PAL material? Answer: You will have your post house convert the footage to NTSC. If you should be hired on an all-PAL project, you will set up your project as a PAL project and get some technical guidance.

# Drop Frame and Non-Drop Frame

Drop frame (DF) and non-drop frame (NDF) are two different methods of numbering and of accounting for videotape frames on NTSC tapes. (PAL and SECAM get by just fine with NDF — lucky them!)

Why two methods?

For years, NTSC videotape was non-drop frame, ran at 30 fps, and was black-and-white only. The addition of color, as mentioned before, slowed the frame rate down to 29.97 fps. This .01% difference adds up to 3.6 seconds after an hour of video. When an NDF tape runs for an hour of real (clock) time, its time code registers as 1:00:03:06. Since television shows are cut to the frame and correct timing is imperative, this is unacceptable. So the NTSC devised drop frame to correct the situation and make timings accurate. How did they do it? They came up with a second way of counting frames: drop frame. Before giving the full explanation, here's the basic difference:

> **NON-DROP** frame is **NUMBERS** accurate.
>
> **DROP** frame is **TIME** accurate.

## The difference between NDF and DF

NDF gives a number to every frame. DF doesn't number certain frames and those frames are not counted; in effect they are dropped. An hour of real time registers as 1;00;00;00 DF and 1:00:03:06 NDF. So how does DF accomplish this? It drops — doesn't number — the 00 and 01 frame on every minute, except for every ten minutes when it doesn't drop any frames. To better grasp this, here's how the two standards advance, frame by frame, when changing from one minute to the next:

| NDF | DF |
|------------|------------|
| 2:06:59:28 | 2;06;59;28 |
| 2:06:59:29 | 2;06;59;29 |
| 2:07:00:00 | 2;07;00;02 |
| 2:07:00:01 | 2;07;00;03 |

## What are NDF and DF good for?

Since NDF is numbers accurate, it's required when you need to verify data. It can be readily identified because it uses a colon or periods between pairs of numbers.

Broadcasters require DF because it is time accurate and they program each minute of the day. DF differs from NDF as it uses a semicolon between pairs of numbers or frequently just the last pair of numbers. A nifty mnemonic: Drop frame drops the colon down (to a semicolon). Table 2.3 illustrates the important differences between DF and NDF and what types of shows rely on each standard.

TABLE 2.3
DROP AND NON-DROP TIME CODE

|  | How TC DISPLAYS | How TC WORKS | How TC USED |
|---|---|---|---|
| NDF | 1:00:00:00 or 1.00.00.00 or 1:00:00.00 | Numbers every frame so it is *number* (data) accurate. | · Commercials and promos (Since they run a minute or less, DF and NDF timings are the same). <br> · Film-finish shows cut on digital systems. <br> · Whenever data verification is critical. |
| DF | 1;00;00;00 or 1:00:00;00 | Doesn't number certain frames so it is *time* accurate. | · TV shows, infomercials. <br> · Shows with a time requirement. <br> · Shows that will be broadcast. |

## Mixing drop frame or non-drop frame tapes

Daily offline tapes should be homogeneous: either all DF or NDF. This makes for accurate and consistent lists and time-efficient shuttling and locating of edits in online. When you receive footage from multiple sources this is not always possible. Make a note of the odd tapes for onlinc so that online editors can adjust their computers to the correct standard and edits can be located swiftly and recorded.

Normally offline and online tapes are the same — all DF or all NDF. The BIG exception: If you shot on film and intend to finish on film and tape, as many TV shows do, you will ingest NDF tapes in offline and produce a DF tape for broadcast. The reason you ingest NDF tapes is because they allow you to verify the accuracy of your telecine transfer. (Chapter 4 discusses how to do this in its "Vital Verifications for Film Finish Shows" section.)

## Frames and fields

Videotape frames play a critical role in the way viewers perceive video images. Every tape frame is composed of two fields which contain vertical lines. Different video standards have different line rates: For instance with SD video, NTSC scans 525 lines-per-frame while PAL and SECAM scan 625 lines.

As a tape plays, a tape deck or other device reads — scans — the lines in the two fields just like we Westerners read: from left to right and top to bottom:

- Field 1 holds the odd-numbered scan lines (1, 3, 5, etc.).
- Field 2 holds the even-numbered scan lines (0, 2, 4, etc.).

There are two ways of scanning these vertical lines: interlace and progressive.

## Interlace scanning, a.k.a. interleaving

This method scans the odd lines of field 1, then the even lines of field 2. Our eyes blend the two fields containing all the lines together as one. However, interlace scanning really only transmits and presents half the lines at one time. Due to the swiftness of the scanning and how the fields are aligned and timed, the human eye sees only whole frames, rapidly, one after another.

## Progressive scanning

This method combines and reproduces all video lines — both odd and even — at the same time.

## SD and HD

Scanning and frame rate are two of the main descriptors that define these two video display resolution (image quality) standards. The third descriptor, frame size, refers to the horizontal lines by vertical lines measured in pixels, e.g., 1280 × 720. The horizontal number is implied by the vertical number so it's omitted most of the time, resulting in three frame-size descriptors: 420, 720, and 1080. They can be interlaced or progressive and SD or HD. Table 2.4 shows the different frame sizes and scanning systems.

TABLE 2.4
U.S. AND CANADA FRAME SIZE, FPS, AND SCANNING TYPES

| FORMAT | 480i | 480p | 720i | 720p* | 1080i** | 1080p |
|---|---|---|---|---|---|---|
| DV (SD VIDEO) | 60i*** | 24p, 30p | Not developed, as it would use more bandwidth to produce a picture equivalent to 480p. | | | |
| SDTV (BROADCAST) | 60i | 24p, 30p | | | | |
| HDV (HD VIDEO) | | | | 24p, 30p, 60p | 60i | 24p, 30p |
| HDTV (BROADCAST) | | | | 24p, 30p, 60p | 60i | 24p, 30p |
| DVD | 60i | 24p, 30p | | | | |
| HD DVD | | | | 24p, 30p, 60p | 60i | 24p, 30p |
| BD (BLU-RAY DISC) | | | | 24p, 30p, 60p | 60i | 24p, 30p |

* 720p is the preferred format for ABC, A&E, Fox, and other networks.
** 1080i is the preferred format for CBS, NBC, The CW, and other networks.
*** 60i means 60 fields per second and is used to denote 30i.
Note: NTSC, an SD-only format, has recently been replaced by ATSC (Advanced Television Systems Committee) for digital TV and HD broadcast in the U.S and includes SD channels.

## 24p

24p is much vaunted for its film look and is the standard Hollywood uses to create DVD and Blu-ray disks. Digital cinema, which runs at 24 fps (or at 48 fps increasingly in the future), currently projects more movies scanned from film than originating on 24p.

Broadcast is a different story. For SD video, most DPs shoot 60i, then change the camera's setting to output 24p video. For HD, they shoot 24P, 30P, or 60i. The rub? U.S. broadcast standards require conversion to 60Hz, a much easier interpolation from 30 fps than from 24 fps. The ability (in the future) to use 24p natively (all the way through) will change things. But for now, 24p is affected by the 60Hz standard which demands complex interpolations from every device — camera, telecine, editing system, broadcast system, etc. — that it touches.

The world of shooting, editing, broadcast, projection, and exhibition on the Web is in flux and will remain so. Stay alert and stay tuned!

# Aspect ratio

Aspect ratio denotes the ratio of width to height and is used to describe formats and screens. *Format aspect ratio* signifies film and video frames, e.g., 16:9 for film and 4:3 for SD video. It is your project's shooting format and is decided by the client or producer, usually in conjunction with the director and DP (director of photography, a.k.a. cinematographer).

*Screen aspect ratio* is the width to height ratio of the screen that the film or video format will be exhibited on, the most common being 1:78 for an HD television screen and 1:85 for a movie theater screen. It is your project's delivery format and a major consideration in deciding the format aspect ratio.

The most common aspect ratios for broadcast and projection worldwide are:

| FORMAT | TV SCREEN | FILM SCREEN |
|---|---|---|
| SD video | 4:3 equivalent to | 1.33:1 |
| HD video | 16:9 equivalent to | 1.78:1 |
| Super 16mm film | | 1.66:1 |
| 35mm film (Europe) | | 1.66:1 |
| 35mm film (U.S.) | 16:9 equivalent to | 1.85:1 |
| IMAX (projects 70mm sideways) | | 1:43:1 |
| Cinemascope (Super 35mm) | | 2.40:1 |

Format and screen aspect ratios don't always match. For example, film shows have been broadcast on SDTV (4:3) for years. To accomplish this, the film aspect ratio (16:9) is retrofitted to the 4:3 ratio, as outlined in Table 2.5, via four different methods.

**TABLE 2.5**
**RETROFITTING A 16:9 TO A 4:3 ASPECT RATIO**

| METHOD | ILLUSTRATION | DESCRIPTION | USE |
|---|---|---|---|
| PAN AND SCAN | | Moves and adjusts 16:9 image within the 4:3 frame. | Popular as it can keep most of the critical action in frame. |
| LETTERBOX | | Shrinks 16:9 image to fit 4:3 frame and inserts black at top and bottom to fill unused portion of frame. | Popular since nothing is lost, just shrunk. |
| PILLARBOX, A.K.A. CROP | | Crops sides of the 16:9 image to fit 4:3 frame. | Not popular or desirable. Cuts out action on both sides of frame. |
| WINDOWBOX, A.K.A. SHUTTERBOX | | Combines letterbox and pillarbox, cropping sides, top, and bottom to fit 16:9 image into 4:3 frame. | Not popular or desirable. Cuts out action on both sides of frame plus top and bottom. |

As HD video and HDTV sets eclipse SD video, format and screen ratios will be the same and need no adjustment. But when "old" 4:3, SD shows are broadcast, they will continue to require retrofitting.

## Editors and aspect ratio

It's a good idea to view and edit your show the way your audience is going to see it. This means using a 16:9 monitor if you're cutting HD or finishing on a film.

If your show has a film finish, the colorist can letterbox your dailies during telecine. The resultant black bars on the top and bottom are perfect for burning in time code and other critical film, tape, and sound data. The drawback to letterboxing your dailies is that the whole film frame is not visible. This becomes a problem from time to time when you need to see the whole frame to reposition a shot. The solution? View the original source material to see what is in the frame and decide what repositioning is possible. Some editors choose instead to receive their dailies full frame and use their editing system's letterbox feature to approximate a 16:9 aspect ratio. If you go this route, make a test before dailies pour in to be sure that the added black bars don't cover the burnt-in data.

## *What Exactly Happens in Telecine*

Telecine used to mean the transfer of film to tape and required the colorist to sync the picture and sound first. It took place at the beginning of a show and produced a daily tape for editing. Due to technological advances and the resultant change in workflows, telecine is expanding from a film transfer process to a film scanning process. The colorist now scans in the film frames first, then syncs picture and sound. Alternatively, to save money, the assistant editor syncs the dailies in the cutting room. More on the technical details as well as editorial's responsibilities (wherever syncing takes place) as we get to them in upcoming chapters.

A bigger change today is that the colorist spends more time on the look of the show and its images, saving the scanned frames in the computer to be refined during color grading. Telecine is shifting to the end of a show and merging with the DI process where the main goal is to create the best looking deliverable possible. Here's a rundown of how the telecine process unfolds:

**2.e** Colorist in a telecine bay works on film dailies using the Spirit Classic DataCine (left) threaded with a camera roll. *Photo courtesy of Digital Film Technology and The Mill Post facility.*

## It's all in the data

On the set of higher budget shows, a DIT (digital image technician) lives in the Video Village[6] and creates the LUT (look up table). This software chart contains the color values for each frame of film (or video). The colorist, DIT, director, and DP rely on the LUT along with their artistic sense to perfect the lighting, color, and look of the show on both film and video shows.

## Pre-telecine prep

The film lab processes the negative (OCN) and sends it over to the telecine bay at the post house. The negative is handled extremely carefully throughout telecine and vaulted afterward.

## Loading the picture and sound

The colorist (telecine operator) preps the picture and sound elements:

**Picture**: The negative camera roll is placed gingerly in a dust-free, film-scanning machine like the popular Spirit DataCine. The scanner has glass doors and a wet gate to counteract dust and scratches and keep the negative clean.

**Sound**: It arrives on file or tape and is loaded into the computer or a tape deck.

## Syncing and recording

Cueing up one take at a time, the colorist syncs picture and sound. If a smart slate[7] was used, its time code is referenced to speed up the process. The synced take is played back and scanned to a file or recorded to tape.

## Color grading

The colorist initially sets the color values unless there was a DIT. There are two main ways to go:

1. Low quality telecine — single color correction, a.k.a. one-lite transfer

    This approach saves money initially and gets the dailies to the cutting room on tape, file, or hard drive ASAP. The colorist makes a single color setting for each scene and saves a reference frame to a digital still store device. Should additional footage for the scene

---

6. Cluster of monitors and computers on the set which display the shot being filmed on camera and the data which goes along with it.

7. A digital slate which feeds time code to the picture and sound simultaneously during the shoot.

arrive, the colorist calls up the still store frame to color match the new footage to that of the previously telecined scene.

After online or as part of the DI process, the colorist performs the final, high quality color grading on only the shots in the show. The DP and director (feature films) or AP (TV shows) supervises the sessions. The parameters that they finalize include: color, saturation, lighting, style of the project's look, continuity of the look, gray scale, and white.

2. High quality telecine — multiple color correction, a.k.a. best light transfer

In this scenario the colorist takes the time to manipulate the color on each shot of dailies or on the director's preferred takes. The dailies are kept in a high quality format and final color correction may be eliminated or minimized, saving money on the back end of postproduction.

## An Overview Tour of the Digital Cutting Room

This tour leads you through the basics of how a digital machine operates to take your project from dailies to finishing format. More depth and detail will be added in upcoming chapters. The aim here is to introduce you to digital systems and give you the information you need to choose the right system for your project which is the focus of the last topic of this chapter.

## Digital and Computer Terms

*"The promise of digital nonlinear editing is that it will bring together not only film, video, and audio but also a variety of other media that have never had one common environment in which to coexist."*

—Thomas A. Ohanian, editor and designer of the Avid Media Composer, from his book *Digital Nonlinear Editing*

Ohanian's pre-Millennium words have proved true: As both consumers and film professionals, we nonchalantly jump from a Blu-ray disk to a DV tape to VHS to a Quicktime file to camera card and maybe even film. All of these old and new formats meet up in today's digital system. This variety of formats expands each year as engineers and IT techs write more algorithms, devise more devices, create new apps and protocols, and establish new standards. To stay grounded, here are a few fundamental terms:

### Digital editing system

A computer with editing software used to edit digital audio and video originating on file, film, disk, or tape. Referred to by other names: DES, workstation, NLE, and just plain editor. Most commonly, a digital editing system is called by its brand name, e.g., Avid, Final Cut Pro, Pro Tools or its brand title: Combustion, Flame, Media Composer, etc.

### Media

The material footage: video, audio, or both.

### Non-destructive editing

NLE digital systems spawned this term because they do not change (destroy) a frame of the media or the original source material during editing. Even when you create audio and visual effects, you do not destroy anything; rather, you create new media. The term has been extended to other editing operations such as color correcting and color filtering. Destructive editing is exemplified by film editing, where physical frames are cut and spliced, and linear tape editing, where frames are recorded over and erased.

### Memory card, a.k.a. flash card or card

A re-recordable electronic data and media storage device used in cameras and editing systems as well as in laptops, phones, MP3 players, and video game consoles.

### P2 card

Popular professional memory card produced by Panasonic and short for Professional Plug-In. P2, like other digital file formats such as SxS, is a wrapper for the compressed or uncompressed data inside.

**2.f** P2 card. *Photo courtesy of Panasonic.*

### Ingest, a.k.a. input

Put media, along with data, into a digital system.

## FireWire

Apple's name for its IEEE 1394 interface found in cable, wireless, fiber optic, and coaxial connectors. FireWire, as used from coast to coast in cutting rooms, is a user-friendly, inexpensive cable that allows for real-time data transfer from tape into the DES.

## Resolution, a.k.a. res or rez

The amount of detail an image holds, measured differently according to format. With the DV format, the greater the number of pixels (often measured in megapixels), the higher (better) the res.

## Transcode

Convert from one digital format to another such as SD to HD. Transcoding can take place automatically as when you download a file from a flip camera to a digital editing system. Or you can transcode manually, for instance when you want to change an offline (lower res) cut to a higher resolution.

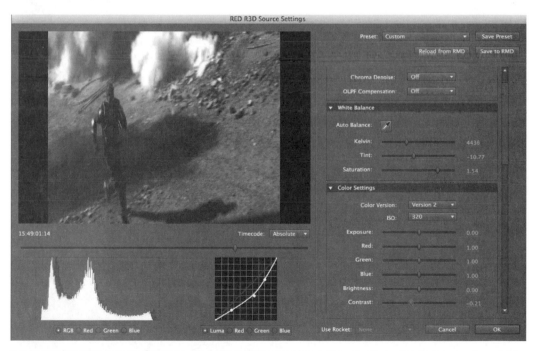

**2.g** Importing RED camera footage with transcoding occurring automatically in the background on Adobe Premiere Pro. *Photo courtesy of Adobe.*

### Uprez, a.k.a. upconvert

Convert from a lower resolution to a higher resolution, e.g., from SD to HD.

### Downrez, a.k.a. downconvert

Convert from a higher resolution to a lower resolution, e.g., from HD to SD.

### Clip

A shot ingested into a digital system.

### Sequence

An edited scene, show, or part of a show on a digital editing system.

### Output

Record a clip or sequence from a digital system to a tape. Also referred to as printing or playing out to tape.

### SAN

Storage area network. Networked servers that allow editors to share and access data and media files quickly and efficiently with other editors, including sound editors, VFX editors, and the post house. Examples: Apple's Xsan, Avid's Unity, and EditShare (by the company of the same name) which works with all systems.

**2.h** Avid's Unity, a widely used SAN. *Photo courtesy of Avid.*

### Import

Bring a file such as a P2, graphic file, CD (or other sound file) into a digital system.

### Export

Send out a file containing a clip, sequence, or data from a digital system.

### Digital intermediary or intermediate, a.k.a. DI

Scanning process that brings together all source formats to create a digital file of the locked cut for the final finishing processes which will produce the show master on film, file, disk, and/or tape.

## Digital Editing Machines Basics

### What exactly is a digital editing system?

It's a computer with editing software made up of:

- An internal hard drive to hold data about shots, edits, and cut shows. Also media, if the project is small.
- External hard drives to store the media — digital images and sound — for editing.
- A monitor or two — SD and/or HD.
- Plug-in hardware for audio, disk backup, signal processing, etc.
- Specialized capture cards for graphics, network, audio, etc.
- A DV deck, audio mixer, mic, and whatever other recording or playback devices you care to connect.

### What does a digital editing system do?

You use a digital editing system to:

- Edit anything from a commercial to a music video to news to a feature film.
- Organize, log, and view footage and cuts.
- Create and import VFX.
- Edit sound and music.
- Capture digital dailies from card, hard drive, or tape and digitize analog tapes.
- Import CDs, DVDs, Blu-rays and other discs.
- Upload or download files from SANs or servers.
- Import audio, graphics, animation and other files.
- Export project files, film cut lists, sound, and video files.
- Output a clip or sequence to tape or file.

### How do you edit on a digital editing system?

In a nutshell: You click with a mouse on menu items or graphic icons and use a keyboard to organize footage, play clips, and make editing decisions. Here are the four major steps:

**1.** *Ingest dailies*

Digitize[8]: To ingest an analog tape into a digital system, its signal must be sampled and converted to digital video, audio, and data. In

---

8. The word digitizing, since it preceded capturing, is habitually generalized to mean ingesting, whether capturing, digitizing, or importing. For clarity's sake, *Cut by Cut* will use specific terms.

other words, since analog video is non-digital material, it must be digitized.

Capture: DV tapes are already digital so technically, they are not digitized. Rather, they are captured, either directly from the camera or from a tape deck.

Import: You select the digital editing system's import command to bring in media from a disk or file from a hard drive or network server.

**2.** *Organize*

You log clips, then organize them in useful ways such as by scene, speaker, subject, location, story, etc.

**3.** *Edit*

You put together audio and video clips using a keyboard and mouse to create a cut. You screen the cut with the powers-that-be — director, producer, or client — after which you re-edit and re-screen the show until it is locked.

**4.** *Finish*

You output the final, locked cut to its delivery format or generate a list of edits for the post house or lab to recreate the cut via online, the DI process, or the negative film cut process.

# Components of the Digital Editing System

The digital editing system is a computer, so many of its components and their functions will be familiar to you. In Figure 2.i the components are labeled and they are described here.

## Internal hard drive

This is the brains of the system and contains your project's data and metadata; it can keep the data for hundreds of projects. Normally you don't put media on your internal hard drive unless your projects are small and you're diligent about media management.

## External hard drive

The external hard drive stores the media files. Part of the editing job is to make sure that you have enough storage space for all your media files. The larger your project, the more storage space you'll need, and the more hard drives you'll need to rent or buy. External hard drives are

**2.i** Components of a digital editing system.

also used to back up the internal hard drive, sneakernet footage from one computer to another, and archive footage.

## Disk drives and files

Digital systems contain the usual drives and inputs for CD, DVD, and memory stick. You use these to import and export files, install software, and make dubs.

### FILES YOU WOULD IMPORT

Databases, telecine logs, CD music, graphics, fonts, EDLs, cutlists, animation, web files.

### FILES YOU WOULD NOT IMPORT

Any software nonessential to editing that may slow down the system or inflict a virus.

### FILES YOU WOULD EXPORT

EDLs, cutlists, graphic files, project data files, audio files, streaming video files, animation files.

### FILES YOU WOULD NOT EXPORT

Anything that is proprietary or that for which copying would be considered piracy.

## Keyboard

You use the keyboard to label clips and perform most editing functions including marking clips, making edits and effects, and trimming sequences. You can customize the keyboard to your style of editing by using the system's software. For a few extra bucks, on Avid, Final Cut Pro, and other systems, you can have a keyboard with candy colored keys imprinted with symbols representing each key's function(s).

## Monitors

Two types of monitors — graphics and video — are routinely hooked up to a digital system. They can be set up on the left or right according to your preference.

### GRAPHICS MONITOR

This screen displays graphics in the form of icons, menus, and text. You click on these icons and menus to make editing and computer system choices. The graphics monitor also displays digital images such as shots and cuts.

Many systems offer two graphics monitors which editors find handy for dividing the work: One screen is used for organizing and the other for cutting. Having two graphic monitors is almost a necessity on multiple camera shows such as rock concerts and sitcoms as well as on shows with huge amounts of footage.

On low budget system setups, the editor makes and views all cuts on the graphic monitor and there may be no other monitors of any kind.

### VIDEO MONITOR, A.K.A. NTSC MONITOR

When you play a clip or a sequence, it runs full-screen on the video monitor, like it's on a TV screen. Multiple-camera shows may have four NTSC monitors, one for each camera. More monitors can be added if need be. It's advantageous to have an NTSC monitor so you can view dailies and your cuts full-screen. Also, with proper calibration, an NTSC monitor will display the image colors the way they will appear to the broadcast audience.

## Mouse

The mouse operates like an ordinary mouse: You click it to select things and drag it to move things. On a digital system you depend on the mouse for many functions, such as selecting clips, sequences, menus, and tools and opening bins (folders) of your footage.

## Mixer, a.k.a. mixing board

Professional digital editing software contains a sophisticated set of editing tools for adjusting and mixing audio levels and adding reverb and other SFX. The result? Many systems — lower budget mainly — are set up without external hardware mixers. Many other systems, however, do include an external mixer as well as a mic for recording VO (voiceover narration). A mixer allows you to closely monitor and manipulate audio as it enters the system and as you output it.

## TBC (time base corrector)

Existing as a stand-alone machine or residing inside a tape deck, a TBC is an essential electronic device that fixes errors in an analog video signal and regulates the signal's video and chroma (color) level, hue, and set-up during playback.

## Black burst generator

An electronic device that generates a reference signal — a black burst — which records as pure black on videotape. Editors, tape operators, and colorists rely on this signal generator to synchronize VTRs, especially analogue decks such as Beta SP.

## UPS (uninterruptible power supply)

Power surges, drops, or outages can damage or destroy the digital system and all your work. Losing data — shots, edits, cuts, and everything else on the internal hard drive — is an editor's nightmare. A UPS prevents this by taking over for a short while so you can back up your work and exit the system before all power, and potentially data, is lost. A UPS is a peripheral which manufacturers highly recommend that system owners add. While you may never need to use it, don't take the chance.

# Features of Digital Systems

## On the positive side

### STATE-OF-THE-ART TECHNOLOGY

Most films and videos are cut on digital editing systems today. The technology, particularly in the area of VFX creation, resolution, and software and hardware compatibility, is continually being developed and improved so that the editor can do more and do it faster and better. Because digital systems allow the transfer of files and media via networks and the Internet, editors can swiftly acquire data from the postproduction facility or information and approval from the director or client.

### Nonlinear + random access = Experimentation to your heart's content

On a digital system you can locate any frame anywhere at any time. With the click of a mouse or press of a key, you can call up and edit the footage any way that you like. Making changes on a digital system is fast and efficient. You can play with frames, putting them in or out of the show, and move shots or scenes around rapidly. When screening a cut for a client or producer, you don't need to make a tape or troop over to a screening room: You can all view the show right on the system. Afterward, if desired, you can all collaborate to make changes right then and there on the system.

### Speed and flexibility = Saving time

Digital systems work as fast as your brain (except when rendering[9] VFX or hanging or crashing like any other computer). Once you've decided where to make your edit, making it is instantaneous. Undoing an edit — or a slew of edits — is equally speedy.

### Multiple versions

You can have many versions (sequences) of a scene or an entire show with a digital editing system. If you are experimenting, first make a copy of your current sequence. Then if your experiment fails, you can go back to the copy.

Suppose you land a job as an assistant or apprentice editor. Since digital systems allow infinite versions, you can edit your own cut. Just make sure it's done on your own time and with the editor's knowledge, that your sequence is properly labeled and saved separately from the editor's sequences, and that you leave the system as you found it.

### Sound

You can bring in many sounds from many sources to a digital system. For example, you can import music from CDs, cassettes, and DAT or plug in a microphone to add VO. Also, digital systems' sound tools have gotten so sophisticated that you can add all the sound tracks you want and mix your cut right on the system.

---

9. Creating new media for a digital video effect or image.

### EFFECTS AND TITLES

On digital systems, you create the majority of VFX in real time[10]. Complex VFX, like 3-D, can take a few minutes to render. With every new software version, the amount of time it takes to make audio and video (A and V) effects decreases and the number of A and V effects offered increases. The advantage of all this is that you can swiftly establish how the effect looks and avoid the costly, time-consuming, trial-and-error process of the film lab.

Additionally, you can readily add titles to your sequence: All manner of fonts and credit styles are available on your system or for import.

### PERSONAL PLEASURE

There may be times when working on a digital system that you will feel as I have, that you're getting paid to operate what is the equivalent of a Rolls Royce: an incredible editing machine on which you would have edited for free, just for the pure joy of editing.

## On the negative side

### COMPUTER OBSOLESCENCE

There will always be new upgrades and systems to purchase on digital systems. Within five years many systems, while still up and running, will be unable to handle the new software and/or hardware and become dated.

### MEDIA MANAGEMENT

This housekeeping chore is a fact of life on digital editing systems. Media management means keeping an eye on the amount of media on your drives and keeping track of which shots and shows are located on which drives. The job entails judicious copying, moving, backing up, archiving and deleting of media so that each show and digital system keeps running efficiently. Media management is a major responsibility on today's systems, most of which have a media manager tool to assist you.

### LEARNING CURVE

To stay current and employable, most editors spend time and money to learn new systems. Learning a digital editing system takes time and money. For example Avid 101, the introductory course, takes three days and costs over $1,000. Practice time is necessary after each course. If you

---

10. An effect for which the creation time equals the time it takes to select the effect and put it in the sequence.

**2.j** Editing on a digital system. *Photo courtesy of Sue Odjakjian.*

don't get on a system right after the course to practice or to work, the knowledge fades away faster than that cool dissolve you made.

Mastering one system doesn't mean you can automatically grasp another. They're all similar but totally different, like French and Spanish. You need training on each system. Also, since systems have many features, there are lots of different courses offered: VFX, media management, film shows, advanced editing, etc. Some features and processes you won't ever use, then blammo! You'll find yourself on a project where you will need to. What to do? Find someone to show you, or, if you know in advance, take a course. You can always learn new tricks from the teacher and often from the other students.

Cutting digitally requires a lot of general knowledge. You need to understand time code and videotape, have solid computer and Internet skills, be able to create VFX on third-party software (preferably), and have experience with film if you're hired on a film show, not to mention know how to edit! Working on a digital system, even when you're totally comfortable, is a constant learning process. Just when you become familiar with the current software, there's an upgrade or new version and more to learn!

If you need to learn how to operate a system, build the training class and learning curve into your project's time and budget. Put yourself through your paces: Practice editing scenes until you find yourself thinking more about the show and less about how you'll make the next edit. The more practice editing you do, the more the editing process and the system will become second nature. You want to feel comfortable and confident about the system on the job. Secure a system guru to work on the project if possible or to take your midnight calls when you or the system get hung up.

## TECHNICAL HELP

Since a digital system is a computer, in time it will freeze, crash, or worse. Routine hang-ups you'll learn to handle; for complex problems, you'll need technical help. Most system owners and rental facilities pay for a service contract that provides for technical help 24/7.

Ordinarily the tech support people can solve your problem over the phone but there are times when they'll need to make a service call. You will appreciate their expertise; down time costs you editing time and can be stressful. Stay calm, focus on the problem, and treat the tech well.

Techs can be helpful for other reasons too. Since digital systems do so much, from time to time you'll need help doing something you've never tried before or did long ago and forgot. Techs can talk you through these operations. Also, when you receive a new software version, you may suddenly have problems with familiar operations. Tech support will usually have workarounds or other solutions to keep you going.

## SCHEDULING — SHIFT WORK

Because digital systems are expensive to rent, often your company will rent only one system. Since two people cannot work on a system at the same time, the editor will assign shifts. This can lead to communication problems between members of the editing crew and feelings of isolation and disconnection from each other and the project. On a feature film, when work print and conforming are involved, there may be a double set of assistants — digital and film. Intricate scheduling is necessary so the situation doesn't deteriorate into chaos.

These problems can be ameliorated with the networking of systems, the sharing of media, and a super job of organization. Commonly, the assistant editor ingests and organizes footage using their own laptop, then transfers it in to the editor's system.

### A DIGITAL SYSTEM'S WORK IS NEVER DONE

Many filmmakers, while positive about digital technology, point out that nothing seems to ever be finished. As with other computer creations, the polishing and re-working carries on until the last moment when the show must air or the negative be cut. Web pieces can be revised and uploaded daily if desired. Some would say this is a good thing since improvements and inspirations can be brought to bear for a much longer period than with film or tape editing; others believe this brings a haze of impermanence to a project, leaving it never really complete since it can always be re-edited and remastered.

## *Last word*

Editing on a digital system is an exciting, cutting-edge place to be. Enjoy your mastery of a system and creating the show you want. A digital system is a tool — *your* tool — and you need to be in control of it to cut the show. Director James Cameron, who learned Avid in order to join the editorial team of *Titanic*, reflects, "The amazing thing is, like any learning experience, it becomes self-defining. When you realize you need something, you learn it. It'll become another arrow in the quiver, and pretty soon you'll be working at a complex level."

# Common Digital Editing Systems

*"Media Composer is my most valued tool as a film editor. My brain and my heart are the only other processors I need."*
—CHRIS INNIS, A.C.E., *The Hurt Locker*

The most commonly used professional digital editing systems today indisputably are Final Cut Pro (FCP), Avid, and Adobe Premiere Pro. Two other professional systems you may encounter — Lightworks and Media 100 — have lost favor and suffered financially but remain afloat and maintain loyal users. (Lightworks, a UK-designed system, has retained its user base in the UK, Europe, Australia, and elsewhere and was used to edit *The King's Speech*).

There are many other low-budget systems around and there are still a few people editing on film, notably, Steven Spielberg's editors. News editors use FCP and Avid, and others systems, notably Grass Valley's Edius and Aurora systems. For the purposes of this book and showing you how systems typically operate, we'll describe the three most popular systems. In order of appearance they are:

## Avid

Avid Technologies, Inc. pioneered digital nonlinear editing in 1989, a time when the most technologically advanced editors were using nonlinear tape systems and the majority of editors cut on film or linear tape. In 1994 Avid won the Academy Award for technical achievement, along with Lightworks.

Synonymous with digital NLEs, Avid is the tool-of-the-trade in Hollywood and across the country. You'll see its logo trailing many a motion picture credit and it dominates television editing as well.

Avid used to offer a lot of systems but currently has pared down to a few. Media Composer remains its tried-and-true foot soldier for everyday editing while its high end digital suites are the "DS" (Digital Symphony)

**2.k** Avid Media Composer on Mac laptop. *Photo courtesy of Avid.*

**2.i** Adobe Premiere Pro. *Photo courtesy of Adobe.*

and the Nitris. Originally a Mac-based system, Avid products now run on both PC and Mac platforms. Nothing beats it for film shows and for the intricacies of fine-tuning (trimming) cuts.

## Adobe Premiere Pro

Premiering in 1991 as a consumer editing system, Premiere Pro upped its market and reputation to attract prosumers and professionals and has gained traction with broadcasters, schools, independent filmmakers, and corporations. In a further pitch to professionals, it was renamed Adobe Premiere Pro in 2003. Clearly a plus is Premiere Pro's ability to interface with Adobe's After Effects, Media Encoder, and Photoshop programs as well as its DVD authoring, sound, and Web software. Also, Adobe bundles it in their Creative Suite packages.

## Final Cut Pro

Apple spun FCP into orbit in 1999 just as the DV evolution took hold. The preferred tool of the Millennium gen and corporate filmmakers, videographers, and independent filmmakers for its low budget, high performance, cutting-edge qualities, FCP is making inroads into Hollywood features and television shows and giving Avid a much needed competitor. With Apple's mighty dollars and brains behind it, FCP has dominated sales, especially among millennials and corporate,

**2.m** Final Cut Pro. *Photo courtesy of Apple.*

reality, and non-Hollywood feature editors. Countering this trend is Apple's disastrous June 2011 launch of FCP X. A brand-new generation of software, X is presently designed for people who work exclusively in tapeless workflows, and not intended for those whose projects use tape or film. Many professionals have jumped ship to Avid or Adobe. The upshot? Currently, the jury is out on the fate of FCP.

## Last word

User groups[11] help spread the word about the latest apps, plug-ins, work-flows, and protocols to keep users informed and excited about these top three tools. I highly recommend connecting with these groups as well as attending manufacturer sponsored events to not only see the latest software version but network. Additionally I would remind you: All systems are simply tools. And you are an editor. Not an Avid editor or a FCP editor or a Premiere editor. Just a plain, proud editor. And you should be prepared and honored to work on whatever tools exist or come down the pike next for editing.

---

11. I've included user groups in the Resources section of this book and on www.joyoffilmeditng.com. But you can easily find them yourself. Just search the Web by typing *user group*, the name of the system, and the name of your nearest big city or town. Even if you live too far away to make a meeting, you can get tons of info at the group's site and pose questions on the online forums.

# Choosing a Digital Editing System

To make your decision, answer questions about these subjects:

## Finishing format & workflow

Does the system allow me to finish on the format(s) I need using the workflow I've designed?

## VFX

Does my project require the editor to make a lot of effects other than the normal dissolves and fades? If so, choose a system that allows you to create the effects you desire or is compatible with the effects software you intend to use.

## Compatibility

Do I need to network with other systems, work with certain plug-in software, import graphic, animation, Internet, sound, or other types of files? Does my project necessitate uploading or downloading cuts or media to or from servers? Be sure that your system is compatible and can perform all the operations you require.

## Budget

Does the cost to buy or rent the system fit my budget? It's worthwhile to visit several post houses and contact more than one seller to see their different price quotes and packages. Make sure you understand the full range of options and what happens should you add a component or make a change after the system is set up. When picking a post house, choose a facility that will calmly and deftly shepherd you through, no matter how roughly or smoothly your project goes.

## Get advice

What do your peers know? Talk to cohorts and other editors about your project's needs to get their feedback and recommendations.

## See the system in action

How do you like working on the system? As you narrow down your choice, get your hands on the system. Check out a demo or better, take a class on the system and visit a cutting room where it's being used. In other words, ask a million questions and become an expert before picking your system.

### Last word

Be clear on your project's requirements and rent or buy the system that does what you need — no more and no less.

### The future: To build a better mousetrap, er, editing system

Systems are getting cheaper and more complex because users — editors, directors, and producers — demand more functions, compatibilities, and speed while manufacturers hustle to outdo each other. The outcome? Systems will continue to flash and fade as they are challenged by others that are cheaper, better, and faster.

## CHAPTER WRAP-UP

With your newfound knowledge of video, digital and film concepts, you can now confidently enter a cutting room and fathom what its inhabitants are talking about. More importantly, you're prepared to set up a cutting room and design your project's workflow, which is what the next chapter is all about.

# PART TWO
# Organizing for Editing

## Introduction

Building on the decisions you made in Part One, Part Two tells you how to turn a jumble of dailies into an orderly collection of scenes and shots. Chapter Three explains everyday organizational practices including workflows, logging, and scheduling. Chapter Four covers how to enter dailies into the digital system and prep them for editing. Once you're finished with Part Two, you'll be ready to begin editing in Stage II.

Following Part Two and Stage One is Appendix C, a form for budgeting this stage of postproduction. You can copy it or tailor it to fit your film or video. You can also download it from the Free tab of www.joyof-filmediting.com.

## CHAPTER 3

# Setting Up the Cutting Room

*Workflows, Labeling Shots, and Other*
*Common Cutting Room Tasks*

## Overview

This chapter could also be titled: "What do you need in the cutting room besides great footage and a good coffeemaker? Organization!" Whether you're an assistant editor or the editor "doing it all," there are organizing practices that are not only customary but essential to running a smooth editing operation. These include dealing with the picture and sound reports that arrive in the cutting room along with dailies and communicating with the many people that you'll encounter in the cutting room. The chapter also covers the universal way to log dailies so everyone understands your shot descriptions, how to design a postproduction schedule, and how to prepare tapes for dubbing dailies.

But first, a few words about workflows...

## Working with Workflows

Welcome to the wonderful world of workflows — the name of the game in planning a project's path through postproduction today. There are workflows for HD shows, workflows for 3-D shows, for low budget docs, for low budget dramas, for animated shows, reality shows, TV dramas, features, for FCP shows, for Avid shows: You name it, there's a WF for it. Workflows are also designed according to editing system, type of show, budget, camera used (Genesis, RED, Viper, etc.), region, and politics among many other reasons. While there are ordinary workflows, it's just as ordinary to deviate from them; each project is different.

How to make sense of it all?

Know the common workflows so that you can create your own. We will lay out the three main workflows: tape, tapeless, a.k.a. file, and film. But even these overlap each other. For instance, you may shoot film and end up on tape or shoot tape but deliver by file.

Understanding these WFs (or at least the first two if you're not shooting film) will ground you in the basic steps and processes of postproduction and enable you to design your own WF. Your workflow will likely deviate from these in one way or another or be a hybrid version of one of them. Last, be aware that you can get input from the post supervisor or, if you're the assistant editor, from the editor in setting down the WF. Here are the three main workflows along with descriptions of the processes involved and the types of shows they're used on:

## Tape workflow — See Figure 3.1

A tape workflow, by definition, entails shooting, viewing, and finishing on tape. However, in this digital age, this workflow will involve files for editing at a minimum, and may use files instead of tapes for shooting, dubs, viewing, etc. So it may not be a strictly tape WF all the way.

### FILMING

The production crew may go single system and put all sound and picture on tape, which is most likely on low budget shows and corporate and event videos as well as on high-budget TV shows. Picture is shot on tape in this WF but sound, increasingly on TV shows, may be recorded on card, hard drive or possibly optical disk. If the crew shoots double system, the editing crew syncs the sound and picture files on the digital editing system — a prime reason for good slates and time code! Or the post house may do this and deliver a synced-up hard drive.

### EDITING

The first order of business is to ingest the dailies into the digital system. Using the ingest tool and a FireWire or USB cable (usually referred to as simply "FireWire" or "USB"), you will capture the tape and import any files, whether on card or hard drive. Unless storage is *not* an issue, you will downrez the media as you ingest it so it will fit on your drives and can be edited.

**FIGURE 3.1**
**TAPE WORKFLOW**

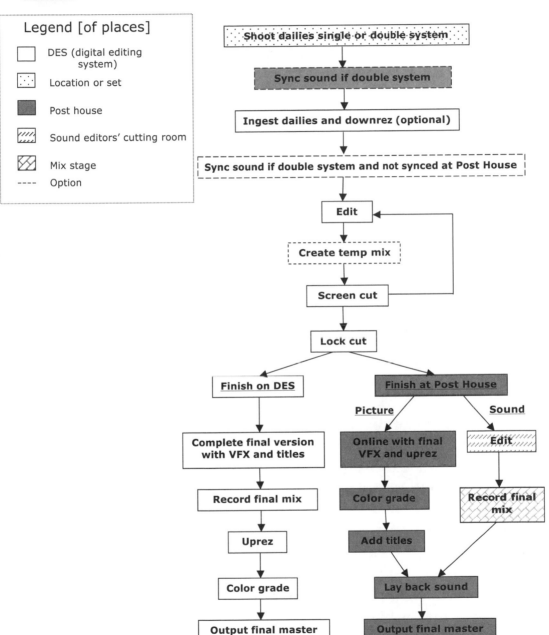

Next, it's frequently editorial's job to make dubs — copies of the dailies — for the director, producer, client, studio, network, and anyone else who requires them. You may dub dailies to tape or disk or to a file (QuickTime ordinarily) for uploading to the viewer's PC, cell phone, smart phone, or other computer device.

Finally, it's time to edit! The editor will build the show each day as new dailies roll in. Invariably, editors will create or lay out VFX on the system or import them from the special effects house. Also, they likely will create a temp (temporary) mix of the sound: dialogue, narration, music, and sound effects.

Soon, the day will come when the first cut is complete and ready for screening with the powers-that-be: director, producer, or client. For those who can't make the screening, editorial will again make dubs. As the show is edited and re-edited, more people will need dubs such as the sound editors, composer, trailer editor, and marketing folks.

At last the cut will be locked and the show will enter the next stage of the workflow.

### FINISHING

A few things — or a lot of things — will be done to the locked cut before the show is put to the final tape for its audience. On low budget shows, the editor will perform all the sound editing and finishing work. Typically, the editor will upconvert the show to HD or a higher res final format. The editor will finalize titles and other graphics as well as VFX, perform a final mix of the sound tracks, and do some color grading to make the show look and sound its best.

If there is money in the budget, sound editors will get cracking on the sound tracks on their Pro Tools or another DAW (digital audio workstation), and the post house will take care of the picture tasks. Editorial will oversee the post house as it onlines the show and the DP, DIT, AP, or post supervisor will keep an eye on the color grading by the post house's colorist. Editorial and/or the AP (on TV shows) or the director (on features) will also watch over the sound mix on the sound stage, along with the sound supervisor.

To enable the post house and the sound editors to do their work, editorial will hand them a file which lists each edit along with its time code and reel number. Editorial will also present the post house and sound editors with a tape, disk, or hard drive of the locked cut for ingesting into their computers.

## DELIVERING

The post house will marry — lay back — the new soundtrack to the master online tape to create the final show master tape and send it to the network for broadcast. In this digital age, however, the tape may well be copied to disk or file and delivered to the audience. So, yes, a tape workflow may in the end produce a file, tape, or disk.

If you are finishing the show on your digital editing system, you will output the final version of your show to tape, disk, and/or file, depending on your delivery requirements, and ship it.

### Tapeless workflow, a.k.a. file-based workflow — See Figure 3.2

The name says it all: a file-based workflow shoots to files and sticks with 'em the whole way through. Tapeless WFs are encroaching on both film and tape WFs and are used on all types of projects from no or low budget to corporate pieces to TV series to feature films. So a file-based workflow is the way of the present and future and will be a part of any workflow you design.

## FILMING

A tapeless workflow shoots double system, generating separate picture and sound files. On higher budget shows, a DIT will set the color and other image values on the set using a LUT (look-up table). The DIT copies the folders of picture files — one scene per folder — from the camera to drives (or tapes if tape WF) for the cutting room and the post house. Frequently the files will require transcoding — converting to an editable file format — before they can be brought into the editing system. To speed things up, Adobe, Avid, and FCP have built tools that allow you to copy tapeless media from a mixture of file formats while the transcoding takes place in the background.

## EDITING

Once dailies hit the cutting room, editorial ingests them into the DES and downrezzes and syncs them if the post house didn't do it. Editing proceeds as with a tape WF: Dubs are made and the editor edits away. Before screening the cut, the editor adds music, VFX, and perhaps a temp mix. After the screening, editorial creates dubs for those who couldn't make the screening as the editing progresses to a locked cut.

Additionally, on tapeless (and tape) shows such as TV series or studio features, there may be a server network, a.k.a. SAN (storage area

**3.a** Avid Media Access (AMA) signifies the new trend: It plays back native file formats such as XDCAM, QT with H.264, and ProRes files as shown here, decoding the footage as it's ingested so you can start editing right away. *Photo courtesy of Avid.*

network) for sharing clips, cuts, and other files, as well as media with other editors and the post house.

### Finishing

Again, the process mirrors the tape workflow: Sound will be mixed on the DES or the mix stage and VFX finalized on the DES or during online. Finally, the show will be color graded and upconverted to HD or the highest SD resolution.

### Delivering

Delivery may be as simple as a final upload to a server for YouTube or the company's intranet portal for corporate shows. Or it may involve sending a hard drive to the network (TV shows) which may also require a tape. With a file-based show, as with any workflow, you may also deliver on disk for home entertainment.

# FIGURE 3.2
## TAPELESS WORKFLOW

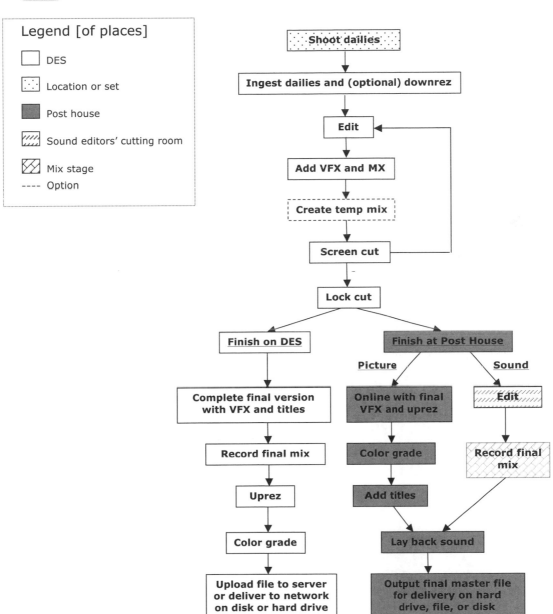

Legend [of places]

☐ DES

▦ Location or set

▦ Post house

▨ Sound editors' cutting room

▨ Mix stage

---- Option

Shoot dailies

Ingest dailies and (optional) downrez

Edit

Add VFX and MX

Create temp mix

Screen cut

Lock cut

Finish on DES

Finish at Post House

Picture                Sound

Complete final version with VFX and titles

Online with final VFX and uprez

Edit

Record final mix

Color grade

Record final mix

Uprez

Add titles

Color grade

Lay back sound

Upload file to server or deliver to network on disk or hard drive

Output final master file for delivery on hard drive, file, or disk

## *Film workflow — See Figure 3.3*

Defining a film workflow appears straightforward: You shoot on film, edit on film, and deliver on film. Not so fast, buckaroos. For starters, most shows edit digitally, on files, not film these days. Secondly, while many feature filmmakers still shoot film for its superior look, these days a film deliverable is often achieved by shooting with a digital camera on 24p video or files and constructing a release print through the DI (digital intermediate) process. Furthermore, the DI process may create a print as well as a file for projecting.

Yes, we live in a polyglot world of media formats and it has invaded the traditional film workflow! Tim Burton's 3-D film *Alice in Wonderland* is a good example. Additional editor J. C. Bond reports that, "the bookends, which take place in 'the real world,' were shot on film. The stuff in Underland, or Wonderland, was all shot digitally."

Bottom line, when you construct a film workflow you will be paralleling parts of tape and tapeless workflows.

### FILMING

Shooting on film professionally has always been a double system operation and it continues that way today. The camera captures the picture on film negative and the digital sound recorder puts the audio to file via card, disk, or hard drive. The film lab processes the negative camera reels, then sends them over to the post house where they meet up with the sound files. The colorist scans them all into the computer, syncs them, and copies the completed dailies to tape, file, or hard drive for the editing crew.

### EDITING

In the cutting room, ingesting, organizing, and making dubs proceed as usual. If the show shoots on film and will deliver on film, the assistant editor verifies time code, film codes, and other crucial data so that the cutlist — necessary for duplicating the locked cut on film — is accurate. (The last section of Chapter 4 details how to do these verifications.)

As editing and completing cuts get underway, screenings will take place in the normal ways. In addition, on big features, there will be previews. Usually before the preview, a temp mix will be recorded on the mix stage. The temp track will be ingested into the editor's digital system and added to the screening version of the cut. If the show previews on tape, the cut will be uprezzed in the cutting room or at the post

# FIGURE 3.3
# FILM WORKFLOW

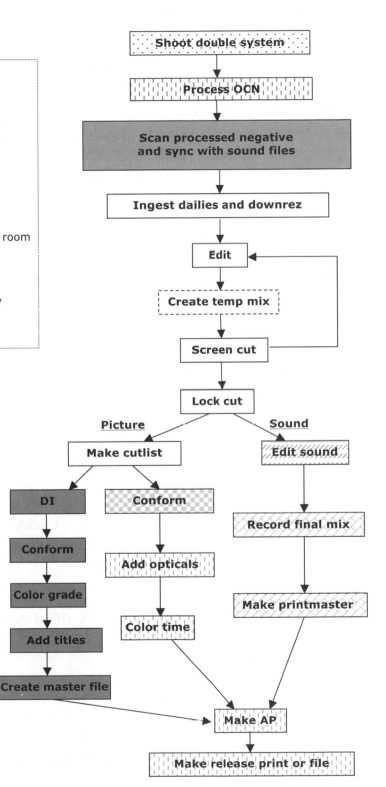

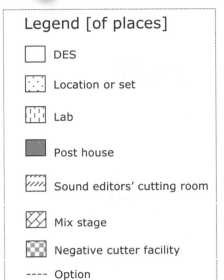

**Legend [of places]**

☐ DES

▫ Location or set

▨ Lab

▨ Post house

▨ Sound editors' cutting room

▨ Mix stage

▨ Negative cutter facility

---- Option

Shoot double system

Process OCN

Scan processed negative
and sync with sound files

Ingest dailies and downrez

Edit

Create temp mix

Screen cut

Lock cut

**Picture**     **Sound**

Make cutlist     Edit sound

DI     Conform     Record final mix

Conform     Add opticals

Color grade     Make printmaster

Add titles     Color time

Create master file

Make AP

Make release print or file

house. If the show previews on film, a film print will be struck via the DI process or conforming to film. Finally, after a series of screenings and a preview or two, the cut will be locked.

## FINISHING

How will your project be projected in the theater? On film or file or both? This will determine how you finish the show.

### Film finish

There are two methods for producing a film release print for projecting: The traditional film negative cutter route or the increasingly popular DI route. Both methods require that the editing crew break the show into reels and make a cutlist for each reel. The methods then split for a few important steps. With the traditional route, the negative cutter sends the cut neg to the lab which processes and color-times it to make a positive film print called an AP (answer print). If you go the DI route, the colorist scans the negative to create a DI which is color graded to make a file known as the digital AP.

The methods converge again as both types of APs are thoroughly reviewed and approved. Then they are married to the sound optical track which the lab has created from the printmaster, a file made by the sound mixers just for this purpose. From the final AP, release prints are struck for projecting in theaters. Don't worry, Chapters 12 and 13 go over these methods thoroughly. For now, to design your workflow, you just need to determine which route your show will take.

### File finish

The post house combines the digital AP with the printmaster to produce a final, master file which is then used to create encrypted files for digital projection.

## DELIVERING

Release prints, divided into reels, are distributed to the theaters for film projection or a file is uploaded and exported to a hard drive for digital projection.

# Setting up the cutting room

It may be a dump or a palace, a closet, a cubicle, or room with enough space for a couch and chair. It could be in your house or the director's, at a studio or post house, in a motel, or a mobile home. Music video editor Dean Gonzalez cut *30 Seconds to Mars* on a bus while touring with the band for months.

Whatever. Wherever. The cutting room is your work home and you'll be clocking a lot of hours in it. You'll experience tense times, fun times, frustration, joy — the gamut of moods and emotions. And, hopefully, you'll create something you're satisfied with — even proud of — in the end. All in the ever-so-humble cutting room.

## Arranging the room

*"Make sure your chair's comfortable and ergonomically sound — your butt's going to spend long hours in that seat."*
—Preditor[1] LES PERKINS, LesIsMore Productions

You may set up the room yourself but more likely it will be set up before you are scheduled to show up. Either way, there are a few things to keep in mind.

### GENERAL APPEARANCE

The room should be friendly. Not so friendly with too comfy couches that people overstay their welcome and usefulness. But not so drab, cold, or dirty that the place hinders concentration and long hours. The room should also be tidy: You want to be able to lay your hands on tapes, paperwork, phone numbers — everything — easily! Sometimes, in the frenzy of ingesting dailies and blasting out cuts, chaos happens. But as soon as there's the slightest lull, make it unhappen. A cutting room that's a pit causes tension and makes you waste time in desperately seeking screening notes or a missing latte. Editing is not for slobs. Organize your cutting room efficiently so you can spend the bulk of your time on the creative part — editing!

### CORKBOARD

A lot of editors like to tack index cards with the show's scenes to a corkboard or bulletin board on the wall. This way editorial and  the director can get an overall flow of the show and easily move cards (scenes) around. Despite this "going green" paperless world and all the descriptions that digital systems permit, the classic card system still works for many filmmakers, giving them the fluidity and ease they need to map out scenes and shows.

---

1. Producer-editor

## COMFORT AND WORKABILITY

Room setup doesn't take place automagically. Think about how you work. What is the best ergonomic arrangement of your keyboard, mouse, mixer, notes, phone etc.? Are there adequate shelves for tapes, drives, supplies, etc.? Are the tools you use — phone, pen, pad, etc. — easily accessible?

Low lighting is usually preferred in cutting rooms so the images on the screen can be seen most clearly. Can you dim the lights for screenings and raise them for discussions? Is the thermostat under your control? Power? There's nothing like an inadequate power supply to darken your epic first cut screening or cause the system to crash and you to lose time and work. Make sure there's sufficient power for all your equipment. And plug a UPS (uninterruptible power supply) into your computer.

## *Test drive your editing system before each show*

Don't assume everything on your editing system works unless you own the system. Put your system through its paces by checking out everything that you will be doing: ingesting and outputting to tape, mixing sound, recording with the mic, making DVDs, importing from CDs, etc. You don't want to wait until dailies are flying through the door to find out your deck isn't reading time code or a channel on your mixer is muted. This is a good time to ingest any stock shots, VFX, or SFX (sound effects) you know you might be using. Testing is particularly critical if you are using a new or upgraded software version.

## LAST WORD

Dealing with potential hiccups in the editing room ahead of time prevents disruptions, lowers stress, and lays the groundwork for a smooth, positive editorial process.

# Communication

COMMUNICATION IS ESSENTIAL between editor and

- Assistant editor
- Director
- Lab
- Music supervisor, composer, editor, and assistant
- Post house: colorist, rep, scheduler, and online editor
- Post supervisor, post coordinator, and post PA
- Producer, co-producer, and AP (associate producer)
- Special effects house
- Script supervisor
- Sound supervisor, editor, and assistant
- VFX supervisor, editor, and assistant

Keep everyone's contact info — phone numbers and emails — prominent in the cutting room, as well as on your computer, cell phone, etc. Things like schedules, screenings, and the arrival time of dailies can change abruptly, so swift communication is vital.

## *Things you need to communicate about:*

- ▶ Where to put what in the cutting room, starting with the espresso machine.
- ▶ Dailies.
- ▶ The schedule.
- ▶ Furniture: The editors' chairs, the client's sofa, and assistant's desk.
- ▶ Parking spaces and passes.
- ▶ How to organize dailies on the digital editing system.
- ▶ Why the photocopier always jams.
- ▶ *Lunch*
- ▶ The lottery: Enter individually or as an editing crew?
- ▶ VFX and SFX.
- ▶ How visitors can find the everlovin' cutting room.
- ▶ Re-shoots and insert shoots.
- ▶ Screenings.
- ▶ Garbage busters: Who do you call when the trash gets rank?
- ▶ *Dinner*
- ▶ Relinking media.

> ▸ Tech help calls.
> ▸ Dubs and viewing copies.
> ▸ Lighting: Getting lamps and dimming the room.
> ▸ Online.
> ▸ The weekend: Who's working and how do they get into the building?
> ▸ Archiving.

## *Communicating during the screening of dailies*

Screening dailies with the director and crew is a sometimes or not-at-all thing these days. If the crew's on location and you're not, the director will view dailies and call you with notes or send them. Or not. I've worked on many scripted shows where I just had the script supervisor's notes and on doc, reality, and corporate shows where I had few or no notes at all. Frequently you watch dailies solo as they're ingested into the system.

If you do watch dailies with the director and crew, each department will tune in to its area: Camera will commandeer you, "Don't use 11-3, focus is soft in the middle;" Wardrobe will steal up and say, "Linda's skirt didn't puff out properly in 11-4;" and Hair will warn, "Tom's toupee was cockeyed in 11-5." Such information can be useful but it's not your main focus.

Direct your attention to the director (or client or other person in charge). Write down what they say or request. Also, take note — if only mentally — of what they're saying between the lines as to how they're approaching and perceiving the project — it's theme, intent, or message as well as its characters, look, pace, etc. Jot down your own ideas and reactions too. Last, write down any sync, sound or other technical issues to be resolved back at the cutting room or post house.

Focus: Whether screened alone or with others, dailies are your first view of the footage. You want to absorb as much as possible so your brain can start percolating about how you're going to put the show together.

# Setting a Post Production Schedule

Every project has a schedule sheet with dates that you must meet. If you're a student or an independent filmmaker, knowing the schedule is doubly important as it's part of budgeting your show. You may make the schedule on your computer using a calendar program or receive it from the post supervisor — or both — but in either case, allow for quick updates as most schedules can and do change. Changes can give you some breathing room or extend your work into the night and through the weekend. Since postproduction takes place at the end of the show, if it's running behind or the schedule gets shortened, editorial gets pushed to work harder and longer!

## Posting the schedule

Many editors mark the schedule on a large erasable calendar and hang it on the wall.

## Typical postproduction schedules

Table 3.1 shows typical schedules for seven different types of shows, from a commercial to a full-length feature film. It lists 24 possible events: No project will include them all. An explanation of each event follows the chart. The table assumes that you will be editing from the first day of the shoot and gives an average range of days/weeks needed for each event. These times will vary from project to project due to budget, delivery dates, project requirements, and the unexpected occurrences that wreak havoc on a schedule.

## TABLE 3.1
## TYPICAL POSTPRODUCTION SCHEDULES

| # | EVENT | COMMERCIAL (60 sec) | MUSIC VIDEO (5 min) | CORPORATE VIDEO (1/2 hour) | DOC (1 hour) | SITCOM (1/2 hour, multi-cam) | TV EPISODE (1 hour) | Feature (90-120 min) |
|---|-------|---------------------|---------------------|----------------------------|--------------|------------------------------|---------------------|----------------------|
| 1 | SHOOT DAYS | 1-2 days | 1-3 days | 4-7 days | 8-10 days | 1 day | 8-10 days | 18-35 days |
| 2 | FIRST CUT | 1-5 days. | 1 day | 1-2 days | 1-3 days | 1 day | 1-2 days | 1-5 days |
| 3 | DIRECTOR'S CUT | Editing often takes place with director and/or client supervising. | 1-5 days | 1-3 weeks Director and producer cut by mutual agreement. | | 1 day** | 4 days** | 6 -10 weeks*** |
| 4 | PRODUCER OR CLIENT CUT | | 1-3 days | 1-3 days | | 2-5 days | 1-3 weeks | |
| 5 | TEMP ONLINE (TAPE) | NA (not applicable) | 1 day | NA | 1 day | 1 day (pilots only, usually) | 1 day | 2 days |
| 6 | TEMP MIX (FILM) | NA | 1 day | NA | NA | NA (pilot 1 day) | NA (pilot 1-2 days) | 1-3 days |
| 7 | FINAL CUT APPROVAL | 1 day | 1 day | NA | 1 day | 1 day | 1-2 days | 2-3 days |
| 8 | PREVIEW SCREENING | NA | 1 day | NA | 1 day | NA | NA | 1 day per preview |
| 9 | FILM OPTICALS, INSERTS, VFX, & FILM TITLES | VFX and inserts are created during editing on editing system or at VFX house and insert stage, respectively. Titles are created during editing at a title house or on the editing system or as part of online or the DI process. | | | | | | |
| 10 | PICTURE LOCK (DAYS FROM FIRST CUT) | 1-7 days | 1-8 days | 1-3 weeks | 2-3 weeks | 2-7 days | 6-14 days | 3-8 weeks |
| 11 | ONLINE (TAPE) | 1 day includes file finish. | 1 day | 1-2 days | 1-2 days | 1 day | 1 day media preload 1 day online | 2-3 days |
| 12 | COLOR GRADING & FINAL TITLING | 1 day | 1 day | 1-2 days | 1-2 days | 1 day | CG 2-3 days Titles 1 day | CG 5-14 days Titles 1 day |
| 13 | SPOTTING MX & SFX | 1 day | NA | 1 day | 1 day | 1 day | 1-2 days | 2-4 days |
| 14 | ADR | 1 day | 1 day | NA | 1 day | 1 day | 2-3 days | 3-10 days |
| 15 | FOLEY | 1 day | 1 day | NA | 1 day | 1 day | 1-2 days | 3-10 days |
| 16 | SCORING STAGE | 1 day | 1 day | NA | 1 day | 1 day | 2-3 days | 3-10 days |
| 17 | PRE-MIX | NA | 1 day | NA | NA | 1 day (pilots only, usually) | 1 day | 1-14 days |
| 18 | MIX | 1 day | 1-3 days | 1-2 days | 1-3 days | 1 day | 1-2 days | 3-21 days |
| 19 | DI PROCESS | 1-2 days | 2-4 days | NA | 4-5 days | 2-4 days | 4-5 days | 1-2 weeks |
| 20 | NEGATIVE CUT | 2 days | NA | NA | 3-6 days | NA | NA | 3-6 weeks |
| 21 | CONVERTING & FORMATTING | 1 day | 1 day | 1 day | 1 day | 1 day | 1 day | 1 day |
| 22 | DISK AUTHORING | NA | NA | 1-7 days | 1-7 days | 1-3 days | 1-3 days | 1-7 days |
| 23 | WEB STREAMING | 1-3 days | 1-3 days | 1-3 days | NA | 1-3 days | 1-3 days | NA |
| 24 | DELIVERY DATE | 1 day | 1 day | 1 day | 1 day | 1 day | 1 day | 1-2 weeks |

* Days of editing after editor screens first cut which is typically turned in 1-3 days after shooting finishes.

** DGA (Directors Guild of America) contract stipulates # of days.

***DGA requirements tied to budget.

## *Events in the schedule*

Events 2–24 will be fully explored in Stages II and III but here's an overview.

**1.** Shoot days

Shoot days are the dates you start and end principal photography. The editing staff usually reports to work on the first day of the shoot or a few days earlier to prep the cutting room.

Regarding shoot dates, editorial needs to know:

▶ When to expect dailies: regular days and times.

▶ About any night or weekend shoots: irregular days and times.

▶ If there will be major second unit, post house effects, inserts, or CGI (computer generated images); and when to expect delivery.

**2.** First cut

The first cut, a.k.a. the editor's cut, is the first complete version of the show. If you are cutting on a digital system, the editor normally turns in the first cut the day after receiving the last day's dailies. If cutting on film, the editor will need a few more days. In either case, the editor screens the first cut for the director.

**3.** Director's cut

The cut that is produced after screening with the director. On feature films there are many screenings and re-cuts before the director's cut is finished; with TV shows the time is contractual.

**4.** Producer and client

The producer is the overseer and coordinator of the show and is responsible to the financial backers. The producer approves the final show unless it is a feature and the director is powerful enough to have final cut rights. When a client has ordered the show — usually a commercial or a corporate video — the client has input and the final say about what goes into the show.

**5.** Temp online (tape)

A temporary online may be done in order to screen a new show at its best for the network, or to preview a high-budget feature.

**6.** Temp dub (film)

A temporary sound mix.

**7.** Final cut approval

A production company or a studio produces the show. The network broadcasts the show. Both are responsible for the completed show. Therefore, executives at the studio or production company and network must see and approve the final cut.

**8.** Preview screening(s)

Many feature films and television series are screened for test audiences, a.k.a. focus groups, to gather more input.

**9.** Film opticals and titles, graphics, post house effects, and insert shoot

Sessions are scheduled for color grading, adding titles, creating GFX, or shooting inserts.

**10.** Picture lock

The picture cut is completed: not a frame can be changed.

**11.** Online (tape)

The offline cut is reproduced from the original tapes to make the show master.

**12.** Color grading and final titling

The show master is color graded scene by scene and approved by the DP, director, and/or the AP. Titles and credits are finalized.

**13.** Spotting

In separate sessions, the sound designer and music composer meet with the director and spot (view) the show to lay out the show's sound and music.

**14-16.** ADR, Foley, and scoring stage

New sound and music are created on the ADR, Foley, and scoring stages and cut into the show's sound and music tracks.

**17.** Premix

Preliminary mix of background sounds such as wind and ocean wave sounds.

**18.** Mix

Mixers mix all sound and music tracks into the final soundtrack.

**19.** DI process

The post facility will import your cutlist or EDL, scan your media — film, file or tape — add or perform color grading, add VFX, and layback the sound mix to produce your master(s) on film, tape, file, or disk.

**20.** Traditional negative cut

The negative cutter assembles the film negative and the lab creates an answer print (AP) to establish settings for the final release prints that will be sent to movie theaters.

**21.** Converting and formatting

Your show may need to be upconverted or transcoded to HD. If your show is destined for broadcast, the post house will format it to the network's technical specs.

**22.** Disk authoring

Depending on how long your project is and how complex its disk's menus, chapters, and buttons are, as well as how many people will have a say in its final outcome, authoring can be a short or lengthy process.

**23.** Web streaming

Most shows end up on the Web eventually, if not immediately. A host company will do the posting or it could be you posting your webisode or video to the Net.

**24.** Delivery date

This is the day your completed project — in its final format(s) on film, disk, file, or tape — is handed over either to the network for airing, the distributor for sending out to theaters, the client for circulating (corporate or training projects), or your IT department for uploading to the company portal. Consider your delivery date fixed. While it can change — to an earlier or later date — you want to hit your deadline. Even if the network decides to air your show on President's day instead of Martin Luther King day, your delivery date will usually remain the same.

Sometimes you have no firm delivery date, such as when there's no distribution deal yet in place. This can be a good thing because you don't have a deadline but also a bad thing because editing can drag on and take your budget along with it, not to mention your life and time!

## Make your own schedule

Appendix B at the end of this chapter is a blank form for creating your own schedule. Select what applies to your show and fill in the days and dates. Feel free to adapt the form to your project. You can also download it from www.joyoffilmediting.com by clicking on the Free tab.

# Dailies' Reports: What you will receive in the cutting room

*"In the real world there are rarely any two productions which have the exact same requirements for dailies. The postproduction facility doing the dailies has to make a variety of alterations, large and small, to the way they operate for each production they work on."*

—MONKSFIELD, STUART and Lindenkreuz, Morris, Bones, DFT Digital Film Technology

For each day that the production crew shoots, you will receive reports via email, fax, FedEx, or on hard copies along with dailies. The kind of reports you receive will depend on your shooting format (tape, file, or film), type of show (scripted or doc), and the professionalism of the crew.

On scripted shows and those with higher budgets and more professional crews, you will receive reports from the script supervisor as well as the camera and sound departments.

On non-scripted shows, reports are essential for identifying who and what you're seeing as well as where you're seeing them. How can you tell a Komodo dragon that inhabits the island of Rinca from one that lives on Gili Motang if the location crew doesn't bother with notes? Kathleen Korth recalls that when she edited the IMAX film *Africa's Elephant Kingdom*, "The producer embedded a person from the shoot in the editing room to help me identify and keep track of all the elephants and their families."

You should expect to receive some or all of the following dailies' reports:

## Tape show reports

Optimally, you should get a logged report for each tape with each location and its shots identified. Sometimes you won't receive any reports at all. Why does this happen? Usually it's due to an inexperienced or overtaxed camera crew. Single system tape shows don't require a clapped slate for syncing so the crew may do little or no slating or logging. The crew may be under the gun to capture all the action — reality shows are a prime example — and grab a ton of footage but neglect to number and log the who-what-where for each shot. This is a problem because poor or no reports, along with a lack of slates, cost time — and therefore money — as editorial must then locate, correctly identify, and label shots in the cutting room.

## Tapeless show reports

Whether the post house delivers your dailies on a hard drive, you pop them out of the camera on card or disk, or they arrive via some other file-based format, you should receive reports like those pictured on the next page. As with tape shows however, depending on the nature of the production crew, your reports may range from non-existent to professional.

## Film show reports

See Handwritten department reports section below.

## Handwritten department reports

### 1. SCRIPT SUPERVISOR'S PAGES AND NOTES

*Editor's daily log, a.k.a. one-liner*

The one-liner contains a one-line summary of each take of dailies and runs 1–2 pages. Assistant Rachelle Dang remarks, "I use the edit log to make sure all my dailies have arrived: Sometimes the lab runs out of time because so much footage was shot that I don't get all my dailies that day and have to wait until the late afternoon or next day."

*Production report*

This one-page report summarizes the day's shoot as illustrated by Figure 3.b.

*Lined script pages*

These are script pages shot that day on which the script supervisor draws vertical lines indicating where each take starts and ends. See figure 3.c.

*Script notes*

On the page opposite the lined script page, the script supervisor marks the circled and uncircled takes and the timing of each take. These notes give a brief description of each take as well as its sound roll and camera

## SCRIPT SUPERVISOR'S PRODUCTION REPORT

THE CAPE  Day _Wednesday_  Date _3/30/2011_  Day _7_ of _18_

Crew Call _7:30 am_

1st Shot _8:16 am_  1st Shot _2:43 PM_

Lunch _1:30 → 2:00 PM_  Dinner _____

1st Shot _____

Wrap _9:25 PM_

ADDED SC. #'S _____  OMITTED SC. #'S _____  ✕ ALTERED SC. #'S _43 = + 3/8_

✱ AS PER DOUBLE, BLUES

TOTAL SCENES _80_  ✱ TOTAL PAGES _52 3/8  53 2/8_ SCENES RE-SHOT _____

SCENE #'S SHOT TODAY _32pt, 36pt, 42pt_

SCENES SHOT _0_  PREVIOUS _14_  TOTAL _14_  REMAINING _66_

PAGES SHOT _1 7/8_  PREVIOUS _12 2/8_  TOTAL _14 1/8_  REMAINING _39 1/8_

SET UPS _32_  PREVIOUS _190_  TOTAL _222_

TIME SHOT _3:00_  PREVIOUS _15:50_  TOTAL _18:50_

WILDTRACKS _____

CAMERA _A 46-65  B 50-53  C 16-19  F 8_  SOUND _11_

SCHEDULED, NOT COVERED | _43* 52 47_ | STARTED, NOT FINISHED _____
COVERED, NOT SCHEDULED | _48, A3a_ | ✱ SC. 43 - moved to stage

NOTES:  32pt = 0/8
    36pt = 1 1/8  1:00 (owe Dana)
    pt 42 = 6/8 (of 1 0/8) 2:00

3.b Script supervisor's production report.

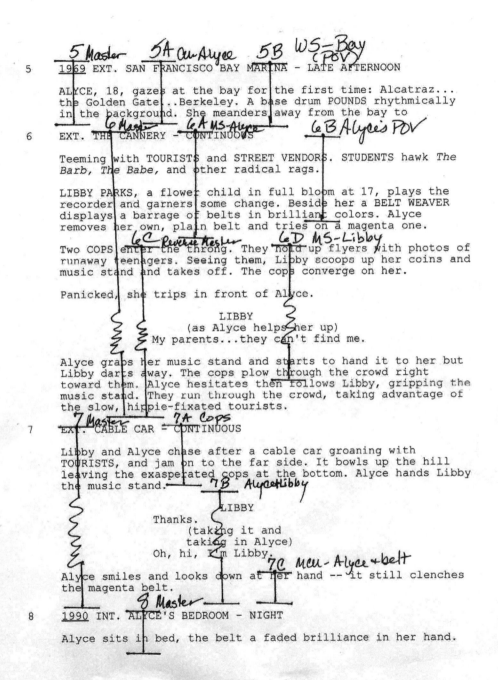

5 Master   5A CU-Alyce   5B WS-Bay (POV)

5   1969 EXT. SAN FRANCISCO BAY MARINA - LATE AFTERNOON

ALYCE, 18, gazes at the bay for the first time: Alcatraz...
the Golden Gate...Berkeley. A base drum POUNDS rhythmically
in the background. She meanders away from the bay to

6 Master   6A MS-Alyce   6B Alyce's POV

6   EXT. THE CANNERY - CONTINUOUS

Teeming with TOURISTS and STREET VENDORS. STUDENTS hawk *The
Barb, The Babe,* and other radical rags.

LIBBY PARKS, a flower child in full bloom at 17, plays the
recorder and garners some change. Beside her a BELT WEAVER
displays a barrage of belts in brilliant colors. Alyce
removes her own, plain belt and tries on a magenta one.

6C Reverse Master   6D MS-Libby

Two COPS enter the throng. They hold up flyers with photos of
runaway teenagers. Seeing them, Libby scoops up her coins and
music stand and takes off. The cops converge on her.

Panicked, she trips in front of Alyce.

                    LIBBY
               (as Alyce helps her up)
          My parents...they can't find me.

Alyce grabs her music stand and starts to hand it to her but
Libby darts away. The cops plow through the crowd right
toward them. Alyce hesitates then follows Libby, gripping the
music stand. They run through the crowd, taking advantage of
the slow, hippie-fixated tourists.

7 Master   7A Cops

7   EXT. CABLE CAR - CONTINUOUS

Libby and Alyce chase after a cable car groaning with
TOURISTS, and jam on to the far side. It bowls up the hill
leaving the exasperated cops at the bottom. Alyce hands Libby
the music stand.   7B Alyce+Libby

                    LIBBY
          Thanks.
               (taking it and
                taking in Alyce)
          Oh, hi, I'm Libby.
                              7C MCU-Alyce+belt
Alyce smiles and looks down at her hand -- it still clenches
the magenta belt.

8 Master

8   1990 INT. ALYCE'S BEDROOM - NIGHT

Alyce sits in bed, the belt a faded brilliance in her hand.

**3.c** Script supervisor's lined script page. Squiggly line denotes character's dialogue on a take. *Photo courtesy of
Chris Senchack.*

info such as camera roll and lens used, e.g., 27mm, 50mm, etc. A good script supervisor also writes down any director's comments and other special notes.

## 2. CAMERA REPORT

*Take names*

The script supervisor assigns these and the camera assistant slates them.

*Circled takes*

Takes the director called out to be used. With film, this means that these takes will be printed by the lab.

> 16mm: All takes circled — and uncircled — are printed.
> 35mm: Due to lab costs, only circled takes are printed.

*Uncircled takes*

From time to time these takes are called up during editing when the director or editor decides to look at them. The hope is that they will yield useable footage. With film these takes are also referred to as B Neg.

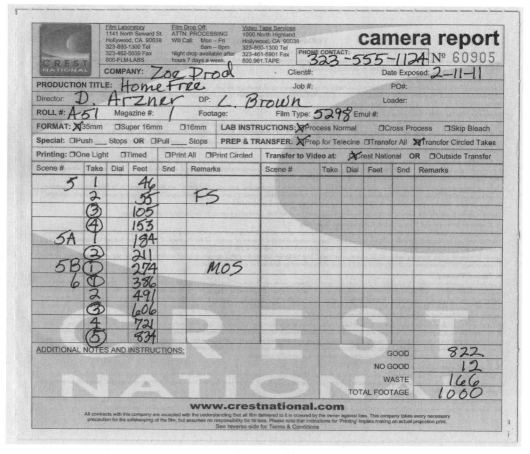

**3.d** Camera report on film show.

*FS*

False start. Look in the feet, duration, or time code column and see how little was shot. This take went nowhere.

*MOS*

Without sound. No sound was recorded on this shot.

*TS*

Tail slate. Slate clapped after the action was completed at the tail of the take.

## 3. DIT REPORT

The DIT keeps track of tons of data including camera info, slates, files, drives, and much more as the sample report from a commercial shoot indicates in Figure 3.e.

## 4. SOUND REPORT

The sound report's circled takes should match the circled takes on the camera report and the script supervisor's one-liner. This report will also include WT (wild track) and room tone. See Figure 3.f.

| | | | | | | GENERAL NOTES | | | | | |
|---|---|---|---|---|---|---|---|---|---|---|---|
| PRODUCTION CO: | LOLLIPOP | | | | | MATERIAL THAT HAS NOT | | | | | |
| PRODUCTION: | GUM DROP 45" spot | | | | | ALREADY GONE TO EDIT: | | | | | |
| DOP: | J FROST | | | | | | | | | | |
| DIT: | TOM TURLEY | | | | | DATE: **12/12/10** | | | | | |
| FORMAT: | 5dmk2 H264 / STILLS CR2 + JPEG | | | | | A CAM - MAG 27 | | | | | |
| FPS: | 24 | | | | | B CAM - MAG 25 | | | | | |
| RESOLUTION: | 1080x1920 | | | | | C CAM - MAGS 2,3,4 | | | | | |
| ASPECT RATIO: | 16:9 | | | | | | | | | | |
| RECORDING: | | | | | | ALL MARKED IN GRAY | | | | | |
| | | | | | | ON DRIVE | | | | | |

DESTINATION DRIVES: 'LOLLIPOP MASTER' + "LOLLIPOP BACKUP'

| MAG # | # OF CLIPS | STILL/VIDEO | NOTES | SC# | GB | LENS | STOP | filter | LH | Distance | Incline |
|---|---|---|---|---|---|---|---|---|---|---|---|
| A1 | 8 | VIDEO | plane landing | 9 | 7.67 | 50 | 4 | nd6 | 4'1 | 6'6 - 7'8 | 4deg down |
| B1 | 1 + odd stills | VIDEO + STILLS | | 2 | 1.23 | 50 | 5.6 1/2 | - | 3'8 | 1'10 | 26deg down |
| A2 | 30 stills | STOP MOTION | Disregard: use A3 | 4 | .9 | 50 | 4 | nd6 | 4'1 | 6'6 - 7'8 | 4deg down |
| B2 | 1 | LIVE ACTION | | 2 | .9 | 50 | 5.6 1/2 | - | 3'8 | 1'10 | 26deg down |
| A3 | 65 stills | STOP MOTION | Extended vers A2 | 4 | 1.93 | 50 | 4 | nd6 | 4'1 | 6'6 - 7'8 | 4deg down |
| B3 | 4 | LIVE ACTION | | 2 | 5.64 | 60 | 5.6 1/2 | - | | | |
| A4 | stills/video | PLATES | Plates for giraffe | 4 | .3 | 50 | 4 | nd6 | 4'1 | 6'6 - 7'8 | 4deg down |
| B5 | 1 | LIVE ACTION | PLATE | 10 | .96 | 60 | 5.6 1/2 | - | 3'9 | 1'9 | |
| C1 | 20 | STOP MOTION | | blind opens | .8 | 28 | 4 1/2 | | | | |
| B6 | 93 | STOP MOTION | | 10a | 2.71 | 50 | 5.6 1/2 | - | 3'10 | 2'2 | 14.7 down |
| B7 | 93 | STOP MOTION | | 10b giraffe | 2.6 | 50 | 4 1/2 | ND3 | 4'0 | 2'8 | 25 down |
| B8 | 5 | PLATES | Plates for giraffe | 10b giraffe | 4.58 | 50 | 4 1/2 | ND3 | 4'0 | 2'8 | 25 down |
| B9 | 48 | STOP MOTION | curtains | 5b | 2.52 | 85 | 5.6 | ND3 | 4'4 | 3'8 | |
| A6 | 2 | LIVE ACTION | | child reaction | 3.02 | 85 | 8 | - | 2'8 | 4'0 | |
| A7 | 1 | LIVE ACTION | | mom reaction | 2.59 | 85 | 8 | - | 2'8 | 4'0 | |
| B10 | 1 still/1 movie | LIVE ACTION | | 13 plane | 1.91 | | | | | | |
| B11 | | STOP MOTION | | 12 car | 0.6 | | | | | | |

Sheet1

**3.e** DIT report for commercial where DIT worked as camera assistant and technician and data coordinator to match the look of a Canon 5D DSLR still photos and videos.

## Wild lines

These are non-sync, non-scripted, audio-only lines of dialogue snagged on set from an actor that can prove critical in making scenes work in the cutting room. Wild lines are also frequently added after production — temporarily during editing or permanently during sound editing — to bridge, bolster, or clarify scenes.

## Computer-printed department reports

### 4. LAB REPORT

The lab usually preps the negative for telecine and sends it over to the telecine bay at the post house along with this computer-generated report. You will receive it if your show is making work print dailies for editing. The report lists the timing lights used to process the negative and make a one-lite daily[2]. It should match the circled takes on the camera report. If the lab missed any circled takes, call right away and provide the information (scene and take numbers along with camera roll) of the overlooked takes.

### 5. TELECINE REPORT

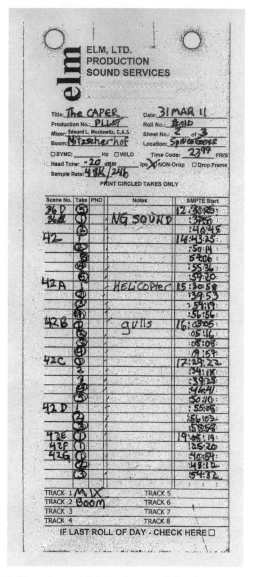

**3.f** Sound report lists tracks recorded at bottom.

The colorist generates this computer report about the transferred dailies. On tape or tapeless shows, the report carries downconverted video time codes and the original audio time codes along with the video tape roll number or file info. On film shows the reports list the time code for each take along with its negative key code, camera roll, and audio info.

---

2. A one-lite is the daily work print that the lab processes using the same printer light setting to time (develop the color for) all film reels.

## What to do with the reports

### 1. CROSS-CHECK 'EM

It's absolutely crucial to cross-reference all reports to confirm that you received all the takes that you're supposed to. This means all the takes the director ordered circled. It's part of editorial's job to ensure that all takes get to the cutting room and are available for editing. You don't want to find yourself in a screening without a certain take cut into the show, have the director question where it is, and have to admit ignorance of its existence. Your ignorance may cause the director to lose trust that you're on top of the footage and are putting together the best show.

### 2. ORGANIZE 'EM

Normally, you arrange the script supervisor's notes and pages chronologically in a three-ringed notebook. You may also put sound, camera, lab, DIT, and other reports in binders or in folders. But customarily these reports are stuffed in manila envelopes and pinned to the wall or two-hole punched and placed on clipboards hung on the wall since horizontal space is precious in cutting rooms. The goal is to meticulously organize all reports and paperwork so that info is easily accessible at any time, especially when a director, client, producer, and/or others are present.

## Planning dailies based on the reports

From the reports, you will have a good idea of the amount of dailies you will receive and what scenes and locations are involved. This helps you plan for ingesting them into the digital system.

## Scripts and transcripts

### SCRIPTS

On scripted shows, the lined script is the editor's blueprint for cutting. Many editors place the script in a script stand — a homegrown affair akin to a music stand — and keep it handy on their desk.

### TRANSCRIPTS

On non-scripted shows, a transcriber usually uses a DVD (or possibly a tape, file, or other disk) created from dailies to type up the interviews. The transcript should include the time code every minute. If it doesn't, write it down yourself. This way you can enter the time code into the system to locate content in a nano and maintain your train of thought in the heat of editing. Put the hard copy of the transcript in a binder and keep the transcriber's word-processed file in your editing system.

A transcript is invaluable for locating lines and sections when editing, and well worth the fee. It also serves as the basis for a paper cut, an editing outline made by the editor, producer, or the director which may include the reel number and time code of the desired line or shot. Some editors make index cards from the transcript and move the cards around on a corkboard to come up with a paper cut. If you can't afford a transcript, use the markers (FCP) or locators (Avid) to mark and describe lines in your digital system for reference points. Many systems let you key in markers while ingesting the footage.

### SCRIPT AND TRANSCRIPT PROGRAMS

There are several programs that allow you to import the script or transcript into the editing system. For instance, Script Sync, Avid's proprietary program, syncs up clips with the writer's preshoot script or with the doc's transcript. Adobe's Transcriptize works on many systems to bring in a roughly accurate version of a transcript. And there are various voice recognition programs for finding words or phrases on the digital editing system. All these programs are continually improving and require some extra set-up work but can speed up searching for lines and comparing takes.

## Shot terms: How to label shots

An indispensible part of good communication in post is to use the universal language for labeling shots. Here's how to call the shots when you're logging them:

## Master

The master includes all the action in a scene from beginning to end. Although the master often starts framed on a small object, the majority of a master is usually a wide-framed shot.

## Pick-up master (PU master)

Sometimes a master shot does not last the length of the scene. This may be because the director planned it this way or due to repeated camera or actor problems. Whatever the reason, a new master is then picked up (continued) from before where the incomplete master left off. The director shoots coverage to allow the editor to bridge from the master to the pick-up master.

## Reverse

An angle shot from the exact opposite angle of the action in the master. Frequently the reverse is a wide shot and is labeled the reverse master.

## Point of view (POV)

A variation of a reverse shot, a POV shot corresponds exactly to where a character is looking; it's *what* they're seeing.

## Wide shot (WS)

A shot framed wide that encompasses much if not all of the action.

## Long shot (LS)

A shot framed long that focuses on the action from a distance.

## Overhead (OH)

Often shot from a crane, an overhead looks down on the scene from above.

## Over the shoulder (OS or OTS)

Shot from the waist or chest up, an OS includes the shoulder of one character while focusing on the other character. "Overs" as they're referred

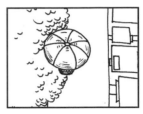

**3.g** From top to bottom: Master Shot, Overhead, and Reverse Master.

**3.h** Here's a matching pair of over-the-shoulder (OS) shots.

to, are shot in pairs so they can be cut together. "OS Chip" means we're seeing Chip over Dale's shoulder — it's Chip's OS shot. OS Dale (Dale's over) means we're seeing Dale over Chip's shoulder.

**3.i** Two-shot.

## Two-shot

A shot with two characters' faces that's usually framed medium.

## Raking shot

A tight form of a two-shot filmed from the side that favors one character. Raking shots are usually shot in pairs, e.g., a shot labeled "raking Isabel" would favor Isabel and the companion shot, "raking Elise," would favor Elise. Raking shots are habitually used in bed scenes and interior car scenes where it's impossible to make a reverse shot or OS.

**3.j** Raking shot.

## Full shot (FS)

A shot framed to include the whole person, animal, or object being shot.

## Medium shot (MS)

A shot framed from the waist or chest up through the top of the person's head.

## Medium close-up (MCU)

Between a CU and an MS, a MCU is shot from the shoulders up through the top of the person's head.

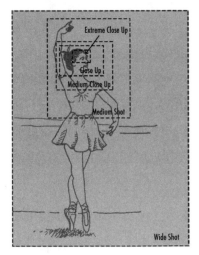

**3.k** Framing for WS, MS, MCU, CU, and ECU.

## Close-up (CU) or Close Shot (CS)

A shot framed close, usually on the face and neck of a person. When framed so that you barely see the neck, it's frequently referred to as a *choker*.

### *Extreme close-up (ECU)*

A shot framed so tight that if it's on a person's face you just see their eyes.

### *Cutaway (CA)*

Any shot that can be used to cut away from the main action, most often the master shot. They're called CAs but best described by how they're framed, usually by MS, MCU, or CU.

### *Insert shot*

Shot of some small but significant detail in a scene. It may be the crab the chef is plunking in the pot of cioppino, the scribbles on a treasure map, the gun in the killer's hand, or a pair of ruby slippers. An insert is shot during post on an insert stage or picked up on the set. As with a CA, an insert is described by how it's framed, usually as a CU.

## Preparing Tapes for Dubs

When you make dubs of dailies or cuts, you may well be copying them to QuickTime files for uploading to a server or exporting to a disk. You may however, dub to tape. To do this for dailies, you'll simply stick in a tape and dub away. However, if you're dubbing a cut, or string of sequences, or anything that needs to be timed — such as a scene for the composer — you will want to black and code a few tapes.

### *A tape is born blank and codeless*

A tape arrives blank from the factory with no code on it. Play it and white dots teem all over the screen, like there's a blizzard on your monitor. Fittingly, this is called snow. You cannot edit a tape with snow on it. So control track — a series of evenly spaced electronic pulses — is laid down on the tape. This is called blacking. Control track allows you to insert audio and video to a tape but it is not frame accurate. This is fine if you're making a viewing tape and are not concerned with exactly how long your show is. When timing is important, you need to add time code to be frame accurate. So you black and code the tape, commonly called pre-striping. Before we discuss how to do this via assemble editing, a little background:

## Pre-striping

You can buy pre-striped tapes from your post house but it may be more cost effective to stripe your own. Usually you code a tape starting at time code 58:30:00. This leaves a minute and a half of run-up before your show starts at 1:00:00:00. But you can set any time code you'd like. Customarily, people code different acts with successive time codes: Act 1 at 1:00:00:00, Act 2 at 2:00:00:00, and so on. Whatever system you devise, make sure to advise everyone in the editing room and at the post house.

## Bars and tone

At the head of your daily tape you often will see 30–60 seconds of color bars and hear an audio tone. "Bars and tone," as they are called, are video and audio level signal references recorded in the field or by the post house. They are part of the network's technical requirements and must be recorded to spec (specification) on your master show tape. When pre-striping or dubbing tapes, you can add bars and tone from your digital system.

**3.1** Color bars on monitor (on right). *Photo courtesy of AlphaDogs.*

### BARS

Editorial depends on bars to make sure that colors are consistent from tape to tape and across the entire show. When you enter a tape into a digital editing system, there are menus for setting bars and tone. For offline editing, keep your tapes and your video monitor consistent; you're making adjustments for your own sensibility and viewing copies. For online or finishing directly from the digital system, these settings are critical and will be scoped (calibrated using color scopes) as they determine what your viewers see.

### TONE

The sound recordist on set or an employee at the post house records an audio tone for 10" to 30" so that when the tape is used for editing or recording, its level (volume level) is consistent. When you dub to tape, you can add tone using your digital system's menu.

While we're on the subject of tone, let's apply it to ingesting dailies. When you prepare a tape for ingest, you reference this tone and adjust a setting with the system's audio tool. The setting varies from one digital system to another, but all are equivalent to 0 dB on an analog VU (volume unit) meter. Inputting a consistent level of audio is important. If your levels are out of whack, i.e., one character speaks loudly and the other can barely be heard, it distracts from a scene and your work. You can compensate by adjusting the levels within the cut but it's much more efficient to get the levels right from the beginning.

## Pre-striping — the process

To black and code a tape, access the menu on your tape deck or digital editing system. There are two different ways to physically record onto a tape: assemble edit and insert edit. The menu on your tape deck or digital editing system will give you both choices. Additionally, the editing system allows you to add bars and tone, a countdown leader, and other goodies.

## Assemble edit

From the point the edit starts, everything — control track, video, and audio — is erased when you assemble edit. A new control track, video and audio track are laid down. When you assemble edit, you record from the beginning of the tape or show to the end. Assemble editing is best for anything that will be recorded from beginning to end without stopping. Consequently it is employed to black and code tapes and is how you will make dubs of dailies and cuts for screening.

Assemble editing does not permit you to stop, restart, or make any changes during or after recording. This is not a practical way to edit most of the time. Say you've put your show to tape and want to add music to it from another tape. You can't do this via assemble editing because it will record the music as well as the picture (even if it's black) from the second tape. To do this, you need to insert edit.

### Insert edit

Insert editing utilizes the time code and control track you laid down when you blacked and coded the tape by assemble editing and allows you to record video-only edits, audio-only edits, or both.

### How assemble and insert edit work together

Assemble edit and insert edit comprise an important pair of practices in the world of videotape. At the start of a show, tapes are blacked and coded and daily tapes are recorded by assemble editing. Insert editing is then employed during offline and online editing to make time coded dubs from a digital system. After the show is onlined, dubs are made via assemble edit.

### Assemble and insert editing on digital systems

Insert and assemble editing come into play when you're outputting a sequence to tape or blacking a tape. In FCP the assemble edit command is "Print to video;" on Avid it's "Crash Record" or "Assemble Record." To insert edit on FCP click on "Edit to Tape;" on Avid select "Insert Edit."

### Real time record and high speed dubs

Both assemble edit and insert edit are real time records, meaning if the show is 22 minutes long, it will take 22 minutes to record. Assemble editing can be performed faster than real time if a high speed deck is used.

### Storing tapes and other footage

After ingesting daily tapes into the system, you may need the tapes for dubbing, onlining, or re-inputting should media be corrupted or destroyed. Your post house can store your original tapes in a nice, cool vault. Or you can devise your own vault — a box, a shelf, an area — that is off limits to everyone but you. You want to protect all footage that arrives in the cutting room be it on tape, disk, hard drive, or card. Label all media and keep it in a safe place. Don't destroy, delete, or recycle any footage or data until the project's been delivered and everything has been archived.

## CHAPTER WRAP-UP

You've designed your workflow, posted your project's schedule, put your system through its paces, and organized the cutting room so neatly that you're testing the coffeemaker with a fresh café Americano while sitting on your newly installed couch. Sounds like you're all set for dailies. Good! They're arriving next, in Chapter 4.

# Appendix B

## Post Production Schedule

| SCHEDULE | SHOW | | DATE | PAGE OF |
|---|---|---|---|---|
| # | EVENT | DAYS | DATES | |
| 1 | Shoot days | | | |
| 2 | First cut | | | |
| 3 | Director's cut | | | |
| 4 | Producer or client cut | | | |
| 5 | Temp online | | | |
| 6 | Temp dub | | | |
| 7 | Final cut approval | | | |
| 8 | Preview screening | | | |
| 9 | Opticals, inserts, VFX, & film titles | | | |
| 10 | Picture lock (days from first cut) | | | |
| 11 | Online | | | |
| 12 | Color grading & final titling | | | |
| 13 | Spotting MX & SFX | | | |
| 14 | ADR | | | |
| 15 | Foley | | | |
| 16 | Scoring stage | | | |
| 17 | Pre-mix | | | |
| 18 | Mix | | | |
| 19 | DI process | | | |
| 20 | Negative cut | | | |
| 21 | Converting & formatting | | | |
| 22 | DVD authoring | | | |
| 23 | Web streaming | | | |
| 24 | Delivery date | | | |

CHAPTER 4

# Preparing Dailies

## Overview

Threset has been struck, the location wrapped, and the crew sent on its merry way. You've cross-checked all your reports and now dailies are staring you in the face. What do you do? The first section of this chapter tells you how to begin by labeling and logging. It then covers the decisions to make before you ingest a frame, starting with a few fundamentals such as codecs, resolution, and storage. Following this, the chapter walks you through how to ingest dailies into the digital editing system and organize them so you're all ready to edit. The final section demystifies the vital data verifications required for projects finishing on film and discusses how these apply to shows shooting 24p.

Let's get moving. As John Wayne's character Wil Anderson famously said in *The Cowboys*, "We're burning daylight!"

## LABELING AND LOGGING REELS FOR INGESTING

Labeling and logging is like locking and loading: Skip it and fuggedabout locating shots easily or editing efficiently. Your show may not be a huge enterprise like *Star Wars* or *Star Trek* but you will have an increasing amount of footage to keep track of as the days go by. So label everything: projects, disks, tapes, notebooks, shelves, and the cutting room door. These you will label before ingesting.

# LABELING

As soon as a tape enters the cutting room, label its cassette and box. Write down the tape's reel number, the name of the show, and any other descriptors you desire such as episode number or a summary of the tape's footage. Store the tapes on racks and/or shelves. Label each rack with the show name, e.g., 30" iPhone spot and each shelf with the reels on it, e.g., Reels 1-15.

Your reel-naming convention depends on the type of show you work on. Commercial editors label reels differently from feature editors who differ from documentarians. If you archive footage — which all newsrooms and many TV shows do — labeling is crucial: You want to create a system that makes future searching clear and straightforward.

Who assigns reel numbers? A lot of people: The production crew, insert stage crew, post house, stock house, VFX house, graphics designer, and oh, yes, you! No matter who assigns the reel number initially, editorial is responsible for keeping track of reels and reel numbers. This means you are the gatekeeper. When assigning reel numbers, use the following guidelines:

## Reel names rules

No matter what type of project you work on, here are the golden rules:

1. Give everything a unique name that clearly and succinctly describes what it contains.
2. Maintain an up-to-date master log of all reels and their contents. Keep a master file in your computer and a hard copy in a notebook.
3. Make sure your naming system is clear to all who touch the project: Your editing crew, post house, sound editors, VFX house, editors on segments or episodes if you're working on a series, film librarians, etc.

## What's in a file name?

As the world moves toward file-based workflows and deliverables, the number of characters you can use to describe a reel parallels computer file name restrictions. Presently this means sticking to 32 characters (or fewer) and using numbers and letters only: no dots, dashes, or symbols.

Practically, most editors assign six characters or less since 32 characters are way too many to read. More importantly, older online and offline systems can't decipher more than six characters and will simply cut off the label so that every reel will read the same, e.g., reel00, instead of reel001 or reel002 or reel003 as intended. To solve this problem, label reels R001, R002 or better, just 001, 002, etc.

## Give each tape a unique ID

Never name two tapes the same. It is crucial that each tape has its own unique ID in your digital system. Why? Two tapes with the same reel numbers will cost you time, money, and aggravation whenever you have to locate either tape during offline and finishing. If the two tapes have the same time codes, this exacerbates the problem and may result in the wrong shots getting in your show master tape or file.

### DEALING WITH DUPLICATE REEL NUMBERS

Since reel assignment is not always in your control, you will probably receive two reels with the same number. This happens when you receive reels from other shows or post houses, from the insert stage or from stock houses, VFX houses, etc.

What should you do?

Change the duplicate number before ingesting the reel. Change this number everywhere: on the tape itself, on the tape box, and on all files, logs, and records. And make certain that the place you received it from changes the name in their files and on their copy of the tape. Just in case they don't, be sure to enter the original name in your master file of reel numbers and contents.

## Typical naming conventions

*"[File naming] is an incredibly UNDERVALUED issue. If you can't find a file, you can't work... period."*

—MARK RAUDONIS, VP of postproduction, Bunim-Murray Productions

If you inherit a naming convention, follow it to the letter — and number! If you get to devise your own scheme, here are a few conventional naming methods to consider:

### SIMPLE METHODS

For reels 1, 2, 3... use 001, 002, 003...or R1, R2, R3... This method is used on everything from TV shows to feature films. News shows label and archive reels by slug (story) name.

## NON-SCRIPTED SHOW METHODS

There are many ways to label nonfiction shows, from the simple method outlined before to a more detailed system when multiple series, shows and/or segments are being edited. Table 4.1 gives a rundown of methods from the least to the most complicated:

### TABLE 4.1
### REEL LABELING METHODS

| METHOD | LABEL | WHAT LABEL MEANS |
|---|---|---|
| LOCATION | Jer10 | Jerusalem reel #10 |
| SUBJECT OF INTERVIEW | Madonna intvw. | Madonna interview |
| TYPE OF FOOTAGE | B: oil spill | B roll of oil spill |
| | Ins. cats jug | Insert reel of cats juggling |
| DATE, CAMERA LOAD, AND SHOW ID | 1127B2IRT | November 27, B camera, second load, Ice Road Truckers |

### EPISODIC TV AND MTV METHODS

The production company designates a number for each series and the episode number and reel number are tacked on to it. Table 4.2 demonstrates this method and a simpler series method. The table also shows how multi-cam shows — sitcoms and music videos — include the camera name when labeling reels.

### TABLE 4.2
### TV SERIES AND MULTI-CAM SHOW LABELING METHODS

| METHOD | LABEL | WHAT LABEL MEANS |
|---|---|---|
| SERIES (DRAMA) | 79112R5 | Series#79, episode #112, reel #5 |
| | 105R01 | Episode #105, reel #1 |
| MULTI-CAM SHOWS (SITCOMS AND MUSIC VIDEOS) | 01A | Reel 1 Camera A |
| | 01B | Reel 1 Camera B |
| | 01C | Reel 1 Camera C |

# Logging

As with labeling, you can log before, during, or after entering dailies and other footage into the system. Whenever you log, it's best to do it before you start to edit. "Why bother?" you ask, "I'm short on time." True, but think again. Here's why: Logging allows you to instantly laser in on every last line, look, cutaway, and frame of footage. As you log the footage, you get to know it better and feel like you're on top of it, not vice versa. Logging also gets your mind working; your show starts to take form as you think about order, structure, and building to that spectacular snow board flip you logged in the middle of reel four. If you're short on storage and not going to ingest all the production footage, logging is a necessity as it helps you determine which footage not to ingest. Lastly, if you will be sharing your footage in the near future or archiving it for posterity you'll need to have it logged. At many companies, logger is a starting or contracted position.

## Logging footage on shows with paper cuts

When cutting news, documentary, segments, or other short pieces, you may have a paper cut (outline of shots and/or subjects) from the producer. The paper cut may include the shots' time codes, in which case you may only be ingesting these specified shots. So you should only log these shots, right? Of course this is tempting, especially if you're under time pressure. However, you should log everything. Why? Because you never know when you'll want to dip into this footage. A log can save you time as it will refresh your memory about what's on the tape (or other daily medium) and help you decide whether to try editing it into the show.

## Logging tapes

Every tape should have a log so you can identify and find the footage on it. In days of yore, a log was always kept in the tape box, but with today's mini-cassettes you should keep the log in your binder, and of course, in the computer for quick reference, and if you can fit it in the box or attach it somehow, do it. Daily tapes on scripted shows arrive with a log made at the set, stage, or post house and usually require no further logging. Put their logs in a binder and keep the master list there and on the computer. If there are any insert or stock shots in addition to the scenes on the tape, note them in your records and on the tape box. On non-scripted shows, creating a tape log is crucial. The field log, if it exists, will not give you the shot details you'll need for editing.

## What to do with all the logs

First, keep a hard copy of each daily tape's log in a binder, organized in reel order, e.g., Reel 1-17. Also include a log of all non-daily tapes: inserts, VFX, animations, music, graphics, stock footage, etc. Second, maintain a master file of all logs on your computer for easy searching, e.g., plugging in the word "swan" to locate all the reels with swan footage. If you're using the digital system's database, it allows you to search rapidly for words, phrases, time code and other data entry fields within a project. Keeping logs in a binder as well as on your computer is the handiest way to find footage.

## The Database Log

*"Logging has always been a part of editing but the big difference now is that a database is created. This makes retrieval of footage a simple matter."*
—ALAN MILLER, Editor and VP at Moving Pictures, a post house in NYC.

Before starting to log, you can create a database on your digital editing system from its log and capture tool and enter the data about each shot. Then you'll use the database to batch capture (automatically ingest) each shot. Photo 4.a shows the Log and Capture tool on Final Cut Pro.

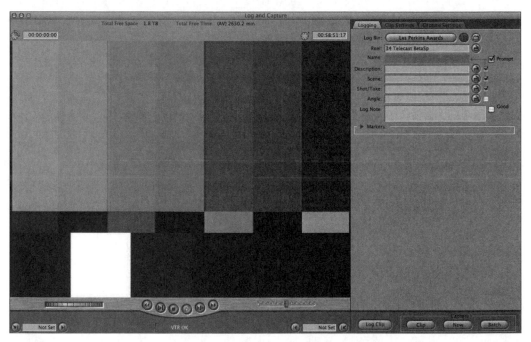

**4.a** FCP's ingest tool displaying a tape's color bars. Notice the logging area in the upper right corner and the capture commands at lower right.

Alternatively, you can create a database on your PC using Excel, FileMaker Pro or another database program. Or you may receive a database from telecine and add shot descriptions, comments and other info. Whatever path you take, know that the database will serve your show by organizing footage for facile searches and storing essential data for finishing your show.

## What to log

You can log any information you want such as date, time, location, and disk location. If you receive a long take labeled "animals" you can divide it into "lions" and "tigers" and "bears." Also, you can eliminate ingesting unusable footage by not logging it into the database at all. To create a database before ingesting, you will view the tape in the tape deck. Here's how:

1. Play to where the take starts on the tape and enter the time code number into the computer.

2. Play through the take and stop at the end. Enter the ending time code, label the take, and type in any descriptions, data, or notes. You can also add comments such as NG (no good), fair, poor, etc. Many editors like to * good takes.

Now you've made your first entry in the database. This entry will become a clip when input. Continue logging takes until you've finished the tape. Then don't forget to label and save your database!

## 24-fps HD finish shows

Table 4.3 is a typical database for a TV show that shot 35mm and is finishing HD 24 fps.

# TABLE 4.3
## DAILY DATABASE FROM TELECINE

| FIELD_DELIM | TABS | | TRACKER_VERSION | | 3.2.003 | | Sort Order: [Video TC In] |
| --- | --- | --- | --- | --- | --- | --- | --- |
| VIDEO_FORMAT | NTSC | | | | | | |
| FILM_FORMAT | 35mm, 4perf | | | | | | |
| AUDIO_FORMAT | 48kHz | | | | | | |

| Name | Tracks | Tape | FPS | Start | End | Cam roll | Sound TC | Sound roll | Comment |
| --- | --- | --- | --- | --- | --- | --- | --- | --- | --- |
| DATA | | | | | | | | | |
| 32-4 | VA1 | 105R01 | 24 | 01:00:00:00 | 01:02:16:10 | A1 | 11:43:43:24 | 52 | |
| 32A-2 | VA1 | 105R01 | 24 | 01:02:16:10 | 01:03:24:20 | A1 | 12:00:30:10 | 52 | boom in |
| 32A-4 | VA1 | 105R01 | 24 | 01:03:24:20 | 01:05:35:15 | A1 | 12:04:30:00 | 52 | |
| 32B-1 | VA1 | 105R01 | 24 | 01:05:35:15 | 01:07:25:15 | A1 | 12:08:20:21 | 52 | |
| 32B-2 | VA1 | 105R01 | 24 | 01:07:25:15 | 01:09:28:05 | A1 | 12:11:07:24 | 52 | airplane |
| 32C-1 | VA1 | 105R01 | 24 | 01:09:28:05 | 01:11:05:15 | A1 | 12:31:43:12 | 52 | |
| 32C-2 | VA1 | 105R01 | 24 | 01:11:05:15 | 01:12:40:00 | A1 | 12:34:57:25 | 52 | |
| 32D-1 | VA1 | 105R01 | 24 | 01:12:40:00 | 01:15:13:10 | A1 | 12:38:25:06 | 52 | |
| 17-3 | VA1 | 105R01 | 24 | 01:15:13:10 | 01:16:28:25 | A1 | 13:37:16:10 | 52 | |
| 17-4 | VA1 | 105R01 | 24 | 01:16:28:25 | 01:18:32:05 | A1 | 13:39:09:28 | 52 | |
| 17A-1 | VA1 | 105R01 | 24 | 01:18:32:05 | 01:20:07:15 | A1 | 13:46:37:15 | 52 | dolly creak |
| 17B-2 | VA1 | 105R01 | 24 | 01:20:07:15 | 01:20:44:25 | A1 | 13:58:20:02 | 52 | |
| 17B-3 | VA1 | 105R01 | 24 | 01:20:44:25 | 01:21:22:05 | A1 | 13:59:32:05 | 52 | |
| 17B-4 | VA1 | 105R01 | 24 | 01:21:22:05 | 01:21:55:25 | A1 | 14:00:44:08 | 52 | |
| 17C-2 | VA1 | 105R01 | 24 | 01:21:55:25 | 01:23:06:10 | A1 | 14:21:44:15 | 52 | dirt in gate |
| 17C-3 | VA1 | 105R01 | 24 | 01:23:06:10 | 01:24:08:20 | A1 | 14:23:47:11 | 52 | |
| 17D-1 | VA1 | 105R01 | 24 | 01:24:08:20 | 01:25:33:05 | A1 | 14:26:54:00 | 52 | |
| 32-4 | VA1 | 105R01 | 24 | 01:25:33:05 | 01:27:48:20 | B1 | 11:43:44:26 | 52 | |
| 32A-2 | VA1 | 105R01 | 24 | 01:27:48:20 | 01:28:54:20 | B1 | 12:00:31:04 | 52 | |
| 32A-4 | VA1 | 105R01 | 24 | 01:28:54:20 | 01:31:03:15 | B1 | 12:04:30:25 | 52 | |
| 32B-1 | VA1 | 105R01 | 24 | 01:31:03:15 | 01:32:50:10 | B1 | 12:08:21:18 | 52 | |
| 32B-2 | VA1 | 105R01 | 24 | 01:32:50:10 | 01:34:50:05 | B1 | 12:11:08:13 | 52 | |
| 32C-1 | VA1 | 105R01 | 24 | 01:34:50:05 | 01:36:26:00 | B1 | 12:31:44:21 | 52 | |

## 24-fps film finish shows

Telecine creates the database and sends it with dailies. Table 4.4 shows that the colorist transferred the film negative to tape and entered the key codes into the database. The 3/2 Fr column displays the video frame — A — that the telecine transfer started on. (Step 5: Vital Verifications for Film explains this in detail.)

TABLE 4.4
**DATABASE FILE FOR TELECINED NEGATIVE**

| DATE: JAN 7, 2012 COLORIST: LZ | | | SCENE 6 | | PRODUCTION: BEACH HOUSE GANG | | | | PAGE 1 OF 1 |
|---|---|---|---|---|---|---|---|---|---|
| SC | TAKE | TIME CODE | 3/2 FR | CAMROLL | KEY CODE PREFIX KEY | | +FR | SND ROLL | SOUND TC |
| 6 | 3 | 03:00:00:00 | A | A12 | KT467682 | 4102 | +09 | 5 | 17:23:44:11 |
| 6 | 4 | 03:01:53:24 | A | A12 | KT467682 | 4283 | +15 | 5 | 17:37:57:06 |
| 6A | 2 | 03:03:47:19 | A | A12 | KT467682 | 4463 | +13 | 5 | 17:51:01:22 |
| 6A | 3 | 03:04:49:04 | A | A12 | KT467682 | 4526 | +03 | 5 | 17:57:35:28 |
| 6B | 1 | 03:06:01:15 | A | A12 | KT467682 | 4590 | +12 | 5 | 18:03:19:04 |
| BLK | EOR* | 03:06:38:02 | | | | | | | |

* End of reel.

Normally telecine produces a database in one of three file formats: Flex file (the most common format), Keylink, or KeyLog, a.k.a. Evertz. You may need to convert the file to a format your system recognizes, e.g., an ALE — Avid log exchange — though ALEs are used so universally these days that many post houses create them for you. Whether you convert the file or the post facility does, the end result is the same: You save the database to your system's internal hard drive and use it for batch capture.

Note: You can create a film database yourself on your system, e.g., by using Cinema Tools on FCP or Film Scribe on Avid. You will need a time-coded tape with a burnt-in film data and video time code. This demands time, absolute accuracy, and a clear understanding of what you're doing; pay the money and leave it to the telecine pros is the recommended course.

## Last word on logging footage and entering data

All shows that finish via online, DI, or negative cut depend on accurate numbers being entered into the digital system. Bogus numbers can result in a fouled-up online or DI that must be re-done at great expense, or worse, a miscut negative, which can be irreversible. These disasters are avoidable. It cannot be more plainly stated: Make sure valid numbers are entered or you will indeed have garbage out.

## INGEST ESSENTIALS

*"Ask, ask, ask. You won't know everything on any show so don't be afraid to ask."*
—RACHELLE DANG, assistant editor, *Bruno*, *Tilda*, and *Pushing Daisies*.

You connect a FireWire to a camera or tape deck, play it back, and presto! The tape transmutes into editable pictures on the digital system. What's behind this mysterious transformation? Read on!

### What happens to a shot in a digital editing system?

A shot, once it's ingested, is known as a clip, and consists of two files: the media file and the data file.

#### MEDIA FILE, A.K.A. MATERIAL FILE

Consists of the clip's picture file and/or sound file(s), preferably stored on an external hard disk.

#### DATA FILE

Stored on the internal hard drive, this file performs two essential functions: 1) It holds critical data and metadata about the clip; and 2) It points to where the clip's media file(s) are stored.

### Resolution, a.k.a. res or rez

Resolution, simply put, is how good your digitized image looks on your editing system. Of course you want to edit with the best looking image possible but…Yes, there's a big but and it has to do with compression. When you ingest images in their original — raw — format, they are uncompressed. They look great, all dressed up in their hi res, uncompressed pixels, but they can take up a lot of disk storage space. And they can strain the computer's processors, thus slowing certain editing functions, e.g., playing back layered (complex) VFX.

| | | | | |
|---|---|---|---|---|
| Uncompressed image | = | higher res | = | more storage required |
| Compressed image | = | lower res | = | less storage required |

So ordinarily, you want to compress — sample and squeeze — the images for editing and then decompress them — return them to their native format — once the cut is locked and you enter the finishing stage of your project. The standard of compression behind all this is MPEG which comes in different flavors according to what type of format is being compressed. MPEG-4 is used to compress video. But how exactly do you tell your system to compress the footage? Enter the codec.

## Codec

Abbreviated from <u>c</u>ompressor/<u>dec</u>ompressor, codec is a two-step process that: 1) Compresses video, audio, and file formats on your hard drive and then 2) Decompresses them to their original size so you can view, edit, and play them back efficiently on a digital system.

There are codecs for cameras, graphics, 3-D, animation, speech, text, the Web, and more. FCP and Avid have their own codecs, Apple ProRes and DNxHD respectively. Each year brings more video and file formats and with them, more codecs. Although there are a lot of choices, you'll probably use only a small handful of codecs in your work. Photo 4.b shows a partial list of codecs you can choose from on a digital system.

### CHOOSING THE CORRECT CODEC

There are no set rules but your workflow, since it should state whether you're transcoding or downrezzing, will help determine your codec.

**Tape workflow**: Normally you pick the codec that matches the video format that you're editing, e.g., DV, DVCPRO50, or DVCPRO-HD. However, some camera codecs are poor for editing so you will need to transcode them to Apple ProRes or another edit-friendly codec.

**File-based workflow**: Typically you'll stay with the codec that the camera uses, e.g., REDCODE RAW codec for the R3D files from the RED camera. When you're shooting HD, choosing the camera codec is your best bet. If you're using a high-end HD format, you'll need a high quality capture card in your

Animation
BMP
Cinepak
Component Video
DV – PAL
DV/DVCPRO – NTSC
DVCPRO – PAL
DVCPRO HD 1080i50
DVCPRO HD 1080i60
DVCPRO HD 1080p25
DVCPRO HD 1080p30
DVCPRO HD 720p50
DVCPRO HD 720p60
DVCPRO50 – NTSC
DVCPRO50 – PAL
Uncompressed 10–bit 4:2:2
Uncompressed 8–bit 4:2:2
Graphics
H.261
HDV 1080i50
HDV 1080i60
HDV 1080p24
HDV 1080p25
HDV 1080p30
HDV 720p24
HDV 720p25
HDV 720p30
HDV 720p50
HDV 720p60
Apple Intermediate Codec
Motion JPEG A
Motion JPEG B
MPEG IMX 525/60 (30 Mb/s)
MPEG IMX 525/60 (40 Mb/s)
MPEG IMX 525/60 (50 Mb/s)
MPEG IMX 625/50 (30 Mb/s)
MPEG IMX 625/50 (40 Mb/s)
MPEG IMX 625/50 (50 Mb/s)
MPEG–4 Video
None
Photo – JPEG
Apple Pixlet Video
Planar RGB
PNG
Apple ProRes 4444
Apple ProRes 422 (HQ)
Apple ProRes 422
Apple ProRes 422 (LT)
Apple ProRes 422 (Proxy)
TGA
TIFF
Video
XDCAM EX 1080i50 (35 Mb/s VBR)
XDCAM EX 1080i60 (35 Mb/s VBR)
XDCAM EX 1080p24 (35 Mb/s VBR)
XDCAM EX 1080p25 (35 Mb/s VBR)
XDCAM EX 1080p30 (35 Mb/s VBR)
XDCAM EX 720p24 (35 Mb/s VBR)
XDCAM EX 720p25 (35 Mb/s VBR)
XDCAM EX 720p30 (35 Mb/s VBR)
XDCAM EX 720p50 (35 Mb/s VBR)
XDCAM EX 720p60 (35 Mb/s VBR)
XDCAM HD 1080i50 (35 Mb/s VBR)
XDCAM HD 1080i60 (35 Mb/s VBR)
XDCAM HD 1080p24 (35 Mb/s VBR)
XDCAM HD 1080p25 (35 Mb/s VBR)
XDCAM HD 1080p30 (35 Mb/s VBR)
XDCAM HD422 1080i50 (50 Mb/s)
XDCAM HD422 1080i60 (50 Mb/s)
XDCAM HD422 1080p24 (50 Mb/s)
XDCAM HD422 1080p25 (50 Mb/s)
XDCAM HD422 1080p30 (50 Mb/s)
XDCAM HD422 720p24 (50 Mb/s)
XDCAM HD422 720p25 (50 Mb/s)
XDCAM HD422 720p30 (50 Mb/s)
XDCAM HD422 720p50 (50 Mb/s)
XDCAM HD422 720p60 (50 Mb/s)
Avid 1:1x
Avid DNxHD Codec
Avid DV
Avid DV100 Codec
Avid Meridien Compressed
Avid Meridien Uncompressed
Avid Packed Codec
Blackmagic RGB 10 Bit
H.263
H.264
JPEG 2000
R10k RGB 10 Bit
Sorenson Video 3
Sorenson Video

**4.b** Partial list of the ever-growing number of codecs.

computer for smooth ingestion along with large, fast hard disks to play the large files properly. Incidentally, the RED — like a few other digital cameras — can record to several different resolutions simultaneously. Once ingested, these low res files — called proxies — allow you to proxy edit on your laptop or desktop and then link back to the original hi res files when you're ready to screen a cut or finish your show.

**Film-based workflow**: If you telecined offline-quality media, you'll likely pick an offline-quality codec. If you telecined online-quality media, you can stick with an online codec or you can downrez and go with an offline-quality codec.

A last major criterion for choosing a codec is to let your final output format dictate it, e.g., Blu-ray (disk) or YouTube (file).

### STAYING NATIVE, A.K.A. NATIVE EDITING

Staying native means using the same codec to ingest, edit, and output your original data and is the way to go if possible. If you compress your media for ingesting to save storage — as many do — just know that you will recapture (a.k.a. conform or re-conform) the media later on the system or the post house will do it during online or the DI process.

### WORKING WITH MIXED FORMATS

It's commonplace to receive dailies and other source footage from different file and tape formats. Mixing formats while editing can cause your system to crash regularly. Since codecs affect how the clips will play in your system, it's best to stick with one codec for all the footage. This means you may need to transcode a lot of footage to stay native and edit effectively. Talk to your post house and fellow editors and ping user's groups online to arrive at the best solution before you start. Technological advances promise to improve this issue in the future.

### LOSSY AND LOSSLESS

Depending on how much of the original image quality they preserve, codecs are deemed "lossy" or "lossless." Both are data compression schemes which are used on a variety of video, audio, graphic, and Web files. Lossy codecs compress the data so that the image loses quality from the original source material and cannot be restored fully to the original. Most codecs — and all video codecs — are lossy. Examples: Apple ProRes, and DNxHD. Lossless codecs retain the data so that when the image is decompressed it is indistinguishable from the original. Example: animation codec.

# Preparing Dailies for Editing in Five Steps

The rest of the chapter details the steps that will take you from dailies to a project fully prepped and ready to be edited. If you aren't finishing on film, you'll be done after step four. Here are the steps:

Step 1: Set up your project

Step 2: Log footage and enter data into the digital system

Step 3: Ingest

Step 4: Organizing after ingest

Step 5: Vital verifications for film finish shows

## Step 1: Set Up Your Project

Ask and answer these three questions before creating a project and ingesting a frame of footage on your digital system:

1. How much footage will be shot?
2. What is my show's finishing standard: 30 fps (tape, filc, or disk) or 24 fps (film, tape, file, or disk)? HD or SD or 3-D?
3. Sound editing: How will it be done?

### 1. How much footage will be shot?

Every clip takes up megabytes of space on your external hard disks; clips with video claim more space than clips with audio only. Clips add up to gigabytes or even terabytes of storage space. So you need to figure out the amount of footage that will be shot in order to acquire sufficient disk storage space for your media. You can and will add more storage as you go because this is cost-effective. But you should calculate storage ahead of time in order to effectively organize the material and manage your media. This is particularly important when there is so much footage that it can't all be available for editing because all the disk drives cannot be hooked up at the same time. In this case organize the media on the disks by episode, section, or scene(s), so that all their clips can be accessed and edited.

To find out how many hours of footage will be shot, ask. The director or your post supervisor, or AP should have the answer. If they don't know or are hazy, work with them to come up with an amount. Impress on them that ordering the right amount of storage makes for a time- and cost-efficient cutting room. Another approach: Determine the TRT (total running time) of the finished show along with how much footage this director or company typically shoots and make your calculation based on the time allotted for shooting.

## SCRIPTED SHOWS

On a scripted show the rule of thumb is: One script page equals one minute of cut footage, so a 30-page script would be 30 minutes of cut footage. This method is chancy, especially if you have action scenes, musical numbers, or any scenes with multiple cameras as they will boost the amount of footage. Consider this sentence in a script: "The platoon goes over the hill and takes the town." Does this mean a five-day shoot, a two-week shoot, or a simple master shot?

## NON-SCRIPTED SHOWS

Every doc, commercial, and music video is different. The footage may start as a trickle and soon become a monsoon. Before it floods the cutting room, ask questions and do your best to gauge the oncoming tide so you have enough drives on hand and a plan for organizing the footage. The dirty truth is that on reality TV and similar shows, there's barely enough time to screen all the dailies, let alone ingest them all. Since these shows run long on footage and short on deadlines, editors routinely "grab and run," high-speeding through the footage and throwing it in the system. Storage space is at a premium so estimating the amount of footage is still important.

## CALCULATING STORAGE

Once you have the daily footage number, estimate the amount of footage from other sources such as: pick-up shoot, overshoot, re-shoot, insert shoot, B roll, VFX from the special effects house, stock footage, and archival footage. When you know the total amount of footage, you can go to each digital system's manufacturer's website and search for their storage calculator. Once you input your parameters, the software will tell you how many gigabytes or terabytes you'll need. You can also download calculators online for free such as VideoSpace or AJA DataRate — see figure 4.c.

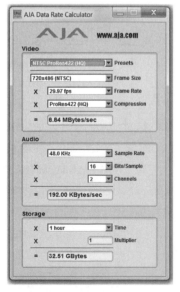

After you establish how many gigabytes or terabytes of storage you'll need, tell your storage supply house or post house. Also, if you'll be adding more storage as the show moves on, let them know so they can feed you drives as you're ready for them.

4.c Downloadable AJA storage calculator. *Photo courtesy of AJA.*

## 2. What is my show finishing on: film, tape, or both?

It's crucial to know whether you're finishing on film or tape or both so you can set up your project correctly on the digital system. If you choose a film finish, you'll create a 24-fps project. This means your cuts will calculate and play at 24 fps and you can prepare a cutlist for negative cutting or the DI process. When you make a 24-fps project, the system will allow you to convert your cut to 30 fps if you need to finish on tape in addition. So when you create a 24-fps project you can finish on all formats: film, tape, disc, or file.

If you select a tape finish, you will normally set up a 30-fps project. Your cuts will calculate and play at 30 fps and you can finish on tape as well as disc or file. However, a few disk and Web companies as well as networks are demanding 24-fps output to fulfill 24-fps HD delivery requirements. If this is true, you'll need to create a 24-fps project.

The lines continue to blur between film and tape. It may be better these days to think 24-fps finish vs. 30-fps finish instead of film vs. tape finish. What remains true is that if there is *any* possibility of a 24-fps finish, set up a 24-fps project as you can easily derive a 30-fps finish from a 24-fps project but not vice versa.

### SYSTEMS AND 24-FPS FINISH

Some systems do not allow you to finish 24 fps. If you think you might finish 24 fps, you have three options:

1. Rent a system that will make a 24-fps project (strongly recommended).
2. Finish via a DI. Certain DI machines can make a film print from a 30-fps cut but check first that the company you're hiring has done this successfully. This is not a time to cut corners or costs.
3. Make certain that your 30-fps system has matchback software or reliable third-party software. Matchback allows you to make a cutlist from your 30-fps final cut and requires familiarity with the negative cutting process and extra time to painstakingly check the cutlist for the negative cutter. This method is not recommended because it requires more time, knowledge, and complete accuracy on the back end.

## 3. Sound editing: What do the sound editors want?

It's easy to overlook sound in the flurry to get dailies ingested and the show edited. But this is a disservice to the project and the sound crew.

Look ahead: Find out what the sound editors need. The main questions to ask them are: 1) How they would like you to capture the tracks and 2) What kinds of sound files they require. The answers will prevent either of you having to re-do work and make for a smooth transfer of files and sound tracks from your system to theirs.

### TRACKING AUDIO

It's important to keep complete records of where all your sound comes from so the sound editors won't have to hunt for it or bug you later. "The more information you can give us, the better," says Suhail Kafity, sound editor on *Apocalypto, The Chronicles of Narnia,* and *Armageddon.* Identify the source of all audio, even if it's temp in case the sound editors — or you — needs to locate it later. Talking with your sound editors goes a long way toward achieving a smooth sound editing process and ensuring the best sounding show possible.

Make sure that the audio time code and sound reel numbers get entered into the system. Audio that arrives with dailies on file, hard drive, or tape should have time code and this information will be entered automatically during ingest. Other audio may not have time code such as music and SFX from CD, DA-98[1], DAT, or DVD. In these cases, note down as much data as you can, e.g., CD title, song title, and track number. You may need this data for onlining and finishing, also for legal reasons if you need to license the music.

## *Set Up Your Project*

Once you've answered these three major questions, log on to your system and create your project with your chosen parameters. Photo 4.d shows where you enter project properties on Final Cut Pro.

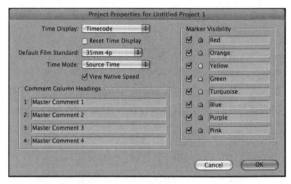

**4.d** Project properties set-up window on Final Cut Pro.

---

1. The Tascam DA-98 is a digital hi 8mm, 8-track audio recorder used in post houses and mix stages. While Tascam has replaced their DA-88 and DA-98 recorders with a digital disk recorder, as with other discontinued devices and formats, you may still receive recordings from them.

# Step 2: Enter Data into the Digital System

*"Garbage in, garbage out."*

—ANONYMOUS

The above maxim is as true for digital editing systems as it is for computers in general. For a tape finish, this translates to correct time codes and reel numbers IN, correct time codes and reel numbers OUT. For a film finish this means correct key codes, camera rolls, time codes, and video reel numbers IN, correct key codes, camera rolls, time codes, and video reel numbers OUT.

## *Daily tapes*

In order to edit, original field tapes — especially HD tapes — are down-converted to files or dubbed to a lower res tape format and ingested into the digital editing system. Commonly, editors ingest original tapes directly from the camera or tape deck into the system. This is risky. Why? *Because every time you run an original tape you risk damage or destruction by the device playing it.* Re-shooting is an unpopular and often non-feasible option. Minimize playing your originals so that you'll never lose hard-won, irreplaceable footage.

## *Tapeless workflow*

When you're ingesting from cards or hard drives, it's essential that you transfer all the information and folders intact and complete to your media drives. Don't just input the media files or QuickTime files because they don't contain the vital metadata that the system needs for finishing. It's equally critical that you retain the original file names and time codes of the original source media and files for future re-linking. You can copy the files and change the names for editing, but do not change the original, root file names.

## *How codes, reel numbers, and other critical data enter the editing system*

*"Forget the images. In the end, editing comes down to code numbers."*

—FILM LIBRARIAN

A skewed view perhaps, but with a bit of truth to it: When finishing and referencing images, you locate images by their code numbers, not their aesthetic or narrative qualities. Codes, reel numbers, and other data enter the internal hard drive in three ways: automatically as you ingest, via a database created by you or telecine prior to ingesting, or via entries you make after ingesting. You can correct or add data afterwards, but typically it's entered as shown in Table 4.5.

**TABLE 4.5**
**HOW DATA TYPICALLY ENTERS THE EDITING SYSTEM**

| DATA | HOW DATA ENTERS | WHEN |
|---|---|---|
| TIME CODE | Automatically | During input |
| TAPE REEL # | By editor or database | Before, during, or after inputting |
| NOTES, COMMENTS, AND SHOT DESCRIPTIONS | By editor and/or database | Before, during, or after inputting |
| SOUND ROLL AND SOUND TIME CODE | Database | During input |
| KEY CODE, CAMERA ROLL #, AND OTHER VITAL FILM DATA | Database | During input |

## Tapes without time code

If a tape has no time code, the digital editing system adds its own time code to each clip as it's ingested. This time code is useful for searching for clips within the system, period. If you need to transcode, uprez, or online, the system's fabricated time code is useless. Dub to a pre-striped tape before ingesting if you need to reference a time code for finishing.

## Tapes or files with breaks in time code

Due to inexperienced camera people, you may receive footage with non-continuous time code. You should always set your editing system to detect time-code breaks so it will stop ingesting and alert you to this problem. If there are lots of breaks, as with non-coded tapes, you may want to copy the reel to a pre-striped tape. Otherwise, you will need to manually stop and restart ingesting with each break. A further problem is that with each break in time code, the camera resets to the same time code. This means you'll have multiple repeated time codes so searching by time code will bring up many clips to dig through.

## Scripts

You can bring in the file of a script or a transcript with special software. Avid's Script Sync, which has been around for years and is used primarily in TV, works by lining up the script supervisor's numbered takes with dialogue in the script. Adobe's Story embodies the latest innovations. The file, once imported, carries essential script elements as metadata and analyzes speech, enabling you to search for keywords, lines, phrases, etc., on fiction and nonfiction shows.

### Film finish shows

It's crucial that telecine burn in the following to each tape, drive, or file: time code including the fields, videotape reel number, camera roll, and key code or ink code depending on whether negative or work print is being telecined. In addition, burning in the sound roll and time code is highly recommended.

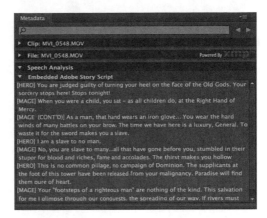

**4.e** Adobe's Story, a speech analysis app. *Photo courtesy of Adobe.*

Accurate window burns and databases are crucial to ensuring a valid cutlist and should only be created by an experienced telecine team. If the crew you're dealing with has little or no idea how to do this, pick one that does. Do not economize in this area; you will pay for it with time and dollars along with a large dollop of stress.

## Step 3: Ingest

When you ingest picture and sound from cards, hard drives, QuickTime or other files, you click on Import and the media and data are copied in. To ingest media from tape, you capture (digitize) it. Digitizing is one of the defining aspects of digital editing. It's also part magic as you watch the images stream in that you will click on and play to create with. Outlined next are the seven general steps for inputting a tape. You'll need to hop on a system and control every step yourself to really experience the magic.

### 1. ENTER TAPE INFO

1. Identify the tape's reel number.
2. Select time code to make sure time code is entered into the system.
3. Select channels to input — V, A1, A2 — by determining what channels of video and audio are on the tape.

### 2. SET VIDEO PARAMETERS

1. Analog tapes: Set video levels with:
   - External scope if you're finishing on the system for broadcast.
   - Internal scope if desired for finishing off the system.
2. Select a resolution and/or codec.

### 3. SET AUDIO PARAMETERS

1. Set audio level via system's internal audio tool or external mixer. (With file-based dailies the system may do this automatically.)
2. Set audio sampling rate*. This is SET FOR THE PROJECT and cannot be changed once you input a frame of media.
   *There are two choices for sampling rate:*
   a) 44.1 kHz = 44,100 audio samples per second
      — Minimum rate at which tapes, CDs, & DAT are sampled for editing.
   b) 48 kHz = 48,000 audio samples per second. Recommended.
      — Gives more samples. Uses more space but negligible.

* Rate at which an audio signal is sampled (read) during capture.

**4. SELECT OR PRESET A DRIVE TO INGEST TO**

Practice savvy media management

1. Make sure you will always be able to access the clips you need to cut a scene or a section and input footage to drives accordingly.
2. Drives fill up faster than you'd like. Don't fill up any drive completely or you may have trouble accessing shots. Free drive space leaves you room to maneuver should you need to reorganize, copy, or move shots between drives.

**5. SELECT SHOTS TO INPUT FROM**

a) Database

OR

b) Tape, drive, disk, or file. Play down on the tape to the first shot you want to input.

**6. INGEST**

Automatically, via database
Select the correct command.
Ingest starts automatically.

Manually, without a database
Select "Start Record" icon on the system.
Press "Play" on the tape deck.

As a shot is captured, you may enter notes, comments, descriptions, etc.

**7. STOP INGEST**

- With a database
Ingest stops automatically once all the shots in the database have been ingested. If there's a problem, stop ingesting manually and pick up from where you left off.
- Without a database
Stop manually via screen command or keyboard and stop the tape.

Once you've mastered the art of digitizing, settle in and let the dailies roll!

# Step 4: After Input: Organizing on the Computer

*"The hardest part was coming up with the system. Once we came up with a great system and the communication lines were all open…it went incredibly smoothly. How we were going to track these shots — and how we were going to live our lives every day for a year and a half — was a great challenge…It was a huge film. To be able to say we got it done and that I organized it all was a good experience."*

—Assistant editor MARY PAT PLOTTNER, on organizing *Star Wars Episode One, The Phantom Menace*

Now that you've ingested the footage, you'll want to organize your clips in bins so they're easy to locate during the editing phase. You also may need to sync audio and video. If telecine syncs your dailies, you will want to check their work and re-sync the occasional take as necessary. (If the whole batch is out, give them a call and have them redo it.) So first, a word on syncing and slates.

# Syncing

## Syncing methods

When you sync an audio and a video clip, you merge the two clips to make a new — third — clip. Keep the original clips and move the new clip to your dailies bin (and/or another bin for editing as outlined in the bin organizing section that appears later). If you have multiple cameras on takes, as you will on most sitcoms and many music videos, you can use "group clip" (Avid) or "merge clip" (Adobe and FCP) to sync all the takes to one audio track. This allows you to "edit on the fly," i.e., play all cameras and press one key to cut from one take to another. Some editors use the multi-cam clip function to group all the clips in a single camera scene and order them together, starting with the master. This big "clip of clips" is referred to as a KEM roll since film dailies were organized this way for KEM editing machines.

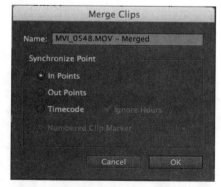

**4.f** Methods (sync points) for merging QT (.mov) clips on Adobe Premiere Pro. *Photo courtesy of Adobe.*

If the audio and video clips have matching time code, then you will sync to the time code or, possibly, an auxiliary time code. If not, you will use the clapped slate. There are several types of slates or stix, as they're commonly called. All slates provide a picture and sound reference for syncing, identify the take number, and give other useful info. You will encounter some or all of the following types of slates during your time in the cutting room.

# Slates

## Clapboard slate

These are the most common slates and supply a lot of information: director, scene and take number, date, production, production number, camera, camera roll (A, B, C, etc.), sound roll. The clap sticks come together for one frame which is the sync frame — the frame you will use to sync the V and A tracks.

## Smart slate

An electronic clapboard that is highly useful because it generates time code and jam syncs (matches) it to the audio recorder. This speeds up syncing tremendously. A smart slate displays time code on a red LED and can generate TOD (time of day) time code which is useful to news reporters, editors, and others concerned with the precise time of an event.

**4.g** Example of a time code "smart" slate. *Photo courtesy of Denecke, Inc.*

## Tail slates (TS)

An upside down clapboard indicates a tail slate is coming. A tail slate is used with children and animals, if the action has to be grabbed and there's no time to head slate it, or when the head slate has been bypassed for one reason or another.

## Closed stix = MOS take

An MOS (without sound) take is a picture-only take. Stix are closed and not clapped.

## Second slate, a.k.a. double stix = twice clapped slate

When the camera crew realizes that the first clapped slate was not in frame or that sound was not up to speed when it was clapped, they remedy this by clapping the slate a second time. You may hear a crew member yell "second stix" on your track and/or see two fingers held up on your picture. Use the second stix for syncing.

## Bloop slate

It earns its name from the bloop sound it makes which occurs simultaneously with a flash of light on the sync frame. Bloop slates provide no label or information and are for syncing purposes only.

## Impromptu slates

I've synced dailies to hand claps, an ax chopping wood, and drumsticks among other improvised slates. Better than nothing and fun for the crew perhaps, but often a time-consuming puzzle for editorial.

## No slates

No excuse. No three strikes. You're out of the industry. Forever... Sigh. I wish. If only you had to sync your own dailies....

## How to sync without slates

Syncing without slates is always a challenge but satisfying once accomplished. If you're close but still flummoxed finding sync, slip (move forward or backward) the sound, one frame or less at a time until you're in sync. There are syncing tools on your system as well as third-party software that may come to your rescue.

### NON-SLATED DIALOGUE

If there is no clapped slate on a dialogue take, you will need to lip sync it. Look for where the speaker's lips make a hard sound like the letter P, K, or B at the beginning of a word. You can use your system's locators — colored markers — to mark the same spot on each track and then line up the two tracks. Play the synced take and adjust it until it's in dead sync. This method also works when a sound recording problem causes sync to drift in and out during a take (which may or may not have been slated). Drifting sync ordinarily requires you to sync the take in several places to maintain sync throughout the take.

### NON-SLATED, NON-DIALOGUE FOOTAGE

Sync these takes by using a door close, footsteps, or any other short, distinct sound-and-picture action.

# Bins

*"Organization is the key to creativity!"*

—MARK RAUDONIS, VP of postproduction, Bunim-Murray Productions

Bin is a term carried over from editing on film where you organize footage in physical bins. On a digital system, a bin sports a folder icon and is the basic organizing unit for all your clips and sequences. Every project dictates its own organizing strategies but here are some common methods.

## *Creating and labeling bins*

### DAILIES BIN

When you ingest or import dailies, send them directly into a dailies bin and label it by date and/or reel number. Each day's dailies should have their own bin. To edit, it's convenient to sort clips by scenes or subjects. Since a clip can live in many bins, you can quickly copy the shots from the dailies bin to as many bins as you care to create and organize. Below are some tried and true methods.

### SCENES BIN

Create a new bin and label it by scene number, e.g., Scene 1, Scene 2, Scene 3, etc. Depending on the amount of footage, you can group scenes in bins, e.g., Scenes 1-5, etc.

### SUBJECT BINS

You can categorize subject bins any way you'd like. For example, you can designate bins according to:

Location: Paris bin, London bin

Interviewee: Dr. Livingston bin, Stanley bin

Category: birds bin, bees bin

Routinely, editors make bins for stock footage, B roll, graphics, VFX, SFX, and music. You may also wish to create a gag reel bin where you collect bloopers from the shoot for editing a short sequence for the wrap party. This assumes the wrap party hasn't already happened before editorial is brought on, which is the case on most projects.

### SEQUENCES/CUTS BIN

A cut is called a sequence[2] and is made up of clips and is represented by a different icon than a clip. Some editors keep their sequences together

---

2. Sequence is used only when working on certain digital systems. When you screen your show with a director, producer, client, or anyone else, you will screen a cut, not a sequence.

with the clips of the scene but most will create a separate sequences bin. If you build up a lot of cuts on a show, it's a good idea to have an old cuts bin and current cuts bin. This way you don't confuse sequences and start re-cutting the wrong one. That can happen easier than you think!

Tip: If you have a long list of bins, there are a couple of ways to easily locate the most used bins. Type "0" or "1" in front of the bin's name to put the bin at the top of the sort list. Put "z" at the head of the bin's name to place the bin at the

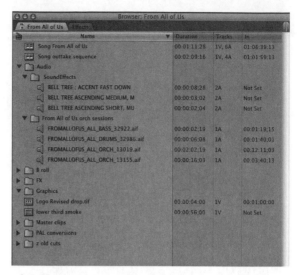

**4.h** Folder icons represent bins on FCP and other systems. Labeled bins pictured here include an Audio bin, B Roll bin, and FX bin. The Audio bin is open and contains an SFX bin and a music bin, both of which house audio clips. The two icons at the top signify that these are sequences. Notice how the old cuts bin is at the bottom due to being labeled with a "Z."

bottom of the list. This way you can always find it at the bottom of the list or bring it to the top by doing a reverse sort.

## You're breaking me down: subclips

Sometimes, after you input clips, you want to break them into smaller segments for more efficient searching and editing. For instance, if you didn't make a database beforehand and sub-divide that lengthy animal shot, you can do so now by subclipping it into lions, tigers, and bears. Subclips have their own special icon and behave similarly to clips.

## Viewing shots in bins

You can view clips, subclips, and sequences in a bin in two main ways: 1) image and label and; 2) icon and data. Both views can be used to rearrange clips and to access them for editing. You will probably prefer one view but you will use both at one time or another.

### ICON VIEW, A.K.A. PICTURE VIEW OR IMAGE AND LABEL VIEW

Icon view, depicted in Figure 4.i, displays your clips as postage stamp-sized frames. Referred to as thumbnails, icons, snapshots, or representative frames, these frames should instantly prod your memory about each clip's content. You can play a clip to view it or change its representative frame. In icon view you can re-order your clips like a storyboard to start visualizing how you will put a scene together. You can even drag the storyboarded clips to the timeline and start editing.

### LIST VIEW, A.K.A. DATA OR DATABASE VIEW

In list view (figure 4.j) you see the clip icon followed by the clip name and all the data you and/or the computer put in. The data is divided into columns such as notes, description, notes, reel number, time code, camera roll, key code, etc. This view swiftly gives you information about your clips and subclips. Opening a bin in icon view is speedier than opening it in picture view because retrieving data takes less time than retrieving images.

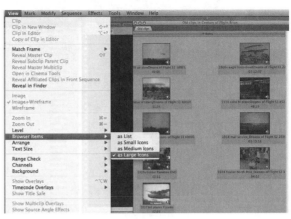

**4.i** Picture (icon) view on Final Cut Pro.

## Searching for bin items

You can search for clips, subclips, or sequences in a bin

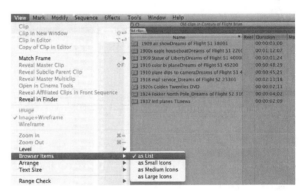

**4.j** Data (list) view on Final Cut Pro.

by typing in the name, reel number, time code, creation date, notes, descriptions, comments, and more. You can also call clips up by one or more categories. For instance you could combine three categories to call up all the close-ups of Dr. Livingston in London. All your diligent organizing work pays off when you access shots quickly and efficiently during editing.

## Future of bins

FCP X does away with bins and the viewer, replacing them with an events browser and a tool that automatically analyzes content and meta data during input, making for quicker searches. Since this method is new and FCP X is aimed at prosumers, not professionals, it's unclear whether other systems will follow these innovations. What is safe to say

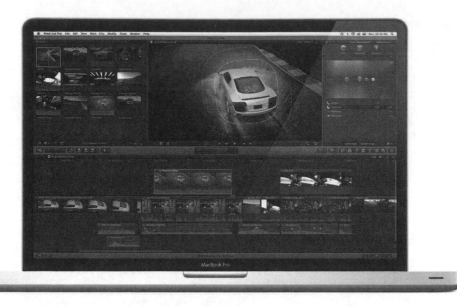

**4.k** FCP X does away with the viewer and bins. *Photo courtesy of Apple.*

is that searches will improve and background operations will increase in the future, streamlining logging and organizing.

## Backing up

A lot of shows shoot dailies on reusable media such as hard drives or cards. After ingesting (bringing in) dailies to the digital editing system, editorial will erase the media and send it back to the production crew for more recording. It's crucial to back up the reusable media to another source before erasing it. This protects you should a disaster of some kind (computer failure, fire, mudslide, etc. — it happens!) wipe out the media in your digital system. Some shows shoot video tape as a backup.

## Last word

Congratulations! You're done! You've prepped the digital editing system for editing. You've logged and input dailies and organized your bins on the system. If you're finishing on film or 24p, you need to read on. (For 24p, read section B to understand 3:2 pulldown, then skip to the next-to-last section, "What if I'm shooting 24p?") If you're ready to set a budget for dailies, see Appendix C which follows this chapter and completes Stage I. Otherwise, you can proceed straight to Stage II: Editing!

# Step 5: Vital Verifications for Film Finish Shows

You had your film telecined to an NDF tape, you've set up a 24-fps film project, and you've captured the footage from a database; now it's time to do one more important thing before beginning to edit: verify! You must check all the data that will be used to cut your negative so that you can create a perfect cutlist to be used for the traditional negative cut or the new DI film-scan process. Yes, you can do this after editing, but if there are problems, which there inevitably will be, you want to catch them the same day you receive the dailies. If you wait and then discover that many clips have inaccurate data, you may have to re-input shots and re-link the clips in your cut and your database, a time-consuming chore.

# Review

A cutlist uses the film data — camera rolls and key code[3] — on the database you brought in from telecine. Because this data is entered by both machine and human beings during telecine, it needs to be checked. It cannot be emphasized enough: Incorrect data in your cutlist leads to a miscut negative which can be irreparable. (More on why in Chapter 13: Finishing on Film and via Digital Intermediary.) To refresh your memory, here are the film and tape numbers that came on the database from telecine and should be burnt in to your tape and therefore your clip:

1. Key codes (negative telecine)
2. Camera roll number
3. NDF time code including fields
4. Video reel number

### The issue: true film frames

Telecine transferred your film footage, which runs at 24 fps, to video-tape which runs at 30 fps. The result is that your videotape has six added frames per second that do not exist on your film. You then ingested this tape into your 24-fps film project. The crux of the issue: When editing, you want to ensure that none of these added frames get cut into your sequence. If only film frames get ingested, then only film frames will be cut and only film frames will show up on your cutlist.

---

3. If you telecined workprint, your cutlist will use ink numbers. Since this process is going the way of the dodo bird, go to the Free tab of www.joyoffilmediting.com to learn about it.

## *Why an NDF tape?*

Remember the difference between drop frame time code and non-drop time code? Drop frame is time accurate, non-drop frame is numbers accurate. Since you are checking numbers, NDF tape is mandatory.

# Verifying Film Numbers: The ABCs

Verifying film numbers is a matter of making sure that the data telecine provided is correct. Editorial is responsible for the cutlist and the data that gets entered into and output from the digital system. That's right. You. Not telecine, even though they may have caused the problem. Below are the ABCs of how to do it.

## *A) Check the database and the clip against the tape time code*

Look at the first shot in the database in Table 4.6. It will have a column for the starting time code. Looking at the entry in the database file below, for 7-1 the time code is 1:00:00:00, a normal starting time code.

### TABLE 4.6
### TELECINED NEGATIVE DATABASE FILE ENTRY

| Date: March 12, 2012 Colorist: JL | | | Scene 7 | | Production: Zoe and the Hedge Rows | | | | Page 1 of 1 |
|---|---|---|---|---|---|---|---|---|---|
| Sc | Take | Time code | 3/2 Fr | CamRoll | Key code Prefix | Key | +Fr | Sound Roll | Sound TC |
| 7 | 1 | 01:00:00:00 | A | A9 | KL723151 | 2106 | +04 | 13 | 13:04:17:02 |

Clip 7-1's time code, which has been captured along with the tape's A & V, should match the database time code. They should both be 1:00:00:00. Actually the clip will be 1:00:00:00.1 as it shows the field which the database will not.

Go to where the clapper closes (or to a distinctive frame on an MOS shot). Check to make sure that the time code on the clapper frame matches the time code of the clapper frame on the tape. (If telecine synced your dailies, this is a good time to make a note if the clip is in sync. If it isn't, you can re-sync it later, before editing. This will not affect your film data verification.)

Go to the next clip and repeat the verification. Check every single take this way. Don't skip any. It's possible that one take could be out and the rest match just fine.

### IF THE TIME CODES DON'T MATCH

If the database time code does not match the clip time code, then telecine has made a mistake. Let telecine know ASAP. They will fix the database or the tape, depending on which is wrong. Then you will need to re-import the database or the clips with the correct numbers. If the database is incorrect, you can type in the correct numbers yourself from the tape. However, since telecine made the mistake, it's best if they fix it at their expense.

So far you've just checked time code numbers to make sure that they came in correctly from the tape to the clip and that they match the database. Now it's time to look at the film data found in the database and burnt-in to the tape.

## B) Make sure the 3:2 pulldown sequence is correct

So what in the name of Quentin Tarantino is the 3:2 pulldown sequence?

Each videotape frame is composed of two fields, remember? When film is transferred to video, in order to make up the difference between film running at 24 fps and video running at 30 fps, film frames are repeated as fields. Precisely at every other field, an extra film frame is repeated or *pulled down.*

Okay, so now I understand pulldown, but what is a 3:2 sequence? Let's examine how the film frames are pulled down to videotape. Since four film frames are repeatedly pulled down to five video frames, (the ratio derived from 24 fps to 30 fps), we'll look at a sequence of four film frames and what becomes of them.

| 4 film frames | **A B C D** | become |
|---|---|---|
| 5 video frames | 1 2 3 4 5 | pulled down become |
| 10 video fields | AA BB <u>BC</u> <u>CD</u> DD | |

See how film frame

**A** becomes two A fields
**B** becomes three B fields
**C** becomes two C fields
**D** becomes three D fields

**A** and **C** fields are pulled down *two* times, **B** and **D** *three* times. This is where the term 3:2 comes from. (Yes, technically it should be called 2:3 but near universal misusage keeps it 3:2.) Notice that BC and CD are different fields that share the same frame. This is why they are under-scored and referred to as mixed frames or shared frames.

## 3:2 pulldown sequence and film frames

In order to check the pulldown sequence, telecine conveniently adds A, B, C, or D at the end of the film key code (or ink code) to specify the film frame.

    4-frame key code sequence:    KT47 1220 1509 + 11A
                                  KT47 1220 1509 + 11B
                                  KT47 1220 1509 + 11C
                                  KT47 1220 1509 + 11D

## Punching the camera roll

At the beginning of each camera roll, (and each take if you request it), telecine punches the A frame. This establishes the required relationship between film frames and video fields.

## Pull-in frame

To make it easier to check, telecine lines up the A frame with time codes ending on the 00 frame and multiples of 5 frame. This is called the pull-in frame and will be listed in your database in the 3/2 Fr column.

Look at your tape one field at a time. The first A frame on the burnt-in film code should show up at the end of the burnt-in film code at time code 1:00:00:00, 1:00:00:05, 1:00:00:10, 1:00:00:15, 1:00:00:20.1, 1:00:00:25, 1:00:01:00, 1:00:01:05, etc. So this is what five frames of time code and film codes burnt into the tape look like, field by field:

| TAPE TIME CODE | FILM KEY CODE |
|---|---|
| 1:00:00:00.1 | KT47 1220 1509 + 11A |
| 1:00:00:00.2 | KT47 1220 1509 + 11A |
| 1:00:00:01.1 | KT47 1220 1509 + 12B |
| 1:00:00:01.2 | KT47 1220 1509 + 12B |
| 1:00:00:02.1 | KT47 1220 1509 + 12B |
| 1:00:00:02.2 | KT47 1220 1509 + 13C |
| 1:00:00:03.1 | KT47 1220 1509 + 13C |
| 1:00:00:03.2 | KT47 1220 1509 + 14D |
| 1:00:00:04.1 | KT47 1220 1509 + 14D |
| 1:00:00:04.2 | KT47 1220 1509 + 14D |
| 1:00:00:05.1 | KT47 1220 1509 + 15A |
| 1:00:00:05.2 | KT47 1220 1509 + 15A |

# C) Check pull-in sequence on a digitized clip

Normally you input a tape at an offline resolution, not a high, finishing resolution. This saves on storage because only every other field is digitized. A digital system is either Field One dominant and digitizes only field ones, or Field Two dominant and digitizes only field twos. So here's how the sequence above would look on a Field One dominant system:

| TAPE TIME CODE | FILM KEY CODE |
|---|---|
| 1:00:00:00.1 | KT47 1220 1509 + 11A |
| 1:00:00:01.1 | KT47 1220 1509 + 12B |
| 1:00:00:02.1 | KT47 1220 1509 + 12B |
| 1:00:00:03.1 | KT47 1220 1509 + 13C |
| 1:00:00:04.1 | KT47 1220 1509 + 14D |
| 1:00:00:05.1 | KT47 1220 1509 + 15A |

Check a few sequences on each clip to make your verification. If they're correct, you're done. If they're not, check the tape frame by frame. If the tape is fine, telecine made an error and you must alert them and have them re-do the tape and database so you can re-input the shots before they're cut. In the unlikely event that the tape is correct, then the digital system has captured it incorrectly and you need a system expert.

## *Other pull-in frames*

It must be stated that technically, telecine can use the A, B, C, or D frame as the pull-in frame. And telecine can change the pull-in frame for each take. The sequences are fine and you may save a few bucks but this is counteracted by the extra work it takes to decipher and verify each clip. So insist on consistency and have telecine pull in the A frame only, especially when you have a lot of footage. Always, to echo that famous jazz tune, "Take the A Frame."

**4.1** A telecined frame. Top: Sound time code and roll. Bottom: Video time code and film key code.

## What a 3:2 pulldown sequence looks like

Now that you understand how the pull-in frame must correlate to the burnt-in time code on a clip, let's examine the 3:2 sequence more closely. The sequence looks different, depending on if the system is Field One dominant, a.k.a. lower, or Field Two dominant, a.k.a. upper. The result in film frames is no different, as you can see below. Depending on what system you're using, you will see this as your sequence:

| System | Field dominance | Videotape fields | Ingested film frames |
|---|---|---|---|
| Avid, FCP | 1 | AA/BB/<u>BC</u>/<u>CD</u>/DD | A B **C** D |
| FCP, Lightworks | 2 | AA/BB/<u>BC</u>/<u>CD</u>/DD | A B <u>**C D**</u> |

**Bold** fields are ingested; non-bold fields are not ingested. You can see that Avid drops (hides, doesn't count) the second B frame (BC) and Lightworks drops the second D frame (DD). FCP allows you to select lower (even), upper (odd), or none for field dominance though you're most likely to follow what telecine sets up.

### How to check the 3:2 pulldown sequence

There is only one correct sequence with the four true film frames: ABCD. Go field by field through each clip and verify that you've got A B C D or A B C D frames. All other sequences, such as ABBC or BCDD, are incorrect. You can fix them on the system if you've digitized in all five video frames and the wrong field is hidden, e.g., ABCC can be adjusted to ABCD. Check each clip to verify that each has the correct sequence and change it if it doesn't.

### What if I'm shooting 24p?

Due to the bandwidth and storage space that 24p consumes, many people have telecine downconvert 24p to 30-fps tapes which means that the 3:2 pulldown gets added automatically. Adding pulldown allows the material to be viewed properly as NTSC monitors can't directly display a 24p signal. In order to finish your project and create an EDL (edit decision list) — the video equivalent of a cutlist — you will need to remove the pulldown. Called reverse telecine and accomplished via a tool on your system, e.g., by Cinema Tools on FCP, this process deletes the added fields and restores your cut to being 24p.

Sounds simpler to stay native and use the uncompressed 24p files, and some do. However, in addition to requiring major bandwidth and storage as mentioned above, this method necessitates special hardware and system configuration. The future will hopefully improve this situation, but this is where it stands now.

## Sound Verification

You can also verify the sound numbers in your database. This is a huge help to the sound editors, but again, communicate with them to see what they want. Have telecine enter the sound roll and the sound time code into the database along with the film and tape numbers and make sure they burn these numbers into the tape. Verify that the burnt-in sound time code on the tape matches the sound time codes on the database.

## CHAPTER WRAP-UP

Congratulations! You've prepped the footage for editing. If you want to set a budget for dailies, see Appendix C, which completes Stage I. Or, if you're ready to roll up your sleeves and go into creative mode, advance to Stage II: Editing!

# Appendix C

## Stage I: Budget for Dailies

Now that you're clear on how to set up your project and prepare dailies, you can budget for this stage of postproduction. You can photocopy this and all budget forms or download them from the Free tab of www.joyoffilmediting.com. Then you can tailor this budget to your project, as not all categories will apply. You can also enter this form into Excel or another spreadsheet program to perform the calculations. Alternatively, you can fork out for a budgeting program such as Movie Magic that professionals use.

### *Purpose of a budget*

- To determine the personnel, equipment, and services your show will need.
- To become an expert on your project — know its requirements, path, and schedule inside out.

### *Before beginning a budget*

- Study your project's script, outline, or storyboard closely to define the details and parameters of your project.
- Create a schedule and estimate how much it could possibly change or be extended.
- Make an accurate list of your delivery specs and format(s).

### *When making a budget*

- Get bids on everything.
  Meet with vendors and post facilities to determine which deals and services best suit your project's needs and budget.
- Know what you're paying for.
  If you don't understand something, ask questions until you do.
- Be generous with your estimates.
  "Anything that can go over budget, will go over budget" could be the subtitle of many a movie.
- Keep tidy records.

| ACCT # | DESCRIPTION | AMOUNT | UNITS | X | RATE | TOTAL |
|--------|-------------|--------|-------|---|------|-------|
| | BUDGET FOR DAILIES | | | | | |
| 2000* | PERSONNEL | | | | | |
| 2001 | Editor | | week | | | |
| 2002 | Asst editor | | week | | | |
| 2003 | Apprentice editor | | week | | | |
| 2004 | Post supervisor | | week | | | |
| 2005 | Editorial runner (PA) | | week | | | |
| | | | | | TOTAL FOR CATEGORY | |
| 2100 | ROOM & EQUIPMENT | | | | | |
| 2102 | Offline system rental | | week | | | |
| 2103 | Tape deck system rental | | week | | | |
| 2104 | UPS rental | | week | | | |
| 2105 | Other peripherals rental | | week | | | |
| 2106 | Moviola or flatbed rental | | week | | | |
| 2107 | Equipment purchase | | allow | | | |
| 2108 | Editing room rental | | week | | | |
| 2109 | Gb/Tb storage (rental) | | week | | | |
| 2110 | Supplies & expenses | | allow | | | |
| | | | | | TOTAL FOR CATEGORY | |
| 2200 | TAPE DAILIES | | | | | |
| 2201 | Downconvert & dub | | hour | | | |
| 2202 | Stock | | tape | | | |
| | | | | | TOTAL FOR CATEGORY | |
| 2210 | TAPELESS DAILIES | | | | | |
| 2211 | File conversion/copy | | hour | | | |
| 2212 | Syncing | | week | | | |
| 2213 | Drive rental | | week | | | |
| | | | | | TOTAL FOR CATEGORY | |
| 2250 | FILM DAILIES | | | | | |
| 2251 | Prep & process negative | | feet | | | |
| 2252 | Print dailies (work print) | | feet | | | |
| 2253 | Coding (ink code) | | feet | | | |
| 2254 | Sound mag stock | | tape | | | |
| 2255 | DAT stock | | tape | | | |
| | | | | | TOTAL FOR CATEGORY | |
| 2270 | TELECINE DAILIES | | | | | |
| 2271 | Negative | | hour | | | |
| 2272 | Positive (work print) | | hour | | | |
| 2273 | Syncing negative | | hour | | | |
| 2274 | Flex files | | disk | | | |
| | | | | | TOTAL FOR CATEGORY | |
| 2300 | DAILIES SCREENING | | | | | |
| 2301 | Projectionist | | hour | | | |
| 2302 | Screening room | | hour | | | |
| 2303 | Daily dubs: DVDs | | disk | | | |
| 2304 | SAN/server rental | | week | | | |
| 2305 | Transcripts | | hour | | | |
| | | | | | TOTAL FOR CATEGORY | |
| 2500 | MISC. EXPENSES | | | | | |
| 2501 | Parking fees, photocopy | | week | | | |
| 2502 | Fax, phone, coffee, etc. | | allow | | | |
| | | | | | TOTAL FOR CATEGORY | |
| | | | | | GRAND TOTAL | |

* Account #'s shown are sample numbers, not established accounting numbers.

# Editing

*"Shooting is like buying groceries and the real cooking is at the editing table."*
—ANG LEE, director, *Brokeback Mountain; Crouching Tiger, Hidden Dragon;* and *Sense and Sensibility*

## Introduction

There are no rules for how to edit yet there are cuts that work better, worse, and not at all. Truth is, you don't know exactly how you're going to edit something until you actually sit down with the footage. The goal of Stage Two is to give you guidelines — field tested by thousands of editors over the years — to help you edit.

Part One spotlights how and why editors make the cuts they do. It focuses on how to approach editing the footage, including how to make the first cut, the last cut, make matched cuts, and edit different genres such as drama, music videos, and documentary.

Part Two shows you how to apply this newfound knowledge by detailing how to cut on a digital editing system and get from first cut to locked cut.

# How to Approach the Footage

*The Editor's Prayer*
*Our perfect director who art in heaven,*
*Showered with Oscars be thy name.*
*Thy Lifetime Achievement will come, thy will be done*
*In the editing room as it is on location.*

*Give us this day our dailies on time and*
*Forgive the missing footage as we also forgive*
*The person in charge of continuity.*

*Lead us not into frustration*
*But deliver us from the talent-free director,*
*For ours is the splicer, the mouse,*
*and the objective eye.*
*Forever. Amen. Rewind.*

## Introduction

Part One illuminates the twists and turns you may encounter on the path to editing your film or video. It's composed of three chapters. Chapter 5 explains how to tackle your first edits and deal with mismatches, then dives into the thorny subject of modern "MTV" style editing, comparing it to traditional, Hollywood style cutting. Chapter 6 clues you in on how to cut action and dialogue scenes and conquer a host of other everyday editing challenges. Chapter 7 centers on the unique challenges editors face on different types of shows including animation, comedy, music video, documentary, and many more. Throughout Part One you will hear from professional editors about how they tackle the footage.

## CHAPTER 5

# To Cut or Not to Cut

*Where to Cut and Why*

*"As the editor begins his task, he has thousands of feet of small individual scenes which have been photographed out of continuity and at various angles, close-ups, full shots, two shots, silent shots, reaction shots, point-of-view shots, inserts, etc... for the ultimate selection as to performance, quality, and timing."*

—JACK W. OGLIVIE, A.C.E., first Laurel and Hardy films, *Heidi*, *Pony Express* TV series

## Overview

A screen full of digital images stares you in the face: Your dailies are ready to be edited. What do you do? How do you start? This chapter covers why and where you cut, beginning with picking the first shot and making your first edit. You'll discover which angles traditionally match, which don't, and how to deal with the pros and cons of making matched and unmatched edits. The second half of the chapter demystifies everyday editing challenges such as establishing rhythm in a cut, making reaction shots count, and cheating shots. It reveals the power of overlaps and gives you several practical exercises for trying them yourself. The chapter finishes with an extensive look into classical cutting style and modern cutting style, exposing their good, bad, and overlap points. Have fun with the chapter and have more fun making your own creative editing decisions! Also, enjoy the frames from well-known shows that illustrate key editing principles.

# GETTING STARTED

*"But you gotta know the territory."*
—CHARLIE, a salesman, *The Music Man*

You've got to know your raw material in order to have an idea of how you're going to edit it. View the footage for the scene and make mental and/or written notes about shots, lines, angles, or cutting ideas. Also, review any notes you took when screening dailies or that you received from the director. The late Dede Allen explained how she edits: "If you have a great deal of coverage, you really can't just go plowing through the whole thing, you'd never remember all of it... I make massive notes which I have if I need them, but I memorize the material so thoroughly that I seldom even look at my notes." Bottom line, you want to be able to access the footage in your mind at all times, so use your notes or commit it to memory like Dede Allen.

# Read the Script or Outline

## Scripted show

You've already read the script but now you have the real, filmed version of a scene along with the lined pages that the script supervisor labored over for your benefit. As you approach cutting the scene, familiarize yourself with it as well as the scenes before and after it. Since you usually edit a show out of sequence, it's important to be clear on what the scene is about. Ask yourself: What led to this scene? What does this scene lead to?

Another question to ask is: "Whose scene is it?" Usually the scene belongs to the main character or to the character with the most lines. But it may belong to the character who listens and reacts. Why? Because in the next scene this character may do something important. Perhaps the farmer listening quietly to the bloviating politician will rebel in the next scene and burn the bum's headquarters down.

## Documentary, reality, and other non-scripted shows

Review the paper cut and keep it and your logs of the shots handy as you edit. Since a non-scripted show typically has fewer guidelines than a scripted show, your editing will have a major impact on its content and structure. Initially you will be the one who decides what the audience sees and learns and when they see it and learn it, so you want to know your shots and laser in on the story you're molding from them.

### Last word

Doc or drama, you need to know where you're coming from and where you're going to before you begin to cut a scene or a section.

# Audience, Purpose, and Motivation

*"I start every picture thinking that I'll fail, that I'll never be able to do it, that I'll forget how to cut, I won't know how to do it, I'll let it down… I still bite my finger nails."*
—DEDE ALLEN

Before starting to edit, you need to be clear on the purpose of the project you're editing and who will be seeing it. Is it a training film for navy recruits or a cereal commercial aimed at kids? Is it a muckraking documentary on the food industry or a drama about Navajo code talkers in World War II? You get the idea.

### Why does an editor cut?

"Editing is not a technical process. It's an artistic process. It's about storytelling," says Jack Tucker, A.C.E., *Shogun* and *Winds of War*. "What editors do is the final rewrite of the script." Tucker states the view of most editors. Telling the story is your primary purpose, no matter what kind of film or video you're cutting. You need to know the story you're telling and tell it with each cut in every scene. So why does an editor cut? Answer: To move the story forward.

### Motivating a cut

Just as you must be clear on the purpose for each scene, so you must be clear on the purpose for each cut. "Each cut should be motivated," is an oft-repeated caveat in editing. Each cut should advance the story, the action, the flow, the thought process. Don't put a shot in solely because it looks nice, is arty, or seems cool. A cut should link to the cut before and after it, knitting the story together, cut by cut.

The subject of what motivates a cut — why and what to cut to next — will come up on every editing job you do. Correspondingly, it will pop up again in this chapter and be expanded on, but for now, consider yourself introduced.

### *Roughing it out vs. fine cutting*

These are two methods to putting a scene together.

1.  Rough cutting: When you rough out a scene, you work through it without pausing. This can be a wonderful organic cutting experience as you are going with the flow of the shots. When done, you review the scene. Then you smooth it out by tightening edits (making them leaner by dropping frames), and loosening edits (letting them breathe by adding frames), as well as by making overlaps, adding cutaways, etc. This method is known as roughing out a scene and then fine tuning it.

2.  Fine cutting: To fine cut a scene, you cut in each shot precisely — with the exact starting and ending frames you desire — before moving on to the next edit. Editors who operate this way feel that editing is a delicate, painstaking process. They finesse each edit, believing that its timing and length affect the timing and length of the next edit.

Each method is perfectly acceptable. Most editors use both, according to the demands of the scene and show. No matter which method they use, editors always review and refine a scene after putting it together. Depending on the situation, the refining takes place as soon as the scene is complete or several hours or days later. As the show progresses and is screened, scenes are fine tuned with each re-cut. Angus Wall comments on how he and Kirk Baxter edited *The Social Network* for which they won the 2011 Oscar: "From the start, Kirk and I cut the scenes very tightly, using faster performances and generally keeping the pace of the film high. When the first assembly was completed, we were at a length of 1 hour 55 minutes — actually a minute shorter than the final version. Unlike most films, we were able to relax the pace and put some air back into the performances during the fine cut."

# Making your first edits

*"Editing is not so much a putting together as it is the discovery of a path."*
—WALTER MURCH

You've looked at the footage, reviewed your notes, and know the scene's script or outline. Now you need to choose the shot to be cut in first. To be conventional, let's say you decide on a master shot. You have three masters. Which one should you use? In order of priority, here are your criteria:

> 1. Dramatic quality
>    — *Choose the take that is best acted/experienced/felt.*
> 2. Action
>    — *Select the take that most clearly tells the story.*
> 3. Pace
>    — *Decide what rate most suits the flow of the story.*
> 4. Technical quality
>    — *More critical: camera, lighting, sound, composition, continuity.*
>    — *Less critical: hair, makeup, wardrobe.*

## Making the first edit

Now that you've selected your first take you are wondering: "Which frame do I start on?" Start where the drama starts, where something begins to happen, where information is given out, where the story begins — no sooner, no later. If you're at the head of the show, you'll probably want to fade the first shot in, so make sure that you have enough frames at the head of the shot to make the fade up. (More on this in the visual effects section of Chapter 8.)

## Cut from the gut

Most editors go with their gut more than their head when cutting. You don't dryly reason out each edit. You use your heart and instinct to cut. Sergei Eisenstein, the esteemed Russian director, deemed the "author of film editing theory," reflected about *Potemkin*: "The filmed material at the moment of editing can sometimes be wiser than the author or editor. I realized the emotive scenes as the Holy Scriptures say, 'without seeing my creation,' that is, I realized them thanks to the feelings which the events inspired within me."

## Start off on the right frame

Look at the footage and take the time you need to find the right point for your first shot. At first it may seem like you're taking forever, but with experience, your ability to pick the right cut point will accelerate and become self-assured and natural. Try this experiment: Watch the first take to get a feel for where you'd like to cut it in. Then play it and stop where you'd like to cut. Do this a few more times. You'll find you've picked the same frame (or close to it) each time. Once you're confident with your choice, make the cut.

# To cut or not to cut and why

*"The art of editing occurs when the combination of two or more shots takes meaning to the next level — excitement, insight, shock, or the epiphany of discovery."*
—KEN DANCYGER, *The Technique of Film and Video Editing*

Now that you've cut in your first shot, how do you decide where to cut out of the shot? Begin by playing the shot. Watch for where it stops being interesting and effective and ask yourself: When do I want to see, know, learn, or reveal something else? There is no correct answer to this question just as there is no single way to put a show together, no set rules for editing. However, there are more effective and less effective ways to cut. Cutting for the right reasons and in the right place has the effect of:

- Sustaining the viewers' interest, involvement, and investment in the show.
- Setting a pace other than the real time pace set by the master shot.
- Keeping continuity: The cut will appear seamless to the viewer even though it's a change in angle.

## Five reasons to cut

*"At all times my editing is driven by story, not by style."*
—JILL BILCOCK, editor of *Moulin Rouge, Elizabeth, The Dish*

Here are five reasons to cut away from the shot you're in:

### 1. TO MOVE THE STORY FORWARD

It's time to show and tell the audience something new:

*Example #1:*
The audience has eyeballed evidence of dinosaurs in *Jurassic Park*, it's time to see the critters themselves.

*Example #2:*
Rick looks up and loses his cool as someone enters his Casablanca club. The audience needs to see who that someone is.

*Example #3:*
With the drop of an olive from above, in three inventive, economical cuts, we're plunked into the start of this comedy show in Figure 5.a.

## 2. THE SHOT YOU'RE IN NO LONGER CARRIES THE ACTION

You must change shots because you've used up the shot or it has a glaring problem with camera, continuity, performance, etc.

## 3. TO IMPART INFORMATION TO THE AUDIENCE WHICH IS CLEARER IN ANOTHER SHOT

You've cut in a shot of two gangsters hatching a plan. The audience won't know the plan's doomed until you cut to a rival gangster eavesdropping at the keyhole. Editor and director Edward Dmytryk writes: "… cutting should always be conceived to show the viewer what he should see at every point in the film. Sometimes it is what the viewer, whether or not he is aware of it, wants to see; sometimes it is what the viewer, whether or not he likes it at the moment, should see; and sometimes (quite often, really) it is what the director and/or cutter manipulate him into thinking he wants to see."

Figure 5.b shows the *Avatar* audience what's happening back at the military base following the first blitz of Pandora, the Na'vi homeland.

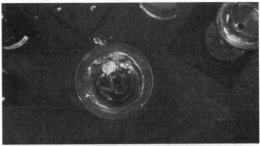

**5.a** Jonathan Ames (Jason Schwartzman) and George Christopher (Ted Danson) meet at a ritzy bar at the start of an episode of *Bored to Death*.

**5.b** Military personnel react differently to the attack on the Na'vi in *Avatar*.

## 4. You want to see/show something different and/or are bored with the current shot

You, the editor, set the pace of the show with the lengths of the cuts you choose. The instant the visual and informational contribution is complete, cut away! It's time to show something else before the story and pace bog down.

## 5. Respect for the footage and the show

Editing is a powerful process of refining the raw footage. You can show how a person thinks and feels. You can show the joy or horror of an era. You and the viewer may breathe as one with the characters or a situation. Director John Huston said: "Film is like thought. It's the closest to the thought process of any art." Walter Murch, A.C.E., elaborated on Huston in a May 1999 *New York Times* article: "Film is a dramatic construction in which…the characters can be seen to think at even the subtlest level… This power is enhanced by two techniques that lie at the foundation of cinema itself: the close-up, which renders such subtlety visible; and the cut, the sudden switch from one image to another, which mimics the acrobatic nature of thought itself."

## Five reasons not to cut

*"It's much more important to learn what not to cut. That's the hardest thing for any young editor starting out; it was for me."*

—Tom Rolf, A.C.E., *Jacob's Ladder; New York, New York;* and *Taxi Driver*

It's equally important to know when not to cut. Here are five reasons *not* to make a cut:

## 1. You think you should

Never cut arbitrarily. Remember: motivation, motivation, motivation. So what effect does an unmotivated, unwarranted cut have? It weighs down the show, particularly if there are a lot of unnecessary shots edited in. This can put the show off kilter and distract, annoy, or possibly lose your audience.

## 2. You think you shouldn't — the shot's sooooo beautiful!

Don't stick with a shot due to its stunning scenery or camera work. When the locale has been established, the moment made, the information conveyed, it's time to move on.

True story: Yours truly worked on a TV show where the plot centered on a teenage boy learning to drive. The opening shot of the show, a master shot, included a long pan of a junkyard from which I cut out at an appropriate place. The director, for his cut, insisted I stay on the shot until it panned past an upturned wheel. To him this symbolized the whole show: the kid and his first set of wheels. Nice concept but I got it from the director, not the footage. The producers didn't get it either. The wheel went out and we all explained why to the director.

**3. THE SHOT TOOK THE CREW A WHOLE DAY ON THEIR BELLIES TO GET. IT'S EXPENSIVE. IT TOOK MONTHS OF NEGOTIATING AND PLANNING. IT MUST GO IN.**
No way. This is what you're paid for: To be detached from the location shoot and to tell the story in the most polished, well paced fashion possible. You don't want to drag the audience down with shots that say, show, or do nothing for the story or subject. In *Film Editing Nutz and Boltz,* editor-author Film Guy puts it bluntly: "Basically the audience could care less what you had to go through to bring off a scene." The effect of cutting in unneeded footage drains the vitality from your film and taxes the patience of your audience.

**4. THE DIRECTOR HAD THE TAKE CIRCLED, IT MUST BE USED**
Nothing doing. Again, if the shot slows the story down or doesn't add crucial information that could be gained more smoothly and engagingly, leave it out. However, if the director asked to see the shot cut in, unless you two have a long-standing relationship, you probably should cut it in. It's often better to try and make a cut work and let the director see that it doesn't, than to merely say it doesn't work. Yes, a picture, even a miscut one, can be worth a thousand words. And your job.

**5. YOU'RE THE EDITOR. YOU'RE SUPPOSED TO MAKE CUTS**
You don't get paid by the cut. You get paid to shape the material into the most moving, breathtaking show possible. If a scene plays in the master, leave it. Too many edits can be the sign of a novice editor and look *cutty.*

## Last word

We'll leave it to Lee Unkrich, who edited all the *Toy Story* movies and won the Oscar in 2011 for directing *Toy Story 3.* He asserts that "editing is not about deciding when to cut but often when not to cut. Sometimes the most powerful moments come from the editor just sitting back and allowing it to play."

# Match Cut: Angles and Places to Cut for Smooth Editing

When looking for the right place to cut, editors habitually look for a match point — a place in the first shot that is duplicated in the second shot. There are many elements to match. The primary elements are: action (movement), screen direction, eyeline, camera angle, and framing. Secondarily, you should aim to match props, sound, weather, wardrobe, hair, makeup, lighting, and color, as they often can be corrected (lighting, color, weather) or masked (the rest) later in post. Table 5.1 shows angles that you'll routinely encounter and what angles they cut to — match — best.

**TABLE 5.1**
**SMOOTH CUTTING ANGLES**

| TYPE OF ANGLE | WHAT ANGLE CUTS TO |
|---|---|
| ELS, LS, WS | FS, MS, MCU, CU, insert |
| FULL SHOT | MCU, CU, ECU, insert |
| MEDIUM LONG SHOT | MS, MCU, CU, insert |
| MS AND CU | ECU, insert |
| ANGLE ON LEFT | All angles on right and vice versa. |
| MOVING SHOT: PAN, TRACKING, DOLLY, OR CRABBING SHOT | Cut to themselves if pacing and visual continuity match. |
| OVERHEAD SHOT | Cuts to almost anything. Minimizes continuity problems. |
| OVER THE SHOULDER OR RAKING SHOT | Cut to each other in matching pairs and to CU, insert, MLS, LS, and WS. |
| POV SHOT | All shots with matched eyelines and directions. |
| TWO-SHOT | CU, insert, LS, WS or two-shot of different people. |

## *Match cutting on movement*

*"Whenever possible, cut in movement… A broad action will offer the easier cut, but even a slight movement of some part of the player's body can serve to initiate a cut which will be 'smooth' or invisible."*

EDWARD DMYTRYK from his book *On Film Editing.*

Cutting on motion makes for slick, vibrant cuts and is used regularly to prod the story along or prolong moments. Here are a few everyday examples:

## CUTTING ON MOVEMENT TO TIGHTEN THE ACTION

**1.** Character goes through a door

Shorten a character entering a room by starting her in, say, a medium shot, and then cutting to a wide shot as she starts to push the door open. This speeds up this mundane bit of business. Or you can cut to the reverse angle from inside the room she's entering to compress and complete the action.

**2.** *Character gets up from a chair and crosses the room*

Cut as he gets up, just before his eyes leave frame, to move things along.

5.c Depicts a regularly used action cut.

## CUTTING ON MOVEMENT TO EXTEND THE ACTION

**1.** *Two people kiss*

Extend the kiss by playing it as long as it lasts in one shot and then cutting to a second shot where it's just started.

**2.** *Champagne toast — raised glasses*

Cut from the MS of one character proposing a toast with raised glass to a WS of everyone joining in. Then cut close on the character you want to focus on next as they retract their glass from the toast to take a sip and react or utter a line. You can shorten or lengthen time this way. The frames in figure 5.d illustrates this.

**5.c** The movement in a simple head turn makes for a common action match as illustrated by the foreground character in this scene from the detective spoof *Hot Fuzz*.

**5.d** The clink of the glasses forwards the action from one shot to another in this anime feature *Paprika*.

### *Last word on match cuts*

Match cuts comprise the majority of cuts editors make. Why? Because they push the story forward seamlessly, maintaining the continuity — physical relationships (characters, geography, props, etc.) and narrative flow — of the action. When you make smooth match cuts, viewers won't notice them. This "invisible" editing, as it's called, leaves your audience engrossed in the story and its players — precisely your intention! And leads seamlessly to our next topic.

## Invisible vs. Visible Editing

*"An editor is successful when the audience enjoys the story and forgets about the juxtaposition of the shots. If the audience is aware of the editing, the editor has failed."*
—KEN DANCYGER, *The Technique of Film and Video Editing*

"Seamless, invisible editing" as the oft-used phrase goes, is what filmgoers are used to. Just as the symphony audience hears the orchestra and seldom singles out individual instruments, so the movie audience views the film, taking in the whole show and not the individual edits. Now and then, the audience may notice the cut, distinguish the oboe, but most of the time it takes in the whole, be it a film or Beethoven's Fifth.

When you don't match cuts, you risk turning off viewers, who may become disoriented, if only momentarily, or drop out of your show. You want to keep them engaged. This does not mean that you must match every cut. Good editors make jump cuts and other in-your-face edits routinely, as the show demands. They do not make flashy cuts to prove anything or because they're the latest, hottest cut, but to support the movie's essence — its theme, story, rhythm, and meaning.

To achieve invisible editing, make smooth edits that dynamically and purposefully tell the story, following the guidelines outlined earlier (cut for dramatic quality, clearest action and storytelling, pace, and best technical quality). Invisible editing is not the rule; I differ with Dancyger's statement above. Serving the story and the material is the rule and means that most frequently, the editing, like the editor, is invisible.

# Mismatches and How to Fix Them

Everyone has gleefully noticed a mismatch during a movie, but many more have been put over on us than we've ever detected. Mistakes in continuity and getting around them are a fact of life for an editor. Here are a few typical types of mismatches:

## *Mismatches between elements*

| MISMATCH | EXAMPLE |
|---|---|
| Lighting, makeup, hair, or wardrobe | Eyeglasses on in one shot and off in the next. |
| Position of limbs or props | A telephone in the left hand in one shot and the right hand in the next. |
| Weather | Rain in one shot; sunshine in the next. |
| Sound | Wording, volume, or pacing of the dialogue or sound changes from one shot to the next. |

Figure 5.e shows a mismatch from a movie that took the Academy Award for Best Editing.

**5.e** This mismatch in the characters' positions and direction of movement from *The Aviator* is one of many mismatches that go unnoticed in the skillful hands of Thelma Schoonmaker, a triple Oscar winner.

## Mismatches due to directing

| MISMATCH | EXAMPLE |
|---|---|
| Screen direction | A person or an object does not exit from the right side of one shot and enter from the left of the next shot so they appear to have jumped across the room. |
| Screen position | A group of people or objects on the right side of the screen in one shot are on the left side in the next shot. |
| Eyeline | A person looks right and down in one shot, and left and up — in a totally different direction — in the next shot. |
| Conversation | When two people are talking to each other, screen reality requires that they face each other, unless, of course, one turning his back or looking down or away from the other person is part of the drama! |
| Pacing of shots | Camera tracks, pans, or dollies faster or slower in one shot than the other. |

In Figure 5.f you can see what matching and non-matching eyelines say.

**5.f** The eyelines of these two cops on stakeout in *Dexter* tell a different story about their relationship in Frame 1 than their eyelines in Frames 2 and 3.

## Cutting around the mismatch

Normally it's most effective to make a properly matched cut, but letting that be the driving force of your editing is not always practical or desirable. Yes, you will be making mismatches! To assuage a bad match, you want to make the most sensible, least discernible cut. How to do that? Dmytryk advises: "Cut for proper values rather than for proper 'matches.' Ignore the mismatch. If the cut is dramatically correct, it is remarkable how often the bad match will be completely unnoticed by the viewer." Many editors run a scene by their assistant to see if they catch the mismatch problem. Frequently, the assistant will find other problems or have other suggestions and miss the mismatch entirely!

**FIVE WAYS TO GET AROUND MISMATCHES:**
1. Cut earlier or later where there is a better match.
2. Let time mitigate the problem: Cut away to another shot and then back.
3. Cut to a tight close-up, overhead shot, or an insert shot.
4. For a screen direction problem:
   a. Cut to a shot coming straight at you (see Figure 5.i) or away from you.
   b. Cut out of the first shot when the person's eyes pass the edge of the frame on the left. Then cut to the second shot approximately six frames before the person's eyes enter the frame. This allows the viewer's eyes to adjust and makes the person appear to be moving in real time.
   c. Reverse the shot.
5. Sound mismatch: Equalize the volume or cross fade to balance disparate volumes or sounds. To ameliorate wording and pacing problems, find an acceptable cut point, put in a cutaway, or overlap.

With practice, you'll make all these edits and more — reflexively — and come up with tricks of your own.

Veteran editor Ralph Winters, A.C.E., whose pictures include *Gaslight, The Pink Panther, 10,* and *Victor Victoria* states, "You've got to learn where the audience's eye is going to be... Nobody does anything twice the same way, so the trick is to get in and out at those times when you don't think an audience is going to be disturbed... You put them where you want them to be. They'll watch action, they'll watch movement."

Figure 5.g illustrates clear screen direction.

**5.g** Follow player #5 down the field in this example of well-matched screen direction from *Friday Night Lights*.

## *Mismatched angles: Why shots don't cut and how to fix them*

There are always going to be problems — er, challenges — in editing, and there are always going to be solutions: This is part of what you get paid for. Invisible editing calls for angles that match but not all do, as you will see when putting them together. So which angles don't match? Table 5.2 lists them, along with cutting solutions.

### TABLE 5.2
### MISMATCHED SHOTS AND HOW TO FIX THEM

| SHOTS THAT DON'T CUT TOGETHER | REASON IT'S A MISMATCH | SOLUTION |
|---|---|---|
| SHOTS WITH TOO SIMILAR ANGLES | Too similar angles make for obvious jump cuts, mismatches, no new information, and a lack of visual variety. | Use angles that cut together (see Table 5.1). Or enlarge — blow up — one shot up to a cuttable close-up |
| SHOTS WITH DRASTICALLY DIFFERENT FRAMING | It looks poor, unsettles the viewer, and can make a person appear to be a giant or a dwarf, i.e., to be disproportionate. | Cut to an MCU, CU, LS or overhead shot before going to the angle. |
| TWO-SHOT TO TWO-SHOT IN A THREE PERSON SCENE | The person common to both shots will appear to jump and most likely will cause a continuity problem. | Bridge two-shots by cutting to an MCU, CU, LS, or overhead shot. |
| MOVING SHOT OF MOVING SUBJECT TO STATIC SHOT | Subject will appear to jump. | Before cutting to the static, allow the:<br>– Moving shot to stop.<br>– Subject to stop moving.<br>– Subject to exit frame. |
| CROSSING THE LINE | People or objects jump from one side of the screen to the other. | Cut to an overhead shot or other cutaway shot. |

Figure 5.h is a jump cut because it crosses the line.

**5.h** Jump cuts suit this scene from *The Constant Gardener* as the couple is, well, jumpy due to underlying secrets.

## Last word on matching

Dmytryk provides both a summary of match cutting and a challenge: "If it is necessary to correct a fault, or if it is possible to improve the dramatic quality of a sequence, and the proper material is not at hand, explore all possibilities or invent a few. The odds that some workable solution can be found are so overwhelming that one should never stop trying, no matter how difficult the problem. Always remember that film is the art of illusion, and the most unlikely things can be made to seem real." For more examples of match cuts, mismatches, and many other types of cuts, click on "Cut of the Month" at www.joyoffilmediting.com

# Everyday Editing Challenges

## Rhythm

*"It's the editor who orchestrates the rhythm of the images, and that is the rhythm of the dialogue, and of course the rhythm of the music. For me, the editor is like a musician, and often a composer."*

—MARTIN SCORSESE, director

## Rhythm: What is it?

*"There are things an editor injects into a film: structure, pace, symmetry, the little gaps in between cuts. All of this is a rhythm."*

—MICHAEL KAHN, A.C.E., *Saving Private Ryan, Schindler's List, Jurassic Park*

Everyone talks about rhythm in editing but what do they mean? Rhythm is the duration of shots and the number of shots in a sequence, e.g., short and many or long and few. Rhythm is the pace of the cuts and is similar to music. Just as musicians refer to beats in a composition, editors talk about beats in a scene. To editors, a beat is a plot point or an action — where something happens or changes in a scene. A beat may be subtle or grand. There are beats of action within every scene; for example, soldiers advancing and retreating or a character stepping into madness. Here's a short example of beats in a scene:

> We see a small town. A stranger walks down the street. Beat. Enters a cafe. Beat. A townie sits on a stool. Beat. Accosts the stranger. Beat. The stranger orders a beer. Beat. Patrons react. Beat. And so on.

While cutting, you may be unaware of subdividing a scene into beats. However, as characters circle each other and eventually make physical contact, whether they fight, make love, or become BFFs, rhythm and beats are evident.

## Expanding and contracting time using rhythm

We've all seen the shot where the basketball leaves the shooter's hands just as the buzzer goes off at the end of a tied game. Will the ball go in the basket? The shot is slo mo. The editor cuts around to the bleachers, the coach, the players. The moment is elongated, time is stopped, expanded… and the basket whooshes through the hoop.

On the other hand, an editor can compress time as battles are fought and lost and a 100-year war is over in ten minutes. It's all in the pacing of the footage, the timing of the cuts…the dance of the movie. Figure 5.i exemplifies the shortening of time.

**5.i** Slo-mo shots contract time as a samurai gallops across the desert in *Hero*.

### *Cut tight or cut loose*

If you leave very little room between actions or lines of dialogue and narration, you are cutting tight. Leave a breath or beat and you are cutting loose. The tightness or looseness of a scene affects its rhythm and is dictated by the action and purpose of the scene.

#### CUT TIGHT

Expository scenes are frequently tightly edited in order to deliver information rapidly and hook the audience. Conversely, the start of the show may be cut loosely to allow viewers to get immersed in the world being presented.

#### CUT LOOSE

Just as composers write rests into their music, so you may need to extend a shot or shots within a scene or add an establishing shot after a frenzied scene so that the audience has a breather. And you may want to vary the length of cuts — make some short and some long — so that just as viewers relax, a monster jumps out, or contrarily, when they're on the edge, a clown rolls out of a barrel.

If the audience is lacking key information, you may have to "open up" cuts and scenes in your show. This means adding frames back in between characters or actions. For instance, if you're cutting a comedy, you may need to add frames back in so the audience finishes laughing and doesn't miss the next joke or bit of the story.

## The impact of the reaction shot

Screenwriters, actors, directors, editors — filmmakers of every stripe — be aware: A reaction is worth a thousand words. The reaction can be a wide shot of Cary Grant trying to outpace a crop duster, a medium shot of Kate Winslet, arms outstretched, on the prow of the Titanic, or a close-up of Meryl Streep, who, with her face alone, can say more than a page of dialogue.

Editing in a reaction or series of reactions can be extremely powerful as reactions show human emotion and thought, and key viewers' emotional response: Should they hold their breaths, laugh, cry, worry, or get angry? Often, it's more important to show viewers how a person, group, or crowd of people is reacting rather than to cut to what's happening. At least right away. This can be true for drama as well for documentary as figures 5.j and 5.k demonstrate.

**15.j** The grandfather in *Modern Family* reacts differently than the rest of the family (frame 2) to the arrival of the new baby (frame 1).

In Francois Truffaut's book *Hitchcock,* Alfred Hitchcock recalls, "I had a car accident, as the basis for a trial, in one of my recent television shows. What I did was to use five shots of people witnessing the accident itself. Or rather, I showed five people as they heard the sound of it. Then I filmed the end of the accident just as the man hits the ground after his motorcycle had turned over and the offending car is speeding away. These are moments when you have to stop time, to stretch it out."

Reactions, along with cutaways, also regularly serve a practical purpose. On a documentary they can facilitate a cut from one part of an interview to another. On a scripted show, they can cover re-ordered or deleted lines, before the scene completes

**5.k** In *Fahrenheit 9/11* Michael Moore relied on reactions to portray the WTC tragedy and did not show the towers collapsing.

in scripted order. Last, a reaction — or series of reactions — can trump words in a dialogue or narration scene. This means that you may focus part or all of a scene on the listener(s) instead of the speaker.

# Finding and cheating shots

Editors routinely take reactions and other shots and cut them into places they weren't intended for. This is known as *cheating* or *stealing* shots. Here are a few examples:

1. Using an actor's reaction to line seven for line twelve.
2. Taking a shot from before the director yells "action" at the start of the scene or from after the director yells "cut" at the end of the scene.
3. Freely mixing crowd reaction shots from several courtroom scenes.

Cheated shots are usually short so to find them you may have to slog through a lot of footage. Your show will be better for it and you may receive praise from actors and directors alike for digging them out.

## Cheating reactions

When cutting in reactions, first check out the spot where the actor or crowd reacted to the line or situation. If the reaction doesn't fit the scene as it's taking shape, look through the rest of the take and then other takes until you find a better reaction.

## Cheating dialogue

It is also possible to cheat dialogue and "put words into the actor's mouth" as it's referred to. This practice is a bit tricky because you must make the picture and the sound appear to be in sync when they're not. (Use the same method you did to lip sync dailies: Line up a word starting with P, K, or B or some other hard sound with its corresponding lip movement.) Conrad Gonzalez, editor on *The Sopranos* and *Dr. Quinn, Medicine Woman,* relates, "…there are often times when I have a great picture with a great facial expression but only the first half of the dialogue delivery works… When that happens, I go into other takes, steal dialogue and place it into the actors' mouths. No one is the wiser, not even the actors. Then the whole performance works."

## Cheating action scenes

Try this exercise: Watch an action scene. Then turn the sound off and watch it again. If you want, go back and slo mo some parts. You are dissecting the scene and now can glimpse some of the editor's sleight of hand. You'll see mismatches and jumps in location or background most probably. Also, the scene may not make much sense without the sound.

When cutting action, if possible, you want to maintain continuity and geography — even if it's cheated — so that the viewer stays with the scene and doesn't become confused. But when it's not possible or desirable, you'll be amazed at what you can cut together that will work, even though it was shot on different days and in different locations.

### Cheating on documentaries

It's acceptable to cheat shots and reactions on docs *if* they accurately portray people's responses and the situation. If they don't, this is unethical. For instance, showing Reverend Pat Robertson performing a same-sex marriage would be a fantasy — perhaps a comedy! You must maintain integrity on non-scripted pieces with every image, dialogue, and narrative choice that you make.

## Straight Cuts and Overlaps

What is an overlap? First, you need to understand what a straight cut is. To make a straight cut, you cut picture and sound at the same time, that is, you edit so audio and video start at the same time. To create an overlap, you cut to picture and sound at different times, i.e., the audio and video edit do not start at the same time.

### Overlap scenario 1

Kumar and Harold are conversing. If you cut from the *picture* and *sound* of Kumar talking:

- ▶ To the picture and sound of Harold talking, you've made a straight cut.
- ▶ To Harold's picture early, while Kumar is still speaking, you've made an overlap.

Film editors gave us the term overlap as well as pre-lap and post-lap (for overlaps at the beginning or ending of a line respectively). Video editors called them L cuts, delayed edits, or split edits due to the way they showed up on their screens. Digital system editors use any of these four terms. We'll stick with overlap to be consistent.

### Overlap scenario 2

Editors overlap constantly. How come? Because in dialogue scenes, the listener usually reacts to the speaker before the speaker finishes, as does the audience. Here's a typical scenario: Tony is talking to Maria as they sit on a park bench. It's obvious that he's leading up to a marriage proposal. We know from his tone and words that he's head over heels but what about her?

Cutting to Maria before her lines gives us a clue. We see that she cares for him but is not in love with him. Simply straight-cutting to Maria when she says yes deflates the tension in the scene and does not set up the future conflict. Seeing Maria react to Tony's words prior to giving her answer is the key part of the scene. Her reaction establishes her ambivalence and foreshadows trouble ahead for the pair. And you accomplish all this with a simple overlap!

## Using overlaps: Exercises to try yourself

### EXERCISE 1: OVERLAP AN ENTIRE SCENE

Cut a two-character scene: When X is speaking, show Y. When Y speaks, show X. Never show anyone speaking on camera but always be on the other person listening and reacting. This will free you from thinking in straight cuts only. Additionally, this lets you check the involvement of the actors in the scene: You'll see who's engaged and reacting in the scene and who drops out when they don't have a line. This is also a good test of your ability to manipulate the digital system.

### EXERCISE 2: OVERLAP TO MAKE ONE CHARACTER INTERRUPT ANOTHER

If you want one character to interrupt another, you must have two tracks of audio, one for each character. Cut in X's line for as far as you want it to go on Track 1. Then, on Track 2, cut in Y's interrupting line, lining it up where you want it to start in relation to X's line. Now you have an audio overlap positioned over two tracks and you can hear both lines as Y interrupts X. Adjust volume as needed and you're done.

### EXERCISE 3: OVERLAPPING AUDIO AT THE END OF A SHOT OR SCENE

Editors habitually overlap a word or a few frames of audio from the outgoing shot, called the *A side* of the cut, over the incoming shot, called the *B side*. Try it and see what it does for your show. You'll find that overlapping sound softens the transition from one shot to another, especially when you're cutting between scenes. Since the ear beats the eye in perceiving information, when you lead with sound, the ear will adjust to the new angle, easing the way for the eye and the picture change. In addition, by making the cut smoother and less visible, the overlap helps the audience take in the whole story and not the individual cuts. Not surprisingly, sound overlaps are regularly used to disguise mismatches. Try a few and see how many you get away with!

### EXERCISE 4: OVERLAP AUDIO TO EXTEND OR CONTRACT TIME

Overlapping audio can set a scene's pace. The prelapped and postlapped audio throughout *The Social Network* help this primarily dialogue flick achieve its brisk pace. If you have a lot of information to get across, overlapping the dialogue or narration speeds the action along. Cop, lawyer, and hospital dramas routinely deliver rapid-fire audio to divulge the details of the crime/injuries. Likewise, expositional scenes at the start of many movies employ audio overlaps to get the action rolling fast.

Overlapping usually has the effect of tightening a scene — shortening time — but it can also be used to expand time in a scene. Comedy regularly relies on the overlap to extend jokes. When the big laugh comes, the editor extends the sound and cuts around to everyone in the scene: major characters, minor characters, the usher, the waiter, etc. Each reaction should sustain or increase the laugh. To see a great example of this, check out the deli scene in *When Harry Met Sally*. For a dramatic example, pick any courtroom or sports victory scene such as when Gene Hackman's team finally wins at the climax of *Hoosiers*.

Take a crack at it yourself: Cut the dialogue or narration on a scene as tight as makes sense, then overlap the picture and see what you think. After reviewing the cut, you can loosen up parts that need more air — frames — to be understood and tighten it more as you see fit.

### Last word

Overlapping gives you extraordinary power as an editor. Use overlaps to show reactions to lines, strengthen performances, expose characters, manipulate time, and control the pace. Overlap as often as you need to in order to support your show's flow and bolster your characters and subjects.

## Cutting patterns

There are cutting patterns — an order of shot types — to how scenes are edited. To analyze a pattern, watch a sitcom, a documentary, drama, or whatever genre interests you. Take notes on enough scenes to be able to see what the cutting patterns are. For each scene:

- Write down the scene's purpose and type: expository, dialogue, action, montage, bridge scene,[1] etc.
- Describe each picture cut.
    - Its shot type (CU, master, etc.).
    - What happens.

Notice the pattern of the shots. What type of shot begins and ends each scene? Why does the cutting pattern work or not work? What else stands out to you? Check out other shows and genres and see what patterns they follow.

## The conventional cutting pattern

The convention over the years is that you start wide with a master shot or long shot in order to orient the viewer and because that's typically where the action is best covered. The master shot sets the geography: The viewer sees who's in the scene, where they're located, and gets a sense of their relationship to the action. From the master, conventionally you then cut to a medium shot, then to a close shot. You are working your way closer to the character(s)/the emotion/the subject/the theme/the conflict.

Why would you cut this way? Because this tried and true cutting pattern frequently works the best. However it will not always work and it is in no way to be taken as a formula. All cuts should be approached with the main storytelling goal in mind along with a keen sense of openness as to how to accomplish this.

## Countering the conventional

Feel free to counter the conventional, not out of rebellion but because it suits your show. "Some people are almost married to the fact that you go from a long shot, to a medium, to over-the-shoulder, to close-up and gradually build a scene in a very dramatic fashion," observes Tom Rolf. "On *Black Rain*, which is about a man caught in an alien culture, I desperately tried to make the cuts a little more unbalanced, to go from a big close-up to an over-the-shoulder, because it just makes it a little more jarring, more unsettling. That also carries over into telling the story. I think it's much more dramatic."

---

1.  Utilitarian scene that moves character(s) from one place or time to another.

## *The best approach*

Cut to the angles that best fit the tale you're telling, whether they produce a conventional or non-conventional cutting pattern. This leads us to a big topic of discussion in the editing and filmmaking community for years now: conventional/classic editing vs. modern/MTV editing.

# Editing styles
## Old Hollywood, traditional editing vs. MTV style editing or Silver screen vs. Computer screen

*"…recent American cinema has seemed so rushed and frazzled, desperate as it is to hold its ground in the losing battle between the haughty silver screen, that decrepit diva who insists on your silent attention, and the accommodating computer screen, the loyal manservant whose command is your every wish."*

—JESSICA WINTER, *"The Lost Art of Editing"* from *The Boston Globe*

Up until now, we've talked about matches, mismatches, cutting patterns — all the shots and angles that are supposed to cut well together to create seamless, invisible cuts. This is the traditional, Hollywood approach to editing and these concepts are still sound. However, there is a new type of editing and filmmaking that has been evolving for over a half century; the MTV or modern style. Since 1981 and the launch of MTV, filmmakers have been complaining, arguing, and embracing the effect of MTV on cutting. So what is this modern style and where did it come from?

### *Modern style cutting — Look what they've done to my cuts, Ma*

They've multiplied them, split them, and sped them up; they're backed by green screen, racked with titillating effects, and tracking multiple stories all while pulsing to a beat, beat, beat. Although a lot of MTV videos run as weak-storied, background visuals on home, computer, and bar screens, MTV continues to change filmmaking, and nowhere is this more evident than in editing.

Steve Hamilton, editor of commercials, promos, and independent filmmaker Hal Hartley's films, comments about the current environment, "There is much more pressure on an editor to try to do something noticeable, or perhaps there are more editors who've grown up thinking that they have to make edits that are noticeable, whereas before the goal was simply to tell the best possible story and to do so relatively invisibly. I think this mentality is leading to a mistrust of the shot." Andrew Weisblum, A.C.E., *Black Swan* and *Fantastic Mr. Fox* corroborates this in explaining his editing style: "…I like to…explore a lot of things that go beyond the footage, in terms of digital solutions and split screens and tricks and gags and things like that."

## Effect on TV editing

*"No time, no money, hand held."*
—SCOTT PALAZZO, producer-director *VH1 and MTV*

Executive producer and director on *The Shield,* Scott Brazil dubbed their method "desperation shooting" and claims that it engages the audience and brought about innovation. John Cassar commented on producing and directing *24*: "MTV tells the story with pictures, not dialogue, like most TV shows. We give the audience the picture and trust them to be intelligent and get it. And they do."

The underlying belief of the modern style filmmakers is that we live in a multi-media world and have become multi-tasking people: We drive (still!) as we talk and text on smart phones, we work on our PCs with the ball game running and lots of apps minimized, and we do any number of things while watching TV. So why the brouhaha about a spike in split screens and a lot of line-crossing action? We're used to taking in oodles of info in a short time. Further, we disengage in nanoseconds these days, swiftly losing interest in the latest war, scandal, or national crisis: They become like a TV show that's run too long and should be replaced. Which is exactly why modern shooting and editing styles work hard these days to keep us plugged in.

Opponents would argue that the MTV style comprises mindless, escapist images that bloat us with eye candy and futz the lines between entertainment and news while starving our brains, hearts, and souls. Whatever your belief, the MTV effect persists and evolves nightly on the tube.

## Roots

Doug Ibold, A.C.E., believes that MTV has had "a huge impact on how people treat the storytelling process. If anyone doubts that, just look at how many episodic TV shows now end the episode with a dramatic song rather than the score." Slushy on you if you didn't immediately think *Glee.*

However, modern style editing didn't just spring up with MTV in the 1980s. It germinated in the 1950s French new Wave filmmaking. It kept on growing in the 1960s with pop art, the madmen world of commercials, the music counter culture, and movies like *A Hard Day's Night*, *Help*, and *Easy Rider*. The 1970s made its mark with the split screens of youth and music in *Woodstock*, the multiple storylines of *American Graffiti* and *Nashville*, and the soundtrack of *Apocalypse Now*. The 1980s contributed MTV as well as the movie *Flashdance* and the TV series *Miami Vice*. In subsequent decades the styles have been extended by films, games, YouTube, social networking sites, and editors who influence and inspire each other.

## Comparing styles

Table 5.3 details the differences in the two styles of editing.

**TABLE 5.3**
**EDITING STYLES: CLASSIC VS. MODERN**

| CLASSIC STYLE | MODERN STYLE |
|---|---|
| INVISIBLE EDITING: Audience unaware of cuts — sees whole show. | IN-YOUR-FACE EDITING: Audience aware of cuts and that they're watching a show. |
| SLOWER PACE: Longer shot durations, except for action scenes. | FASTER PACE: Short shot durations in every type of scene. |
| LINEAR STRUCTURE, typically. Effortless to follow timeline due to synchronous events. | NONLINEAR STRUCTURE frequently. Often takes effort to follow timeline due to asynchronous events. |
| ONE OR TWO PLOTLINES, usually. Plot driven, usually. Narrative and dramatic arc reign supreme; side trips eschewed. | MULTIPLE PLOTLINES, commonly. Feeling and senses first; plot second. Narrative a series of set pieces; dramatic arc less important. |
| MUSIC ENHANCES THE STORY. Songs sung on stage and ordinarily backdrop to plot.<br>— Studio tried to remove "Somewhere over the Rainbow" from *Wizard of Oz.* | MUSIC DRIVES STORY. Songs often central to show and may end show. |
| CONTINUITY RULES! Editors maintain continuity via match cuts (matching eyelines, action, angles, etc.). | CONTINUITY — WHATEVER! Often observed but not THE WAY. |
| JUMP CUTS SHUNNED. | JUMP CUTS EMBRACED. |
| SPARE USE OF EFFECTS the audience is aware of: Time transition effects such as dissolves and fades most common.<br>— Composites and mattes, slo mos and speed-ups as needed. | CRAZY-FREE USE OF EFFECTS. Audience aware of all types of dazzling wipes and other transitions.<br>— Green screen and varispeed frenzy. |
| SPLIT SCREENS RARELY EMPLOYED. | SPLIT SCREENS ROUTINELY EMPLOYED. |
| ESTABLISHED CUTTING PATTERNS that move from wide shots via medium and O/S shots to close-ups. | CUTTING PATTERNS UPENDED in a myriad of ways such as not starting with or including wide-shots, employing lots of close-ups, and using multiple non-matching angles. |
| 180° RULE OBSERVED AND PLANNED FOR except for chaotic scenes such as war scenes. | 180° RULE OFTEN IGNORED and regularly broken. |
| MONTAGE USED AS NEEDED to give info quickly, advance the plot and show passage of time. | MONTAGE UBIQUITOUSLY USED; sometimes whole show can be montage. |
| EXPENSIVE CAMERAS, FEWER SET-UPS, LOW SHOOTING RATIO. Shows tightly scripted with complex camera moves and blocking planned and possible due to big crew. | HANDHELD CAMERA, MANY SET-UPS, HIGH SHOOTING RATIO. Shows loosely scripted and rapidly shot with little or no blocking by small crew. |

## *Where are things headed?*

*"Modern movies may be more engrossing — we get 'lost' in them more readily — because the universe's natural rhythm is driving the mind."*

—JAMES CUTTING, Jordan DeLong, and Christine Nothelfer, Cornell University

No rules and bad footage do not have to translate to bad editing. The task for the editor is still to sift through the footage, structure the show, and tell the story. Scott Powell, editor of music videos, docs, and television shows, comments on editing *24*, "I've never received so much footage and paid so little attention to the script. I read the film." Here's some intriguing research that may foretell the future of editing and filmmaking.

## *Research — What grabs and holds the mind in movies?*

*"Our unit of investigation was the shot."*

—JAMES CUTTING, professor at Cornell University

Cognitive psychology professor James Cutting, along with two of his grad students interested in the human mind and its attention span, studied 150 popular Hollywood movies filmed between 1935 and 2005 in five genres: action, adventure, animation, comedy, and drama. The team used .avi (video-only) files to measure the duration of each shot in each scene. They researched "Hollywood style" editing and filmmaking which they defined as the invisible style that "...is designed to suppress awareness of the presentational aspects of the film while promoting the narrative."

The psychologists applied a concept from chaos theory — the 1/f fluctuation — which describes a pattern of attention that, according to their analysis, occurs naturally in the human brain. They found that films made after 1980 matched the 1/f pattern of the natural rhythm of the mind. The trio deduced that this pattern has developed during the 125-year life span of filmmaking as the edited rhythms of shot sequences succeeded or failed to create clear and engaging movies. Their results also indicate that "Hollywood film has become increasingly clustered in packets of shots of similar length." Action flicks, with their short shot durations, are closest to the 1/f pattern, followed by adventure, animation, comedy, and drama.

The researchers' predictions? "We suggest that over the next 50 years or so, and with action films likely leading the way, Hollywood film will progress toward a shot structure that more generally matches the 1/f patterns found elsewhere in physics, biology, culture, and the mind." Acknowledging that viewers do not rate movies based on shot duration, they conclude, "Good storytelling is the balancing of constraints at multiple scales of presentation… film editors design shot patterns with care, generating a visual momentum in the viewer, who tracks the narrative."

## Vive la difference or how to make the best edits possible

*"That [MTV] revolution pushed us into an evolution that's still going on. When MTV appeared, it seeped into mass consciousness and now is part of everyday life — like Starbucks."*

—MARK GOLDBLATT, A.C.E., *Xmen: The Last Stand; Armageddon;* and *Terminator 1 and 2.*

Traditional editing is highly effective and still apparent in many a movie today. *The King's Speech* and *Made in Dagenham*, two conventionally edited, top-nominated dramas prove this point just as *Black Swan, Blue Valentine,* and *Slumdog Millionaire* epitomize the modern style. Most movies and shows of all types fall somewhere in between. It is the story and the filmed material that dictate how to edit a scene.

Chris Dickens, who won the editing Oscar for *Slumdog Millionaire*, typifies the current attitude which blends the traditional sensibility with the modern approach with his remarks about the editing of the sizzling action-comedy *Hot Fuzz*: "A lot of the cuts are nearly invisible and others are intentional, such as jump cuts. We wanted the cutting at times to draw attention to itself. There are also other invisible things, like hidden split-screens in a shot to pick up the pace within that shot."

As with all creative arts, good editing originates from absorbing the elements and drawing out the best possible piece. For an editor, the main elements to absorb are: 1) Picture (framing, lighting, movement, angle); and 2) Sound (dialogue, narration, sound effects, and music). Just as some accomplished authors talk about how their characters speak to them, so many experienced editors relate that the footage speaks to them. On dramas and other scripted shows, this means engaging with the actors and their voices, looks, pauses, and nuances; on non-scripted shows it involves concentrating on interviews, narration, MOS footage, and wild sound.

## Last words

*"I don't really have a definite style. Each project brings with it a new set of challenges that must be met."*

— Jim Clark, Academy Award-winning editor, from his book *Dream Repairman: Adventures in Film Editing*

If some of the reasons to make an edit seem contradictory — stick with the master/cut away from the master, go with your gut/don't be too cutty, modern vs. traditional — well, I hope you understand that your job as editor is to serve the story every cut of the way. There will be times when you question yourself, fight the footage, or take a wrong path. This is a good moment to go away from the scene — shelve it, to use an old film term — and come back later for a fresh attack.

Whether your show is a doc, webisode, commercial or comedy, etc., you want to tell the story in the most effective way possible. On one show this may mean mysterious, languid shots that set up the flash mob video followed by energetic, on-the-beat cuts as the crowd gets into the spirit of things. On another show it may entail a lot of extreme close-up reactions, e.g., Garbo in *Camille* or Harpo in any Marx brothers' flick. On a third it may be as simple as an engrossing, tell-all shot like Orson Welles' famed three-minute master at the head of *Touch of Evil*. Or it may be a series of split screen shots like those that kick off *127 Hours* which blink on and off as the main character doggedly drives through the night.

On every project, you want to sculpt the footage and the story. It is your job, your challenge, your joy, your privilege to do so. Editing becomes a very personal thing as you live and breathe with your creation and put your heart and soul into it. You have the pulse of the film — its life — in your hands. Respect and honor it with all the caring, ingenuity, and stamina you've got.

## CHAPTER WRAP-UP

You've faced the footage and are well-versed with why and where to cut so now you're primed for learning more about wrangling the footage. Chapter 6 introduces you to the types of scenes — such as action and montage — that challenge editors on a daily basis, and how to handle them.

# Everyday Editing Challenges

*"Forget theory; each film presents a different case."*
—John Dunning, editor, *Show Boat* and *Ben-Hur*

This chapter takes on the types of scenes that confront editors on a daily basis and how to deal with them. It jumps right in, talking about how to cut action scenes with a special section on 3-D. Next, it looks at creating montage sequences, beginning with a brief history and including a chart of types of montage. Moving on, the chapter probes how to finesse dialogue scenes and the editor's relation to the actor — friend or foe? It then segues to dealing with narration and wraps with a section on editing music.

Threaded throughout the chapter are frames from familiar shows and movies that exemplify the different editing techniques along with words of wisdom from editors on how they approach cutting all these different types of scenes. So warm up the digital system and the coffee and let's get cracking!

## Cutting action

*"… however good the director's raw material, it is the editor who makes or mars a sequence of action."*
—Karel Reisz and Gavin Millar from their book *The Techniques of Film Editing*

## Approaching the action scene

"All hell breaks loose when the crowd realizes the mayor has run off with the till," reads the script. "A series of shots of climbers summiting

Everest," says the paper cut. Doc or drama, the action scene is only a sketch until the editor creates it. It's up to you to cut the action so that it achieves the thrills, laughs, or pathos the scene demands. An action scene such as a horse race, car chase, or pie-throwing scene, is propelled by pictures and amplified by sound effects: hoofs clattering, glass shattering, pies splattering. You choose the order of the shots, their length, and their pacing.

## Be organized and know your shots

Action scenes are routinely shot with three or more cameras. For instance, eight cameras were used to capture many of the boxing match scenes in *The Fighter*. On *The Hurt Locker*, four handheld 16mm cameras ran every day. Documentaries for surround theaters, like those exhibited at Orlando's Epcot theatre, can use up to 30 cameras. 3-D shows require that two cameras be mounted in parallel for converging in post. Music videos are synonymous with multiple cameras. Reality TV shows shoot non-stop. So you're going to be deluged with lots of footage, often of different formats.

To cut scenes with ginormous amounts of material, you need to be on top of the footage, able to access it pronto so you don't lose your flow of thought in the heat of cutting. You must be familiar with the material — know all the angles, literally. If you forget critical shots, you will struggle to edit the scene. Re-cutting and integrating shots later won't be a matter of simply dropping them in. Adding shots usually affects the timing of a scene, forcing you to adjust edits — lengthen, shorten, delete, and/or re-arrange them — to make the scene work.

## Approaching the footage

*"When you have big scenes with multiple cameras and lots of film…rather than let yourself be overwhelmed, I do it a shot at a time. If it isn't obvious what the first shot is, pick your shot. Then I say, "What do I want to see next?" You know from the script what the objective of the scene is and you can work your way through to the end. Then I go through the process of examining all of the existing material very carefully and weave it into that basic framework."*

—WILLIAM REYNOLDS, A.C.E., *Sound of Music*, *The Godfather*, and *The Sting*

A scene with tons of footage means you have tons of choices, so it's best to work one beat at a time.

## Scenario

You're cutting a football scene with extensive coverage of the game. There's also a goodly amount on the two main characters — a father and daughter — who have significant dialogue as they watch from the stands. And you have lots of B roll footage of the crowd, the benches, the scoreboard, etc.

To cut this scene, your thought process might progress something like this: "First I'm going to get the team out on to the field. As the team runs in, I'll cut to the fans, the coach, and the father and daughter to establish their presence and moods." After editing this first beat you think, "Okay, now it's time to cut in the kickoff — the start of the game." After that you'll cut to the quarterback, the first hint of friction between father and daughter, the first touchdown — you get the idea.

Some editors like to slug (leave space) for shots of the crowd because it's easy to lose concentration on the drama and pacing of a scene while searching for a good cutaway. Later they go through all the crowd footage and drop in the appropriate reactions. Figure 6.a displays a typical "cutting around the horn" pattern that keeps the team, coach, spectators, and scoreboard in play.

**6.a** A game unfolds on *Friday Night Lights.*

## Putting the people in action scenes

*"All the scenes [in The Hurt Locker] are intimate character scenes, even the big action ones. That's what sets this apart from other films that just have random things that go 'boom' in them. We had to keep the character drama alive during the action sequences, just as much — if not more — as in the quieter more intimate moments."*

—CHRIS INNIS and ROBERT MURAWSKI, winners of the Academy Award for Best Editing for *The Hurt Locker*

### Compelling characters + well shot scenes = best action scenes

Cutting in characters' reactions heightens the emotional intensity of an action scene. It also forwards the drama as characters respond and act to send the plot in unexpected directions. Reactions can also help bridge locations and continuity gaps, liven up slow sections, and skip over unwanted action bits. Ideally you want to put in reaction shots from participants and bystanders as well as all the vital characters in a scene.

True story: I was the assistant editor on a sitcom with Dann Cahn, a television editor famous for innovative comedy editing on *I Love Lucy*. We

**6.b** Reactions to destruction intensify this scene from *Avatar*.

worked on an episode where a boy got a tractor going and couldn't stop it until it smashed into a partially constructed house. There were many cameras and takes of the action but no reactions of the boy. Dann caught this omission and brought it up to the director. The director agreed but said it was too late — there was no time to go back to the location. "Put him in a chair," Dann persisted. So the crew went outside the sound stage, hoisted the actor in a chair above their heads, and wiggled it from side to side against the sky while the camera caught him in a close-up. When cut in, the boy's reactions made all the difference in the scene.

In Figure 6.b the action drops back for a reaction on Pandora.

# Pacing the Action Scene
# What Makes the Action Scene Move

*"...while it's great to talk about how revolutionary* Avatar *is, we were still making a movie...when you come down to it, all this technology is just there to make the images more compelling and to tell the story better. Ultimately, we're asking the same questions editors always ask: Does this shot work? Does this scene serve the story? It's all about performance and story. Things just take a little longer to get done when you're on the moon Pandora..."*
—JOHN REFOUA, A.C.E., co-editor, *Avatar*

The pace of the action scene is produced by the type of shots (LS, CU, etc.), their length, and their placement. Inexperienced camera operators sometimes believe that keeping shots in motion by shifting the camera around creates the pace of a show. Not true. Pans, dollies, and zooms don't usually move at the same rate and if cut together may result in a gut-wrenching scene of the wrong kind. The editor sets the pace from a series of static and moving shots.

## Shots and the information they convey

Long shots and wide shots contain more information, so to register, they are held on the screen longer. This is true for 2-D as well as 3-D shows. Since the audience grasps close-ups and medium shots quicker, you can cut them shorter. Intercutting wider and closer shots in a scene results in a varying of its pace. It also heightens the dramatic tension and keeps the audience on the edge of their seats.

The cutting and pacing of an action scene is similar to music with its fast and moderate tempos, staccatos, and rests. To get a cutting rhythm going, some editors crank up the rock music; others turn off all sound and cut in silence. Also, you'll find that the cuts in action scenes tend to get shorter and the angles closer until you pull back for the next strike, the next score, the next pratfall. For example, the notorious shower scene in Hitchcock's *Psycho* lasts two minutes and contains a whopping 50 cuts. But it's not the number of quick cuts that make an action scene effective. Buster Keaton's train sequence in *The General* spans 18 minutes and a mere 160 cuts. It's the juxtaposition of shots — short and close, long and wide — that determine the show's pace.

## Repeating the action

Sometimes you cut an action scene so that the same action is repeated in two or more shots. This is commonly done to milk the incredible event: the bomb blast, the bridge collapse, the train smash, etc. By inter-cutting different angles and slo-mo shots, the editor repeats the action in the shots and spins out the action.

Editors also regularly repeat frames between certain shots because viewers' eyes don't instantly catch up between shots. If you repeat a few frames of the action at the tail of a long shot and the head of a close shot, the result is a smooth cut that the viewers perceive as continuous action.

### Overlapping action

Sometimes the repeating of action is obvious because the editor duplicates longer por-tions of the action over a series of shots, frequently from dif-ferent angles or points of view. This overlapping amplifies the action for dramatic or comic impact and expands time. In Figure 6.c the hero's descent from the helicopter repeats over three cuts to increase the drama and the viewer's enjoyment.

# Parallel action and cross cutting

Even if we don't recognize the terms, we recognize these two types of editing when we see them on screen. Both create conflict and intrigue and are seen in all genres: drama, docu-

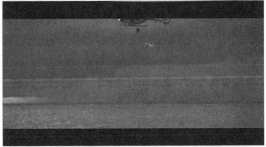

**6.c** Extending a stunt on *Burn Notice*.

mentary, comedy, commercials, etc. Parallel action frequently kicks off a film, revealing strangers going about their separate lives, unaware of each other. It leaves us wondering what they have in common and itch-ing to see them meet. In Figure 6.d passengers, terrorists, and pilots are living parallel lives as United Flight 93 takes off.

Cross cutting is used after characters have met or are aware of each other. We watch them react to each other in separate scenes: the lovers' attraction creeping toward romance, the gunslingers' repulsion escalating to a showdown, the hapless tourist flailing in the quicksand. Cross cuts make us lean forward in our chairs, anxious to find out: Will the lovers ever get together? Will the good guy trounce the bad guy? Will the rescue squad rope the victim to safety in time?

When you cross cut, you bring characters and situations together. This tightens the pace and ratchets up the conflict so editors cross cut reflexively to build the film's climax. Figure 6.e depicts a familiar cross cut as Sioux warriors face the U.S. military.

Table 6.1 summarizes parallel action and cross cutting and gives examples of each.

**6.d** Parallel action dominates *United 93* until the terrorists seize the plane. (Selected cuts).

**6.e** Cross cutting is invariably part of battle scenes like this one from the TV drama *Bury My Heart at Wounded Knee*.

## TABLE 6.1
## PARALLEL ACTION AND CROSS CUTTING

| | DESCRIPTION | MOVIE EXAMPLE |
|---|---|---|
| **PARALLEL ACTION** | • Editing two (or more) independent lines of action together where characters, settings, or subjects do not interact directly and are unaware of each other.<br>• Scenes run independent of each other and rely on viewers to make the connection. | 1) *Roger and Me — non-scripted*<br>Michael Moore attempts to bring together the CEO of General Motors, who makes decisions about auto plants, and the autoworkers who are affected by these decisions. Moore fails, but successfully demonstrates, via parallel action, how the lives of the CEO and the workers don't intersect.<br>2) *Crash — scripted*<br>Los Angelenos go about their separate lives until they begin to collide with each other. |
| **CROSS CUTTING** | • Editing two (or more) dependent lines of action together so that the characters, settings, or subjects interact directly and are aware of each other.<br>• Scenes are dependent on each other and don't function without being cross-cut. | 1) *The Cove — non-scripted*<br>Filmmakers wielding cameras are cross cut with a village fishing crew to expose dolphin killing in a local, "off limits" cove.<br>2) *Toy Story 3 — scripted*<br>As the plot gets going, there are many cross cuts between the toy gang and their antagonists: humans, evil toys, and a trash dump conveyor belt, to name but a few. |

# Cutting Action: A Sample Scene

You're cutting a robbery scene. The frames to the right represent your cutting sequence so far. You could change this sequence in a couple of ways:

1. Add more shots.
   ▪ Before Edit 1 — Establish the bank and show the robber entering.
   ▪ After Edit 1 — Show the bystanders' reactions.
2. Cut the scene with fewer shots by losing (eliminating) Edits 1–3 and starting with Edit 4 as the robber flees and jumps in the getaway car.

How do you decide? How much to show depends on many factors: Do you want a stylized stick-up with a minimum of shots or is it critical to see more shots and more details? Should you cut in a shot of the robber's face or reveal the robber's identity later? Or is it even necessary to know who the robber is? From the script or outline and discussions with the director, you will know what to do.

1

2

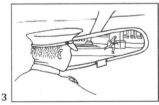

3

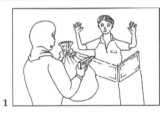

4

5

If you're intimidated by cutting an action sequence, just remember that an action scene is a mini-story and each cut, no matter how long or short, must be motivated and advance the story.

# Cutting 3-D

*"You don't cut a 3-D movie just like you don't write a 3-D movie or compose shots in 3-D. There are some small accommodations to the stereo that need to be made, but they should always be downstream of the dramatic edit. I don't think we shifted one cut because of it. More people are going to see* Avatar *in 2-D anyway, so the edit is the edit; it has to stand on its own."*

—JAMES CAMERON, director and editor on *Avatar*

A stable percentage of movies are shooting 3-D or being bumped from 2-D to 3-D. It is a part of today's cinema landscape and likely to increase as technical processes become cheaper and faster. So how does 3-D affect editors?

## *Editors and 3-D*

Editorial benefits from a show going 3-D because it's brought in during preproduction (earlier than usual). Due to 3-D being so costly, editors are hired during the storyboard phase to put together sequences. Editors are on board for the creation of the characters, lines, and the story as well as the previz. They get to collaborate with the director, writers, cinematographer, production designer, lay out, and others they normally wouldn't.

Collaboration, as well as organization, is also key on 3-D shows within editorial itself because there are so many editors: picture, VFX, sound, assistant editors, etc. Other factors of 3-D editing are:

- Master shots are cut longer than usual so moviegoers can take in the action and the world being created.
- Camera movement must be well-defined because fast paced, blurry camera moves are too much for viewers to take in.
- More time is allotted for editing due to:
  - Large amount of footage: VFX, CGI, 3-D modeling, and virtual capture.
  - Having to create multiple versions: 2-D, 3-D, and IMAX 3-D.

## Editing 3-D on the digital system

Since stereo (3-D) projection works by converging two images — one for each eye — that have been captured at slightly different angles, editors must view the two images properly converged in 3-D. Most editors cut in 2-D lower res proxy versions and screen scenes or cuts later in 3-D due to the tremendous amount of storage 3-D devours. They use software that combines the left-right eye images or splits them horizontally, placing the left eye image on top. Figure 6.g depicts an editor's-eye view of 3-D:

**6.g** 2-D view screen which synchronizes both eye images, left eye on top to simulate 3-D. *Photo courtesy of Avid.*

J. C. Bond, additional editor on *Alice in Wonderland* reflects on the difference between cutting 2-D and 3-D: "… you get used to the fact that you're looking at something in stereo. And then you just cut it like a regular movie. There's no major difference beyond that. There are minor considerations. You can do some cheats in 2-D where you may cross the line, and things like that that are a bit more jarring in stereo. But from a creative standpoint, you should try to avoid those things — even in regular 2-D."

## Last word

3-D is part of the continuum of the melding of technical and theatrical worlds to immerse the audience evermore deeply in the world they're seeing. As more techniques are invented, what is "wow" today will continue to become "so what" or archaic tomorrow. 3-D is another aid to storytelling that lets viewers experience your show in more emotional and sensory ways. If the story's good, well done 3-D will enhance it. If the story's NG, no amount of 3-D or HD will help — it will just deserve a plain old D.

We'll give the last word to Joyce Arrastia. One of three editors on the 3-D animated feature *Monsters vs. Aliens,* she crossed over from the 2-D live action world with some reluctance: "For me, it's been a revelation. We were able to use it [3-D] to emphasize key story points and a character's emotional arc simply by adding it or lessening it. A lot of filmmakers maybe don't realize that 3-D really is just another tool that helps you tell a more compelling story — just like the choice you make in camera composition or using color or music or pacing to help set a tone and a style. The end result was a much more compelling story, and so now I've really embraced it. I think it's not a passing phase; 3-D is definitely here to stay for a while."

# Cutting Montage

What is montage? Definition: A succinct, self-contained sequence of images inserted to convey or recap facts, feelings, or thoughts. To understand it better, we'll take a quick trip through the term's history. As film editing and theory developed in three different countries, montage evolved through three distinct definitions.

### Soviet Union and montage — 1920s

To revolutionary Soviet filmmakers, montage was synonymous with editing and meant the juxtaposition and manipulation of shots. It was an extension of Marxist philosophy and the Hegelian dialectic. The filmmakers translated Hegel's philosophy of how human thought advances — thesis, antithesis, synthesis — into montage as set-up, conflict, and resolution, e.g., boy meets girl, boy loses girl, boy gets girl.

Vsevolod Pudovkin, the filmmaker and film professor who greatly influenced this generation of Soviet filmmakers, saw montage as the *linking of ideas* through the linking of one shot to another. His student, pioneer filmmaker Sergei Eisenstein, viewed montage as the *conflict of ideas* derived from the opposition of one shot to another. Eisenstein wrote: "The general course of the montage was an uninterrupted interweaving of diverse themes into one unified movement. Each montage-piece had a double responsibility to build the total line as well as to continue the movement within each of the contributory themes."

### France and montage — 1950s

The French gave us the word montage, translated as to "assemble," "put together," or "mount." However, the New Wave filmmakers and theoreticians of the 1950s French cinema threw over Eisenstein's montage theories for their own theories of "realism" which exposed the director's manipulations by using jump cuts. Montage in the credits of a French movie means editing and stands for the editor; *son montage* is the sound editor.

### United States and montage today

Montage has come to be defined as a sequence of images used to convey facts, feelings, or thoughts that functions as a transition in time, knowledge, or place. Montage is a way to succinctly deliver or sum up a lot of information and can be used to inform, entice, amuse, and always, to advance the story.

## How montage works today

Montage scenes are self-contained and frequently function as bridges between dialogue or action scenes. Documentaries, commercials, infomercials, dramas, and comedies all use montages. The opening credit sequence for most TV shows and many movies is a montage. Figure 6.h shows three cuts from the long montage which begins *When the Levees Broke: A Requiem in Four Acts* and serves as an elegy to New Orleans.

A montage can be one of three types: dramatic, comic, or informative. Table 6.2 gives several examples of each type.

**6.h** Part of the three-minute montage which begins *When the Levees Broke: A Requiem in Four Acts.*

**TABLE 6.2**
**EXAMPLES OF MONTAGE TYPES**

| TYPE OF MONTAGE | EXAMPLE |
|---|---|
| **DRAMATIC** | |
| GRIEF OR RECOVERY | The character walks the old, familiar path on the beach or in the city, stares out the window on a rainy day, or lies in bed unable to move. After the montage, the character returns to life by taking a first step or making a choice of some kind. |
| LOVE | The lovers enjoy sunsets, romantic dinners, rolls in the hay, etc. before emerging from their cocoon and addressing the realities lurking around the corner. |
| WAR | A soldier goes through the travails of boot camp, acquires helmet and weapon, and sets out for the field of battle. The montage sets the scene for battle and the testing of the soldier. |
| SUCCESS | A rock band jams in a garage and by the end of the montage is playing at Madison Square Garden. |
| **COMIC** | |
| JOB | A college grad is interviewed by a series of bizarre employers. |
| DATING | A woman goes out with a string of loser dates. |
| CLOTHING | A man tries on a succession of ridiculous ties. |
| **INFORMATION** | |
| HISTORY | Immigrants arrive in Manhattan and erect the city. |
| PROCESS | A mayfly hatches, grows, mates, and dies. |
| SEARCH | A reporter travels to different holy sites, seeking enlightenment. |

# Putting a montage together

The montage arises from the script, the outline, the director, or the editor. A script or outline for the montage typically reads like these examples:

- A series of shots as Jack and Jill go up the hill.
- A montage of newspaper headlines condemning the murder.
- Archive footage of tornadoes in the Midwest.

The rules for cutting a montage are the same as for cutting anything else. The main difference is that cuts are usually separated by dissolves, wipes, or other types of transitions. Few montages are silent; most contain little or no sync dialogue and are set to music though some use wild sound or deliberate, recurring manufactured sounds. Often you'll cut the montage to music. But just as often you'll create the montage and add the music later.

Constructing a montage is freeing and rewarding as you work to assemble a cohesive whole and stumble across random connections. You'll put shots together from different times, sources, locations, and angles. The juxtaposed shots will delight you and lead you down cutting paths you never imagined. Accidentally, you'll insert a shot at the wrong place and be happily surprised by the result. When you finish editing the montage, you'll find you've created a scene that is much bigger than the sum of its shots.

# Cutting Dialogue

*"Dialogue dictates how a scene should be cut."*
TOM ROLF, co-editor on *The Right Stuff* and *Taxi Driver*

Dialogue is a pulse that you cut to and can drive a scene or even an entire show: *The Social Network* is a fast-paced dialogue picture. While the dialogue — the spoken words — is important, it's the interactions between people, be they real or fictional, that keep the audience engaged. Carol Littleton, A.C.E., *The Rum Diary, E.T.,* and *Places in the Heart* explains: "One-to-one dialogue scenes are difficult [to cut] because it's literally about the very thin connection between two people and that connection can't be violated. You have to be aware of it all the time. They may be connecting or not connecting emotionally, but you have to be aware of what's happening between them the whole time."

When you edit a dialogue scene, you are forging relationships between characters using the actors' words and looks. These relationships, whether they wither or grow, are integral to the development of your show and must be carefully constructed. In figure 6.i the second season of *Nurse Jackie* culminates in her husband and her friend confronting her over her drug addiction.

**6.i** The jig is up for Jackie in this climactic, final dialogue scene from Season 2 of *Nurse Jackie*.

## *Arc and pacing*

With narrative and dialogue scenes, building the growth and movement — the arc — of each character or documentary subject is vital. Conrad Gonzalez, A.C.E., puts it this way: "Although I want to facilitate the director's choices, sometimes the preferred take may not fit the overall arc of the performance and I can't use it. It's important to make every cut connect in terms of what I've built before and after it."

Part of building a character arc is cutting the looks and words at the pace the scene demands. The words set the pace 80% of the time in dialogue scenes. Proper pacing requires tightening words and lines in some places and loosening them in others. This is particularly true when cutting comedy but also applies to drama. Gonzales describes cutting *The Sopranos*: "Sometimes, since the actors are listening to each other closely and responding to each other very quickly, I have to create pauses that put spaces in between their lines... some actors are plodding in terms of how they deliver their dialogue; I have to tighten up their pauses."

Once you're absorbed in cutting a dialogue scene, you'll become keenly attuned to this subtle but crucial pacing and will live and breathe with your characters.

### Off-screen dialogue, a.k.a. off-camera lines

You've got a dialogue scene between Terry and Sean. During Terry's coverage, Terry was miked, that is the microphone was placed to pick up Terry's dialogue and Sean's dialogue was secondary. This means that all Sean's lines spoken during Terry's shots are off-screen lines. Never cut in off-screen dialogue. If you want to use Sean's dialogue while Terry's on screen, take it from one of Sean's takes. This way Sean is properly miked and you will have the best sound and best performance.

If you're roughing a scene together, it's all right to leave the off-camera lines in temporarily. When you're done with the scene, go back and replace them with the on-camera lines before anyone views the scene. When you cut in the on-camera lines, you will probably find that Sean did not deliver the lines exactly the same way on camera as off camera, so you will need to make adjustments. It's not unusual to find that the energy and pace of the on-camera dialogue is superior to that of the off-camera dialogue. (Actors know their off-camera dialogue won't be used and sometimes act accordingly.) For these reasons of timing adjustments and performance, you may prefer to cut in the on-camera dialogue as you go.

# The editor is the actor's friend

*"An editor is very much like an actor in a film. You are the actor's actor, in that your responsibility is to take the most interesting moments from all of the performances and find ways to make them hang together in a way that enhances and clarifies everything even further."*

—WALTER MURCH from his book *In the Blink of an Eye*

"Left on the cutting room floor;" that's the popular conception of what an editor does to an actor. Au contraire, I would counter, the conscientious editor is the best friend of the actor (or whoever is on camera). Editors work hard to bring out the best performance from every actor in every scene. They polish great performances, upgrade mediocre ones, save poor ones, and rarely delete them. Writer-director John Sayles, who always edits his own films, lays out the editor's approach: "You usually give yourself one or two cutting points so you can put together the best of the actor's work. You might be able to cut three different takes together. One take was very strong in the beginning, one was very strong in the middle and another was very strong in the end."

Editors coordinate the actors' timings and reactions so that each performance is consistent and attains its dramatic purpose. Sometimes this means holding a beat on an actor to expand the emotion and time. Sometimes it means cutting tight to sustain a performance and keep a taut pace. Always, it means molding the best performance to fit the character and the scene. Chris Innes and Robert Murawski, husband and wife and co-editors on *The Hurt Locker,* reflect on the film: "The through line of the piece for us was the clash of wills between the characters…Sometimes it is as simple as two characters exchanging glances that another character doesn't see. If audiences care about the characters then they will be willing to submit to almost any film structure or rhythm."

## *Left on the cutting room floor*

The decision to lose a line, a scene, or, more rarely, an entire character or interview subject, is made by the director and/or the producer, usually with the editor's input. There are many reasons for the decision, but it mostly isn't attributable to a weak performance or interview, rather it's made because the performance or interview slowed down, confused, or otherwise negatively impacted the show. For example, a character is axed or minimized because a scene or a plot line is axed or minimized;

an interview is jettisoned because the point is covered by another interviewee or the narrator.

True story: An MOW (movie of the week) I worked on had a script which the director and producer realized was convoluted after the third cut. After many re-cuts, conversations with the writer, and screenings, they were running out of ideas and the show was running two weeks behind schedule. They decided to drop a minor character in an attempt to salvage the script problem. The producer called the actor, praised his work, and made sure he got a copy of his big scene.

### Final word

In the course of a show, the editor hardly ever meets the actors or interviewee. Therefore, to an editor, an actor is a character, an interviewee is a subject. The editor deals objectively with each character or interviewee's words, lines, looks, and total presentation with an eye to the purpose of the scene and the show as a whole. Feature and television editor Nina Gilberti sums it up best: "Understanding the core issue of the characters — finding it in a look, creating it in a moment — is my joy in the editing process."

# Cutting Narration

For editing purposes, narration is defined as an unseen speaker whose voice is heard as visuals play. It's also referred to as voice-over narration, voice-over, or VO. VO can be spoken by the show's narrator, by a character, or by an interviewee. To record the VO, a narrator is hired or the actor brought in to a recording studio.

There are two common approaches to editing narration: You can cut the picture first and then add the narration or lay out the narration and then add the pictures. Both approaches necessitate some frame adjustments after the second element is added to make the sequence work perfectly.

### Approach 1: Cut narration, add pictures

#### STEP 1: PUT THE NARRATION TOGETHER

On documentaries it's quite common to start by stringing together the words of the person being interviewed or the narrator narrating. You cut and paste sentences, phrases, and words and may jump around parts of the interview or between takes of the narrator. Since you're ignoring the picture for the moment, some people call this a radio cut. While you're constructing this cut, you'll "pull out the air" — remove pauses, false starts, and the "ums" and "uhs." Your goal is to piece together a coherent, well-paced VO that accurately states what the interviewee or narrator said.

### PAY ATTENTION TO SYNC

While editing the narration, you must be mindful of the picture so you don't throw your scene or show out of sync. You can slug picture (fill video channel with black) to match the duration of the narration. Or, if there's sync picture of the interviewee, narrator, or character, you can keep it in along with the words.

### VIEWING THE SCENE

Watch the scene to see how the narration works. You'll notice that some of the pictures will be jump cuts and/or poor cuts. Don't worry about them for now but concentrate on perfecting the audio flow. Once you're satisfied with the narration, you are ready for Step 2.

### STEP 2: CUT IN AND ADJUST PICTURE EDITS

Now you want to cover up the slugs or picture jump cuts with your visuals. In some places, the shots of interviewees will work fine on camera. In other places, you'll want to drop in cutaways. For instance, as the interviewee or narrator talks about erecting a house, cut in your nice early morning house-framing shot. When they describe the labor involved, insert shots of people sawing and hammering. You get the idea.

## Approach 2: Cut picture, add narration

Ordinarily you cut the picture first and the final narration for your documentary[1] or drama is recorded and laid in after you've completed and screened a few cuts. The narrator's track usually lays in well because you've anticipated it with scratch track. Scratch track is a temporary narration track recorded for the purposes of editing. The scratch track narrator is the director, producer, editor, or someone else recruited for their suitable speaking voice. Scratch track is immensely helpful for timing visuals and making certain that they fit the narration and have the desired impact.

---

1. On docs, the narration is usually scripted after the shoot.

# Cutting Music

*"When you work with sound, you have to think about what works for the picture and how to manipulate the audience's emotions. I love to intertwine music and sound effects to create a 'soup' that is very atmospheric—so you can't tell the difference between the music and the effects."*

—CHRIS DICKENS, *Slumdog Millionaire, Hot Fuzz,* and *Shaun of the Dead*

It's always amazing to experience what laying in a piece of music does to a scene. Suddenly your documentary comes alive. The shots in your montage flow together. Those boring seconds where the heroine crosses the hall have life and purpose and finally seem joined to the rest of the picture. Serendipity! A song can boost a film and, if over end credits, leave a positive final impression of the show. We can all think of at least one film where the theme song was more memorable than the movie. Film Guy writes in his book *Sound Editing Nutz and Boltz*: "As far back as silent movie days, film music has always been used as the 'cosmic glue' to save scenes that are not happening pix-wise." Many shows go overboard with music, spreading the cosmic glue everywhere, but there's no denying that music can keep a show alive and breathing, like an audible heart beat.

## Cutting in music

Time and again when you lay in a song, you'll be surprised at how key actions miraculously fall on beats. Sound engineer Tomlinson Holman, the "TH" in THX sound, asserts in his book, *Sound for Film and Television*: "Music imposes its own order on a scene, whether the picture is cut to the music or not. It is surprising how many times music will be laid underneath a scene of someone walking, for example, and the walk appears to be 'on the beat.' Somehow our brain searches for order out of chaos and imposes it, finding order where none was intended."

## Which comes first, the picture or the music?

You can cut the picture first and add the music or lay down the music and then add the picture. The situation determines the correct line of attack. Figure 6.j shows a few selected frames from the extraordinarily popular TV show *Glee*, where the bed of music is laid down and the pictures cut in afterwards.

Whichever cutting method you use, you'll most likely make adjustments to the picture by fiddling with frames here and there. You can

**6.j** Selected cuts of the *Glee* cast dancing to a Madonna song.

also finesse the music itself by dropping out or repeating stanzas or lines as long as you make an aurally acceptable cut. Table 6.3 gives several typical scenarios for each cutting method.

TABLE 6.3
SCENARIOS FOR CUTTING PICTURE AND MUSIC (MX)

| | SCENARIO | HOW IT'S HANDLED |
|---|---|---|
| CUT PIX TO MX | Pre-approved MX with rights secured or not needed. | When a specific piece is definitely going to be used in the final show, the editor lays MX in and cuts to it. |
| | Temp song or piece of MX. FYI: Sometimes temp MX is preferable to final MX but rights are unobtainable. | Editor adds temp music to help a scene, section, or montage. Temp MX occasionally becomes or leads the way to the permanent choice. |
| | Musical, dance number, MX video, or MX concert piece. | Song or music is decided before pix is shot. |
| | Promos, commercials, and documentaries. | Often MX is selected before the picture is shot or cut. |
| CUT MX TO PIX | A montage or scene is already cut. | Editor adds temp MX before running the show for the director/producer/client. |
| | Temp mix. | Any MX is possible because the show is still a work-in-progress. |
| | Picture is locked. | Scenes are timed for MX and the composer composes or the MX editor hunts down music and cuts it in. |

## *Last word*

When you cut music and picture seamlessly, you'll leave people guessing: Did the picture or the music come first?

## Chapter Wrap-Up

Now that you're grounded in current editing practices, advance to Chapter 7 and hear from editors about how they put these skills to work every day to cut music videos, dramas, documentaries, news, comedy, and a variety of other genres.

# From Animation to Reality

*Editing Different Genres*

*"Editing film is really a combination of instinct and experience with a lot of experimentation thrown in."*

—JIM CLARK, from the foreword to his book *Dream Repairman: Adventures in Film Editing*

## Overview

This chapter conveys a series of snapshots of genres and how they are edited, starting with animation and ending with reality TV, with stops at comedy, commercials, corporate videos, news, and music videos along the way. The guidelines laid out in Chapter 6 apply to all genres of cutting. However, each genre has some different requirements and areas that demand special expertise. Unfortunately, editors are often typed by genre, i.e., they become known as a music video editor, feature editor, or commercial editor. This can make it hard to break into another genre. Most editors and knowledgeable filmmakers believe that if you know how to cut, you can cut anything as long as you put your heart, mind, and energy into it. So if you want to cross to another genre, learn its requirements and go for it!

## Cutting Animation

There are many different kinds of animation: hand-drawn (*The Illusionist, Persepolis*); stop-motion with puppets (*Fantastic Mr. Fox, Corpse Bride*) or clay figures (*Wallace and Gromit* films); and computer modeling and motion-capture (*Shrek* and *Toy Story* movies), to name the three main types. All rely on computers these days and start with a storyboard and a script. On feature films, the editor is hired at this previz stage; on TV cartoons the editor is onboarded with the filming of the first episode.

## Animation vs. live action

*"…when people ask me about the difference between editing live action and animation, I tell them that the goal is the same: to control the pacing, performances, and structure in an effort to end up with an entertaining, riveting film. It is just that the path to get there is wildly different."*

—LEE UNKRICH, director-editor, A.C.E., *Toy Story 1, 2,* and *3, Finding Nemo,* and *A Bug's Life*

Editing animation semi-reverses the live action workflow. Live action shows shoot first and then edit. With animation, the editor edits the dialogue and/or the storyboards before the shoot. A live action film starts with a few people during pre-production, builds to a large number of people during production, then drops to a medium-sized crew during post production. An animated feature starts with a small crew for the script stage, balloons to a big crew as storyboards are created, and keeps this huge crew working for most of the show with editing taking place during all stages of the process.

## The process

Here are the fundamental steps for creating animated shows:

**CREATING ANIMATION**

Note: These steps often overlap.

1. Script
2. Storyboard = comic strip drawings of scenes to be animated with scripted lines, SFX, VFX, etc.
3. Dialogue
   a. Feature: Record scratch track.
   b. TV cartoon: Record actors.
   c. Add natural pauses (where a speaker would naturally pause) of 3-4 frames as part of the editing in Step 3 (cartoons) or Step 4 (features).
4. Story reel, a.k.a. animatic = edited dialogue + storyboard and serves as blueprint for show.
   Note: Cartoons skip this step.
   a. Shoot storyboard to nail down timing, perfect designs, test characters and dialogue, etc.
   b. Edit with dialogue.
5. Design: Create characters, foregrounds, and backgrounds.
6. Layout: Complete all drawings: camera moves, foregrounds, backgrounds, characters, key frames, in-between frames.
7. Shoot: Film final, animated version.
8. Post production

## Strict organization

Animated features require strict scheduling and organization since there are many editors and assistants and much footage. A big feature can have hundreds of hours of voice recordings and over 100,000 storyboards. Lee Unkrich remarks, "The thing about doing an animated film — especially computer animation — is that every last little element, except for the actual recordings of the actors' voices, is synthetically created. It all has to be neatly catalogued and organized in the Avid. It's an enormous amount of material — scratch dialogue, final dialogue, storyboards, sound effects, music, etc."

## Editing

Just as with 3-D, on animated shows, post production starts early, during preproduction, allowing the editorial team to collaborate more fully on the show. Jonathan Lucas, editor on *Corpse Bride,* reports, "The storyboards are all JPEG images, and they shoot almost to the frame what's on the storyboards. At one point, we had five or six storyboard artists working ten hours a day, six days a week. Do they play it in a close shot? A wide shot? It's fine-tuned for months on end until the director says he's happy."

**7.a** Guess where (at which studio) this animation cutting room is. *Photo courtesy of Sue Odjakjian.*

### DIALOGUE TRACK

Cutting the dialogue track is crucial because the animation will be shot to match it. One challenge is the lack of handles. In live action there are always handles — seconds or frames after an actor finishes speaking — because the camera doesn't stop right after the actor utters the last syllable. With feature animation, the animated pictures are created and shot to match the dialogue cut; there are no handles. To shoot handles, even only a few frames in length, can take a day and ups expenses. Contrarily, on television cartoon series, scenes are animated slightly long so the editor has the leeway to cut out footage and bring the show "to time" (the network's required length).

Editing the dialogue track challenges editors and gives them power. Lee Unkrich reveals, "Many of the lines are the price of many little pieces of several different takes. Some of them are recorded at multiple recording sessions. One of the luxuries in editing for animation is that we have a degree of control over how to shape the actor's performances that is really nearly impossible in live action."

### COMPLETION

Once the director approves the dialogue cut, the animation is filmed and the editor brings the animated pictures and dialogue together. The edited material replaces the storyboard and the show progresses bit by bit toward completion. SOP is that writing, shooting, storyboarding, cutting, voice recordings and screenings continue from the beginning of the show until it's locked.

## Last word

*"At the end the editor's responsibility is the same in live action and animation. He manages the narrative structure and flow of the film as well as orchestrates the sound and visuals to create an engaging experience for the audience."*

—LEE UNKRICH

The high demand for 3-D today combined with the ever-improving and cheapening of computer and film technology are making animation a stronger, more lucrative player than ever in the movie biz; it's always had a home on TV. Hey! It even has its own Oscar category finally. Animation is de rigueur in docs lately and a familiar sight on YouTube, corporate, and training videos. So we'll be enjoying lots more of it and th-th-that's all for now, folks!

# Cutting Comedy

*"…editing comedy is first, about looking and finding the best performances and second, about finding the rhythms. Comedy, more so than almost any other genre, needs delicate timing."*

—SKIP COLLECTOR, editor-director, *10 Things I Hate About You, Brothers,* and *Seinfeld.*

Cutting comedy is similar to performing comedy: It's all in the timing. Sometimes you let the scene "play" (run as filmed); other times you shorten time by accelerating the action to earn the laugh. For example, you may speed up a scene or delete bits that drop the energy or simply cut tight to sustain pace and interest. Usually, you want to cut lean — not linger on frames.

However, there are times when you want to milk the moment or, as veteran comedy editor Dann Cahn called it, "cut around the horn." This means you extend "the laugh" — the audience's enjoyment of the scene — by cutting to people's reactions…maybe even the parakeet's. Just think of how a mudslinging scene builds and sustains momentum. Figure 7.b shows an epic vomit scene from *The Office* which is punctuated by reactions of the egg-eating character whose actions instigates the laughs. The scene goes on much longer — I've cut it down to a few, select frames.

**7.b** Building laughs via reactions in *The Office*.

## *Rule of Three*

Customarily, editors show three instances of something — say a woman trying to make a soufflé — before paying if off with a smoking oven. Three's funny, and the viewer stays with it and can remember the gag; four or more is not — unless the cuts are very short. How does this work? The first soufflé — the set-up — should be funny, the second attempt — reinforcing the first — funnier, and the third conglomeration — the punch line or payoff — the funniest — and often the most unexpected.

The rule of three often arrives in three verbal beats:

Example 1: "I celebrated Thanksgiving in an old-fashioned way. I invited everyone in my neighborhood to my house, we had an enormous feast, and then I killed them and took their land."
—Jon Stewart

Example 2: "There was a priest, a rabbi, and an imam…"

Example 3: "I used to be Snow White…but I drifted." —Mae West
The pause in the middle after Snow White stands in as the second beat.

Figure 7.c exemplifies the Rule of Three with a character who enjoys a piggyback ride while at work (frame 1), a character who is disgusted that his co-workers are horsing around (frame 2), and a character who conducts city business while riding piggyback (frame 3).

## Comedy style today

The mockumentary style, where characters address the camera, as seen on *Modern Family, The Office,* and *Parks and Recreation,* is in vogue today and can be traced back to Rob Reiner's two 1980s films: *When Harry Met Sally* and *This is Spinal Tap. Curb Your Enthusiasm* editor Steve Rasch, A.C.E., maintains that "the written joke is no longer funny to viewers. They don't want to hear it. They are more interested in story and character-based comedy."

**7.c** Rule of Three demonstrated in a scene from *Parks and Recreation.*

With comedy you cut from your funny bone, functioning more deliberately as both creator and audience than in any other genre. You learn to sense when the materials needs to be snappier, take a breather, or be ratcheted up. Frequently you can show hard truths about the human condition, political issues, and social mores, and reach more people through comedy than drama or documentary. Here are a few TV and movie examples: *Thank You For Not Smoking, Religulous, The Colbert Report, The Daily Show, Monk, Nine to Five, Election, Wag the Dog, In and Out, Tootsie, Blazing Saddles,* and *M*A*S*H.*

While comedies today are cut in traditional as well as modern style, one aspect remains the same: Sitcoms are shot either single camera or multi-cam.

## Multiple-camera comedy

Multi-cam shows are recorded from first scene to last in front of an audience, with three or four cameras labeled A, B, C, and D. A cabled gang of four camera operators maneuvers up and down the stage to nab their assigned shots which are radioed in to them during the shoot by the TD (technical director). D camera, referred to as X camera or the iso-cam, is an isolated camera which often shoots independently of A, B, and C, and may run only 50% of the time.

Once the show is recorded, the multi-cam editor receives:
- A hard drive of low res HD dailies or a tape for each camera: A, B, C, and D.
- The script supervisor's script with A, B, C, and D camera's angles marked with the line cut.
- The line cut.

### LINE CUT AND Q SPLIT

The line cut is a tape or file of the switches from one camera angle to the other that the director called out to the TD during the shoot. The line cut represents the director's desires for cutting the scenes and is a guide for the editor. It displays all four cameras on a monitor where it is called the quad split (Q split).

### PREPPING THE MULTI-CAM SHOW FOR EDITING

Whether you're cutting a comedy, a rock concert, or other multi-cam show, the procedure is the same. You sync all camera angles by time code, common points, or slate, take by take. Next, you use the digital system's multi-cam function to group (gang) four or more takes and make a multi-clip. Multi-clips enable you to cut freely and easily from camera to camera "on the fly," i.e., while playing at normal speed.

### EDITING MULTI-CAM

To start, you lay down the best and longest audio track from one of the cameras, usually Camera A. After this, you cut video only from camera to camera on the fly, then review the scene and adjust the cuts. However, if you're changing the audio track in any way — shortening it, repeating it, or slowing it down — you may want to use the normal "stop and start" method of cutting where you park on your last desired frame and then choose the incoming frame. You will need to re-sync cameras from time to time with each method.

### MATCHING MULTI-CAM

Since multiple cameras capture all the action simultaneously, there are no matching problems for the editor, right? Wrong. This assumes that no filmed lines will be dropped during editing and that the camera ops always made it to their assigned spots during shooting. Both nice fictions. When the camera is out of position, the actor will be shot off camera, partially on camera, or with the camera moving and settling on a critical line. If the director or TD doesn't catch this, there is little chance of picking up the shot since by the time the editor receives the footage the next week's show is already being blocked. To fix these problems, the editor will have to cut earlier or later than the camera gaffe and dodge to a reaction shot to cover the muffed line.

### CHALLENGE OF MULTI-CAM

The multi-cam editor doesn't just tidy up the line cut and retire for the day. Multi-cam comedy brings a special challenge for the editor: the audience. Though unseen during the recording of the show, the audience is not unheard: If the show is good, audience members do their job — they laugh. These laughs are miked and sent to the cutting room, where the editor incorporates them into the show.

Sometimes, however, the audience doesn't laugh or it laughs and laughs and laughs, exceeding what is sustainable for an edited scene. What to do? The editor must take advantage of the audience's response by cutting in the laughs but must also keep the drama going. So the editor becomes expert at finessing the laughs in and out of the show. This finessing is called feathering the laughs, dialing the laughs in or out, or ramping them up or down. The audience is thus a boon and a challenge, because it functions as a character — verbal, reactive, and unseen — that the editor must attend to while editing.

### PROS AND CONS OF MULTI-CAM COMEDIES

Studios shoot multi-cam for two main reasons:

1. It can be done live, e.g., *Letterman, Leno, Ellen.*
2. It's cheaper and faster than single camera. The long list of multi-cam shows includes *The Big Bang Theory, Everybody Loves Raymond, Friends, Frasier, Cheers, Maude, All in the Family, The Dick Van Dyke Show,* and *I Love Lucy.*

The downside of multi-cam comedy is the limitations of the proscenium arch stage which restricts the shooting area to 180° of the action. This means that reverse angles, outdoor scenes, 360° shots and others are avoided or shot before or after the live audience recording. Also, multi-cam shows tend to be plot-driven and rely on jokes and their rhythms first and characters and situations second. However, this doesn't preclude their being popular, well done, or getting below the surface. Figure 7.d shows a typical multi-cam sitcom and some of the types of shots, starting with the establishing shot, that are possible.

**7.d** Types of over-the-shoulder shots possible with multi-cam shows demonstrated by *How I Met Your Mother.*

## Single-cam comedy

Single camera shows are shot and edited like dramas and most other TV and theatrical shows: Out of scene order, with several set-ups for each scene, and by a single camera, except for stunts or heavy action scenes. The camera is free to roam outdoors, make elaborate master shots, tracking shots, close-ups, over-the shoulder shots, and generally be more visually creative. In fact there's more freedom to create for everybody: lighting, sets, sound, etc. The editor has more latitude to create the timing, build character, etc., as with a drama or dramedy. Examples of single-cam comedy include *Modern Family*, *30 Rock*, *The Office*, *Weeds*, *Ugly Betty*, *Desperate Housewives*, *Curb Your Enthusiasm*, *The Bill Cosby Show*, *Get Smart*, *The Beverly Hillbillies*, and *Leave It to Beaver.*

## Laugh track

A show is "laffed" after the dialogue mix or after the entire mix. The laughs start when the "laffer" wheels the laff box in. Whoa... hold the talking horse...That was then. Now Charley Douglass' original laugh machine from the 1950s, like everything else, comes in a digital format. Today files contain all the titters, guffaws, snickers, and chuckles that editors need.

### WHY LAUGH A SHOW?

To sweeten it. Sweetening, in this instance, means that laughs are inserted to bridge and bolster audience response or lack of response.

### CONTROVERSY

Laugh tracks have been disdained since the 1970s but still they persist. Many beloved shows have them — *I Love Lucy, M\*A\*S\*H,* and *Friends* to name but a few.

The worst offenders are single cam shows such as *Gilligan's Island* and *Hogan's Heroes.* With no audience and no laughs, a laugh track was inserted at the network's insistence. The track came across as canned due to the rarely varying volume, length, and strength of the laughs. The current trend with single-cam comedies is to leave out the laugh track. Most multi-cam shows today take the natural laugh track created by the audience and simply sweeten it — a much lighter touch than in the past.

**7.e** Comedy editor cracks up. *Photo courtesy of Sandip Mahal.*

### Last word

*"It seems like there are no rules now. Every show is different."*

—STEVE RASCH, A.C.E., *Important Things with Demetri Martin, Curb Your Enthusiasm,* and *Spin City.*

If you can cut comedy, you can cut anything because you understand timing, characters, reaction shots, and how to start, build, sustain, and end laughs and therefore, scenes. So have fun — a lot of fun — cutting comedy. And it's okay if you cut up yourself!

## Cutting Commercials, Promos, Trailers, and PSAs

*"I think some young editors tend to want to operate the machine as fast as they can....What gets you a good cut is understanding the concept and idea of the piece and building a spot from there....You also need to be able to pick the best scenes and the best performances. Over time, as you edit more and more, you'll get better and faster."*

—OWEN PLOTKIN, commercial editor

Promos, (short promotional pieces), trailers (movie previews), and PSAs (public service announcements) are forms of advertising like commercials. All four have the same cutting challenge: Tell a lot in a little amount of time. Commercial editors regularly cut under pressure — less than a day for a 30 second spot

**7.f** A promo editor eyes the monitor. *Photo courtesy of Chris Senchack.*

isn't unusual. They put together such compelling images, text, and stories that, after 60 seconds or less, viewers run to the phone, store, or computer and spend money!

### Daily life

The commercial shooting ratio, upwards of 70:1 (shot footage compared to edited footage) has always been among the highest in filmmaking. The editor can expect to receive a storyboard and multiple takes and be surrounded by many people such as the client, producer, and director. In today's market, the commercial editor needs to know how to create and/or integrate complex effects on a digital system, think coolly in a pressured atmosphere, and make tight, innovative cuts — "freak the film" — as some call it.

### Creative challenge: So many shots, so little time

Owen Plotkin comments about cutting three Office.com spots: "I often imply things with fragments. All three commercials are very linear, and there are a lot of elements to the story that have to be conveyed, so it seems natural to use jump cuts to compress time. Those cuts also help to create tension, which works well with the release of humor… That said, I would just as soon not use jump cuts and cut a spot with as few cuts as possible. It depends on what works for the particular spot."

**7.g** A web video marketing shooter-preditor. *Photo courtesy of Andika Duncan.*

### Cutting the infomercial

Cutting an infomercial is like cutting a long commercial or corporate video with one-tenth the budget. The infomercial always includes testimonials and demonstrations as well as countdown times for viewers to call in and order. An infomercial may contain graphics and docudramas as well. Knowing how to cut music, drama, comedy, and commercials is useful as infomercials can include all of these. Word of warning: Often the production house collects a percentage of the profit if the product takes off. This means that an underpaid producer with a stagnant profit deal may try to slice your wages, so watch it!

### Trailers

*"If a film is a distillation of life or an expansion of an imagined life, trailers are compressed versions of them."*

—LISA KERNAN, from her book *Coming Attractions: Reading Movie Trailers*

To create a trailer, the editor pulls footage, then pieces it together to distill a movie and spark moviegoers to catch it before the DVD comes out. Unbound by the story order of the movie, trailer editors use music, VO, wipes, and other effects, plus titles along with clips and shots from the movie, in ways that usually reflect existing editing styles and occasionally break through to a new style.

## CHALLENGE

The challenge of cutting trailers is to tell and sell the story of a story in 90 seconds or less. Hired by a company contracted by the production company, the editor receives the edited scenes for the majority of the movie and has a week or two to cut them to trailer length. A trailer editor benefits from a knowledge of music and knowing how to seamlessly segue lines of music together since fractions of different types of music are routinely used to pull the trailer together and highlight its action and scenes.

## ATTITUDE

*"They give away too much of the movie." "They're better than the films." "They only show the spectacular parts." "All the best jokes are in the trailer." "They lie." "They're the best part of going to the movies." "They're too loud."*

—LISA KERNAN, from her book *Coming Attractions: Reading Movie Trailers*

Most of us have contradictory attitudes toward trailers. Trailers are a bonus — we get to see a part of another film — for the price of seeing the movie we just paid for. They help us get in the mood for the feature. We can use them to reject a movie and save ourselves time and money. Yet we dismiss them as crass commercials and don't worry about entering a theater in the middle of them. Still, as filmmakers, we can appreciate them as incredibly condensed movies. The Independent Film Channel (IFC) puts it this way: "…trailers provide a version of cinema that's essentially utopian, in which every film is perfect, if only for two and a half minutes." As such, they provide another avenue for editing expertise as the ingenious frame in Figure 7.h proves.

**7.h** This trailer for the Austrian film *Import Export* consists of multiple matte shots and frames of text on a horizontally split screen that move — like filmstrips — in opposite directions (top strip to left, bottom strip to right).

# Cutting a Corporate Video

*"I look at editing as being a great big jigsaw puzzle and you're the one who pulls all the pieces into one nice, big cohesive story."*
—LES PERKINS, Les is More Productions

Editing a corporate video is like editing an educational film and a commercial. The piece can be short or long and about a process, person, or product that the corporation decides is worthy of such an expenditure. Designed to educate or promote, it will be shown in-house, at trade shows and demos, or sent to prospective customers. Many companies have editors on staff, but they also regularly outsource projects.

An editor works with some or all of these people: instructional designer, director, producer, and client. The goal is to create a video that gets the information across in the most effective way, be it by drama, documentary, comedy, animation, or demonstration. If it's a marketing piece, the target audience will affect whether it's jazzy, funny, informative, down to earth, etc.

**7.i** Corporate training editor gets creative. *Photo courtesy of David Mallory.*

Often the editor is also a producer on the project and referred to as the preditor. Preditor Les Perkins of Les is More Productions explains that he assists clients with all sorts of issues: He helps determine the camera codecs, editing system, audio recording, and color grading to name a few. Perkins insists that post be part of preproduction. "Before you shoot a pixel or a frame, you have to plan your postproduction workflow all the way through delivery," he asserts. But problems happen anyway and are all part of the job, he acknowledges, adding, "I love problem solving — finding editorial solutions for production problems so the client doesn't have to re-shoot."

# Cutting a Documentary

*"Docs are an editor's medium. You've somehow got to figure out from the mountain of stuff you're handed exactly what you're going to cut."*

—TIM TOBIN, editor, *The Miles Davis Documentary, The ACLU Freedom Files,* and *The Cutting Edge: The Magic of Movie Editing.*

When cutting a documentary, no matter how useful the outline, the editor frequently functions as the primary shaper of the story as well its visual style and sound designer. Doc editing can be, therefore, an extraordinarily creative, collaborative, and rewarding experience. And its subjects are astonishingly varied: You may re-create a time in history, illuminate the consequences of fiscal recklessness, or acquaint the audience with a community it would never otherwise meet. A doc, like any good show — scripted or non — is essentially a mystery. It raises questions that intrigue viewers such as: Why is our food unhealthy? How did she really die? What was he actually like?

Former commercial editor and owner of his own commercial house Dan Swietlik, who segued to the doc world when he cut *An Inconvenient Truth* and *Sicko,* reflects: "The awakening for me was how much the editor has to write in documentaries. And how much you have to live and breathe that topic."

## *Process*

Since a doc is scriptless, you will start with any or all of the following elements: transcript, markers on a digital system's time line of important lines, index cards of lines and/or scenes, or a paper cut.[1] The editor's first move, typically, is to lay down a bed of interviews and narration, then double back to drop in cutaways that bridge speeches and illustrate points. Habitually on documentaries, editors tighten words, cut and paste interviews, and arrange images to clarify the thought process and points of view. They usually create a montage or two, add music, and work in narration and often some graphics and animation.

Editing a documentary requires sitting with the footage, running it in one's head, memorizing it, and tucking it away so that images and ideas can ferment and connect. In addition, it calls for viewing and re-viewing the footage and experimenting — cutting the same shots together in different versions. Swietlik believes that "the hardest thing

---

1. Note: A paper cut is just that, a cut on paper, not with the footage. The footage does not always mesh with the paper cut; it will always dictate its own course.

about a documentary is not figuring out what you want to say, but realizing what you don't have the time to say. You struggle. You have to abandon some of the initial ideas that you had and find the focus that makes it as entertaining and palatable as possible. You don't want to overwhelm the viewer."

## Special challenge: Integrity

*"… in documentary the important thing is to prevent editing decisions compromising the validity of the material — not showing the truth."*

—ROGER CRITTENDEN, director, from his book *Film and Video Editing.*

The documentary camera stands in for the viewer as it witnesses the documented event and records the documented subject. No matter where the camera is positioned, it can always be subject to different interpretations. Millions of people saw the Rodney King-LAPD video yet there were distinct and opposing interpretations of what it exposed. Documentary editing charges the editor to present all the significant footage and represent all the viewpoints to tell the most truthful tale.

When there is integrity in the shooting and editing of a documentary, it can win hearts, minds, and awards such as those garnered by *The Inside*

**7.j** Documentary editor selects the next shot. *Photo courtesy of Matthew Tucker.*

*Job, The Cove, Man on Wire, Hoop Dreams, Chicks in White Satin, The Last Days, The Civil War, Scared Straight, 7 Up, The Life and Times of Harvey Milk*, and *Streetwise* to name but a few.

## The bliss of creation

Let's close with the eloquent words of Mathew Tucker, editor of a documentary on a year in the life of the musky rat–kangaroo, which he cut on a Lightworks: "I've often felt that editing is a process akin to painting… As I selected shots and clipped out the "good bits," I couldn't help but feel that I was assembling a series of rich palettes with which to work… The screen… was my canvas, but what was more fun was that my "painting" was in not two but four dimensions… height and width, naturally…then movement within these two and in the implicit screen "depth." However the dimension unique to editing was time-space and I sometimes imagined this dimension as one that extended out of the screen towards me and beyond… Moreover as the edit progressed, the time line… became a visual and tactile overview of this time-structural dimension. Using placeholders in the (mostly unused) audio tracks gave a neat visual clue to the overall shape and rhythm of the film, much as stepping back from a canvas reveals balance and composition…

I was delighted to watch my palettes changing subtlety in color and light as the scenes and the seasons progressed. Scattered amongst the rich reds, browns, and yellows of the decomposing humus and the dark glossy greens of the rainforest understory were the intensely colored rainforest fruit that the musky rat–kangaroo prefers to eat. My Lightworks became a jewelry box from which to adorn the growing painting."

## Cutting movies

Since editing features was the focus of Chapter 6, we'll let Carol Littleton, A.C.E., *The Rum Diary, E.T.,* and *Places in the Heart* sum it up: "A good editor needs to be aware of the other contributions and heighten them, to bring out their best qualities in performance, art direction, cinematography, or the direction of the film. It's really my job to be interpreter of other people's work and ultimately to rewrite the film using images and sound."

## Cutting News

*"Morning meeting at 10 a.m., assignments are given, reporters out in the field bring tapes in throughout the day for digitizing into an Avid system, airtime is at 6 p.m."*
—SUSAN PERLA, CBS news editor, New York City

Cutting news is a special type of editing due to its relentless deadlines and its unique lingo, schedules, staff titles, and workflow. News cutters have to be fast and flexible, ready to switch or update stories as priorities shift with the daily ebb and flow of news.

## Footage sources

Material arrives in the news editing room from two main sources on a variety of formats:

1. Inside sources:
   — Footage shot by in-house shooters.
   — Archive footage.
   — Formats: P2 cards or tape from XD cams, usually.
2. Outside sources:
   — Footage (news and archive) shot by out-of-house shooters.
   — News feeds.
   — Formats: Any. Usually transferred to tape.

## Getting material in and out

All material is uploaded to a humongous server. The editors download the material for each story to their Grass Valley Aurora or Edius, Avid, FCP, or other news editing system and cut in hi-res HD.

> **NEWS LINGO**
>
> *Field tape*
> Contains: Location shots, shots of people being interviewed by reporter, and/or reporter telling the story and NAT sound.
>
> *NAT*
> Natural audio that is either sync or wild sound.
>
> *VOT*
> Voice on tape. Audio written and recorded in studio by the reporter after returning from the field which the editor receives via a live feed or download.
>
> *SOT*
> Sync on tape or Voice over sync on tape: Reporter's voice recorded on the field tape, performing an interview and/or telling the story. Also referred to as voice SOT or VO SOT.

News producers start their day by "stacking the show," i.e., ordering the stories for broadcast. News is stacked 1-2 hours ahead. Once the editors have a completed story, they upload it to the server or, if they're out in the field, send it back to the station via microwave or satellite. If there are updates to a story or changes to the stacking, they can easily re-cut the story.

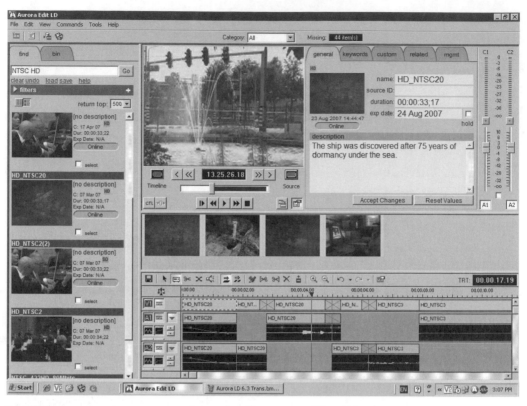

**7.k** Editing screen on Aurora news cutting system. *Photo courtesy of Grass Valley.*

## Jobs and titles

News editors arc part of two unions: NABET (National Association of Broadcast Employees and Technicians) or IBEW (International Brotherhood of Electrical Workers). NABET has been fighting a losing war with the networks and there have been many changes for the worse. At KABC-LA the editor used to choose the footage, now the writer picks the clips and indicates them on the script. The upshot? Many editors have lost their jobs, segued to other jobs, or broadened their scope and become hyphenates. Common hyphenate jobs are: shooter-editor, shooter-editor-transmitter, reporter-editor, and writer-editor.

## Editing process

*"The logistics of editing a news package are not that difficult. You just have to have nimble fingers and keep your logs clear to find the right shots quickly."*
—SUSAN PERLA

More and more, editing takes place in the field as the shooter-editor-transmitter edits on a laptop in a coffee shop or in a truck parked near the unfolding story or even at home. Wherever, the process goes like this: The editor receives the script from the writer. Then "we cut the footage as it comes in," Liz McHale, writer-editor at KABC-LA reports. "We lay down the pieces (pictures) and mark ins and outs on the fly, one clip at a time." The time line on the digital system can mix HD and SD and is set to auto-convert mixed formats to HD.

The editor then cuts in the NAT sound and the voice SOT. Next, any VOT is added. If the editor is also the reporter, the VOT may be recorded and the pictures cut to it. Routinely, editors slo-mo or speed up shots to fit the VO SOT using fit-to-fill.[2] Sometimes anchors talk live to a story during a broadcast. When this is scheduled, the editors add up to 21 extra seconds of picture — enough to cover a slow-talking anchor.

The news cutter must work swiftly and efficiently to get a story approved by the producer so it can "make air." A situation like the one depicted in the movie *Broadcast News*,

7.1 Putting the news together. *Photo courtesy of Chris Senchack.*

where the editor worked up to airtime sweating bullets along with the reporter and producer, can be a daily occurrence.

Occasionally editors have the "luxury" of one to three days to put together a package — a precut story of timely human interest. They enjoy this because they get to stretch and show more of their editing chops. Another regular responsibility is sending clip reels (additional material) along with graphics to the news truck while it covers breaking news. This way the shooter-editor-transmitter can cut a hot story right in the truck and send it over the airwaves.

## Archiving

With all the daily footage coming in and stories being broadcast, there is a tremendous amount of material to store. "We live and die by our archive," editor and media manager at KABC-LA Ryan Byrne affirms. The station stores stories as they are broadcast for legal reasons as well

---

2. Shoehorning video or audio portion of a shot into a certain time slot by either slowing it down or speeding it up. For news, the video would most likely be slowed down due to shortage of visuals.

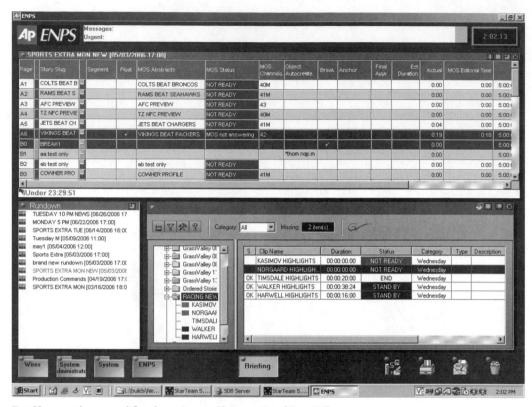

**7.m** News stories queued for air on Aurora. *Photo courtesy of Grass Valley.*

as for future source material but deletes the raw footage due to space limitations. To conserve space, material is archived low res, but when restored, automatically downloads hi res.

## The Challenge: What makes a good news story?

According to Susan Perla, "Pacing, good SOT, and cameramen who shoot footage like cameramen and not wedding video photographers." Liz McHale has found that "the biggest factor in editing a news story is understanding not only the facts but the atmosphere surrounding the story. Understanding what the story means to the community and to the viewer gives me a good framework to choose shots."

Perla recalls her 16-hour days following the obliteration of the World Trade Center: "The images that I could not air were pretty awful. I do think about some of the footage and it disturbs me. I hope that as I work with people, I can bring humanness to any aspect of a news story. There are times when I feel we are vultures, looking for scraps. Then there are times when I finish up and look at the work and it makes me proud of a day's work or a package cut well. It might make an impact or force someone to think about an issue."

# Cutting Concert Pieces and Music Videos

## Rock concerts and other music concerts

In essence, a concert piece is a straightforward documentary of an event from start to finish. Whether it's an evening at the Kennedy Center, Norah Jones' sell-out performance, or The Rolling Stones' latest tour, the concert piece documents the musical performance from the artists' applause-laden entrance through their applause-laden exit. You will lock the cameras in order to cut on the fly from singer to keyboardist to audience while staying in sync with the music. You unlock them to change the timing of the music or put in some audience shots or other cutaways. As long as your cutting room has good soundproofing, you can crank up the music and whale away on your editing system.

### Special skills

Knowledge of music and music editing is crucial since music is the driving force of the concert piece. Often concert pieces are cut at post houses where online and offline merge and editor and director work long hours side by side. But these days they can be cut at your house or the director's. When you work on a good concert piece, at least you'll go home singing at night!

## Music videos

*"The way I see good editing is that you just enhance and bring out what the artist or band is giving you."*
—SCOTT RICHTER, editor of a dozen Dave Meyers music videos including Jay Z's *I Just Wanna Love* and *Do My Ladies* and Mary J. Blige's *Family Affair*

A music video is a promotional documentary of one song, told in free-form fashion, usually with fewer cameras than a concert piece. Again, music knowledge is vital as sometimes you need to cut out stanzas or sections of songs. In addition, a keen sense of sync and rhythm are required since the singer(s) often sing and dance to playback music instead of performing the song live as they would for a concert piece.

To begin, "I listen to the song multiple times and learn to love it," reveals Dean Gonzalez, editor of *Green Day: Heart Like a Hand Grenade* among other music videos and documentaries. He observes that "with commercials and features everything is scripted, storyboarded and well planned

**7.n** Cutting a music video. *Photo courtesy of Dean Gonzalez.*

out. On a music video you get a treatment that the crew didn't completely shoot. So you have to be very creative with the footage." He continues, "I find it exciting and daunting to create something without all the elements — to make a story out footage that isn't always there. I love storytelling. I enjoy capturing the moments and seeing the story unfold."

As for the actual structuring and editing Gonzalez says, "You have to create the arcs. You have a path with the music and certain story elements have to hit at certain times. It's amazing to see an artist's music blend so naturally with a director's vision." Also, he adds, "It's good to cut off beat. I try to find my way inside the music and show that editorially." He believes that "When you get to work with and meet amazing talent, you feel a part of their creative visions."

## CHALLENGE

Scott Richter, editor of Missy Elliot's *Get Ur Freak On,* which won the 2001 MTV music video editing award, recalls, "It was such a cool choreography routine — yes, we were able to shift highlights around a little, just to add some musical highlights to it. But it was more important to let the rest breathe and play out naturally — to let the dance be the focus, not just cuts to cut." Gonzalez expands on Richter, asserting, "The director has the vision but you have more creative freedom to make something different than the director has seen."

# Cutting Television: Dramas, Soaps, and Reality

*"The best editors in the world today cut television. The deadlines are there and it's got to work and you learn how to cheat the film…When you've cut television for a couple of years and you get into features, you can put anything together. When I went with Spielberg, he shot a lot of footage and if I didn't have that experience it would have been difficult."*

—MICHAEL KAHN, A.C.E., *Schindler's List, Saving Private Ryan,* and *Hogan's Heroes*

Some see TV shows as mere filler between commercials. Clearly as there are ever more channels, ever more product is required. So those that toil for the "small screen" edit in all genres: animation, comedy, concert, documentary, drama, infomercial, music video, and news as well as a couple unique to TV: soap operas and reality shows.

## Television deadlines and duties

The sentiment of many TV editors is, "We do everything feature editors do, only faster!" A TV movie of the week (MOW) and other "long form" shows, i.e., mini-series, are shot in less time with less coverage than a feature yet they must be completely edited within weeks of finishing shooting. Feature film editors have more time, though even their schedules are getting squeezed. "Short form" shows like episodic dramas and sitcoms have even tighter schedules.

Most TV editors, whether cutting dramas, comedies, or dramedies, create green screens and other VFX and lay in SFX and music. Editors also create recaps ("previously on…") and bumpers (short recaps inserted between acts on MOWs and mini-series). "What they (producers) expect to see is literally a finished product before it's finished. And that's what we have to deliver; that's the expectation," relates Janet Ashikaga, A.C.E., *The West Wing* and *Seinfeld*.

On the positive side, if you're a staff editor on a TV series, you cut more hours of footage than you do in any other editing arena. You get to edit a lot of different scenes and you gain lots of experience. If you don't like this week's show, the next week will arrive in no time. Since

**7.0** Cutting a dramatic TV series. Notice lined script and notes on script stand. *Photo courtesy of Chris Senchack.*

you're typically employed on a series for months, there's opportunity for professional growth and to form lasting professional relationships.

Farrel Levy, A.C.E., *The Defenders, Criminal Minds,* and *NYPD Blue,* contrasts TV editing with feature editing: "I often think of it as doing many fine drawings, as opposed to one painting. It can be very freeing. The quantity of TV shows being cranked out has some interesting by-products. I think that because television offers a chance to be more experimental from an editing point of view, over time, this broadens what is considered acceptable to the audience, and it will broaden the way we tell stories."

## Soap opera

So what's unique about soaps? The time frame, for one thing. Customarily a crew — lead editor, associate editor, assistant editor, sound mixer, music supervisor, and online editor — start and finish a new one-hour show each day, five times a week. How do they do it?

To start, the production crew shoots 135 pages (30" air time/page) every day, using two redundant stages with dedicated sets. One set is prepped and lit while the other's being filmed, in a constant rotation. "We move the actors to the lights, instead of the lights to the actors" reveals editor Lugh Powers, winner of two daytime Emmys on *Days of Our Lives.* Powers, who as an AD also directs, states that the show uses three primary cameras and, as needed, a floating camera or a gib camera, and shoots on digi beta.

As for post production, Powers contends that "technology is there to serve the story." The editorial crew employs four Avid Symphonys utilizing the multi-cam set-up. Typically the associate editor puts together the first cut and gets notes from the producer before Powers, as lead editor, makes the final cut. Like a multi-cam comedy editor, he uses the director's line cut and the lined script as a guide for cutting. However, there are no audio pre-laps because, as with most soaps, "Dialogue is driving the show so we stay on the actor speaking."

How does he like editing soap opera? Powers is passionate about editing and believes it to be the "best job because you get to create. Where else do you get to indulge that five-year-old child who sees a castle or a spaceship, not a cardboard box?" Further, he firmly believes that it is the [film] industry's responsibility to entertain, inspire, and teach, because "we are the bards."

## Cutting reality

Adam Coleite, editor of reality shows as well as docs and dramas, insightfully appraises the world of reality TV: "We've been conditioned to understand that when the camera's shaky, stuff doesn't match, the dialogue's not so audible and there are strange cuts, that it's real. We allow more leeway for mistakes, for messiness, because they seem more real. Reality and nonfiction TV don't have to have production values because people [viewers] assume it's real and forgive more."

### GETTING STARTED

*"They hand you something called a script, but in reality it's just a shot list."*
—KEN BORNSTEIN, editor, *Bachelorette* and other reality, feature, and documentary shows

It takes five weeks or more to edit a one hour reality show, with multiple editors taking different 2-3 minute segments some call "pods." The process begins with the assistant editors, (AEs), who set up each show as a project on the FCP or other digital system. They prep the bins, log the footage, and put in markers when there are multiple takes. Ordinarily the AEs set up shows one of two ways: They stack takes on the time line or multi-clip the show. This entire set-up process consumes 3-4 days. The editor receives a transcript of interviews marked by loggers who can be in-house or outsourced. Additionally, the editor gets a story outline or script up to 30 pages from the story producer. But this is just a starting point. "A lot of the work is figuring out the show as you go," Coleite reports. "At first I don't know what I'm looking for."

### EDITING

"There's a lot of useless, unusable footage," Coleite admits. "Because there's a lot of footage and not many good script supervisors on set, sometimes I have to look through an hour of footage to find a moment or a response. There are a lot of needle-in-the-haystack moments." Reality editors cannot be slackers: Daily, they spin through a lot of footage to extract the gold and pull out the story. Katherine Bransten, editor on *The Swan, Survivor, Eco-Challenge*, and other reality shows contends, "If you're lazy, forget it. You'll never get a good cut. You need to watch everything, even if is excruciatingly boring. You have to be alert to anything that will help the story. That's where the editor has a very significant role to play."

Editors cut out the curses or bleep them if that doesn't work. Pick-ups may be necessary from the original people in the show and/or the narrator, often at the network's request. Most shows shun re-creations, a.k.a. re-enactments, or alert the audience to them with a caption.

"There's tons of cheating (of shots) that goes on," Coleite divulges. New lines, nicknamed "Frankenbites," are pieced together from pieces of several lines. Why? Because "you're paying attention to the veracity and continuity of the story," Coleite explains. Because the footage can be less than desired, rendering the story less than desired, editors routinely soup-up scenes with a glut of effects such as split screens, fancy wipes, and speed-ups. Bornstein, who dubs reality the "fast food of television," says that, "You can do a whole host of things to dress up truly awful footage, which is why, when you look at a lot of reality shows, they're so tricked up."

Coleite screens the cut on his editing system with the show producer, after which the two of them work together to redo the outline and he re-cuts the show. Bornstein comments, "Often producers have only a vague notion of what they want... until you put it together and they watch it." Bransten confirms this, "On some shows the producers have a strong role, but over the last few years I have experienced exactly the opposite. The editor is the one who tells the story."

Subsequent screenings take place with the showrunner, network executive, and possibly the president of the production company. Once the show is locked, the AEs sort out the audio tracks and send an OMF (more about this sound file in Chapter 9) to the mixer. The AEs also sort out the video files and send them to the colorist as well as the online editor.

## CHALLENGE

"I like reality because I'm not tied to continuity — to temporal or spatial continuity. For example, when someone pulls up to a house and knocks on the door, I can jump cut to take time out," enthuses Coleite. "Reality frees you up to think about a scene and put it together differently. I can start on a line and not worry about what people are wearing or where they are." He concludes, "I'm not just putting shots together, it's a lot more creative. I'm telling a story that didn't exist before I started. I am much more the storyteller because I'm creating the story as I'm cutting it."

## PART ONE WRAP-UP

Part One of Stage II, Editing: It has been a long, varied trip through many different cutting rooms, editing challenges, and film genres. Now it's time for Part Two where you'll pull up your chair and learn how to perform these edits on the digital editing system and take a show from first cut to finish.

## PART TWO

# Getting from First Cut to Final Cut

## Introduction

Film machine, digital system, and whatever is invented next: They're all tools to help you edit your film or video. Chapter 8 applies the editing practices you learned in Part One by addressing how to make edits and add titles, sound, and visual effects on a digital editing system. Chapter 9 then goes over the process for getting your first cut to a locked show. In essence Part Two is the lab for Part One.

Following Part Two are three appendices: Appendix D consists of a continuity form for tape and tapeless shows; Appendix E provides a film show continuity form; and Appendix F is the budget form for editing. Once again, you can download all these forms by going to www.joyoffilmediting.com and clicking on the Free tab.

# CHAPTER 8

# Making the Cuts

*Editing on a Digital System*

*"Happiness is a warm Avid."*
—James Cameron

## Overview

You'll need training and plenty of hands-on practice time to operate any digital editing system proficiently. *Cut by Cut*'s mission here is to prepare you for and supplement your instruction be it at a college, a professional facility, or online. Courses are pricey so you do yourself a huge disservice if you're not prepared. This chapter familiarizes you with the concepts, terms, and techniques of editing on a digital machine. Although specific systems are mentioned, the intent is not to single out any one system. There are plenty of books, software manuals, websites, and users groups to help you master each popular system. Also, each system has tutorials and manuals online. So fire up your system and let's get cutting!

## Getting Started

You've input the material and organized it into bins, now grab your script or outline and go to the bin with the dailies for the first scene you want to edit. To edit, you will play clips, cut them into the time line, and create your sequence utilizing two viewers: source and record. The *source viewer* is where you view and audition all your clips: dailies, stock footage, music, etc. In the *record viewer* you build and screen your

**8.a** Source viewer on left and record viewer on right on Final Cut Pro which calls them viewer and canvas respectively. *Photo courtesy of Chris Senchack.*

sequence. Both viewers can display time code and other metadata, depending on the settings you choose.

## Playing and marking footage

To audition a clip for editing into your sequence, play it in the source viewer. You can make the clip play forward or reverse at normal, fast, or frame-by-frame speed. View your clips in the source viewer until you've decided which clip you want to cut in. Play this clip to the first frame you wish to see in your sequence. This first, starting frame is called an *in point*, *cut point*, or *edit point*. Mark it by using your keyboard or mouse. This mark is called an *in mark* or *mark in*. Next, play the clip to the frame that you want to end your first edit on. This is called the *out point*. Make a mark. This is your *mark out* or *out mark*.

## Making the edit

So far you've just marked the IN and the OUT. You have not made the edit. To make an edit, each digital system has a special icon, key, and/or a button. Choose it and voila! You've made your first edit in sequence. You can play it and watch it in your record viewer.

Now you have an unlabeled sequence. Actually, the system gives it a label like *Untitled Sequence 1*. Label it yourself. Right away! Type in a short, descriptive name such as *Act1 Cut1, Reel 5 Cut 4, Sc56 C2, Widget Spot 30" V2,* (or better, to save space and enable full label viewing, *Wdgt30" V2*). Label every cut with a unique, descriptive name so you can easily locate it and know what it contains. Make labels succinct, leaving out spaces where you can, and be consistent. If you're swapping or passing on cuts to others, add your initials, e.g., *ADK022912gc,* so everyone knows whom to contact.

Exactly how you label sequences will depend on the convention where you work and the type of project you're working on: doc, drama, music video, web series, etc. Never label anything final. You end up with too many final-final-final versions. Type in the date, and if necessary the time of day.

> *We have one simple rule: Never label anything FINAL! That's the kiss of death. Call it final and you can bet your life that it won't be!*
>
> — MARK RAUDONIS, VP of Post Production, Bunim-Murray Productions

## The time line

A distinguishing feature of every digital system, the time line is a horizontal bar graph of all the edits in your sequence. It reads left to right, from your first edit to your last. Each bar of the graph — called tracks, channels, or strips — represents a video or audio series of edits. You can also label tracks, for instance narration, music, SFX1, dialogue 2, etc. Each edit within a track carries its clip name, e.g., "CU-Jose," "Honolulu Aerial 5," "firecracker SFX," etc., and can display a photo of the clip if you select that setting.

**8.b** Time line on Final Cut Pro. Notice the playhead in the middle and that there is a thumbnail frame at the head of each video cut in the two video (upper) tracks.

The time line is a map to your sequence; knowing how to navigate it is part of operating an editing system. A vertical bar — variously referred to as the locator bar, strip indicator, or playhead — bisects the time line and shows you which frame you're parked on in your sequence. Drag this bar on the time line to locate the head of your sequence, the tail of your sequence, or any place in between.

The record viewer shows you visually where you are in your cut sequence; the time line shows you graphically. It also displays the in and out marks you made on the record viewer and can hold a variety of frame rates: 23.97, 24, 29.97, 30 fps, etc., and formats: HD, SD, DSLR, film, etc., as Figure 8.c demonstrates.

**8.c** Time line with mixed formats. *Photo courtesy of Avid.*

## TIME LINE EDITING

To make edits and VFX and perform the countless actions necessary to create your sequence on a digital system, you will click or drag on marks, buttons, icons, tools on the time line, press keys, or choose commands from a menu. Most systems — notably Adobe Premiere Pro and Final Cut Pro — permit you to skip marking and manipulate the time line to make the majority of your edits. You do this by dragging shots to the time line from a bin or the source viewer or dropping and dragging shots within the time line itself. You can also import shots directly into the time line and import time lines from other systems and manufacturers. These are fast ways to rough in material and fine cut it. Increasingly — due to technical advances — you can edit a clip on the time line before it is finished being ingested.

Time line editing uses few or no marks, or substitutes the vertical bar for a mark. You may choose to edit this way primarily. However, it's helpful to know how to cut with marks as you'll definitely use them to measure segments, acts, and scenes as well as to speed up or slow down sections of your sequence. You may also find them useful when dealing with complex edits, especially during recutting and in a myriad of other editing tasks. Additionally, understanding marks helps you grasp basic editing principles.

## Two-, three-, and four-point edits

### THREE-POINT EDIT

Let's mark a second edit. Begin by moving to the tail of your first edit in your sequence in the record viewer. Your locator bar will be at the end of the time line. This is where you will add your next clip. Now do the following:

1. Make an IN mark. You've now told the system where to start the next edit in your sequence.
2. Go to your source viewer and decide on your second clip by again playing and auditioning clips. Make an IN mark at the in point and an OUT mark at the out point.

Thinking of these marks as points, you now have three points:

▶ The sequence has one point, which is the mark IN at the in point.
▶ The new clip in the source viewer has two points: the mark IN at the in point and the mark OUT at the out point.

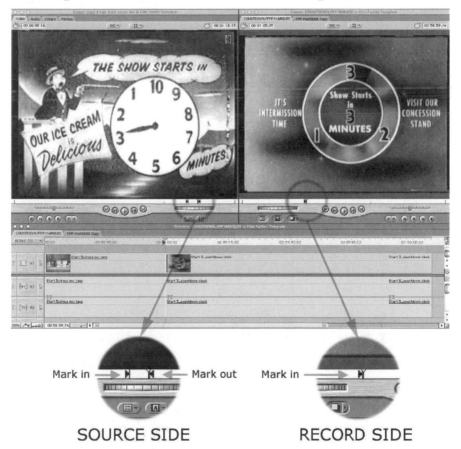

**8.d** A three-point edit. The play head is to the left of the mark out on the source side and the right of the mark in on record viewer. The time line reflects record viewer with play head and mark in. *Photo courtesy of Chris Senchack.*

227

In order to make a cut, the most you need are three points. This is true for all editing, whether you're working on film or a digital system. The new clip, because it has two of the three points, governs the edit's duration. You can mark the two points on the new clip and one point on the sequence or vice versa. Sometimes the sequence will determine the in and out points and therefore the duration, and other times the new clip will determine them.

**EXAMPLES:**

*Sequence decides three-point edit*
While a scientist describes the space shuttle launch, you want to cut away to a clip of the shuttle. You let the speaker's line(s) about the shuttle determine the in point and the out point.

*Clip decides three-point edit*
The shuttle clip is shorter than the scientist's words so its duration determines the in point and the out point.

## Two-point edit

Actually, you need only two points to make an edit. To make a two-point edit:

▶ Make an IN point on your new clip.
▶ Make an IN point on your sequence or if your system allows, place your locator bar where you want the new clip to go.

What you have now is a two-point edit that is an open-ended edit; it has no out point. The digital system will put the clip in from the in point to the end of the clip (where you stopped inputting the shot).

All edits on all systems require two points. Otherwise you do not have enough information to execute the edit on film, tape, or a digital system. Two-point edits are usually made when you're assembling your first cut and don't want to think about your out point. Later in the chapter when we discuss splice and replace, you'll realize why you seldom use a two-point edit during recutting.

## Four-point edit = Two in marks and two out marks

This is a "no-no."

Think about it. If both the new clip and the sequence have an IN mark and an OUT mark, you have two durations. Which one is right? As the editor you must know which is correct and remove the unnecessary fourth point: in mark or out mark.

In reality most digital systems will make a four-point edit; they'll just ignore the OUT mark on the new clip. If this isn't what you want, your sequence will gain an edit you didn't intend. The solution is to hit undo; every digital system has an easy undo icon or button. An undo command takes you back to where you were before you made the unintended edit. Examine the edit to figure out which of the four marks to remove.

### One-point edit

You will always have an in point (via mark or locator bar) on your time line. If you have no marks on your clip, the digital system will simply put the entire clip into your sequence.

## How a clip goes into a sequence: Insert and Overwrite

Once you've marked a clip, there are actually two ways to add it to a sequence. Different systems use different terms for these two methods but they all mean the same thing. We'll use the two most common terms: *insert* and *overwrite*. You will immediately see on the time line what happens when you make an insert and overwrite edit. We'll begin with two clips on the time line and concentrate on the video (top) track as illustrated below in Figure 8.e.

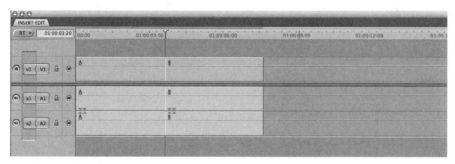

**8.e** Here is the time line with clips A and B on the video (top) track. Figures 8.f and 8.g are based on 8.e.

*Insert edit* (Figure 8.f): When you insert clip C between clip A and clip B, clip B (and all edits to the right) gets pushed down. Your show *gains time* for the amount of clip C's duration.

**8.f** Insert edit: This is the time line after clip C is inserted between clips A and B. Notice that clip B has moved down in the time line and that there is less space at the end of the time line.

*Overwrite edit* (Figure 8.g): When you overwrite clip C between clip A and clip B, B gets partially covered up by C. Your show *does not gain or lose time*. If clip C is the same length as the following clip — clip B in this case — it will be replaced entirely. If clip C is longer, then clip B and part or all of the following clips will be replaced, depending on the duration of all the clips.

**8.g** Overwrite edit: This time clip C is added by overwriting it between clips A and B: Clip B is shorter at the head because it has been partially overwritten by the tail of clip C. Note that the space at the end of the time line is the same as in Figure 8.e since no time has been added to the cut.

Table 8.1 summarizes the properties and uses of insert and overwrite edits.

**TABLE 8.1**
**INSERT AND OVERWRITE EDITS**

| | IN A NUTSHELL | EQUIVALENT TO: | USE IT WHEN | PITFALLS |
|---|---|---|---|---|
| **INSERT** | You *add* a clip and time to your sequence when you make an insert edit. Your show's TRT increases by the amount of your clip's duration. Edits (clips) to the right get pushed down the time line. | • Inserting a word on a computer.<br>• Splicing a piece of film into a reel.<br>• Rippling the list in online. | –You don't want to affect the clips on either side of the place you're inserting the new clip.<br>–Making changes to a sequence.<br>–Building your first sequence. | *1) Inserting video without audio.* This adds time to your video track only and will cause your audio to go out of sync.<br>*2) Insert audio without video.* This adds time to your audio track only and will cause your video to go out of sync. |
| **OVERWRITE** | When you make an overwrite edit, the new clip totally or partially replaces the following clip(s). Time stays the same typically. | • Overwriting a word on a computer.<br>• Replacing picture or track in film. | –You want to replace a clip.<br>–Making video-only edits.<br>–Adding music, sound effects, or any other audio-only media. | Replacing clips unintentionally. |

# Cutting in video or audio only and not going out of sync

Often you will cut video and audio independently. These edits are known as video- and audio-only edits. Creating a video-only edit is the way you usually cut in reaction shots and replace video. For example, you would make a video-only edit to create a montage to music, replace a temp visual effect with a new effect, or substitute one close-up take for another. An audio only edit allows you to add narration, sound effects, or music to an already edited picture montage, or replace a line of dialogue or narration.

## *Cutting in video only*

Let's say a former member of the Blood gang is speaking about how she now has a boyfriend who's a member of the Crip gang and you want to cut away to the boyfriend while she's talking. You've already cut her dialogue and picture so all you need to do is cut away to him. You will make a three-point, video-only edit using overwrite by marking in and out on the sequence in the record viewer. Here's how to proceed:

1. Mark the clips.

   a) On the Source viewer: Mark IN on the first frame of the boy-friend's clip.

   b) On the sequence in the Record viewer:

   Mark IN on the first frame you want to see the boyfriend.

   Mark OUT on the frame you want to see the speaker again.

2. On the Record viewer: Check your sequence's tracks.

   a) Make sure Video 1 is ON (selected).

   b) Make sure all other video and audio tracks are OFF (de-selected).

3. Choose overwrite to make the video-only edit.

Figure 8.h illustrates the results of your video-only edit.

**8.h** A video-only cutaway from the documentary mini-series *Brick City.*

## Cutting in audio only

This time you've cut a series of tsunami clips together. You've received the recorded narration recounting the perils of hurricanes and want to cut it in. Again you will make a three-point edit using overwrite except this time it will be audio-only. Here's the drill:

1. Mark the clips

   a. On the Source viewer: Mark IN on the first frame of the narration.

   b. On the sequence in the Record viewer:

   Mark IN on the first frame you want to hear the narration.

   Mark OUT on the frame the narration ends.

**2.** On the Record viewer: Check your sequence's tracks.

a. Make sure Audio 1 (or Audio 2 or 3 or whichever track you're designating for narration) is ON (selected).

b. Make sure all other video and audio tracks are OFF (de-selected).

**3.** Choose overwrite to make the audio-only edit.

### Pitfalls of adding video- or audio-only edits

Going out of sync. Going out of sync. Going out of sync. Did I mention going out of sync? Always select and de-select your tracks carefully and check the edit afterwards so you won't "throw yourself out of sync" as it's called. If you do make a mistake, undo the edit, make the correction, and redo it.

## Going Out of Sync

You usually go out of sync because you insert or delete a clip accidentally on some tracks and not others. You'll know you're out of sync when:

- A person's lips move but do not match their words.
- Giraffes lope across the frame while the narrator yaks about orangutans.
- Edits no longer hit the beats of the music as they used to.
- The time line no longer lines up and your system's indicators show you're out of sync.

To stay in sync be vigilant as you cut. Should you go out of sync and UNDO doesn't fix the problem, follow this procedure:

- Make a copy of your current edit before fixing it, in case you get yourself into worse trouble.
- Calmly recall the last time you were in sync and remember what you've edited since then.
- Play your edit to find exactly where it goes out of sync.
- Determine what's out: video or audio.
- Use the time line's out-of-sync indicators to help locate and solve the problem. Notice if the indicators all register the same number of frames so that one adjustment in the right place will fix everything.
- Use the system's fix sync or trim function to put your sequence back in sync.
- Make sure the fix does not put anything else out of sync. If it does, re-evaluate the problem before continuing.

### *Going out of sync on purpose*

Actually, it's okay to be out of sync — as long as you realize what you're doing and are in control. Every editor throws their cut out of sync on purpose at times just as paradoxically, every editor dreads going out of sync unknowingly. For instance, on the first cut of a documentary, trailer, or other piece not wholly tied to dialogue or narration, editors frequently build the audio track without worrying about keeping it in sync. They add the video later and put everything in sync then. Most cuts will have parts that are in sync and those that are deliberately out of sync, so, to save time and headache, always be conscious of sync — what's in and what's out.

## Cutting Visual Effects (VFX)

*"Visual effects are just another way of creating film for me to cut. We're used to having the film shot on the set, processed and sent to the editing room and that's it. In the visual effects world, that's just the beginning of making the shot. Instead of the shot being made in one day, it might be made in anywhere from one month to one year. Visual effects are just a tool the same as making a decision to shoot with a Steadicam or on a dolly…One of the nice things is that it allows post to be involved in creating the shot."*

—ZACH STAENBERG, A.C.E., *The Matrix* (all three films) and *Gotti*

Making dissolves, fades, and other effects can add zing to your film or video and bolster your story's purpose. Some shows exhibit effects so stunningly original that they ignite a creative revolution and make their designer the unsung auteur (author) of the film. Conversely, many effects go unheralded — such as wire removals (painting out wires used to make actors fly) and composites, e.g., adding or subtracting buildings from landscapes — but they contribute mightily to the film just the same.

Like many digital terms, VFX has evolved from a film term (optical), has other abbreviations (EFX, FX, or F/X), and has definitions that vary, depending on where you're working: cutting room, post house, or special effects house. For our purposes, VFX will stand for all effects, no matter how simple or complex.

## *Categories of VFX*

VFXs can be categorized by the time and money they suck up:

1. Simple VFX
   - Include transitions, flips, and filters.
   - Most common.
   - Easily created on the digital system by the editor.
2. Complex VFX
   - Layered, consisting of two or more shots, and perhaps some text and a dissolve or superimposition.[1]
   - May involve key frames. Motion effect example: You want a ball (or other) object to move within a shot. For each place you want the ball to move, set a key frame so that it will follow your desired path of motion.
   - Editor creates on the system or by using Adobe After Effects (AE), Boris (Avid FX), or other motion graphics software and imports into editing system.
   - May be outsourced to the post house (wire removal and other routine VFX) or to the VFX house (original, more involved VFX).
3. Super complex VFX
   - Combine many types of effects.
   - Can include live shots, 3-D, CGI, and animation.
   - Created at VFX house by a team of artists, craftspeople, and editors on AE, Combustion, Flame, Maya, or other compositing, motion graphics, or 3-D animation software.

Table 8.2 describes the many types of VFX.

---

1. A superimposition (*super*) is a long dissolve where one shot lingers, superimposed over another.

## TABLE 8.2
## TYPES OF VFX

| TYPE | DESCRIPTION | EXAMPLE |
|---|---|---|
| **TRANSITION** | Shift from one shot to the next without using a cut. | Dissolve, wipe, fade-in, fade-out, or white-out.* |
| **VARISPEED** | Alter the frame rate of a shot by slo mo-ing it, speeding it up, or reversing it. | Reversing the action so that a car squeals to a stop before hitting the baby instead of moving backwards from the baby as filmed.** |
| **FLOP, A.K.A. MIRROR** | Rotate the shot horizontally. | Correcting a POV error: The boy now looks from right to left instead of left to right. |
| **FLIP** | Rotating the shot vertically. | A girl standing on her feet now stands on her head. |
| **REPO** | Reposition an object within a frame by moving the object or the frame. | Adjusting a target so it's at the correct angle to get hit by projectiles. |
| **RESIZE** | Change the size of an object or the entire image within the frame by enlarging or shrinking it. | A blow-up. |
| **COLOR OR TEXTURE** | Change the color or texture of a shot. | Making a scene black-and-white or sepia to reflect the past. |
| **MATTE, A.K.A. KEY** | Cut a hole in a shot and place (key) another shot in that hole. | The witch, chickens, etc. Dorothy sees through her window during the cyclone in *The Wizard of Oz*. |
| **MOTION** | Moving an object within a frame by setting it on a path, and/or by making it spin, rotate or become animated in some fashion. | An object such as a book, arrow, or a title moves through a frame. |
| **COMPOSITE** | Merge two or more shots — referred to as layers — together. | Giant spiders (shot 1) attack the White House (shot 2). |
| **GREEN (OR BLUE) SCREEN, A.K.A. CHROMA KEY** | Composite two shots by keying the foreground shot (subject) over the background shot (green or blue screen). | Weather reporter (subject) points to the approaching cold front on the map (background). |
| **ROTOSCOPE** | Create animation imagery or mattes frame by frame via tracing or otherwise referencing live footage to create new images or repair images. | Light sabers in three original *Star Wars* movies. *A Scanner Darkly* — entire movie. |
| **CGI** | Computer generated imagery. Digital effects created on computers that compose an ever-growing array of visual possibilities for both animated and live-action footage. | *The Matrix* films (morphing, i.e., shape changing) and *The Curious Case of Benjamin Button* and *Avatar* (performance capture). |
| **3-D** | Blend layers of shots on an XYZ axis into one shot so it appears to have three dimensions: height, width, and depth. | *Clash of the Titans* (live action) and *Rango* (animation). |

* When a shot dissolves or cuts to white instead of black, it's called a white-out.
** When reversing a shot, always be aware of lettering on signs, shirts, etc., as letters will read backwards.

# Creating VFX

*"With the current advent of computer graphics, anything you can imagine, from the gross to the extremely subtle, is available to you — for a price."*
—FILM GUY from his book *Film Editing Nutz and Boltz*

The creation of VFX follows two main workflows, depending on whether the editor creates them or they are outsourced. We'll cover the editor's responsibilities for each WF.

## 1. Creating VFX on the digital editing system

Until the digital computer age, VFX were called opticals and created by reproducing the film negative and employing an optical printer. Today, film opticals are made using the DI scanning process and optical printers are all but out of commission. Every day, editors are creating all the VFX for their projects right on the digital editing system; knowing how is part of the job description.

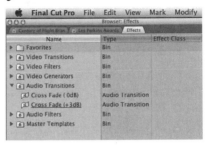

**8.i** The Effects tab on FCP contains bins arranged by type of VFX. The open Audio transitions bin displays two audio crossfade effects.

### REAL TIME AND RENDERED EFFECTS

When you create an effect and can play it back instantly, it is called a real time effect. When an effect can't be played back instantly, you must command the system to render it, that is, create new media for it — so you can play it back. Real-time effects are preferable because you can immediately view them to accept or reject them or determine how to adjust them. System owners frequently add video capture cards such as AJA's Kona or those offered by Matrox and Blackmagic Design to boost processing time and allow for more real-time effects.

Rendering an effect can take seconds, minutes, or longer depending on its complexity. Since rendering eats up time, many editors set their effects to render all at one time, then take a break, checking back periodically to make sure the system didn't hang. Extremely complex effects can take days or weeks to render so they're often sent to the render farm, a roomful of dedicated, networked computers.

**8.j** Building a motion effect. *Photo courtesy of Apple.*

## THE PROCESS

In addition to classroom courses, books, and manuals, there are many tutorials online — free and fee — that detail how to create all types of effects on the widely used editing systems, so we'll just list the four basic steps here.

1. Park your playhead on or near the cut point of the edit where you want to make the effect.
2. From a menu or tab, select the effect or drag it to the time line. You may need to add an extra track beforehand, depending on the type of effect.
3. Render the effect if necessary.
4. View the effect.

Figure 8.k shows five VFX tracks laid out on a time line.

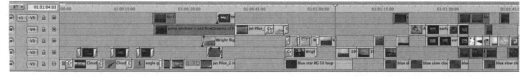

**8.k** Production and green screen background clips on V1 (lowest track) and VFX on V2-V5 tracks.

You can create your own VFX for reuse by labeling them and saving them as favorites. Many editors copy a bin of favorites to a disk or drive and take them from project to project.

## GREEN SCREEN

Green screens have become common effects because they save the expense of going on location. Commonly the editor creates a garbage matte — Figure 8.m below — as part of the process of creating a green screen shot. This rough matte helps remove garbage (undesirable elements such as wires or models). It also helps retain parts of images such as light spills that the green screen might obliterate. Figures 8.l through 8.n show the main steps.

**8.l** Here's the original shot ingested from production with the subject in the foreground and the green screen in the background.

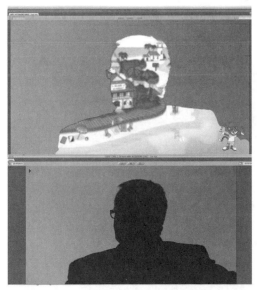

**8.m** You add a matte on two different V tracks in order to precisely cut out the subject in the foreground V2 (top frame) against the background V1 (bottom frame).

**8.n** Next, you bring the subject back in and check it against a black background (top frame). Finally, you key out the black background with your desired background (bottom frame).

## 2. Creating VFX at the post house or VFX house

*"I receive the script, which I break down into VFX shots. I determine how the elements of each shot will be made…With the help of production coordinators I track each shot. I know how much each shot costs and the schedule for completing each shot."*

—MICKEY McGOVERN, VFX producer and editor, *Forrest Gump, Star Wars* episodes 5 and 6, *Contact, Speed*

When an effect is outsourced, editorial's job is to assist the post or VFX house.

1. To start, ask them what their requirements are. For instance, they may specify a certain file format or VFX numbering scheme.
2. Write a precise description of the effect — what it should look like, its frame rate, etc. It's commonplace for editors to create the effect on their system and send a dub for reference.
3. Provide them with all the data — time code, tape reel, etc. (tape shows) camera roll, keycode, etc. (film shows) — necessary to create the effect. Your system's tape EDL tool or film cutlist tool can help you generate this data. Alternatively, you can use FileMaker Pro or another database program, or the post house or VFX house may provide you with their own data form.
4. Send over the media (tape or film shows) or file (tapeless show) to make the effect.

**8.0** Editing VFX at a post house. Notice storyboard of VFX on cards pinned to bulletin board. *Photo courtesy of AlphaDogs.*

5. During the development phases, as the effect goes back and forth between the cutting room and the post or VFX house, keep everyone in the loop with regular status reports.

6. Edit the final VFX into the show.

# Trimming

Trimming has both a broad and narrow definition. The narrow definition, derived from film, means adjusting an edit by removing frames, shortening it as opposed to extending it by adding frames. Some digital systems define trimming more broadly as adjusting an edit by shortening, extending, slipping, or sliding it. It's vital to be able to trim because you'll be making a lot of changes to your sequence from first cut to final to hone the edits exactly the way you want them. A word of warning: When trimming, you need to remain hyper vigilant of sync and maintain the sync relationships on all tracks. If you're only trimming one track — say audio — make sure video and other audio tracks are not adversely affected.

## Deleting and filling

Cutting off frames to shorten an edit — deleting — is the most common form of trimming. Deleting is simple, particularly when you have a straight cut[2]. Once you've made the deletion, check the time line and play the edit to make sure it's correct. You can also take frames out of an edit and replace them with black frames. This is called slugging, adding fill, or filling. Sometimes you slug so you can place and time a shot you haven't yet received such as an effect or stock shot.

## Opening up a shot and using the trim function

You can make simple trims by manipulating the edit on the time line, selecting an icon, menu, button, or a tool (ripple or roll on FCP), or pressing a key on your keyboard. There are times, however, when you want to open up an edit and examine it closely to refine it. This calls for using your system's trim mode, a.k.a. trim view.

Trim mode lets you work with the A side (the outgoing clip) and the B side (the incoming clip) of your edit at the same time. When you enter trim mode, you'll notice that your source and record viewers disappear. Now you'll see two graphic viewers with different selections below

---

2. A cut where A and V tracks are positioned at the same place in the time line.

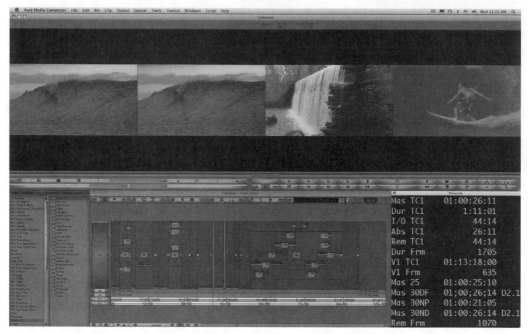

**8.p** Trim view displays the head and tail frames on the A side – two identical wide shots of a surfer at sunset in the sea – and the head and tail frames on the B side – a waterfall and medium wide shot of a different surfer. Notice that video track on time line is enlarged and locator bar is near the center. *Photo courtesy of Avid.*

them. The left viewer displays the A side of your edit; the right viewer displays the B side.

As you move through the edit, the A side and/or the B side move in the viewers. Play around until you're clear on what's happening and you've trimmed the clips the way you want. You can then preview the new edit. Once you're satisfied with it, exit trim function. The viewers revert to source and record viewers and the time line updates, confirming the changes you've made.

# Slip-sliding around

Slip and slide are two common ways to trim edits that do not change the duration of a cut. When you slip an edit, it changes *internally*. When you slide and edit, it changes *externally*, taking place earlier or later in the sequence.

## Slip

You slip an edit to move its starting frame, thereby affecting its ending frame. Select the head of the edit if you wish to decide by the first frame; the tail of the edit to decide by its last frame. For instance if you slip the head of a two-second edit so it begins 20 frames *later*, the tail of the edit will also slip 20 frames so it ends 20 frames *later*. Similarly, if you slip the tail of the edit by beginning it 15 frames *earlier*, the head of the edit will automatically begin 15 frames *earlier*. In both cases the edit remains two seconds long. You can slip video and audio together or separately. The following examples clarify how and why you slip an edit.

### SLIPPING VIDEO AND AUDIO

*Problem*: Your edit shows the monkey scampering up into a tree and starting to swing into the foliage. You want to begin the edit with the swing and see the monkey fly from tree to tree.

*Solution*: Slip the head of the shot so that it starts when the monkey swings.

### SLIPPING VIDEO

*Problem*: The audio (to a song) on the edit is fine. The picture edit, however, shows dancers dancing in a circle, raising their hands together, then circling again. You want the picture edit to end with their hands raised.

*Solution*: Slip video at the tail of the edit so that it ends earlier with the dancers' hands raised.

### SLIPPING AUDIO: TWO EVERYDAY EXAMPLES

1. Slipping narration

   *Problem*: The narration upcuts (cuts off) the first syllable of the narrator's first word.

   *Solution*: Slip the audio a few frames at the head. This keeps the narration in the same place in relation to the video but now you don't clip the first syllable.

2. Slipping audio out of sync

   *Problem*: You've cut in a sync A and V clip of a group of cyclists racing. At the end of the clip is the unwanted sound of a car horn honking.

   *Solution*: Slip the audio at the tail of the edit so it ends before the honk. Now the clip plays naturally and you don't hear the extraneous noise, even though it's technically out of sync.

## Slide

Sliding an edit means that you adjust its position in the sequence by moving it up or down. You can see this occur graphically on the time line. The preceding edit gets shorter if you slide an edit up (forward/to the left in the time line) while the following edit (afterward/to the right in the time line) gets longer by the same number of frames. Often you slide a video edit or a group of video edits to reposition them against a bed of music or narration. Or you cut the music or narration in and slide it into position.

## Pulling up and pushing down

If you slip, slide, or trim an edit so it starts sooner or later, you are pulling it up or pushing it down the time line, respectively. You routinely pull up or push down an edit to hit a music beat or match the narration better. For instance if you delete or tighten narration, you will have to pull up the video so it matches. Conversely if you extend or add narration, you will have to push down the video so it matches.

## Overlapping

You overlap clips by manipulating the time line or accessing the trim function. Start by making a straight cut for audio or video. Returning to the Tony and Maria example from Chapter 6, this means you've straight cut their lines together so he proposes marriage and she answers. Now you want to overlap the second part of his line (A side) on her (B side) so the audience takes in her reaction.

You can do this by adjusting the time line, but to hear and see the overlap while you make it, go into trim view. Before you do, turn *on* the track you wish to overlap, which in this case is the video; turn *off* the track with the straight cut — the audio track in this case — so it remains unchanged. Once in trim view, select the mode that makes the cut interactive, i.e., what you add to the A side gets subtracted from

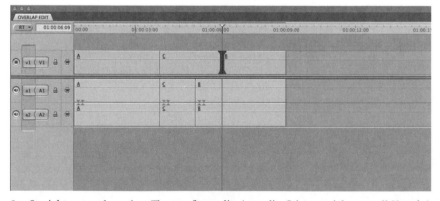

**8.q** Straight cut and overlap. The cut from clip A to clip C is a straight cut; all V and A tracks line up. The cut from C to B on V1 (top track) — indicated by a dark area and the position of the playhead — is an overlap; C's picture track extends beyond its audio track and overlaps B.

the B side and vice versa. You want to see Maria before she speaks so add frames to the head of her shot, which is the B side. Preview and adjust the overlap until you're satisfied, then exit trim view and check your edit.

Since 80% of the overlaps you make will be like this one — making the audio straight cut, then overlapping the video — it's a good idea to practice making them on each new digital system you learn. Take a scene and overlap every edit. This will help cement your knowledge of overlaps and the system.

### Changing and deleting VFX

To change an effect, you can trim it, slip or slide it, or build upon it by putting another effect on another track above it. To extend an effect's duration, you will need to remake it. If you're making changes to a rendered effect, you'll need to delete it and then remake it. Deleting an effect is like deleting any other edit; you can undo if you just made it or you can select it and use mouse or keyboard to delete it.

## Moving and Copying Edits

There are times, especially when recutting, that you'll want to move an edit around in your sequence or copy it to another place. Here are a couple of examples:

*Move scenario*: You want to change the order of clips in your bird montage from flamingo, heron, kingfisher to kingfisher, flamingo, heron.
*Copy scenario*: You put in the sound effect of a phone ringing in one scene and you want to copy it to another scene.

### How to move or copy

There are two basic methods, each of which can be performed by making an insert or overwrite edit.

1. Move or copy via a clipboard
   This is analogous to cut and paste on any computer. You send a marked shot or part of a sequence to the clipboard and then drop it in the cut where you want.
2. Move or copy by dragging in the time line
   With the mouse you select and drag the edit(s) that you wish to move or copy to a different place on the time line.

# Determining the Duration of Clip, Scene, or Show

At different junctures during editing you'll want to know the duration of a clip, scene, or show. For instance, when you're recutting a show that's "over time" (longer than the allotted time), and looking to eliminate shots and scenes, it's helpful to know how long they are. Measuring is easy: Mark IN at the head of the scene or section you want to measure and mark OUT at the tail. This duration will appear on the time line. To find the TRT (total running time) of your show, look at your time line; the figure will be above or below it, depending on the system. You can also use your calculator or the system's to calculate how many hours, minutes, and seconds your video is or how many feet and frames your film is.

# Protecting Your Work and Maintaining the System

Saving your work is part of the job, just as it is on any computer. In this section we'll go over what to back up and when. But first, one more plug for top notch labeling and organization: They will aid retrieval of your work should you need to call on your backups.

## Saving sequences

The ability to make different versions of a sequence (or sections of a sequence) is one of the huge benefits of editing on a digital system. Preserve every version of a cut. Do not recut over the same version: It takes but a nanosecond to make a new version.

Create a new version:

- ▸ Every time you recut a show.
- ▸ When experimenting with a scene, especially if your changes are complicated. This way, if you don't like the changes, you can go back to the old version.
- ▸ Before you combine audio tracks or mix them down (combine the level and perform other adjustments) for a screening. You may use the uncombined tracks version for recutting.
- ▸ To prevent edit file corruption, particularly with a long, complex cut.
- ▸ Before you copy sections from old cuts to new cuts.

Most systems regularly save your sequences to a system-designated space on the internal hard drive (the *attic* on Avid and the *autosave vault* on FCP) so you can retrieve your sequence from a few hours ago. Do not depend on these features. They may bring back only part of your sequence or miss the period when your sequence was in decent shape. Make it a habit to save your project to a local drive and safeguard your work.

## Saving your project: Lunch and leave

You can set your system to autosave your project every so many minutes but you should also save it manually yourself on a daily basis. To do this, make sure everything in your project is located in one folder, then save the folder to an external drive twice every day; at lunch and when you leave for the night. Conscientious editors and assistants save to two drives and take one home. Power outages, natural disasters, burglaries, and accidents can and have destroyed cutting rooms: Backups can and have saved the day.

## Saving media

Since drives normally don't lose media, most editors don't go to the time and expense of backing up their media files. If you lose media, you will re-ingest or re-import it and then re-link it to your clips and sequences. Remember, the internal hard drive holds the data files, including clips and sequences: Once they're re-linked to the media you will hear and see your show and be back in business. The exception: Tapeless shows. The card or hard drive that ushered in the media is reusable, so once it's ingested, the media is deleted and the card/drive whisked back out to the production crew. For this reason it's crucial that you save the original files to a back-up drive before renaming or copying them anywhere on your system.

## Saving SFX, MX, and VFX

The day of the rough cut with minimal sound and music and no VFX is gone with the wind, er, whoosh of the Moviola pedal. Today's editor is expected to deliver a full-blown cut, tricked out with tracks of sound, music, and effects which may lack time code. The result? Many editors build up libraries of SFX, VFX, and MX which of course they protect with regular back-ups.

On episodic shows for web and TV, you'll have stock shots, logos, and other shots that you regularly insert into episodes which also may not have time code. Back up the metadata and the media for all these periodically to save the hassle of locating and reproducing them should they be lost. Also, back up the user settings you've created (computer instructions about how you like your editing desktop arranged, bins to open up, time line setup, etc.) so you can cart them from project to project.

## Crashes and freezes: Troubleshooting your system

The longer you work on a system, the savvier you'll become at dealing with its quirks and issues. From the start, beginning with your training, ask what to do when the system acts up. When you encounter something you can't handle, ask other editors, talk to the technician at the company that rented you the system, or call the technical help line for the system. Stay calm. Remember what you were doing and the steps that led up to it when the system got hung up. If an error message flashed on the screen, write it down. If you've received a new software version and suddenly a function isn't working, there may be a bug and the tech may have a workaround for you. In any case, remember: the problem will be resolved and you will get through it. Regular backups will help ensure that you don't lose too much work.

## Dealing with new software versions

*"Coming to grips with new techniques and features is a constant and never-ending process. You now face an everyday choice of whether to exchange the power of the newest and the fastest for the comfort of the familiar."*

—STEVE BAYES, editor and Avid trainer/consultant from his book *The Avid Handbook*

In order to be cutting edge, competitive, and solvent, digital editing system manufacturers are forever bringing out upgrades and new software versions. You barely do a job on one software version and lo and behold there's another version with the latest, coolest features to learn. When should you jump to the next version and when should you stick with what you've got? Consider these five points, based on many editors' experiences, before you decide:

1. DO keep up on your system's current software version as well as what's coming down the pike by talking to trusted postproduction friends, attending user group meetings, and visiting online sites.

2. DON'T change software versions in the middle of a project unless the new software version is merely a bug fix, absolutely compatible with all software you're using, and can be integrated swiftly. Remember, your mission is to deliver a well-edited show on time,

not be behind because you want to try out the latest, greatest software. Play with it after the project.

3. DO upgrade if you are convinced after polling your trusted peeps that the upgrade will get your dead or ailing system up and running again.

4. DON'T change unless the new software has features you need on your project and until you've heard from editors who have worked with it about its reliability.

5. DO take a hint from digital editing system rental companies: When a new software version comes out they don't rush to install it on every machine. Instead they install it on a few machines and have editors expert in the previous versions work with it. These editors can be counted on to learn, explain, experiment with, and document the good features and the bad. Frequently they discover new ways of working — as well as bugs that the manufacturer wasn't even aware of — and pass them on to everyone.

## Becoming a great media manager

Media management is a huge and ever-evolving part of postproduction. As your show progresses, media builds up on the external drives as you:

- Ingest dailies, stock shots, and VFX.
- Import graphics, music, and SFX.
- Render effects (called precomputes on Avid).
  - The rendered media is not deleted when you delete the rendered effect so you must use your system's media management tool to get rid of it.

You need to keep on top of the amount of media stored on your drives so they don't become overloaded and accessing footage becomes dicey. The best way to manage media is to:

- Organize your drives for the way you will access and edit the footage.
- Anticipate storage needs: Leave room for uprezzing, color grading, VFX, stock shots, and other additional, post-shoot footage.
- Delete footage that was input incorrectly or will never be used.
- Consolidate[3] media when circumstances call for it.

---

3. When you command a system to consolidate, it makes new clips (data files and media) of the edits in your sequence. For example, a two-minute clip, which is a five-second edit in your sequence, will consolidate to a new clip five seconds long. (You can add handles for trimming the edit of up to two seconds at both head and tail.) Consolidating initially creates more media but then allows you to delete the original (old) clips and media off your drives. Consolidate only when a show is locked or close to lock since once it's consolidated, you won't have access to all the footage (unless you re-ingest it).

Most systems have a tool or utility to aid you, e.g., Render Manager on FCP and Media tool on Avid. Your best strategy, however, depends on you, not the system. This means labeling clips, sequences, bins, reels, and projects and properly organizing your projects and media on drives. In other words, knowing where everything lives on your system will go a long way toward managing your media and projects. It also means keeping transparent records, communicating clearly with everyone involved with the project, knowing your media's parameters (aspect ratio, frame rate and size, codec, and audio sampling rate, etc.), and understanding how to and why to link and unlink media. Last, media management comes into play when you need to move or copy your project to another system and when the show's finished and you're wrapping it for the future. Which brings us neatly to archiving, this chapter's final topic.

## Archiving

Television news networks, with a ton of media arriving daily, delegate a media manager whose job it is to set up the computers to automatically delete media on a daily basis as well as archive it to their massive archive systems. Likewise, episodic TV shows worry about archiving with an eye to audience and monetizing. They ask, "How will we guarantee future generations can see *Roots* or *The Simpsons*?" Documentarians depend on archival footage to create their shows. So what are the solutions? While there can be no set rules since media formats and technologies will continue to change, here are some guidelines.

### SAVING PROJECTS

Save your project files with all their metadata about clips, sequences, etc., to CD, DVD, or similar small storage format. This makes it possible to re-create your show at any time by copying it to a digital editing system, then recapturing and re-linking the time coded media.

### SAVING MEDIA

Safely archive all physical source media: tapes, film negative, DI, etc. Save non-time coded media (such as graphics and files you created on the computer) to CD, DVD, hard disk, or a similar storage format. If you need to store media long term and fear it will become obsolete, copy the footage to new formats as they become commonplace. This requires time, vigilance, money, and an evaluation of the significance of your footage. Broadcast networks, studios, and post facilities are gravitating to LTO (linear tape-open), a magnetic tape technology, because it can holds terabytes of media on a single tape cartridge.

From all this, you may conclude, rightly, that there is not a perfect long-term solution. Archiving continues to require thought, preparation, and technical advances, so be aware and keep informed.

## CHAPTER WRAP-UP

Now that you're grounded in how to edit and trim a show on a digital system and manage its media, it's time to put the whole editing process together. Chapter 9: The Process: Moving from First Cut to Locked Show does just that.

CHAPTER 9

# The Process

*Getting from First Cut to Locked Cut*

## Overview

This chapter is divided into the four steps you'll take to go from finishing and screening your first cut to finalizing and locking your show:

1. Preparing for the screening
2. The screening
3. Recutting
4. Locking the show

In addition, the chapter spotlights how editors collaborate with directors and other editors. Let's get rolling!

## STEP 1: PREPARING FOR THE SCREENING

There are a number of things that you'll want to do to make your cut shine before screening it for others. These include: dropping in stock shots, adding music, smoothing out the sound, and writing up a continuity sheet. We'll go over all of them momentarily, but to start, a few words on rough cuts.

The first time a show is edited and screened it's called the First Cut, or the Editor's Cut (contractually required on a union show). The first cut is also commonly referred to as the rough cut. Editors have never considered their work "rough" as they have always worked hard to perfect character, story, action, and dialogue to make the smoothest, best cut. The first cut *is* rough in the sense that it lacks final VFX, stock footage, titles, and the sound mix. But this is true of every cut until the show is locked and finished. With digital editing equipment, an unlimited amount of sound and video tracks are available and first cuts are becoming more and more polished.

So to be accurate and respectful, we will call it a first cut.

## Stock shots, slugs, and banners

You need a shot of a New Guinea village at sunset which somehow the crew didn't shoot when on location in Toronto. You contact stock houses or search online to find the shot. They send it to you for approval so it will be low res or have time code and/or text running through it so you can't possibly use it without paying. No problem. Everybody at the screening understands it's temp.

What if the shot doesn't appear in time for your screening? Again, no problem. Slug it — insert black from your system's menu — for the shot's duration so it's included in your show's TRT (total running time). You can even title the slug "stock shot missing" so everyone's clued in about this mysterious black hole in the show. Better yet, drop in a banner. A banner is a placeholder for missing shots with text that announces what footage will be cut in, e.g., "stock shot missing," insert commercial," "insert main title," "scene missing," etc. You can import a bin of banner clips from show to show to save time titling each slug.

## Color grading

When screening your work, you want your audience to focus on the show and not be distracted or confused by any shots, sounds, or scenes. So in advance of the final grading, which follows online at the post house, you may want to use your system's color grader to tweak your cut prior to screening it. For instance, if a scene shot over several days results in a noticeable lighting mismatch, you may decide to make the shots more uniform. Or if a flashback scene is not obvious, you may want to desaturate it (pull its color down) or throw a sepia, B & W (black and white), or other filter on it. Similarly, you may want to filter a death, dream, or fantasy sequence.

The color grading tools on offline editing systems have become so sophisticated lately that many editors use them to do the final color grading themselves. The tools include built-in video scopes for measuring luminance (brightness and contrast), chrominance (color), broadcast acceptability, and other image properties. You can also use these tools to detect problems; then correct them with your system's color corrector filters.

## Adding leaders and pops

Originally part of film syncing practices, leaders and pops have become digital like so many other parts of post and continue to fulfill the same critical sync functions. Before we discuss how and why you add leaders to your show, a few definitions.

### ACADEMY LEADER, a.k.a. SMPTE leader or countdown leader

Leader is a piece of film or tape or a digital clip attached to the head or tail of a show for the purpose of maintaining sync between picture and sound. Head leader counts down from eight to two in less than eight seconds (12 feet) in a clockwise wipe pattern (or sometimes 12 to 2 without the wipe pattern). The last frame of a head leader is the #2 frame which is always followed by the FFOP (first frame of picture). Since there's only one #2 frame, it's a snap to locate. Tail leader runs for a few seconds after LFOP (last frame of picture).

### SYNC POP

A sync pop is a 1,000 Hz beep tone placed on the audio head and tail leader to keep sync during screenings, sound editing, and sound mixing.

### HEAD POP, A.K.A. 2-POP

A head leader always has a sync pop on the audio track aligned with the #2 picture frame which is why it's nicknamed the 2-pop.

**9.a** Head Academy leader on 35mm which digital leader replicates. *Photo courtesy of Chris Senchack.*

**9.b** Tail leader on 16mm which digital leader replicates. *Photo courtesy of Chris Senchack.*

### TAIL POP

This is a sync pop that appears on the audio track two seconds into the tail leader, often corresponding to a flash frame[1] or a frame with the word "End" printed on it.

### ADDING LEADERS AND POPS

Before you go to a screening it's professional practice to add leaders to each reel of your show. For film projection, head and tail leaders are mandatory and unseen by the audience. With digital projection, you can get away without leaders, but putting both leaders on — which your screening audience probably *will* see — gives everyone time to settle in to the show. Digital systems supply virtual leader as part of their output-to-tape function so the leaders won't be on your sequence's time line. Alternatively, you can download leaders from the Web and add them to your time line or create your own. You can copy leaders from one reel to another. Just make sure to put head and tail pops in the right places on the audio tracks!

**9.c** 2-pop frame at end of head leader. *Photo courtesy of Chris Senchack.*

## Cutting in Sound and Music

Editors want their work to sound as well as look the best that it can. For this reason, many cut in sound effects and music to help the director/producer/client better envision the show. Music and sound effects underscore

**9.d** Flash frame is the light frame at the bottom. *Photo courtesy of Chris Senchack.*

your story and add believability to a cut. They also add more tracks which increase your time and labor in updating them and maintaining sync as you make changes during recutting. You need to evaluate how much sound work can be accomplished for each screening. On some shows, you simply won't have the time or budget to do much work; on

---

1. Frame at the end of a take where light entered the film camera when it was stopped between takes.

others, the expectations will run high and you will do some temp mixes in order to preview the show or sell it.

## Types of sound and music to add

To put your best cut forward, include the narration, wild lines, wild track, and sound effects necessary to get the story across.

### SCRATCH TRACK AND NARRATION

To insert scratch track in your cut, plug a mic into your mixer. Some systems allow you to record your voice right into the time line as you play the scene. This is particularly useful to news editors timing the "on air" narration to come. You can also record to a third party software like Audacity and import the files.

**9.e** Adding scratch track with mic and mixer. *Photo courtesy of Chris Senchack.*

### WILD LINES

Wild lines — characters' non-sync lines — are recorded during production and postproduction. These lines of dialogue are usually integrated into the soundtrack during the sound editing phase but you may receive some wild lines or create your own to cut in during the picture editing phase. Wild lines beef up scenes or cover up plot holes, especially those created when scenes or parts of scenes are deleted during editing. Typically, you cut in wild lines on the character's back or over another character so the lack of mouth movement (sync) isn't noticeable. If you land a job on a live action, talking animal picture like *Marmaduke* or *Babe,* a major part of the dialogue will be wild lines!

### SOUND EFFECTS

It's common for an edit to be motivated by a sound effect, for instance, a gunshot causing a crowd to duck. You may want to cut in the sound effect so everyone at the screening can see that the edit works. You can add also specific effects like phone rings, car crashes, and body slams. You'll obtain the effects from sound houses and SFX libraries online or on CD. As picture editor you have neither the time nor the budget to put in all SFX, but adding crucial ones can help sell your cut. Also, if the sound effect will be duplicated in online, you need to label the audio

**9.f** You can activate a waveform overlay on your time line to help finesse audio. Waveforms help you see where SFX and MX clips start, dip, spike, and stop; you will quickly learn to read them. Note the video track: It displays clips of mixed frame rates from different cameras. *Photo courtesy of Avid.*

clip properly and make sure its time code and reel number or other source data get entered into the system.

### WILD TRACK
Sound effects editors use wild track — non-sync, non-dialogue sound the sound recordist snagged on location — to effect the most realistic sounding picture. You may wish to audition and cut in some of the wild track but normally this job is left to the sound editors.

### MUSIC
Editors routinely add music from files or CDs to their digital cuts. Sometimes the music you pick will be used in the final mix but usually it's replaced. If your show has a music composer who was brought on early, you may have some of the real music to cut in. When a scene or a show depends on music, e.g., a musical or music video, you should have the final music from the start. We'll talk more about music editing and design in the next chapter.

# Sound work

### CLEANING AND FILLING TRACKS

Your sync dialogue track, a.k.a. the production track, is the main sound track you'll be working on. You want to make sure your dialogue track (and all tracks) can be heard clearly. This means you want to *clean the tracks* by removing extraneous, unwanted sounds on the track such as dolly squeaks, dish rattles, planes overhead, and the voices of the director, script supervisor, or other crew members.

Where you remove these sounds, you'll hear a drop in the sound which is referred to as a *hole* in the sound or dead sound. It can kill the energy of a scene and distract your screening audience. You need to fill as many of these sound holes as possible with ambient sound. You can usually find ambience within the take; try around the clapper if you don't find it in the body of the take. If this doesn't work, try another take of the same angle and then other takes in the scene until you find a sufficient amount.

Replacing and filling tracks is part of the editor's job — within reason. You won't have time to fill every hole in the track, particularly when the hole's less than a second long. You don't need to fill any spots that will be covered by a music track. Try and fill the obvious holes and the ones that can easily be filled. Frequently you can use a dialogue overlap to cover holes. Bear in mind that filling track is only temporary since all holes will be filled during sound editing and mixing after the cut is locked.

### BALANCING LEVELS AND ADDING AUDIO EFFECTS

Your show will sound amateurish if the dialogue, music, and sounds can't be heard correctly at one volume setting. You can — and should — adjust levels from section to section, shot to shot, and within a shot. When you have several tracks you may need to lower the music or raise the dialogue, etc., to achieve the correct sound. Digital systems are capable of a good amount of high quality sound editing and mixing: Tracks can be panned (placed left or right), EQ'd (bass and treble balanced), and cross-faded. You can also add all sorts of audio effects including reverb (echo), futz (makes dialogue sound like it's coming through a telephone), and varispeed (speeds up or slows down audio).

## LAYING OUT AND MIXING TRACKS

Laying out tracks means ordering them on your time line. Invariably you put the production track on top as it's the first one you'll receive and needs to be the handiest since you'll be working with it the most. Conventionally, editors lay out tracks in this hierarchy:

- Production
- Narration
- SFX
- MX

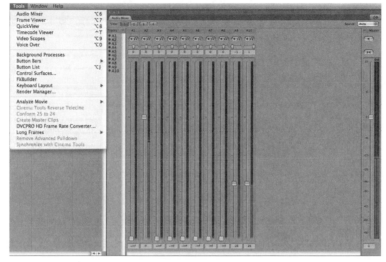

**9.g** Audio mix tool.

So you'll always know where tracks are, choose an order you like and stick with it from show to show. Many systems let you freely color code your audio and video tracks. For example, if you make your music track(s) orange on every show, they will be instantly recognizable to you. Once you've got all the tracks laid out, you can mix them using the digital system internal mixer or your external mixer.

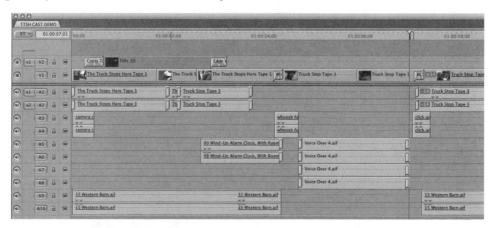

**9.h** Audio tracks laid out on time line.

### OUTPUTTING TRACKS

You can cut as many audio tracks as you'd like but your digital system, mixer, and output format limit the number you can output. So you need to know how many tracks your system can output and how many tracks the tape — or other format — you're outputting to can hold. For instance, FCP allows you to output 24 tracks but DigiBeta tape, which is typical for tape formats, only holds four audio tracks. If you've cut more than four tracks, you will need to nest (combine) tracks and/or assign them to four output channels on your system before playing your sequence out to tape. If you're using a sound mixer, you'll also need to assign and prepare its output channels.

# Show timings — A balancing act

How long is your show? How long should it be? As you prep for the screening, you need to face this reality check. To start, you must know the exact running time (RT) or ideal RT for your show. For example, a feature film can run from 70 minutes (*Duck Soup*) to 227 minutes (*Lawrence of Arabia*) but normally fits in the 90–120 minute range. A documentary can be of any length as long as it holds the audience, but it should fit exhibition standards for shorts or features in order to be seen in theaters and considered for academy and festival awards.

With each screening, you will measure your show and compare it to the TRT (total running time) you're aiming for. Typically, shows get leaner and shorter as the recutting proceeds. At the next screening you'll need to report the new TRT and should be prepared to answer how much time the show lost (or gained) on each act, reel, or segment. Below are some additional considerations for specific types of shows.

### TV TIMINGS

TV shows are divided into acts by the screenwriter, each act playing between commercials. There are seven acts on a MOW (movie of the week), four acts on an hour show, and two acts on a half-hour show. Actually, due to commercials, hour shows run 42–47 minutes and half-hour shows 20–23 minutes. The network specifies the exact length of a show as well as the minimum and maximum length allowable for each act in its delivery requirements. You need to be aware of these specifications as eventually you will have to cut the show "to time" — the exact number of minutes the network requires.

More immediately, you'll need to build the show into acts according to the script and see how the timings measure up against the network specs. If you've been editing separate scenes and dragging them to a scenes bin, now is the time to string them all together in one time-line. As you put scenes together for the first time, check the transitions between them and add a dissolve or other effect if you don't want a straight cut. Slug 2-3" of black between acts.

### BALANCING FOR SCREENING ON TAPE

If your show runs longer than the tape you're outputting to, you'll need to break your cut into two or more sequences. Use marks and duration timings on your sequence to measure and help determine where to put the breaks. Make sure to place any breaks where they make sense in your story at a straight A and V cut so they're not jarring.

### BALANCING FOR SCREENING ON FILM

You screen film on reels of up to 2,000 ft (35mm) or 800 ft (16mm) which translates to 20–22 minutes/reel. (Super 16mm cannot be projected so you will have to go through the DI process to make a 35mm screenable print.) Use your system's calculator or the time line duration numbers to break down your sequence into reels for conforming the film. Each reel should be a separate edit and have a unique name such as Reel 1 Cut 1. More info on conforming in the upcoming section "Screen on Film."

## Continuity Sheet

Continuity sheets help you measure and assess your show. A continuity sheet lists a show's scenes in the order they are edited along with a descriptive phrase or sentence about the scene's action and its RT. Knowing each scene's RT comes in handy when you must drop or cut down scenes to shorten a show's TRT. You create a new continuity sheet for each screening so that everyone can see not only the order of scenes but which scenes have been moved, dropped, or have footage coming.

Making a continuity sheet is especially helpful when you are switching scenes around. The continuity sheet may start out in script order, i.e., scenes 1, 2, 3, 4, 5 and end up rearranged, as cutting and recutting progress, to scenes 3, 1, 2, 4, 5. Here's a sample continuity sheet. It is for a dramatic TV episode but will work for any tape or tapeless shows measuring in *time*.

# Tape/Tapeless Show Continuity Sheet

| CONTINUITY | | SHOW The East Wing, Ep. 204 CUT # 2 | | PAGE 2 OF 5 | |
|---|---|---|---|---|---|
| ACT # 3 | DATE 4/7/12 | COMMENTS: Sc 24 split in two, sandwiching Sc 23. | | | |
| SC # | TIME | DESCRIPTION | | RUNNING TIME OLD | NEW |
| 20 | N/X | Bluebird café. Slugged: Waiting for stock shot. | | :03 | :03 |
| 21 | N/I | Robin runs into Sandy inside a café. | | 1:01 | 1:01 |
| 22 | N/I | Love scene at Robin's loft. | | 2:23 | 2:01 |
| 24 first half | D/I | Sandy ignores Robin at the press conference. | | 3:48 | 2:44 |
| 23 | N/I | The aftermath at the loft: Sandy storms out. | | 4:13 | 4:13 |
| 24 last half | D/X | Robin exits press conf. early, upset. | | Part of Sc. 24 | 1:26 |
| | | | RT | 11:28 | 11:08 |
| | | | GAIN/LOSS | | -:20 |

**Key**

D/I = Day Interior        D/X Day Exterior
N/I = Night Interior      N/X Night Exterior

This second example is for a documentary cutting on film but will work for any show measuring in feet and frames. To figure gain/loss, calculate using the previous cut's continuity sheet.

# Film Show Continuity Sheet

| CONTINUITY | | SHOW Apocalypse in Paradise | | Page 1 of 1 | |
|---|---|---|---|---|---|
| REEL # 2 | DATE Aug 17 | COMMENTS: Scene 10 dropped | | START MARK = 0 | |
| SC # | TIME | DESCRIPTION | | SCENE FEET + FR | SCENE END FEET + FR |
| 6 | D/X | Hawaiian islands exist, free of rats, gnats, newts. | | 186'04 | 186'04 |
| 7 | D/X | 1100-1330: Polynesians arrive. Bring animals & plants including dogs, rats, coconuts, & bananas. | | 157'08 | 243'12 |
| 8 | D/X | A few native animal and plant species become extinct. | | 228'12 | 572'08 |
| 9 | D/X | 1778: Captain Cook visits, deposits first Western flora, fauna, and disease. | | 95'09 | 665'01 |
| 11 | D/X | Intro today: Number of plant & animal species becoming extinct & endangered grows daily. | | 41'13 | 707'14 |
| | | | | RT | 707'14 |
| | | | | GAIN/LOSS | -93'+02 |

Appendices D and E follow this chapter and provide blank forms of each of these continuity forms. You can also download them by visiting www.joyoffilmediting.com and searching under the Free tab.

# Screening format

How will the director/producer/client view your cut? On tape, film, file, disk, or on your digital system? Here are the special preparations you make for each circumstance.

## Screen on the editing system

There's not a whole lot to do to prepare for screening on the system in the cutting room. Get in a couch or some chairs and check their sight-lines to the viewing monitor(s). Make sure your audio levels are set, the system's up to snuff, and that you can readily access all your clips. Some editors like to have snacks and make folks comfy; others want to get back to work and don't bother with amenities, subtly encouraging exodus.

9.i Ready to screen. *Photo courtesy of AlphaDogs.*

### REMOTE SCREENINGS

A few editors are running cuts remotely from their systems using Slingshot or other software which allows for screening cuts and recutting with the director. As technology improves, there will be more remote screenings of cuts as well as dailies, VFX, and other footage.

## Screen on file

There are three avenues to screening via file: 1) You create an uncompressed file — QT most likely, or another movie file such as .avi, .mov, etc. — and send it to a screening room, first testing to ensure that the facility can run it correctly; 2) You take your hard drives to a screening room that has the same digital editing system you're cutting on. This involves copying your project files onto the screening room's system from a portable hard drive or fast thumb drive, connecting your media drives to the screening room's system, and then making certain your cut can be played and projected properly; 3) You upload the file to a server for viewers to download. Currently this method is used mainly to distribute cuts when everyone can't meet up for a screening but this will change as remote and file-based communications improve.

## Screen on tape

To do this, you either make a file and put it to tape or use your system's output tool to record your cut sequence to a tape. Recording your cut sequence from the time line to tape is variously referred to as outputting, printing to tape or video, or playing out to tape, depending on the system.

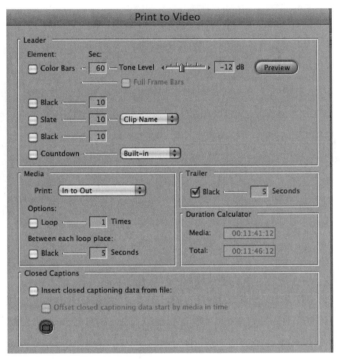

**9.j** Print to video tool on Final Cut Pro.

Before getting started, make sure your tape deck is connected properly to send audio and video from your digital system. There's nothing like a screening deadline and an ill-prepared tape deck to up your stress level! If you have an external sound mixer, you can set a level before playing out the cut and adjust levels if necessary during play out. Table 9.1 outlines the three methods for playing out to tape.

TABLE 9.1
THREE METHODS TO PLAY OUT TO TAPE

| METHOD | BASIC METHOD | COMMENTS |
|---|---|---|
| -1-<br>MANUAL RECORD,<br>A.K.A.<br>CRASH RECORD<br>OR<br>"DOWN AND DIRTY,<br>I'M IN A HURRY" | 1. Press the record button on the tape deck or camcorder.<br>2. Press play on your sequence.<br>3. Hit the stop button on the tape deck or camcorder when you're done. | Before recording<br>a) Perform rendering manually.<br>b) Slug 5" or more of black at the head of your sequence to prevent the first frames of your show from being clipped during recording and to quiet the audience at the start of the screening.<br>c) Slug 30" at the end of your sequence. Otherwise, once you stop the recording, the tape signal will drop out and cut to snow, bringing your show to an abrupt, undesirable end.<br><br>*During recording*<br>You cannot stop down to make any changes. If you see a problem, you must stop and begin all over again. |
| -2-<br>ASSEMBLE EDIT,<br>A.K.A.<br>PRINT TO VIDEO | –Same as #1 except the system controls the process, auto-rendering FX as needed.<br>–System adds color bars, a countdown leader, and a title if you select them. | a) The system adds its own time code which is useless for timings.<br><br>b) You cannot play out a section by marking IN and OUT.<br><br>c) Useful for recording to tape in deck or camcorder. |
| -3-<br>INSERT EDIT,<br>A.K.A.<br>EDIT TO TAPE | –Requires a pre-striped tape and control of deck or other device.<br>–System controls everything.<br>–System adds leader, bars, etc. like #2 and can add black at end. | a) This method makes a frame-accurate tape that can be used for timings by music editors and others if you select visible code.<br><br>b) You may play out a section by marking IN and OUT or pick it up as in #2. |

Whichever method you use, review the tape to make sure your show gets recorded flawlessly. On a long show, spot check the tape from beginning to end, making sure to inspect any pick-up points. From this tape, dubs can be made for producers, the music editor, the composer, the sound editor, the network, and anyone else who needs to see the cut.

## Screen on disk

You'll make an uncompressed file of your cut and export it to DVD or Blu-ray or export your sequence directly to disk. You will view the cut in a screening room or, more likely, the disks will be distributed and you'll get notes or discuss the cut later with the director.

## Screen on film

Screening on film means that you reproduce your digital cut on film and project the reels. To accomplish this, the film is conformed — matched cut for cut — to the digital cut from a cutlist you make on the digital system.

### Making a cutlist

You imported key code numbers along with time code and camera roll data when you imported the telecine database to ingest dailies. Now you'll call up this data to make a cutlist using your system's film tool (Cutlist tool on Avid, Cinema tool on FCP). The cutlist shows the key code for the start and end (in-point and out-point) of each edit in your sequence. It also provides the camera roll number and the length of each shot in feet and frames. You will send this negative cutlist to the lab or post house to make a workprint for viewing. The workprint will be conformed to your sequence, cut by cut, by film conformers or the DI process. Once the reels are conformed and checked, they're ready to screen.

Although others may be handling the film, it's up to the digital editor or assistant to verify the data and provide perfect cutlists. For more details, please see Chapter 13, which goes over the "film out" process. Also, within the Free tab of www.joyoffilmediting.com there is a lot more information about editing on film and working with a workprint.

### Pros and cons of screening on film

On the plus side, since you are screening the show in its true medium and aspect ratio — the way your audience will see it — you can judge better how the cuts play. Additionally, sometimes subtle focus and sync problems become apparent which could not be seen on the digital system monitor or when screening on tape. The downside is the cost of the conformers or DI process.

## STEP 2: The Screening

This is what you'll need to take to the screening:

- Tape, disk, file, or film reels of your cut, if not delivered ahead of time.
- Continuity sheets with TRT.
- Notepad.
- Optional: Script, outline, or paper cut and notebook of transcripts

### *Frame of mind*

It's important to be in the right state of mind at a screening. No matter how nervous you are, never apologize for a cut. This is your best work, there's no need. You may mention certain problems beyond your control — missing shots, scenes, lines, effects — but they shouldn't be a litany.

Keep your eye on the show and always remember that you are fostering the director's/producer's/client's vision. Your employer has put time and money into this project and ultimately it's their baby. Hopefully you share their sentiments about its merits and demerits, but if you don't, (and sometimes you won't), keep your smart, incisive opinions to yourself. You want to come from a place of serving the footage and molding the story as best you can. In addition to supporting the project, your goal in every situation is to learn and grow creatively and technically, make connections for further work, and collect a self-respecting paycheck. If you hit all three on a project you're lucky!

## When the lights go down

Eventually, laden with lattes, the powers-that-be will arrive. You will view the show all put together for the first time. Everybody will see what the planning, writing, directing, shooting, and editing have accomplished. Let the darkened room work its magic. The best approach is for all to watch with a pair of fresh eyes. Typically you screen the show straight through without comment. If it's a less formal screening and you're running on a digital system, you may need to ride the volume control from your mixer where needed. In any case, you'll initially screen for one person— the director usually. As recutting proceeds, the audience may grow to include the producer, client, studio execs, etc., or there may be a series of small, targeted viewings to get sign-off from executives and others.

## When the lights go up

*"Great editors... understand, like a great diagnostician in medicine — this is the problem, this is how we can treat it, but you're going to have side effects. They'll see the whole picture."*
—BO GOLDMAN, screenwriter, *Scent of a Woman, The Rose,* and *One Flew over the Cuckoo's Nest*

After the screening, you will run the cut from beginning to end, stopping and starting for the director/producer/client to give notes of the changes they'd like. This après screening session can be long or short, depending on how much work there is to do

**9.k** Screening a cut. *Photo courtesy of Chris Senchack.*

and how efficient the director or "the committee" (if it's a group screening) is at giving notes.

### Taking notes

For the first cut, you will receive notes from one person: the director. If you're screening on your editing system, the director may stick around and work with you to make the changes. Some editors like to insert a locator on the time line at each change so it's easy to spot on the time line.

As recuts and screenings progress, you may receive notes from producers, writers, execs, or the client. Each show has a different hierarchy of people you will be interacting with. Typically the final say on the final cut belongs to the client (corporate videos, commercials), the director (features, documentaries, concert pieces, music videos), or the producer (television, features, documentaries, concert pieces, music videos).

Take the time to make clear notes so that you can decipher them later. The notes may be sparse and specific or lengthy and contradictory. Editors often say that they listen to the spirit and the intent of what the director/client/producer is saying, not just the words.

### On a non-scripted show

It's not unusual for everyone to re-comb the transcripts, logs, or footage itself for fresh ideas and connections. A new paper cut may be formulated, sections dropped or rearranged, or narration rewritten.

### On a scripted show

You all may refer to the script to cross out or rearrange lines. Some ADR lines may be called for as well as pick-up or insert shots.

### Dubs

After the screening you will make copies of the cut for those wishing to review it as well as for those who couldn't make the screening. You may receive additional notes. At some point during the screening and recutting process you'll also deliver time-coded cuts to the music composer and possibly the sound designer so they can begin their work.

## Collaboration

Following the screening you will be asked your professional opinion on scenes, structure, story, and shots. When you respond, remember: You are the person with the most intimacy and knowledge of the footage. The story is in your hands and you want to put it across in the best way possible to produce the best show possible. Point out the show's strengths as well as its problems and provide solutions. If a scene isn't working right, suggest a fix such as eliminating or rearranging lines or shots, adding VO or a pick-up shot, resizing a shot, etc. If there's no obvious resolution, promise to give the scene and its footage another look.

No matter how inexperienced an editor you are or how experienced the director/producer/client is, every show is unique and no one will have all the answers. In the best of situations you will work as a team, all contributing ideas. In the worst, they may scream, contradict, or micromanage your cut to the frame. If the worst occurs and you are reduced to being "a pair of hands" — it's happened to many of us, usually due to the insecurity or inexperience of our employers — perform the cuts quickly and try to make a game of anticipating their needs with positive suggestions. Sometimes they will even trust you after a cut or two and then leave you to it. If you're a beginner, this can be a way to learn. In any case, your employers will rely on you to know if the footage is there to make the changes they want and they will have the final say.

And while we're on ugly realities, let's talk about politics. Sometime you may find yourself caught in a fracas between director and producer or others. Stay as neutral as possible and let them work it out while keeping an eye to your future alliances — and paycheck. Here's Jim Clark's advice from his book *Dream Repairman: Adventures in Film Editing*: "An editor can best make his points by skillful demonstration. I have never believed in arguing with a director, which usually ends in bad feelings and hurts the film. But I do believe in cutting many versions of a scene to prove a point."

## *Editors and directors*

*"…[the editor is] the end of the relay race, and she and her director share one certain knowledge that binds them in a way no screenwriter can ever be: They both know they're on the* Titanic *together…"*

—WILLIAM GOLDMAN, screenwriter, from his book *Adventures in the Screen Trade*

As editor, you've had your way with the show on the first cut. After this, during the recutting process, you'll work closely with the director. In the best of situations, this is the collaborative phase of editing and can be stimulating and rewarding for all involved. Many editors and directors have strong, positive feelings about this partnership as the quotes scattered throughout the next section demonstrate. In these times of accelerated schedules on TV shows as well as features, editors also collaborate with each other. Dan Swietlik comments on editing *Sicko*, "the edges were very blurred between who cut what because we were modifying so much. It got handed around a lot."

## STEP 3: RECUTTING

Now you're back in the cutting room, hopefully after lunch or a good night's sleep or a breather of some kind. The time line of your first cut is glaring at you from the monitor. Suddenly all the excitement and the good ideas that the screening inspired seem to drain out of you...

## The Process

*"The process of turning a first cut into a finished film always proceeds one reel at a time. Each scene is carefully tuned before the next one is tackled. It's the way I imagine a cobra ingests a crocodile, the dead beast going through the snake's digestive system inch by inch, the head being completely transformed by the digestive juices before the neck arrives. "*

—RALPH ROSENBLUM, editor *The Producers* (1968), *Annie Hall, The Pawnbroker,* and *A Thousand Clowns,* from his book *When the Shooting Stops... the Cutting Begins.*

The first cut may indeed seem like a dead crocodile being ingested by a cobra — both dead and ready to bite you at the same time. Take heart and pick up your screening notes. No matter what you screened on — film, tape, disk, or digital system — the recutting process begins with making a new version of your sequence. Breathe deeply and attack the time line with the first change...

In a little while, time will have passed and your concentration will break. You may have made one change or several but you'll find you've been just as engaged as during the first cut. Mark off each change you make on your screening notepad. Jot down any ideas and be sure to write why you couldn't make a change (i.e., not enough footage, no other takes, a mismatched performance, etc.). Otherwise you may forget at the next screening and have to revisit the area all over again.

A show's first cut is usually loose; it gets tightened up with each recut as extraneous words, lines, beats, and scenes, are dropped. You'll find that like the proverbial stone hitting the water, when you make changes to a scene there's a ripple effect: Trim one shot and others will have to be trimmed, extended, slipped, or slid. It's a fine-tuning, balancing process that, as the show improves, is quite satisfying. And you will appreciate that you have the framework of the first cut to build upon. As screenings continue, and scenes are changed, moved, and deleted, you may have to rebalance acts or reels — split or move scenes from one act or reel to another — and reconsider "act outs" (act endings) in order to satisfy timing requirements and dramatic hooks.

The director (or client or producer) may sit beside you in the cutting room for the changes or may return in a few hours or days to screen the changes with you. You may send recuts out on tape, file, or disk and then wait for more changes. You may screen some recuts on the system and preview others on film or tape, especially as the time escalates toward locking the show. Whatever the screening routine, the editing process will continue this way: Screen, get notes, make changes; screen, notes, changes…until eventually you'll bring the show to a reasonable state and it will be locked.

> "Certainly no director can claim to be an 'auteur' unless he can edit or fully supervise the editing of his own films, and the extent to which a director's films approach the full potential of excellence will depend as much on this mastery of the editing craft as on his knowledge and practice of story and filming techniques."
>
> —EDWARD DMYTRYK

> "The film editor has pulled the director out of more scrapes and has helped him out of more weaknesses than any other person in the industry."
>
> —CECIL B. DeMILLE

> "I have learned the most that I have about directing from editors, from hanging around them in the *Rawhide* days, and watching them work."
>
> —CLINT EASTWOOD

> "There is a brotherhood in filmmaking… between the film editor and the film director. It's a brotherhood of trust and interdependence, and it is a sanctuary. It is for me where the filmmaking really gets started, and it's where I feel most comfortable."
>
> —STEVEN SPIELBERG

## Lifts

Often during recutting, you will cut out — lift — sections, scenes, or parts of scenes, which are called lifts. Some editors consign lifts to a special lifts bin, a habit leftover from editing on film where a lift was a physical roll of spliced pieces of film stored in a box or left hanging on the Moviola trim bin. As long as you have saved a sequence with the lift intact, there's no need to save it elsewhere.

## *Previews*

A preview can be pricey, taking place at a theater and gathering verbal and written responses from the audience or a small "focus group." Or a preview can be a matter of inviting friends and trusted cohorts over to sit on your couch and view your work-in-progress. Or it can be somewhere in between. Big, medium, or small, a preview can give you valuable info about your movie, so you want your cut to appear at its best.

### UPREZZING

You want to run your show at its uncompressed best so you will take the time to uprez your sequence and put it to HD tape.

### TEMP MIX, A.K.A. TEMP DUB, SLOP MIX, ROUGH MIX, OR SCRATCH MIX

> "When a director is filming, he's not making a movie, he's making the material from which a movie is going to be made, and it's going to be made in the editing… I see the job as trying to get the best possible version of the film that the director wants. You always have to keep in the forefront of your mind that it is the director's film."
>
> —EDITOR WILLIAM REYNOLDS, *Sound of Music, The Godfather,* and *The Sting.*

> "[Editing *Sicko*] was completely collaborative. [Director] Michael [Moore] is the type who lets the editors do the initial shaping of the film. Then he watches from the approach of an audience. That's how he shapes it. He gives a lot of freedom to the editors to put things together and write the film."
>
> —DAN SWIETLIK, *An Inconvenient Truth* and *Sicko.*

A temp mix of music, dialogue, and sound effects is often performed during the picture editing phase in order to preview to a test audience, the network, or a potential buyer or distributor. If the production company can afford it, you'll go to a soundstage and engage sound editors and mixers to do the job. You can also do the temp mix right on your editing system. Since the audio tools on current digital system are capable of pretty slick work, money is not always the issue as James Cameron makes clear: "A lot of filmmakers go to [the trouble of preparing] a true "temp mix," where you go on a dubbing stage for several days and have mixers and all that. We previewed *Titanic* all three times with our Avid audio tracks, which you can appreciate on a film of that cost, if nothing else. Those preview screenings were absolutely critical, and we previewed with a mono track mixed out of the Avid's four tracks. And it played fine."

After the preview, you will cut the mixed track into your sequence. You should keep tabs on the music and effects used; they may be needed for another temp dub or liked so much that they're included in the final mix. Also, keep track of which tracks these temp effects and music are on in your sequence; the sound and music editors may want to use them and ask you to strip them out from the locked cut before handing it over to them.

> "What I do is interpose myself between the director's vision of what they think they shot and what they really shot."
>
> —ALAN HEIM, A.C.E., *Lenny*, *Network*, and *All That Jazz*.
>
> "I've always been concerned when editors get awards and directors don't. It seems wrong to me because without the material we can't do a thing. We are only interpreting what we're given. We are the dream repairmen. That's what we do. We repair other people's dreams."
>
> —JIM CLARK, *Vera Drake*, *Nell*, *The Killing Fields*, *Marathon Man*, and *Charade*.

## Film Shows: Recutting and Change Lists

On film shows, following the first screening, you will make a new version on the digital system and recut it, just as you would if you screened on the system or on tape. However, Cut 2, and all subsequent cuts that will be screened on film, must be reconformed by making changes to the film reels. A list of changes, called a change list, is made by the picture editor or assistant on the digital system and handed to the film conformers. The change list program works by comparing the current, new cut with the previous, old cut on a reel-by-reel basis. Table 9.2 shows a sample change list and includes both ink code and key code so you can see how both can be used for conforming.[2] Study it to understand how a change list compares cuts and provides information for the recut.

While you may not be doing the film reconform yourself, you are responsible for rebalancing the reels and creating the change list. Check it thoroughly and add your own notes to help the conformers. Also, it's helpful to inform the conformers of the overall nature of the changes, e.g., "A lot of shots were dropped and all of scene 7," or "Scene 63 and 79 were swapped and other than that there were just a few shot extensions."

---

2. A real list shows either key code or ink code. Normally you reconform workprint (never the film negative!) so your change list would have to use ink codes. However, a change list with key codes might be required in the DI process or if the negative cutter uncovers mistakes in the cutlist.

**TABLE 9.2**
**SAMPLE CHANGE LIST**

| HOME FREE | REEL 004 | PICTURE TRACK 1 | | |
|---|---|---|---|---|
| Old duration 1592+13 | 156 events | 65 insertions | All counts are inclusive | Page 1 of 14 |
| New duration 1302+12 | 88 deletions | (inside/inside) | Date: 2/22/12 | |
| Total Change -290+1 | 3 moves | | | |

| EDIT | AT THIS FOOTAGE | FOR THIS LENGTH | DO THIS | FIRST/LAST KEY CODE | FIRST/LAST INK CODE | CLIP NAME | TOTAL CHANGE |
|---|---|---|---|---|---|---|---|
| 1 | 45+04 111+15 | -66+12 | Delete 2 shots | KR 24 7568-4644+01 KQ 26 1047-1370+06 | 012 -2343+11 031 -1187+06 | 12-5 A31-2 | -66+12 |
| 2 | 45+04 73+13 | +28+10 | Insert shot | Opt 5-0000+00 Opt 5-0028+09 | Opt 5-0000+00 Opt 5-0028+09 | Opt #5 | -38+02 |
| 3 | 73+14 117+14 | +44+01 | Insert shot | EH 51 0414-5023+01 EH 51 0414-5067+01 | 600 -1013+00 600 -1057+00 | Aerial forest | +5+15 |
| 4 | 127+12 131-01 | -3+06 | Delete shot | KQ 26 4476-4078+10 KQ 26 4476-4081+15 | 031 -1565+10 031 -1568+15 | 31B-4 | +2+09 |
| 5 | 127+12 131+01 | +3+06 | Lengthen head | KQ 26 4481-8505+15 KQ 26 4481-8505+15 | 031 -1779+15 031 -1783+04 | 31D-2 | +5+15 |
| 6 | 134+09 137+09 | -3+01 | Trim tail | KQ 26 4481-8512+12 KQ 26 4481-8515+12 | 031 -1786+12 031 -1789+12 | 31D-2 | +2+14 |
| 7 | 134+09 135+01 | -09 | Trim head | KQ 26 4481-8004+16 KQ 26 4481-8005+05 | 031 -1213+03 031 -1214+05 | 31-3 | +2+05 |
| 8 | 134+09 137+09 | +3+01 | Insert shot | KQ 26 4481-8086+08 KQ 26 4481-8089+08 | 031 -1295+08 031 -1298+08 | 31A-6 | +5+06 |
| 9 | 160+08 163+00 | -2+09 | Move shot to #11 | KQ 26 4481-9119+15 KQ 26 4481-9122+07 | 031 -1396+15 031 -1399+07 | 31F-1 | +2+14 |
| 10 | 161+11 161+11 | -0+01 | Trim middle | KQ 26 4481-9149+10 KQ 26 4481-9149+10 | 031 -1359+10 031 -1359+10 | 31C-3 | +2+13 |
| 11 | 161+11 164+03 | +2+09 | Insert shot from #9 | KQ 26 4481-9119+15 KQ 26 4481-9122+07 | 031 -1396+15 031 -1399+07 | 31F-1 | +5+05 |

# STEP 4: LOCKING THE SHOW

As you get close to the final cut, optimally the picture has reached a point where everyone is satisfied that it's the best that it can be and you're just polishing the marble. (Hopefully it's marble!) Whatever the quality of your show, eventually you'll be told "It's a lock" and you will make your last edit.

Locking a cut simply means that you're done editing — not a frame will be changed. A deadline — air date or exhibit date — often clinches a lock. Once a show is locked, it must be approved by the exhibitor. On a TV show this is the network; on a movie for theatrical release, it's the studio.

### Rating the show

Following studio and network approval, every show must be rated for age appropriateness and type of content. A movie is reviewed and rated G, PG, PG-13, R, or NC-17 by the Motion Picture Academy of Arts (MPAA). A TV show goes to the TV Parental Guidelines monitoring board which bestows a TV-Y, TV-Y7, TV-G, TV-PG, TV-14, or TV-MA rating, and often, a sub-rating of D, L, S, or V[3] for the last three categories. After your show goes to the ratings board, you will make any demanded changes. If it's for TV, you will also bring it to time — cut it precisely to the last second — so that the show meets the network's required running time.

### Unlocking the show

Ordinarily, once the show is locked it remains locked. It's not uncommon however, for it to be unlocked and relocked as final changes and fixes are made. For instance, reels become unlocked on a feature film as the director works to the last minute.

### After lock

Once locked, the show moves into the two final phases of postproduction: sound editing and finishing. At this point you may be kept on to oversee these phases or released to work on another episode or in-house project job or — be prepared — to look for your next gig.

## CHAPTER WRAP-UP

With picture lock, you've completed Stage II and the editing phase of postproduction. You can take time to fill out Appendix F, the budget form for the editing phase, which is also available from www.joyoffilmediting.com under the Free tab. Otherwise it's time to begin Stage III — sound editing and finishing — starting with Chapter 10, where sound design gets underway.

---

3. D (drugs), L(language), S (sex), and V (violence).

# Appendix D

## Tape & Tapeless Show Continuity Form

| CONTINUITY | | SHOW<br>CUT # | | PAGE 1 OF 1 | |
|---|---|---|---|---|---|
| ACT # | DATE | COMMENTS: | | | |
| SC # | TIME | DESCRIPTION | | RUNNING TIME<br>OLD | NEW |
| | | | | | |
| | | | | | |
| | | | | | |
| | | | | | |
| | | | | | |
| | | | | | |
| | | | | | |
| | | | | | |
| | | | | | |
| | | | | | |
| | | | | | |
| | | | | | |
| | | | | | |
| | | | | | |
| | | | | | |
| | | | | RT | |
| | | | | GAIN/LOSS | |

# Appendix E

## Film Show Continuity Form

| CONTINUITY | | | SHOW | PAGE 1 OF 1 | |
|---|---|---|---|---|---|
| REEL # | | DATE | COMMENTS | START MARK = 0 | |
| Sc # | TIME | | DESCRIPTION | SCENE FEET + FR | SCENE END FEET + FR |
| | | | | | |
| | | | | | |
| | | | | | |
| | | | | | |
| | | | | | |
| | | | | | |
| | | | | | |
| | | | | | |
| | | | | | |
| | | | | | |
| | | | | | |
| | | | | | |
| | | | | | |
| | | | | | |
| | | | | | |
| | | | | | |
| | | | | | |
| | | | POP AT: | LFOA | |
| | | | | RT GAIN/LOSS | |

# Appendix F

## Stage II: Budget for Editing

Now that you know how to edit your project, you can budget for this stage of postproduction. Feel free to photocopy this form or go to the Free tab of www.joyoffilmediting.com and download it.

| | | BUDGET FOR EDITING | | | | |
|---|---|---|---|---|---|---|
| ACCT# | DESCRIPTION | AMOUNT | UNITS | X | RATE | TOTAL |
| 4000 | FILM | | | | | |
| 4001 | Picture reprints | | feet | | | |
| 4002 | Sound retransfers | | feet | | | |
| | | | TOTAL FOR CATEGORY | | | |
| 4200 | SPECIAL EFFECTS | | | | | |
| 4201 | Standard opticals | | allow | | | |
| 4202 | Special opticals | | allow | | | |
| 4203 | Film morph effects | | allow | | | |
| 4204 | Matte shots | | allow | | | |
| 4205 | Roto shots | | allow | | | |
| 4206 | CGI | | allow | | | |
| 4207 | Green screen | | allow | | | |
| 4208 | Lab, stock, and transfer | | allow | | | |
| 4209 | Misc. | | allow | | | |
| | | | TOTAL FOR CATEGORY | | | |
| 4400 | ADDITIONAL FOOTAGE | | | | | |
| 4401 | Pick-up shots | | allow | | | |
| 4402 | Insert shots | | allow | | | |
| 4403 | Retakes | | allow | | | |
| 4404 | B Neg | | allow | | | |
| 4405 | Stock footage | | allow | | | |
| 4406 | Stock footage — Search | | hour | | | |
| 4407 | Lab and transfer costs | | hour | | | |
| | | | TOTAL FOR CATEGORY | | | |
| 4500 | PREVIEW PREP | | | | | |
| 4501 | Temp narration/VO | | hour | | | |
| 4502 | Temp online | | allow | | | |
| 4503 | Temp mix | | allow | | | |
| | | | TOTAL FOR CATEGORY | | | |
| 4700 | SCREENINGS & PREVIEW | | | | | |
| 4701 | Screening room | | allow | | | |
| 4702 | Screening dubs | | disk | | | |
| 4703 | Preview theater | | allow | | | |
| 4704 | Projectionist | | hour | | | |
| | | | TOTAL FOR CATEGORY | | | |
| | | | GRAND TOTAL | | | |

# STAGE THREE

# Finishing

## Introduction

Stages I and II illuminated the editor's path from dailies to a locked cut. Stage III leads you through the finalization of all decisions about picture, sound, and music. Part One covers how sound and music are designed, edited, and mixed. Part Two sees the postproduction journey come to an end as your project reaches its finishing format: disk, file, film, or tape. Both parts contain budget charts so you can plan for these final two phases of postproduction.

# Sound, Music, and the Mix

True soldier story

*"…the first thing I thought about was how the war did not sound like war. Having grown up watching Hollywood war movies I expected a lot more sound and much bigger sound. It was not until I was hit that I realized what I was in was real."*

—WW II veteran

## Introduction

The soldier's reaction above was replayed on September 11, 2001, when a New Yorker told a television interviewer that when he saw the first plane hit, his immediate thought was that it was just like a movie. Gradually, our dreams, fantasies, the shows we watch, and our waking lives are intersecting, mixing and melding reality, documentary, and drama. Sound, being the important sense and sense memory that it is, plays a dominant role in this.

The aim of Part One is to expose you to how to design sound and music and mix them into your film or video. Chapter 10 traces sound from its conception by the sound designer to its acquisition by the sound editors. It then follows the parallel process for how music gets from the composer to the music editor and sketches out workflows for both sound and music editors. Chapter 11 relates how sound and music are edited and meet up at the mix where sound mixers blend and record them together. Along the way you will hear from sound designers, music editors, and mixers about how they approach their work.

## CHAPTER 10

# Designing Sound and Music

*"Sound may be the most powerful tool in the filmmaker's arsenal in terms of its ability to seduce."*

—RANDY THOM, C.A.S., sound designer and mixer, *How to Train Your Dragon, The Incredibles, The Right Stuff*, and *Return of the Jedi*.

## Overview

This chapter is devoted to making you aware of the power of sound and music and to grounding you in the sound and music design process. You will learn how to plan for sound and music on your project and become familiar with sound and music editing tools, terms, workflows, and practices. So consider this the warm up — on to the heart and soul of it!

## What Sound Can Do for Your Film or Video

*"...if you encourage the sounds of the characters, the things, and the places in your film to inform your decisions in all the other film crafts, then your movie may just grow to have a voice beyond anything you might have dreamed."*

—RANDY THOM

We've all come to expect realistic, natural sound in movies. In truth, sound in films is anything but realistic or natural: A dozen sound editors and mixers have created and positioned the audio so that we — the audience — will accept it and the movie. We accept that Barcelona sounds like this, the "wild west" sounded like that, and Middle Earth vibrates this way due to the world of sound conceived by the sound designer, editors, and mixers. Sound lets us enjoy the ride, albeit through a twister, typhoon, or game of Quidditch. It enables us to believe in the movie; if the sound seems phony or unreal, we discount the movie.

Well designed and mixed sound — meaning sound effects and dialogue — gives voice to the visuals, adding dimension to the picture that viewers may not consciously perceive. Sound can set the pace for a scene, signal changes in time or place, heighten the action or diminish it, and smooth scene transitions. It can connect characters, images, locations, and ideas. Sound also helps define characters by building their aural persona so we can know what they're feeling and experiencing. How does the character sound when they react to a scream? A song? A misstep into a mud puddle? A baby's cry?

Hitchcock believed that "to describe a sound accurately, one has to imagine its equivalent in dialogue" and gave this illustration from a scene in *The Birds:* "The flock gathers, surveys, and attacks, saying, 'Now we've got you where we want you. Here we come. We don't have to scream in triumph or in anger. This is going to be a silent murder.'" *The Birds* is noteworthy because it relied heavily on sounds — there was no score — to make its farfetched plot plausible.

The buzz words today for sound are "organic," "real," and "natural." *The Hurt Locker*, which won the 2009 Academy Awards for sound editing and sound mixing, typifies this trend. A memorable scene of GIs on a night-search in Iraq depended entirely on the bed of realistic sound the editors built. *Avatar*, the runner-up for the Oscar that year, embodies the other side of the sonic spectrum: Its audio palette paints an imaginary planet where the synthesized sounds are anything but real. What these two sound styles have in common, however, is crucial: They both aurally plant the audience in the movie's environment.

Whether you have many layers of sound or minimal sound, sonics are pivotal to the audience's perception and reception of your show. They transport viewers away from the filming on the soundstage and into the characters' world. Sound sustains and is an integral part of a film's voice and vision. Bear this in mind when you design sound; every sound effect and piece of dialogue should strengthen its purpose.

Lastly, as with all editing, be open to experimenting, to failing or succeeding, but always, to learning. Steve Boeddeker, sound designer and supervisor on *Alice in Wonderland 3-D* says, "Don't be afraid to make mistakes. Any time you want to do something new—and we do on every project—you're going to make mistakes. The trick is to try the experiment and fail as early as possible in the project and as inexpensively as possible."

# The Sound Department

*"You learn that the most important thing that you can do as a sound designer is to make the right choice, for the right sound, at the right moment in the film."*
—Ben Burtt, C.A.S., *Wall-E; Star Wars: The Phantom Menace; Raiders of the Lost Ark; and ET.*

Here is a brief introduction to the members of the sound team. We'll add more details and players as we encounter them in this chapter and the next.

## Sound designer, a.k.a. supervising sound editor or sound supervisor

The sound designer has two main jobs: 1) To work with the script, locked show, and director to map out and envision the show's soundscape; and 2) To lead a team of sound editors and mixers to design, record, edit, and mix the show. Christopher Boyes relates his view of the job in designing the sound for *Titanic*: "I love the way the groans accompany the slowly sinking ship that make you feel as if this incredible creation is resisting death — as if *Titanic* is a huge dying creature that's not giving up on life yet... That's really the function of a sound designer — to weed out what you don't want to hear and create an effect that plays for a specific moment on screen."

It's best to contract the sound designer during preproduction so they can read the script, begin to formulate ideas, and contribute to the storytelling right from the start. This happens on major features, but on most shows the sound designer and crew are hired when the picture is locked or a few weeks prior. On TV and lower budget shows the sound crew starts work after the show is onlined.

## Sound effects editor

Sound effects editors are responsible for placing all the sound effects in the show. They record or otherwise acquire the SFX, manipulate them on their DAW (digital audio workstation), and shepherd them through the mix.

### Foley editor

A Foley effect is a sound effect that is recorded in a recording studio in sync with specific actions on the screen such as the crunching claws of a creature in a sci-fi flick or a warrior deflecting arrows with a shield. The Foley editor oversees the Foley recording session, then returns to the cutting room to edit the Foley into the show. On smaller shows the SFX editor cuts in the Foley.

### Dialogue editor

The dialogue editor labors to produce a pristine dialogue track, cleaning up the production track, adding wild lines, and smoothing everything out with room tone.

### ADR editor

ADR (automated dialogue replacement) is the process by which a line of dialogue is recorded and re-spoken by an actor in sync with the picture to replace the original sync production line. The ADR editor is responsible for cutting in the recorded lines. On many shows the dialogue editor will do this job.

## What Music Can Do for Your Film or Video

*"The final anchoring point of the movie soundtrack is the music. Music provides an emotional bedrock for a film."*

—SKYWALKER SOUND Ltd., George Lucas's sound company

Music can strongly influence how an audience feels about a show's subject, characters, themes, and plot. Well thought-out music sets the appropriate tone for the picture, clueing viewers in as to what to expect: a comedy, a romance, or a chance to rock and roll. Music, like sound, affects our hearts and senses and seals the movie in our memories: John Williams' music in *Schindler's List*, played by the incomparable violinist Itzhak Perlman, evokes the suffering and loss of Jews during WW II.

Music anticipates and foreshadows action, often warning that a villain is just around the corner, or, as in M. Night Shyamalan's *The Village*, hinting that this is no ordinary hamlet. It can also conjure a time or place. Scott Joplin's upbeat piano tunes peppered *The Sting*, rooting the movie in the 1930s and paralleling the characters' optimism. The musical theme in *Somewhere in Time* sustained its time travel plot. Regularly, music accents key and not-so-key points: entrances, exits, scene transitions, and act outs.

Music can counter what's on screen to convey a larger truth. Composer Toru Takemitsu delivered a renowned score for writer-director-editor Akira Kurosawa's epic movie *Ran*. Here's what one scene in the script called for: "A terrible scroll of Hell is shown depicting the fall of the castle. There are no real sounds as the scroll unfolds like a daytime nightmare. It is a scene of human evildoing...The music superimposed on these pictures is, like the Buddha's heart, measured in beats of profound anguish, the chanting of a melody full of sorrow that begins like sobbing and rises gradually as it is repeated, like karmic cycles, then finally sounds like the wailing of countless Buddhas."

Music can let the audience know something before a character does — that good or bad news is on the other side of the door. It can also do the opposite — set the audience up — as the melody at the end of *Carrie* does, lulling the audience so the movie can deliver its final jolt of fright. Music regularly conveys characters' inner thoughts and emotions. Bernard Hermann's score for *Vertigo* heightened its characters' nightmares, dreams, and schemes right from the opening carousel music which mirrored the circular camera movement and the spiraling mystery plot. Sometimes characters even have themes, e.g., Lara's theme in *Dr. Zhivago* or the shark's refrain in *Jaws*.

# The Music Department

The music team consists of some or all of the following members:

## *Composer*

The composer writes long pieces of music, short pieces (stingers), and occasionally, songs for the show, ensuring that the director's desires are realized. A low budget show may not be able to afford a composer or may have the composer fill some of the jobs outlined below.

## *Songwriter*

A show may hire a songwriter to compose a new song or may secure the rights to use an already composed song. Either way, the director and music supervisor will be heavily involved.

### Music supervisor

The music supervisor functions like a producer, chaperoning the music from acquisition to delivery. More specifically, the supervisor secures song and music rights, oversees the budget, and coordinates the music editing process with the music editor.

### Music editor

*"The music editor is a musician as well as a film technician. Being fluent in two languages, namely music and film technique, the music editor is the translator par excellence, explaining techniques in musical terms, and music in technical terms."*

—JACK W. OGLIVIE, A.C.E., first two *Laurel and Hardy* films, *Heidi*, *Pony Express* TV series.

The music editor edits the composer's and songwriter's work into the film or video and is responsible for creating the temp track, making the audio files and cue sheet for the mix, and representing the composer's wishes at the mix. The music editor also supplies the click track[1] for dancers on the set and for the musicians during the scoring session.

## How story translates into sound and music

Like picture cuts, sound and music elements contribute to the story. They pump up POV sequences, help put the noir in film noir, and are the backbone of many a dream and fantasy sequence. Sounds, words, and music can inform a character, prompting an action or reaction or revealing overt or underlying emotions.

Music and sound personnel strive to enhance and support the story with each piece of sound and music they place in the show. But it's not always a matter of "see a bird, hear a chirp effect" or — as in the wonderful world of Disney — hear the robin sing. Sound can represent something or someone unseen — off screen — and comment on or deepen a scene. Yes! Routinely, sound and music bound from the backseat to drive the story. Think of the ways the off-screen kaboom of a bomb or swoosh of an advancing tsunami affects a town of people. Recall how Rick reacts to hearing "As Time Goes By" in *Casablanca* or the Martians respond to the broadcasting of "Indian Love Call" in *Mars Attacks*. Table 10.1 links story elements with their sound and music counterparts.

---

1. Track of clicks or beeps played back on set instead of music to provide a beat and tempo for dancers and musicians to perform to. A click track is used when the scene's music has not been finalized.

**TABLE 10.1**
**TRANSLATING STORY TO SOUND AND MUSIC**

| STORY | SOUND | MUSIC |
|---|---|---|
| screenplay | sound design | score |
| screenwriter | sound designer | composer |
| director | sound supervisor | conductor |
| actors | Foley artists, ADR creators, loop group | performers |
| character | hard SFX | instrument |
| DP | sound editors | music editor |
| theme | repeated hard and background SFX | song or melody |
| era (time) | background sound/ambience diegetic and non-diegetic sound | musical period, e.g., romantic, baroque |
| setting (place) | background sound/ambience diegetic and non-diegetic sound | style, e.g., hip hop, jazz |
| dialogue | cleaned & filled dialogue & ADR tracks | lyric |
| pace | sonic pacing | tempo |
| beat | targeted sound cues | meter |
| exposition | introductory sounds/worldizing | overture/form title (theme) music |
| arc of scene | building up sound over scene | crescendo |
| conflict | counter sounds, e.g., overlaps, shrill pitches, sudden loud noises | dissonance |
| scene/sequence | sound mix | verse or form/sequence |

# Beats: Deciding Where to Change Sound or Music

*"As with picture editing, a sound track should evoke its own sense of logic, rhythm, and dynamic to help drive the forward motion of the image."*

— FILM Guy from his book *Sound Editing Nutz and Boltz*

In Chapter 6 we talked about how a picture editor cuts in beats — changes of action within a scene. Thinking in beats is also useful to sound and music designers in conceiving how a scene should sound, what sounds and music should be used, and when they should come in. A beat can call for a change in tempo, pitch, volume, or intensity of music or effects. As you design sound for your show, the beats in each scene will help you decide where to bring in music or let it fade out, where to punch up a word or take it down to a murmur, and where to plaster the picture with sound effects or restrict them to a single, recurring effect.

And don't overlook the power of silence. Sound design can include planned sections of silence or minimal sound. (No show is entirely silent as there is always ambient sound. If you drop out all sound, you risk an audience's hostile glares at the projection booth or a TV viewer's channel surfing.) Silence, especially during a gripping scene or after a cacophony of sounds, can put the audience on the edge of their seats until they're literally living and breathing with the movie.

## Beats of a familiar movie scene

To discover how beats, sound, and silence work, let's look at a familiar scene from *The Wizard of Oz*: The cyclone scene where Dorothy is transported from Kansas to Munchkinland. If you can, watch this two minute forty-five second scene. Notice how the sound effects work and how the music changes with the action. Witness the effect of silence as Dorothy gets her first glimpse of Munchkinland. Table 10.2 charts what happens with the sound and the music at each beat of the scene. Study it before, during, or after you view the scene.

TABLE 10.2
SCENE BEATS, SOUND, AND *THE WIZARD OF OZ*

| BEAT | SOUND | MUSIC |
|---|---|---|
| 1) BLACK & WHITE film<br>D enters house as a chair crashes. | BG: cyclone/wind<br>FX: chair crash | None |
| 2) D walks thru house to bedroom.<br>D screams as a window knocks her out. | BG: cyclone/wind<br>DIAL: "Auntie Em"<br>FX: window crash<br>DIAL: "Oh!" | MX begins: Warning MX |
| 3) D on bed, unconscious.<br>Superimpose spinning house and cyclone. | BG: cyclone/wind | Unconscious MX (horns & other instruments) |
| 4) Begin montage thru window. | BG: cyclone/wind | Upbeat MX |
| 5) D comes to and views the cyclone thru the window.<br>Sees Miss Gulch on a bike, then on a broom.<br>(End montage scene.) | BG: cyclone/wind<br>FX: animal sounds<br>DIAL: "We must be inside the cyclone."<br>DIAL: "Oh, Miss Gulch!"<br>DIAL: Scream | Upbeat MX<br>Munchkin theme<br>Miss Gulch/Witch theme |
| 6) House falls | BG: cyclone/wind<br>DIAL: Witch cackles<br>DIAL: D screams | Active, big. |
| 7) House lands | FX: crash | MX stops |
| 8) D walks thru house and exits. | Silence except for FX: door open | |
| 9) D opens door to COLOR film<br>and Munchkinland. | BG: birds | "Somewhere over the Rainbow" |

Key
D = Dorothy     FX = Hard (specific) sound effect     MX = Music
DIAL = Dialogue     BG = Soft, background sound effect

**EXERCISE**

Now you try it! Pick a scene and dissect it yourself. A few suggestions: the opening scenes of *The River,* the island arrival scene in *Castaway,* or the last scene in *Babe.* Once you get the hang of it, you'll be ready to start designing sound for your own film or video. But first, a few terms.

# Sound and Music Editing Terms

In film lingo, the music department and its personnel are referred to as "Music," sound department and personnel as "Sound," and the picture editor and department as "Picture," a convention we will observe from now on. Here are other frequently used terms:

## *ADR*

Automated dialogue replacement, the process by which a line of dialogue is rerecorded and re-spoken by an actor in sync with the picture to replace the original sync production line.

## *Balance*

Make sure all the elements — dialogue, FX, and music — blend and can be heard. The balance varies from scene to scene, according to the dictates of the show, director, sound supervisor, and mixer.

## *Clean up a track*

To edit, equalize, level out the track, and remove as much extraneous noise as possible.

## *Cue*

Place where dialogue, music, or sound effect is located on a track, reel, or session.

## *Cue sheet*

A multi-page chart of the cues for each reel of dialogue, music, and effects. The music editor and each sound editor writes a cue sheet.

## *DAW*

Digital audio workstation. Used to record, edit, and mix sound and music. Well known DAWs that sound editors use are: Apple's Soundtrack Pro, Steinberg's Nuendo, and Adobe's Audition. Pro Tools, the most popular system, was designed by DigiDesign, which operates under Avid's

**10.a** Pro Tools, set up for a music editor. *Photo courtesy of Avid.*

umbrella. In addition to Pro Tools, music editors favor Apple's Logic Audio and Steinberg's Cubase.

### Digital audio recorder, a.k.a. digital recorder or recorder

Standard in-studio audio recording device used to record ADR, Foley, FX, dialogue, music, and the final mix that holds 8–48 tracks, depending on the machine. It records to a digital medium such as hard disk, DAT, CD, or DVD or can be saved as a session (a file) for the digital audio editing system.

### Diegetic and nondiegetic sound

Diegetic describes sounds that sync to an onscreen source, e.g., a bat hitting a ball. Asynchronous sounds that do not have a visible source and play in the background are considered nondiegetic, e.g., a river babbling.

### Dynamics

Relationship between low and high volume. If mixed correctly, track dynamics will be uncompressed, differentiate between soft and loud sounds, and contain organic high points and low points.

DESIGNING SOUND AND MUSIC

## Equalize (EQ)

Adjust the volume level of individual frequencies of a sound in order to change its tone. For example, dialogue is always EQ'd so that ADR lines match the production dialogue track.

## Gain, a.k.a. level or volume

Increase or decrease in strength of an electrical signal which is measured in decibels or number-of-times of magnification. Mixers constantly "ride the gain" to ensure a consistent audio level from show start to finish. If this wasn't done, viewers would constantly be adjusting their TV sets.

The gain control is the audio potentiometer that raises or lowers the record, mix, or playback signal strength. Keeping the levels equal is commonly referred to as "leveling out" the dialogue. This means that all the characters sound like they're talking to each other; one doesn't sound lower or further away.

## Hiss

Unwanted high frequency sounds ameliorated through EQ'ing.

## Hot

Loud. The VU meter is in the red. You don't want your levels too hot because when a big, loud sound comes along you will have no gain left.

## LCRS

Left-center-right-surround speaker channels in a movie theater. During the premix and mix, the mixers assign tracks to LCRS speaker channels.

## 5.1

Surround sound with five channels: left, right and center in the front plus left and right surrounds. The "1" stands for the low frequency effects channel or sub-woofer.

## 7.1

The latest surround sound which adds left and right rear channels to 5:1.

## Looping

ADR is routinely referred to as looping and ADR lines as loop lines due to the way ADR was recorded on film in the past.

### Looper

Voice actor brought to the ADR stage to record non-sync lines for unnamed characters in scenes, e.g., bar patrons, soccer fans, crowd of protestors. Loopers are usually part of a loop group which voices all extra lines for a show, working scene by scene.

### Mix down, a.k.a. sub dub

Combine tracks. Used as a noun or a verb.

### Mixer, a.k.a. rerecording engineer or postproduction audio mixer

Person who mixes the sound and music and creates the sound elements for delivering on disk, file, film, or tape.

### Mono sound

As opposed to stereo sound. One track is recorded by a non-stereo mike and the same track is played to each speaker. Dialogue tracks are usually mono as are some SFX tracks but few shows finish mono these days.

### Multitrack

Computer software used instead of DAW to make ADR, Foley, and other post audio recordings on a computer. Developed from a hardware device popular in the 1980s and 1990s and called "the 24 track," since the most commonly used machine had 24 tracks.

### Pan

Direct the sound to the right, left, or center speaker channel. Mixers routinely pan sounds to simulate what a character is hearing or to correspond to a pan shot. Picture and sound editors also regularly pan audio on their digital editing systems. Examples of situations that call for panning: a parade marching by, a bird flapping overhead, a bullet zinging across the plain.

### Pitching audio

How high or low the audio sounds. Pitch is the main way the audience distinguishes sounds.

### Pot

Potentiometer. A mixer may say, "I raised the pot" or "lowered the pot." What they did was move a slider or knob to change the EQ, gain,

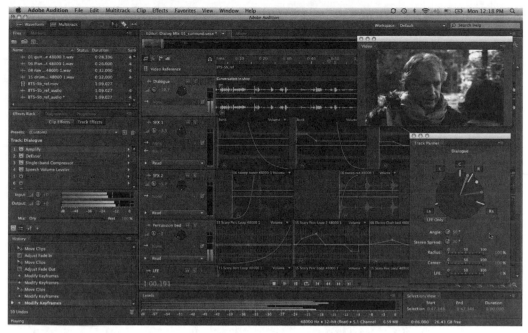

**10.b** Photo of pan & other sound tools on Adobe Audition. *Photo courtesy of Adobe.*

pan, pitch, tone, etc. While adjusting the pot, the mixer watches the VU meter to make sure it stays within normal range. Technically, a pot is a resistor with a range of potential settings. A mixing board has many pots.

## Pre-lay
Transfer the edited tracks to hard drive before the premix or mix.

## Production track
Original sync track recorded during the shoot.

## Punch in
Work on a particular section of a track during mixing and leave the surrounding area alone.

## Rock 'n' roll
Swiftly fix or finish a section of the mix and move on.

## SFX
Sound effects. Routinely shortened to FX just like the term VFX. Context will make the meaning clear.

### Stereo sound

As opposed to mono sound. Identical tracks are separated and played to different speaker channels, usually left and right. LCRS is a sophisticated form of stereo audio and is the standard. Stereo tracks give the audience a wider spatial feel for the sound.

To create stereo, two tracks are recorded at the same time with a stereo mike. Background sounds, such as wailing winds are often recorded stereo so they surround the audience and seem like they are everywhere.

To cut stereo tracks, the sound editor will usually gang them together and cut one exactly like the other.

### Sweeten

Add extra audio elements to an effect to refine it and make it sound just right. This fine-tuning involves playing around with the sound: EQ'ing it, varying its speed or pitch, adding other SFX, etc. For example, one frequently used sound editor trick is to sweeten the sound of an explosion by adding tracks of animal growls. On low budget shows, sweetening substitutes for the mix. On TV shows, sweetening refers to the laying back of the final audio to the show master before it's shipped to the network.

### Tubby, a.k.a. basey

Overpowering, low frequency (bass) sounds that are attenuated (reduced) through EQ'ing.

### Signal

Electricity that flows through a mic — cabled or wireless — to a media storage device such a disk, drive, or tape.

### Level

Amount of signal strength.

### Clip

Distort or overmodulate a signal. Digital signals, which are a lot less forgiving than analog signals, clip when registering less than digital zero.

### Compressor

Device that automatically reduces an audio signal's dynamic range, i.e., decreases the difference between high and low levels or volume.

## Limiter

An analog circuit in a recorder that automatically adjusts volume to prevent clipping when a digital or analog signal surpasses a preset level.

## VU

Volume unit for both analog and digital signals. Recordists and rerecordists use a VU meter to calibrate audio so that levels are consistent throughout the show. The meter displays the dB (decibel) level of the sound during mixing or recording via digital thermometer-type displays, LED lights, or a red needle on a speedometer-type scale as shown in figure 10.c.

**10.c** VU meter on the BF76 plug-in limiter-compressor. *Photo courtesy of Avid.*

# THE SOUND AND MUSIC DESIGN PROCESS

*"When I say sound, that's all of it, that's all the effects, all the detail work, and of course the score, because all of it needs to feel like it's one piece. It has to be able to be integrated and yet set itself apart at the same time, so it's a complicated proposition."*

—KATHRYN BIGELOW, director, *The Hurt Locker*

The spotting session is the kick-off meeting for a show's sound and music design. Sound and Music usually spot separately. The session may take place in a screening room, on the picture editor's system, or on a DAW where notes can be input directly.

# The Sound Spotting Session

*"... I try to enhance the movie, support what the story's telling, and make it a little bit better, clearer, and more interesting."*

—PAUL OTTOSSON, sound designer, *The Hurt Locker, Spiderman 2* and *3*

Spotting brings the sound designer, director, sound editors (sometimes), producer (possibly), and picture editor together to view and discuss the show. The conversation is specific — about certain sound effects the director desires or where ADR is anticipated — and general as the director talks about what a scene, subject, or character should convey. The sound designer (and editors, if present) make notes on what each scene requires. This is the time to set the plan of action, make sure you're in sync with the director's desires, express your ideas, raise concerns, and ask detailed questions.

If you're designing your own show's sound, spot with yourself. Go through the show, stopping and starting to make a list of specific sounds and where they go. You'll also want to form a clear idea of how you want your show to sound overall as well as in each scene, e.g., dark, light, bouncy, ominous, uplifting, sorrowful, dreamy, tense, happy, scary, sexy, etc. Here are six questions to help you decide what kind of SFX to use:

---

### FRAMING SFX

1. What is the sound?
2. Is it a hard (specific) sound or a soft (background) sound?
3. Is it organic or synthetic? Will it require a little or a lot of manipulation?
4. Where (at what time code) is the sound located?
5. How does the sound support the scene? the subject? the movie overall?
6. What does the sound represent? Tension, horror, joy, sorrow or what?

*Example*: The sound of the tanks advancing in *Life Is Beautiful*. The sound signifies not only the arrival of the U.S. liberators but also the fulfillment of the father's promise. It's a moving moment and the climax of the film.

---

Steve Boeddeker gives this advice: "With any film, the first step in sound design is getting a feel for the film and deciding what you want it to sound like. For me it's usually an emotional thing in that I'll watch it and let ideas just come to me and I'll jot them down or even dive right in and try them."

## Spotting notes

During the spotting session all dialogue and SFX notes are made on a laptop, notepad, or note form or entered directly into a DAW.

### DIALOGUE

Dialogue notes will fit into either of two categories:

1. Dialogue that must be replaced by ADR. (More about ADR in Chapter 11's section on dialogue editing.)
2. Dialogue that must be added such as new lines, wild lines, and walla[2].

## SFX

*"We must draw a distinction between those sound effects which are amusing only by virtue of their novelty (which soon wears off), and those that help one to understand the action, and which excite emotions which could not been roused by the sight of the pictures alone."*

—RENE CLAIR, French New Wave writer, from *Reflections on the Cinema*

Each sound effect noted will fall into one of three types and affect viewers in a certain way, as Table 10.3 documents.

**TABLE 10.3**
**TYPES OF SFX AND VIEWER PERCEPTION**

| TYPE | DESCRIPTION | EXAMPLES | VIEWERS... |
|---|---|---|---|
| Sync sounds, a.k.a. diegetic or hard sounds | Sounds that sync with a specific action on screen. | Phone ring, dog bark, champagne cork pop, water splash, glass smash, toilet flush, keys in door, plane take-off, tire screech, car horn. | — Are conscious of hard sounds.<br>— Ordinarily react to sound, e.g., a gunshot, before seeing the action that produced the sound. |
| Non-sync sounds, a.k.a. asynchronous, non-diegetic, or soft sounds | Soft sounds that have a constant presence and do not sync to a specific action. | Ambience, wind, crickets chirping, a brook gurgling, rain, feet shuffling on a dance floor, traffic, windshield wipers. | Are only peripherally aware of soft sounds ordinarily since they play in the background. |
| Foley | SFX recorded in sync with specific actions on the screen that can't be recorded on location or obtained from a sound library. | A kiss, clothes rustle, bubble gum popping, fight noises, body falls, creaky doors, alien hatching, monkey scratching. | Are conscious of Foley though can't distinguish it from hard SFX. |

## *Consider music*

When spotting for sound, it's important to find out where the director plans to put music. If you've already cut temp music into the show, you'll have a good idea where music should appear. When music covers a scene, it doesn't mean there won't be any sound work. You can eliminate Foley but, at a minimum, you will add ambience. Also, since the director will sometimes drop the music during the mix, it's wise to design and edit sound for every scene. Better to overdesign sound and drop out a few cues than madly be adding and cutting in sounds while on the mix stage.

---

2. Non-sync background conversation made up of indistinguishable words voiced by actors.

Sound must always aim to work hand in hand with Music to uphold the story and meet or exceed the director's intentions. Music editor Charles Martin Inouye (*Gnomeo and Juliet, Little Fockers,* and *Smart People*) puts it this way: "Even if a composer has written music for it [the cue], don't fight the picture. If it's not serving the needs of the movie as much as maybe someone's bit of dialogue or some creaky windmill, there's cooperation and coordination between the sound effects and the music people that's very important."

## THE MUSIC SPOTTING SESSION

*"Composers like to be problem solvers. We like to find creative ways to solve problems and our number one problem is often they don't have enough time or enough money."*
—JEFF TOYNE, composer, *Dirty Girl, Box Elder,* and *The Two Coreys.*

The music editor and music supervisor spot the show with the director and producer. The composer and songwriter may be present or, if hired earlier, may have already met with the director and be off composing. The discussion will center on the director's ideas for the music's placement in the show as well as its style and genre. Directors tend to talk in dramatic and emotional terms when describing the music in the movie: the composer and music editor will translate these descriptions into the music. Usually monetary matters, namely music budget and rights, will pop up and play a role in the discussion.

During the session the music editor makes spotting notes. The notes will detail the location and duration of each music cue (piece of music), and how each music cue should sound — melancholy, stealthy, frenzied, etc. The session's goals are the same as for spotting sound: To clarify the overall music design and vision, to set down the musical requirements for each scene or sequence (mood, purpose, duration, etc.), and to develop a rapport between director and music personnel.

It's never too early to start thinking about how music will play in your project. Documentarian Ken Burns relates, "I record all of my music with authentic instruments in a studio before we start editing, doing many, many versions. The music shapes the film as we edit so it has an organic relationship to the content."

## AFTER SPOTTING
# Cueing and Acquiring Sound and Music

Following the spotting session, sound and music editors cue and acquire sound and music in preparation for editing.

## Cueing Sound and Music

Cueing effects or music is also referred to as breaking down a show.

Frequently the sound designer or editor cue ADR and effects on the DAW so they can be input into the DAW and edited. ADR is cued to be recorded on the ADR stage and Foley is cued to be recorded on the Foley stage. The music editor and assistant time each music cue, thereby turning the spotting notes into timing sheets, a.k.a. breakdown notes. Included in the timing sheets are: dialogue lines so that music does not cover them, the number assigned to the cue, and a detailed description of what's happening on screen during the cue.

## Acquiring Sound

*"Every time I hear a new sound, it gives me a new idea — it feeds my creative consciousness. As a result, I did a tremendous amount of field recording on* Titanic *— about 60 hours of raw field recording. We recorded all sorts of sounds: quadraphonic sounds of wind, a tremendous amount of recordings of water in all sorts of environments — water treatment plants, hydrophonic recordings underneath ships, etc. We placed microphones down all sorts of strange places — into hulls of ships to get different types of sloppy water hits."*
—CHRISTOPHER BOYES, *Tron: Legacy; Avatar;* and *Titanic*

### Recording SFX

Sound designers get their kicks from creating, discovering, and manipulating sounds in inventive and memorable ways. They take the time to find and record the specific sound of a 1968 VW microbus, a Brazilian tree frog, or the Garden State Parkway at rush hour. They dig out these sounds from a variety of sources and mediums.

### Sound libraries and production recordings

In addition to recording their own sounds, SFX editors also draw from sound libraries which are available on CDs and DVDs as well as online. Many SFX editors have their own extensive sound libraries which they expand with each job. SFX editors also rely on the production recordings and the picture's cut production tracks. They will dig into alternative takes and search through the wild sound that the on-set recordist made.

## Foley

Foley is another way editors acquire audio effects. It's usually difficult to distinguish Foley sounds from the natural audio recorded on the set during production. This is due to the talent of the Foley artist, a.k.a. Foley walker or dancer who re-enacts the scene in perfect sync with innovative props to create these "natural sounds."

The Foley artist works on a Foley stage, a.k.a. Foley pit or booth, which has audio recording equipment and a screen for playing back the picture. The Foley pit is a purposeful junkyard which contains all kinds of props — invariably clothing and shoes — and all sorts of surfaces: grass, gravel, sand, cement, etc. Foley artists originate realistic sounds from unexpected materials. For instance, crunching snow is Foleyed by walking on kosher salt coated with cornstarch. To create Foley, the Foley artist — properly positioned near a mic — makes the effect in sync to the picture playing on the screen while a recordist captures the sound on a hard drive or digital audio recorder.

Jack Foley pioneered the technique in the 1930s. He never received a screen credit but his artistry improved many a movie and the technique named after him lives on. Today, feature films and high budget TV shows use Foley, but normally it's too expensive for TV, corporate videos,

**10.d** Foley stage. *Photo courtesy of Todd-AO/Ascent Media Creative Services.*

and other shows. To avoid Foley costs, record good location sound and do a top-notch sound editing job.

## Audio formats

There are three uncompressed audio file formats that professionals use: AIFF, WAV, and BWF. Compressed formats like MP3 and QT are also used for temp mixes and on lower budget shows. Sound regularly arrives via hard drive, disk, DAT, videotape, and, decreasingly, DA-88 or DA-98 cassette tapes.

## Last word — a Hitchcock ending

At times the usual sources don't work and the sound designer has to innovate. Danny Greene, sound supervisor on *Psycho* recalls: "The only problem we had was the stabbing sound in the shower. We used our library. We had standard thugs and whacks and socks... Well, Hitchcock didn't like any of the socks. I started to feel like I'd failed. So I asked him to break for dinner and thought, okay, I'll get right down to it. I went to the market down the street and bought the biggest roast I could find. I got a knife from the prop shop, which was ironically the one that was in the picture, and I just recorded stabs. Stabs from the gristle side, stabs from the meat side — something I had never done before. And the sound of that was just vicious. Slicing flesh. It was horrible. So Hitchcock came back... and he just smiled and said, 'Oh, yes. That's lovely.' He just got off on it."

# Typical Sound Workflow

Like picture, sound has workflows. Though no two projects will take the exact same course, here's a typical sound workflow.

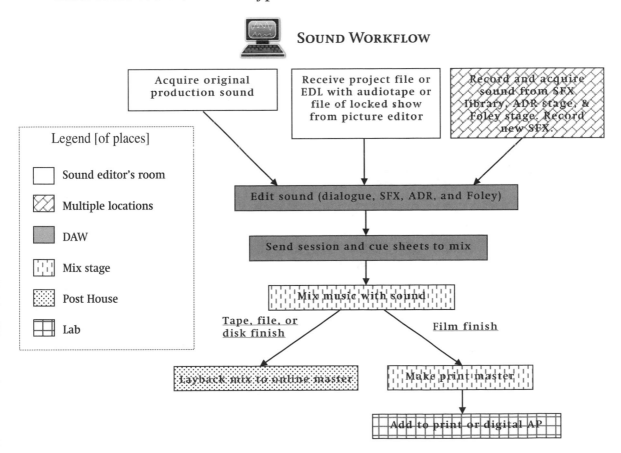

301

# Acquiring Music

*"What you can't do with a camera or dialogue, music has a way of taking care of. It gets at the deeper emotions that aren't always expressible on film. People who are skeptical about film music should be condemned to watch films without it."*

—David Raksin, composer, *Laura, The Secret Life of Walter Mitty,* and *The Bad and the Beautiful*

The music editor (or the picture editor if the show can't afford a music editor) acquires music from a variety of sources and formats. This section describes these sources and spells out how to obtain the rights to use the music in your show.

## Composed music

A show can hire a composer to create a score and/or a songwriter to crank out a song or two. Or if you have sufficient knowledge and instinct, you can create music yourself.

### Composer and score

On low budget shows, the composer will create a score, record it on a synthesizer, and hand it over to the music editor as a session. If the show is more flush, the composer will send the score to a recording session where a conductor will lead a group of musicians in making a recording. (More on the composer's process following the music workflow at the end of the chapter.)

### Songwriter and song

*"No one leaves the theater whistling a two-shot."*

—Anonymous, www.arthousemovies.com

The songwriter will compose the song as well as supervise and deliver the recording of the song. Alternatively, the show may purchase the rights to use a recording of a song or to record a new version of a previously written song. To do this, you must *clear* the song.

Clearing a song involves paying a fee to the record company (owner of the master rights) and to the author's publishing company (owner of the sync or publishing rights). The publisher will then grant you permission to sync the song to a picture image. If your film or video is a student or festival project, the publisher usually gives you a handsome break in the price along with a limited festival license. If your film is subsequently scooped up by a distribution company, the distributor will then renegotiate a commercial license with you. If you want to use a tune from a band — especially an unknown band — you can probably negotiate a deal directly with its manager.

### DIY SCORE

Various software programs are available if you want to attempt your own musical score. Programs like Apple's Garageband and SmartSound's Sonicfire Pro offer an array of different features including sampling and altering the music's tempo, duration, and pitch.

## Music library

Most shows can't spring for a composer so the music editor pulls music from a library such as Associated Production Music or Extreme Music. The music editor auditions tracks for every cue noted during spotting and imports it into their DAW. The director/client/producer approves all music and the company buys the tracks or entire CD. Music libraries have copyrighted all the music so there are no rights issues to deal with. When purchasing music from a library, however, scrutinize the contract for any hidden fees. You can get music free for certain venues, namely podcasts and webcasts, but normally you will license it for a specific time period and type of programming.

## Music tracking

Even when a show has a composer, the composer frequently does not compose for the entire movie. For instance, a scene may be added or the producers may wish to purchase a previously written song. The composer then asks the music editor to *track* that part of the show. Tracking means that the editor cuts up a song to fit the new scene or rearranges music the composer has already composed. From time to time the music editor *tracks the temp*, i.e., selects and edits the music for the temp mix. Some of this music may remain in the final mix but most of it will be replaced during the scoring session. A show that doesn't use original music is referred to as *tracked*.

## Source music

Source music has a clear, visual source onscreen such as a radio, album, or piano. Commonly, source music plays in the background and is purchased but can be composed.

## Needle drop, a.k.a. canned music

Background music — usually source music or a song — that requires a license fee to use in a show. The term dates to the days of vinyl when each drop of the record player's needle required a separate fee.

## Playback music

Playback is music recorded to be played back on the set on each musical take. It enables the performers to maintain sync with the music while singing and/or dancing. The music editor makes sure that the playback music gets recorded and sent to the set.

## Music formats

Music arrives on a variety of mediums, the same as sound: file, hard drive, disk, DAT, videotape, and, decreasingly, DA-88 or DA-98 cassette tapes.

## Rights and licenses

You need to clear each piece of music and all song lyrics that go into your film or video. This is a time-consuming job so start it as soon as you decide what music you want. You need to make certain that each piece of music is *free and clear* before your film or video is released. Free and clear denotes music that does not have a copyright nor require a fee because it's considered public domain (unowned). For instance, all music composed during the classical period is public domain. However, if you use a public domain recording, you will have to pay the person or orchestra who made the recording as well as the recording company. If you play and record public domain music yourself or compose the music for your own film, you do not have to pay any fees. Temp music is also not subject to fees or rights searches, so anything goes!

### MUSIC REPORTING, A.K.A. PUBLISHING CUE SHEET

After the music is cut in and mixed, tally how many minutes and seconds each piece of music runs. Enter this figure on a cue sheet along with the cue number, how the music was used, its title, composer, publisher, and performing rights society such as ASCAP,[3] BMI,[4] or SESAC,[5] and hand them over to the production company along with a disk or file of the music. You can obtain a cue sheet like the sample in Figure 10.e from any of the performing rights societies listed previously.

3. American Society of Composers, Authors, and Publishers.
4. Broadcast Music Incorporated.
5. Society of European Stage Authors and Composers.

| SAMPLE MUSIC PUBLISHING CUE SHEET | | | | |
|---|---|---|---|---|
| Company | | Title of project/ series | | |
| Phone #, email | | Length | | |
| Person to contact | | Network | | |
| CUE INFO | | | | |
| Cue # | Cue title | Use | Timing | Composer(s), affiliation/% | Publisher(s), affiliation/% |
| | | | | | |
| | | | | | |
| | | | | | |

10.e Sample music publishing cue sheet

Do not take music clearance lightly; make sure all your music is cleared. If you don't have time, hire a music coordinator to do the job and don't skimp if it becomes necessary to bring on a lawyer. Publishers and performing rights societies will not take it lightly if you are a slacker.

## Typical Music Workflow

The workflow chart below illustrates the typical path music takes from its origin to the mix.

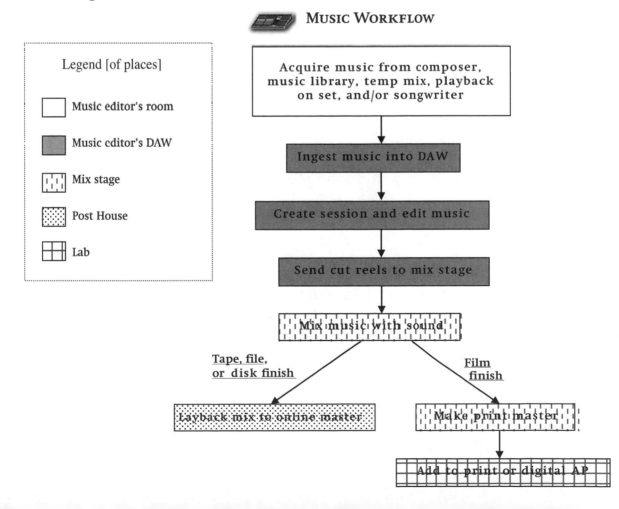

MUSIC WORKFLOW

Legend [of places]

☐ Music editor's room

▨ Music editor's DAW

▦ Mix stage

▦ Post House

⊞ Lab

Acquire music from composer, music library, temp mix, playback on set, and/or songwriter

Ingest music into DAW

Create session and edit music

Send cut reels to mix stage

Mix music with sound

Tape, file, or disk finish

Film finish

Layback mix to online master

Make print master

Add to print or digital AP

# The Composer and the Composing Process

*"It's one thing to write a beautiful piece of music, but it's another thing to have that beautiful piece of music be the right tone and start at the right time and be the right emotional variant that makes sense dramatically."*

—JEFF TOYNE

The director or producer hires the composer who begins work during preproduction (working off the script), or production (working off the script and dailies), or post production (working off cuts in progress). The timing of the composer's hiring depends on the size of the picture, its budget, and the scope of the music.

Once engaged, the composer will spot the show with the director and the pair will talk extensively about the amount and kind of music the show demands. The composer may create music for the temp mix, furthering the conversation. As soon as the cut is locked, the composer will receive a copy of the show on file, disk, or perhaps tape, and start writing in earnest. Before we continue with the composer's process, a few definitions are in order.

**10.f** Composer begins. *Photo courtesy of Kim Bova.*

## Definitions

### SYNTHESIZER, A.K.A. SYNTH

A "band in a box," a synth is an electronic instrument that produces an endless variety of sounds and music that can imitate instruments or create new sounds. There are hard (hardware) synths that plug in to DAWs and soft (software) synths that export the composer's MIDI file into the DAW.

### MIDI

Musical instrument digital interface. Protocol for the types of control signals that one electronic musical device sends to another. In less technical terms, MIDI is a plug-in which enables a musician's computer to communicate with a host of devices such as MIDI sound modules (samplers, synthesizers, etc.) and to send and receive time code. A MIDI score is the representation of the music.

### MIDI CONTROLLER

Keyboard, drum kit, guitar, piano, or other electronic musical device that generates MIDI messages to adjust individual controls like pan or gain on devices in the MIDI network.

### SAMPLE

Take a part (sample) of a recorded instrument, e.g., bass, voice, keyboard or strings or sound to use in recording a song or score.

### TEMPO

Speed, measured in BPMs (beats per minutes), at which a piece of music is performed.

## Creating the music

*"I don't think it's about being a great composer or an amazing musician or anything like that. I'm none of those things. If you're able to feel, and if you're willing to allow yourself to really sit in front of the characters and feel what they're experiencing — and watch them and look into their faces and their hands, and look around the picture — it will start to translate itself in music through you."*

—LISA GERRARD, composer, singer, and musician, *Layer Cake, Whalerider,* and *Gladiator*

Some composers develop music using pen, pencil, and piano but most use synthesizers and a musical composition software, e.g., Cubase or Pro Tools or notation software, e.g., Finale or Sibelius. Working through the show cue by cue, the composer samples instruments on a synth to select the composition's instrumentation and plays the music back through the MIDI controller. The composer may add arpeggio, echo, or other effects and drop or add instruments along the way and will make innumerable decisions on pitch, tempo, accent, beat, key, and modulation (change of key).

When ready, the composer will test the music by playing it back against the picture. Music spotting notes are like picture paper cuts: What works in theory on paper may not meet the playback test. A perfectly conceived piece of music may bog the picture down, not hit

**10.g** Digidesign's Mini Grand composer. *Photo courtesy of Avid.*

the desired emotional tone, or otherwise miss the mark; another piece may give the movie extra zing or add meaning in unexpected ways.

Composing is an intense trial and error process: Every music cue — like every sound element and picture cut — should serve an emotional beat of the story. This may mean the music heightens the drama or runs counter to what's on screen, builds to a crescendo, or lies low and then zaps the audience or does a thousand other things. The style of the music will depend on the film or video's components: time period(s), theme, mood, setting, editing, cinematography, lighting, undertones, characters, and more.

# The Scoring Session

Once the composer has finished the score, the music supervisor schedules the musicians for a scoring session during which the music is conducted, played, and recorded. A file or tape of the show runs on a screen and monitor so the conductor and composer (frequently the same person) can keep an eye on the scene as it's recorded.

## *Preparation*

The composer chooses a tempo for each music cue. The tempo is based on metronome time — more often referred to as *click time* — a method of timing music derived from the frames and half frames of 35mm film. During the scoring session, warning clicks set the tempo in advance of each music cue. Also, a click track plays throughout the cue so the musicians can keep time with each other and the picture.

**10.h** Score editor. *Photo courtesy of Avid.*

## STREAMERS

The music editor or assistant programs a streamer (a colored line) for each music cue so it will stream across the picture as it plays during the session. Depending on what the conductor demands, a streamer can designate:

- The start, end, or duration of a music cue.
- A musical accent or change in tempo.

## SCORING CUE LIST

The assistant music editor fills out the scoring cue list and distributes it to everyone attending the scoring session. The list provides pertinent information for each cue: name, brief description of scene action, start time code, duration, and tempo. The editor numbers the cues by reel or act and cue, e.g., 1m1 stands for the first act and the first music cue; 1m2 would be the first act and the second music cue and so on. The cue system is critical not only for ordering, editing, and scoring music but for mixing music as well as completing the licensing paperwork afterwards.

## Scoring

To create the cue, the scene plays back on the screen, the warning clicks sound, the streamer starts, the conductor conducts, and the cue is recorded. Holed up in the recording booth, the music editor listens to the take as it's recorded for problems such as wrong notes, coughs, or chair scrapes. Barring obvious problems, once the recording is complete, the take is played back. If it's unacceptable to the director, composer, recording engineer, or music editor, it's redone. If the take is a keeper, the music editor directs everyone to the next cue. Similar cues are recorded together, rather than recording cues sequentially from the beginning of the picture to the end.

Every take is timed by a digital counter. There is also a digital clock on the wall that the conductor follows. The timing of the recorded cue must match the original spotting timing as closely as possible in order to fit the picture. Both the sound engineer and the music assistant editor make timing notes and other notes on each acceptable take. The engineer mikes and records each type of instrument — string, brass, woodwind, and percussion — onto a separate track for ease and flexibility during the final mix.

**10.i** Scoring session. *Photo courtesy of Todd-AO/Ascent Media Creative Services.*

## *After the scoring session*

All the instruments on their separate tracks are mixed down to fewer tracks. This mixdown, as it's called, is created in a new session on the DAW. The music editor goes to work, editing the best takes and laying out the tracks. Once done, the music editor mixes the music, creating a pre-mix of the music. Then it's time to send a hard drive of the session to the mix stage where the music will be mixed with the rest of the sound elements, i.e., the dialogue and SFX.

## CHAPTER WRAP-UP

Now that you've familiar with how sound and music are designed, created and acquired, you're ready to move into the sound editing room and on to the dub stage and the next chapter to learn how sound effects, dialogue, and music are edited and mixed.

## CHAPTER 11

# Editing and Mixing Sound and Music

*"Sound is 50% of the experience."*
—George Lucas

## Overview

The first half of this chapter tells you how sound and music are edited. It details the steps and the tools for cutting sound effects, dialogue, and music and explains how ADR is created and edited. Then it's time for the mix. The second half of the chapter takes you to the mix stage and conducts you through the pre-mix and mix process, shedding light on the powerful contribution that the final mix makes to your show. Let's make tracks!

## PREPARING FOR SOUND AND MUSIC EDITING

Sound and music are edited reel by reel, scene by scene, and cue by cue. For each scene of a picture there are multiple tracks of sound effects, dialogue, and music. Why? Because many sound effects, dialogue, and music cues occur near or at the same time. To be mixed effectively, these cues must be spaced out over multiple tracks.

In order to cut sound and music, you need to *see* the locked picture and *hear* the production track (track that the picture editor cut). Together, picture and track guide all sound and music cutting. Indeed, once input into the DAW, the production track is called the guide track. On low budget shows, the picture editor cuts all the sound and music right on the digital editing systems with their fine and ever-improving sound tools. Higher budget shows bring on sound and music professionals and sound editing work stations. This next section details more specifically what they'll need for the job.

# The Handover: What Picture Provides Sound

To get off to a good start with Sound, Picture needs to communicate clearly with everyone about the current state of the show and give 'em the files they want in the format they request via disk, hard drive, or server. Here are Picture's responsibilities for the handover to sound.

## Prep show

*"File management and data management are crucial as it trips up everyone down the line if they can't locate sound."*

—Victoria Rose Sampson, Dialogue, ADR and supervising sound editor, *Scream 4, The Fighter,* and *Sex and the City 1* and *2*

Make certain your project's time line and tracks are in sync and cleanly laid out in an orderly hierarchy, e.g., production track, narration, sound effects, and music. Add head and tail leaders and sync pops as described in the first section of Chapter 9 to enable the sound editors to keep reels in sync.

## Make copy of show

Provide a copy of the show on tape or as a QuickTime file. Make sure that it displays burnt-in time code (and feet and frames if you're on a show finishing on film) starting at FFOP. You should also burn in the audio time code and reel number. You can make these copies and add the burn-in right from your digital editing system. Send material using the codec, frame rate (commonly 23.97 or 29.97), and frame size that Sound requires. Fulfill any other requirements on Sound and Music's list such as eliminating the video tracks from the time line or deleting crossfades (audio dissolves).

## Send the edited audio media

Most commonly, sound editors will demand either an AAF or OMF file because these files readily translate into a session (sequence) on their

Pro Tools. Sound may require an EDL also. Here are some more details about these files.

### EDL (EDIT DECISION LIST) = *Time code and reel number for each edit*

The EDL, habitually referred to simply as "the list," has been around since the 1980s and continues to be a player in onlining and sound editing. An EDL contains the reel number and time code numbers for each edit in the final offline cut. It can also carry the DAT or DA-88 time code and sound roll info — data critical to sound editors. However, an EDL will not contain media or any metadata. (More in Chapter 12 about the roles EDLs play in online.)

### OMF (OPEN MEDIA FRAMEWORK) = *EDL + media*

Introduced by Avid in 1990, the OMF file expanded the EDL to include audio, video, and VFX as well as title re-creation information. Basically, OMFs (and AAFs) re-create the picture editor's time line with all of the edited audio tracks, including many choices like volume and speed changes. OMFs can include media, project data, and metadata and appear as a time line in the Pro Tools, Avid, or whatever editing system they're imported to.

### AAF (ADVANCED AUTHORING FORMAT) = *OMF that links to but does not contain media*

Debuting in 2000, AAF is a newer file format that rivals OMF. AAF files contain editing decisions and links to media but do not hold media. At present, Picture, Sound, Music, and online editors use AAFs and OMFs every day since each file format interacts with systems and devices in different ways. Plug-in software like Automatic Duck and MetaFuze aid in translating sequences like AAF, OMF, and other files between systems such as After Effects, Avid, FCP, and Pro Tools.

## Send original sound files

The sound editors need all the audio recordings from their original file, DAT, or DA-88 source. The dialogue editor will ask for all the original dialogue recorded on set or location including room tone and wild lines. The sound effects editor will require all the wild tracks.

## Send session of temp mix, a.k.a. temp dub

If a temp mix was performed before the sound editors were hired, they will need to get the temp's files or session into their DAWs. Since OMFs and AAFs can pass volume, EQ, and other audio-altering data, check with Sound to see if they need this info or if they want you to strip it from the tracks. Ordinarily, Sound requires handles for each audio cut, so inquire about how long they would like their handles; 150 frames (5 seconds) is typical.

### Paperwork

Send the sound reports from all sound recordings as well as the final continuity sheet and contact list (phone, email, etc.).

## The Handover: What Picture Provides Music

Music's needs are simpler. The composer will request a tape or QT file of the show with burnt-in time code. The music editor will expect an AAF or OMF for importing into their Pro Tools and a list of all source music and songs as well as timing sheets. With these materials, along with continuity sheets, contact list, and spotting notes, Music will be off and running.

## SOUND AND MUSIC EDITING TOOLS

Cutting sound on film faded out with the end of the millennium due to cost and the new digital technology. Today, sound and music are edited on digital systems which provide the latest tools, best interface with digital picture editing, and an expedient path to the mix stage. Sound and music editors cut on a DAW (digital audio workstation) but few call it that. Universally, editors refer to the brand name of the system they're cutting on — usually Pro Tools. Here's a bit more about how DAWs operate and what you can do on them:

### Sound samples and units of measurement

Unlike picture editing systems, which are frame-based, DAWs are based on audio samples, measured in kHz (kilohertz) per second. Currently, sound and music editors edit at 48 kHz which carries 48,000 samples per second. When cutting and cross fading, the editor works with units ranging in size from 1 second to 1 frame to 1/100th of a frame and every size in between.

### Manipulating sound

With the click of a DAW's mouse, you can manipulate audio, reversing, reverbing, or EQ'ing it and pitching it higher or lower in many subtle and not so subtle ways. You can compress (shorten) or expand (lengthen) a sound's duration, repeat it, re-sample it, and copy it to another track. You can also raise and lower the volume of a sound, track, or several tracks. The waveform tool with its graphic plot of the amplitude — loud and soft spots of sounds — is indispensible for getting in between words or syllables and for pre-mixing effects. The innovative software available coupled with the demands of the picture and your imagination give you an enormous array of possibilities.

**11.a** Sound tools on Adobe Audition. *Photo courtesy of Adobe.*

## SOUND EFFECTS EDITING

*"See a sound; hear a sound. Every time you see some action on the screen your mind expects to hear a complementary sound. The support of sound effects helps you 'willingly suspend your disbelief' and become immersed in the movie experience."*

—SKYWALKER SOUND, George Lucas' sound company

### The challenge of SFX editing: The sound of three dogs barking

The sound effects editor receives the plan, the vision, and perhaps the cues from the sound designer and cuts in the most convincing effects possible. The effect can be as routine as putting in a *car by* (sound of a car driving by) or as inventive as expressing a storm on Mars. Before cutting an effect into a reel, the editor auditions it against the picture to see if it works. To work, the effect must do at least one, if not two or all three, of the following:

- Make the picture seem realistic or natural.
  Example: The yipping yelp of a Chihuahua.
- Trigger an emotion.
  Example: The feeling of loneliness induced by a wolf howl.
- Show something novel and imaginative.
  Example: The sound of a lunar dog barking at the earth.

If the show is not a routine show and/or the sound editor and the director haven't worked together before, the sound editor will often run ideas by the director ahead of time. Also, the sound effects editor, like the rest of sound and music editors, will provide alternative SFX for certain cues to give the director choices.

**11.b** Cutting effects on Pro Tools. *Photo courtesy of Dan Weeks.*

### INTO THE DAW

Once the editor determines that a sound effect works, the audition is over and the effect is cut into the reel on the DAW. More commonly today, the editor spots and auditions the reel in the session. Here are the typical steps which are more or less what Foley, dialogue, ADR, and music editors also follow:

---

**Editing Sound on a DAW**

1. Create a session.
   — A session is the place you work and can be a scene, reel, or an entire show, depending on how you set it up.
2. Import QT file of final locked cut.
3. Import sound tracks of final cut via OMF, AAF, or EDL.
   **3A.** Link to media if it did not arrive in Step #3.
4. Lock sync between guide track and final picture cut with time stamp at FFOP or other sync point (to keep sync during editing).
5. Import sound effect file and media via server or disk.
6. Go to where the first sound effect is cued.
   (Or spot and cue if you haven't done so already.)
7. Lay in the imported effect (from Step #5).
   — Laying in an effect means that you put it in the proper place against picture.
   — You may need to slip the effect a few frames and crossfade it in and/or out so that it sounds just right. Routinely you may use several sounds to create an effect.
8. Continue cutting in SFX until you're done with the reel.

---

### Cutting in Foley FX

The Foley editor starts the Foley process by cueing the Foley on the DAW and sending the session via hard drive or server to the Foley stage. The editor also sends a Foley cue sheet which contains the time code location of each cue, its name, number, description, etc. The Foley artist walks (creates) and records the Foley, then sends it back to the editor for fine tuning. The editor makes sure the Foley is in perfect sync and cuts out extraneous noise, cleaning up the Foley tracks. When finished, the editor sends the Foley session to the mix stage accompanied by the final Foley cue sheets.

**11.c** A sound effects editor works on some Foley. *Photo courtesy of Rhapsody Post.*

#### WORLDIZING — ANOTHER WAY TO CREATE A SOUNDSCAPE

Worldizing is defined as the aligning of sound elements — commonly Foley or ADR — to match a character's environment. The Foley or ADR editor worldizes a scene by placing the sound elements in the world — a live room such as a basement or garage — to make them sound more real. In the past the editor played the sounds from a sound booth into speakers placed in the world and re-recorded them via a mic placed in the world. Now plug-ins to the DAW do the job.

## DIALOGUE EDITING

*"Cooperation is important. We need each other. I respect the picture editor's cut and come to the table not just as an editor but as a filmmaker. I learn a movie's scenes and don't just think in reels as some sound editors do."*

—VICTORIA ROSE SAMPSON, Dialogue, ADR, and supervising sound editor *Scream 4, The Fighter,* and *Sex and the City 1* and *2.*

Dialogue editing is a critical part of sound editing that viewers aren't aware of ordinarily. But when they don't understand what an actor or narrator is saying or spy an out-of-sync line, they realize that dialogue work is lacking. Good dialogue editing entails cutting high quality tracks that play perfectly on their own without any sound effects or music tracks. It is meticulous work: The dialogue editor concentrates on every sentence, word, and utterance to makes sure the dialogue, narration, and VO (voice over) is clear and fits the show. This means cleaning out extraneous sounds, then filling any audio gaps with ambience so the dialogue blends into the setting of each scene. When the dialogue cannot be fixed, the dialogue editor works with the director and ADR editor to identify dialogue that must be ADR'd.

# How to Cut Dialogue

Dialogue tracks, as edited by the picture editor, cannot be delivered to the mixer. Why? Because the words are too close together for a mixer to get between them and properly mix the sound. The dialogue editor remedies this by splitting[1] (dividing) the tracks. A feature film can have up to 32 dialogue tracks per scene.

## How to split tracks

Dialogue editors split tracks by camera setups, putting master takes on one track, two-shots on another, Bonnie's close-up on a third, Clyde's close-up on a fourth, and so on. Why? Because each camera setup requires a different microphone setup. Part of any sound editor's job is to organize cues and tracks as effectively as possible for the mixer. Cutting each mic setup on a different track makes things easier for the mixer, resulting in an efficient mix.

## Reasons to split dialogue

*"It's the ambience behind the words that we're editing."*
—Victoria Rose Sampson

**1.** To match ambience between speakers

When two or more people are talking, there's usually a difference in the ambient sound between their two shots. For instance, if Ben and Jerry are talking, you would put Ben on one track and Jerry on another. Then you would extend the ambience at the head and tail of each of their lines so that their backgrounds can be blended during the mix. This is the most important reason to split dialogue. Dialogue editors spend more time matching and manipulating ambience than on the words themselves.

On documentaries, often there's little ambience to choose from so you'll have to steal it from wherever you can. Raw sound is expected on

---

1. Splitting dialogue is sometimes referred to as checkerboarding dialogue since each piece of dialogue is preceded and followed by sound fill and resembles a checkerboard when laid out on the time line.

documentaries and reality shows; it's part of what makes them seem authentic. However, the sound should not be so raw that it impedes the viewer's connection to the doc.

**2.** To adjust and match levels between speakers.

**3.** To single out a word or words for special treatment.

There are times when you want to raise or lower the volume of a word or futz it, (filter it to sound like it's coming through a telephone line). Splitting it off to another track isolates it for futzing; indeed, it's labeled the futz track.

## Common dialogue problems and fixes

*"I like solving a story problem with sound, for example by finding a take that helps you understand the film."*
—Victoria Rose Sampson

To hear the dialogue clearly, dialogue editors wear headphones. Here are some routine problems they encounter and how they fix them.

- Clicks and pops

When they hear a click, pop, actor's lips smack, or other unwanted noise on the production or any other track, dialogue editors get rid of it and cover the sound hole with ambience.

- Damaged lines

Occasionally a line of dialogue is distorted or all but destroyed due to technical or other reasons and ADR is not practical. To fix the line, the dialogue editor pieces it together word by word, at times syllable by syllable, from several takes so that it sounds acceptable and is in sync.

- Upcut line, a.k.a. clipped line

An upcut line is one that's cut off at the head or tail. The picture editor cuts without headphones so a syllable can get accidentally cut off. The dialogue editor finds the original sound take and adds back the upcut syllable.

- Alternate takes

Routinely, dialogue editors prepare additional takes or alternate versions of the same line from the production audio. These add/alt tracks, referred to as the X and Y tracks, give the mixer and director choices. For example, when a director gets to the mix stage and decides to dump an ADR line, an alt line may step off the bench. Secondarily, dialogue editors supply alt lines because while rooting around in the production takes, they discover a reading that's better technically or that they think the director might prefer. In either case, the editor mutes the alt tracks on the session but notes them on the cue sheet. This way the mixer can unmute the tracks and play them back as needed during the mix.

- Transitions between sounds

There are three ways to transition from one sound to another: cut, dissolve, or soft cut. A cut is also referred to as a straight cut or a hard cut. A sound dissolve, where one sound fades out as another fades in, is referred to as a crossfade. A soft cut is a tiny dissolve — 1 to 4 frames — between lines or sounds. Technically, a soft cut is a crossfade, but since it's only a few frames away from being a cut and has the effect of softening a cut, it's called soft cut. Soft cuts are used ubiquitously by sound and dialogue editors to smooth dialogue.

- PFX track

The production effects track (PFX track) consists of non-dialogue sounds like door closings and chair scrapings that are part of the production audio captured on the set or location. In essence, PFX is production Foley (and may help avoid or cut down on Foley expenses). When a film or video has foreign distribution and another language will be substituted for English, a PFX track is necessary. To create the PFX, the dialogue editor strips out all the English dialogue, leaving only the production effects, and adds ambience, crossfades, etc., to perfect the track. The PFX track, along with the music and sound effects tracks (M & E), will be turned over as part of the foreign delivery requirements. (More on M & Es in the mix section.)

### Special circumstances — fictional languages

If you edit dialogue long enough, you may get lucky, as Gwen Yates Whittle did on *Avatar* and get to work with an entirely new language. Here's her response to the challenge: "I loved working with the Na'vi language, and the translating of all the extra crowd dialogue in the film with the inventor of the language, Paul Frommer. It was cool to see how he took what we wanted to say and created new sentences, never heard or said before."

# ADR

The ADR editor or the dialogue editor notes the ADR lines during dialogue spotting. ADR is recorded in order to:

- Replace poor production track.

- Add any new lines that were written after the shoot.
- Change a performance (infrequently done).
- Re-voice a performance with a new actor (rarely done).
- Create walla or wild lines for groups of people or non-starring characters (see Loop Group below).
- Replace the movie theater version of a line, e.g., swear words, with the sanitized TV version.

ADR is not used on nonfiction shows as it would rightfully provoke the audience's distrust of the speaker and the entire show.

## *Preparing for ADR*

The editor prepares for the ADR session by cueing ADR lines and making a session on the DAW for each character. The ADR editor makes the cues directly on the digital audio system like the Foley editor and delivers the session(s) via hard drive or server to the ADR stage. Table 11.1 shows a cue sheet after the cues have been recorded at the ADR session. Appendix G at the end of this chapter provides a blank form for you to create your own. You can also download it from www.joyoffilmediting .com by selecting the Free tab.

# Table 11.1
# ADR Cue Sheet

| ADR CUE SHEET | | | SHOW: Home Free | | PAGE 1 OF 1 | | | |
|---|---|---|---|---|---|---|---|---|
| REELS Reel #= time code hour<br>Reel 2 Reel 4<br>Reel 3 Reel 5 | | | COMMENTS<br>Reason for ADR noted in<br>brackets.* | | DATE/VERSION<br>Aug 17 | | | |
| TIME CODE START | CUE | CHARACTER | DIALOGUE | | RECORDED TAKES | | | |
| 02:13:29:01 | 077 | Lois | We're firefighters too.<br>(overlap) | | NG<br>O | NG | X | NG |
| 03:03:12:11 | 094 | Lois | Truce!<br>(Added line) | | O | NG | X | |
| 04:09:48:23 | 126 | Lois | They're candy, dope.<br>(paper noise) | | NG<br>O | X | NG | NG |
| 05:19:37:22 | 163 | Lois | Can I have a puff?<br>(too much reverb on orig) | | NG<br>O | NG | NG | X |

**Key** (for marking recorded takes)

**X** Printed take          **O** Alternate take          **NG** No Good

*This is optional but helpful in case there's a question as to why a line is being ADR'd.

## Recording ADR

*"I usually have an idea of a performance in my head of what I'd like the actor to sound like, and I've always considered it my job to help them get there, especially if the director is not around at the time. There are reasons the actors are acting and I am not: I stink at acting! But I know how the mood of a scene should feel, and the sound sweetens what is on the screen. I guess you could say I act it in my head."*

—GWEN YATES WHITTLE, ADR, dialogue and sound editor at Skywalker Sound on *Tron*, *True Grit* (Academy Award), *Avatar*, and *The Curious Case of Benjamin Button*.

ADR is recorded on the ADR stage, a small sound stage with a recording booth and screen. On hand are the ADR editor, assistant editor, and recordist as well as the actor, director, and possibly the picture editor and producer. The scene is programmed to start a few lines before the ADR line. Beeps and sometimes streamers are inserted to prompt the actor.

To lay down an ADR cue, the actor studies the line on the cue sheet. When ready, the actor dons headphones, stands at the mic on the stage, and watches the scene play on the screen, commonly via a QT file. As the scene nears the

**11.d** View from recordist's booth toward stage: Prepping for ADR. *Photo courtesy of Todd-AO/Ascent Media Creative Services.*

ADR line, the actor hears three beeps. Where the fourth beep would be, the actor speaks the line. It's important that the actor match sync as well as performance or the viewer will notice the mismatch. Sitting in the recording booth, the ADR recordist monitors and makes notes on the ADR cue sheet about each take and which channel it was recorded to. The recordist saves the take to the editor's programmed ADR session in the DAW as well as to a back-up DAT.

If the take is satisfactory to director, actor, ADR editor, and recordist, the actor moves on to the next cue. If not, the scene replays and the actor immediately redoes the line which is re-recorded over the same spot in the session. The back-up DAT saves all takes in case one of the rejected takes is needed later. On average, an actor can loop ten lines in an hour. Occasionally, two actors will loop a scene together, but usually looping is a solo endeavor. In addition to ADR lines, any added lines for the character are recorded.

## ADR and looping: Why ADR is still called looping

Looping is the way dialogue used to be replaced. The looping editor fashioned three film loops of identical lengths — a picture loop, an audio guide loop (with the line to be redone), and the record loop (for recording the replacement). The loops played in sync as the actor repeated the line and it was recorded over and over until it fit right. This time-consuming process was made obsolete in the 1960s by the dubber, a film sound machine which could playback and hold more than one recording. It in turn was unseated by analog tape ADR in the 1970s which has given way to digital hard drives.

## The loop group, a.k.a. loopers

When lines are needed to simulate a crowd, a loop group — a group of professional actors — is brought on to the ADR stage. Working off the ADR editor's cue sheets, loopers add two kinds of lines:

**1.** Walla

Walla is non-sync background conversation made up of indistinguishable words. For example, you hear barroom walla when characters converse in a bar or angry passenger walla when the airline agent announces a flight delay. Now and again walla is scripted into the original scene as "audience walla, café walla, crowd walla," etc. During spotting, all walla to be recorded is noted. Walla can be created on location as well as by the loop group. The dialogue editor routinely multiplies the walla by cutting it on two or more tracks.

**2.** Wild lines

The loop group also voices non-sync lines for the crowd such as: "No batter, no batter," "Do you believe that?" and "That ump should have his head examined." These lines are routinely placed on actors' backs (or at least with their mouths off camera) so there are no lip sync issues. The wild lines may also be created as off screen lines to "punch up" the sound, i.e., add energy and reality to a scene.

## Advantages and disadvantages of ADR

There are clear advantages and disadvantages to recording ADR. On the upside, you're not stuck with problems from the production shoot, you acquire clean audio, and the line and performance are exactly what the director wants.

The downsides are evident when you sync ADR to picture: Some actors are super loopers, others are not. ADR editors cut parts of different takes together, massage words, syllables, and ambience. They also pitch the ADR, remove recording glitches and add EQ and reverb to make lines work. Despite these heroic efforts by actor and editor, it's near impossible to match a performance perfectly. Another disadvantage is that the ADR studio ambience never matches production ambience and requires skillful massaging to blend the dialogue seamlessly into the production track. Lastly, ADR ain't cheap.

## MUSIC EDITING

*"[Music editing] is about tempo and feel, hitting the right spot in the right key to make completely different types of music, recorded in completely different locations, blend seamlessly together."*

—NICK CARR, music editor, *SpongeBob SquarePants, Modern Marvels,* and *Power Rangers*

Editing music is a joyful and precise art that plays an indispensable role in films and can be extremely inventive. To be a good music editor you need to have a knowledge of music including key signatures and rhythms as well as a willingness to experiment and work to deadline and music cue. The job also requires considerable collaborative ability as you are the one to coordinate the varied requests of the composer, music supervisor, director, and picture and sound editors.

## Preparing to Cut Music

Like the sound editors, the music editor receives an OMF or AAF and a QT file from Picture. Additionally, the music editor gets a mixdown created by the composer of the scoring session. If the music was created on the synth, the composer will send a session or file with the music instead. The music editor will import all the music into the DAW and create a session(s) for each reel.

The music editor will also import non-scored music such as source music, head and tail credit music, and songs. This music is typically found on files or CDs and may not have time code. It's best to code all music because if a cue is destroyed or deleted, its reference points will be lost and it will have to be re-edited.

# Cutting Music

*"Film music used well is so important for the movie; it has thoughts with the small nuances of the little twists and turns in a movie. In a blink of someone's eyes the music can give some phrases with the score. It's important to define these things that are hard to explain and sometimes audiences don't even pick up."*

—PAUL OTTOSSON, sound designer, *The Hurt Locker, Spiderman 2* and *3*

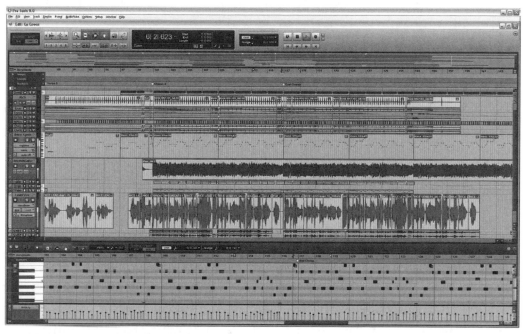

**11.e** Music tracks laid out on Pro Tools. *Photo courtesy of Avid.*

When music editors lay in music, it means that they put in the music from first frame to last to see how it works against cue time and picture. On a scored show or where the picture's been cut to music as with a music playback number, the music should lay in well, although some adjustments may be necessary. On shows or areas of a show where the music has not been timed or scored, the music will not lay in, so the editor will make cuts in the music to fit it to the picture. This means chopping up Chopin or condensing Coltrane — repeating measures, slashing stanzas, and rearranging bars to shoehorn in the music. Usually the editor can camouflage the music edit under a sound effect or a bit of dialogue.

Once the music editor has arranged and laid in all the tracks, the sessions are sent to the mix stage.

# Picture Changes

*"…We were making changes up until the point the negative was being cut — and beyond. I think at one point we had dailies in from a re-shoot, we were final dubbing, we were temp dubbing for a preview, and we were negative-cutting simultaneously. It was quite a balancing act."*

—LAWRENCE JORDAN, A.C.E., co-editor on cutting *Riding in Cars with Boys*

The picture cut frequently bounces from locked to unlocked during sound editing and only finally locks when time runs out. The picture editor (or assistant) therefore regularly provides the music and sound editors with a file of the changes referred to as a change note or change list. Sound and music editors must be vigilant and create a separate session for each new set of picture changes so that they're editing and conforming to the latest version of the picture. Table 9.2 in Chapter 9 shows a sample change list of picture changes only. Sound changes are sent separately and contain a list for each track of dialogue, SFX, etc.; the full list can reach the size of a book.

# Preparing for the Mix

At last the cut is really locked and all the dialogue, sound effects, and music tracks are completely conformed and edited. Before sending the sessions to the mix stage, it's crucial to make sure every reel and track is properly prepared. This means: 1) Laying out tracks 2) Labeling each reel; 3) Adding head sync pops; and 4) Making a cue sheet. Here are the details:

### 1) Laying out tracks
Different facilities and mixers have different tools and ways of working. So sound and music editors always ask the mixers how they want the tracks laid out and do their best to accommodate them.

### 2) Reels
You label reels in several different ways, depending on the mixer's preference, or more likely, on your DAW's cue sheet program. Here's a traditional scheme, carried over from editing sound on film:

| SOUND AND MUSIC REEL NAMES | | | |
|---|---|---|---|
| REEL TYPE | REEL 1 TRACK 1 | REEL 1 TRACK 2 | REEL 2 TRACK 1 |
| EFFECTS | R1FX1 | R1FX2 | R2FX1 |
| FOLEY | R1Foley1 | R1Foley2 | R2Foley1 |
| DIALOGUE | R1D1 | R1D2 | R2D1* |
| ADR | R1ADR1 | R1ADR2 | R2ADR1 |
| MUSIC | R1MX1 | R1MX2 | R2MX1 |

*Sprocket of film history: Once George Lucas overheard a dialogue editor ask for R2D2 and thus a robot star was born.

A variation on this is R1FXA, R1FXB, R1FXC, etc. Today, editors usually let the digital system do the labeling (or devise their own spreadsheet). For example, Pro Tools provides the show's name (abbreviated as initials), reel #, version of cut, and type of effect as seen in the following box:

| REEL NAMES ON PRO TOOLS |
|---|
| MB_R1_v18_BG.A-B |
| MB_R1_FX.A.B.C |
| MB_R1_Foley.FS_LYBK |
| MB_R1_Foley.PROPS_LYBK |
| BG = background    v = version    FS = footsteps    LYBK = layback |

## 3) Sync pops

Cut in a sync pop at 6 seconds (9 feet) at the #2 frame at the head of each track which is 2 seconds (3 feet) from FFOA. On the tail of each track, place the pop at 2 seconds (3 feet) after LFOA. You can quickly copy pops from one track to another on the DAW.

## 4) Cue sheets

Mixers today are reading the sessions from the DAWs and not always requiring cue sheets. Another reason to layout and label your tracks, reels, and cues clearly! Still, creating a cue sheet often remains an important component of the sound editor's job so we'll go over how to make one.

You will fill out a cue sheet for each reel and its tracks. Cue sheets show each track as a column from left to right. A cue sheet can contain up to 24 tracks. However, to make them easy for editor and mixer to keep track, sound editors generally keep them to 15 tracks or fewer. For the mix, the editor tapes the sheets together so it's easy to scan across an entire reel and see which cue is coming up next.

There will be separate cue sheets for each reel of ADR, dialogue, effects, Foley, and music. If the mix is a stereo mix (the norm for TV shows, features, and many other shows), the editor pairs the reels for the left/right (L/R) speakers and the mixer assigns them to two mix channels. The DAW automatically generates cue sheets from the editor's cut tracks. Each cue sheet should show:

- The date
- Show's name
- Reel name and number
- Sync pop's location
- Name of the cue
- Brief description of the cue
- Time code at start and end of cue
- Instruments required for the cue (music cue sheet)
- L/R (odd and even) speaker pair assignments for stereo mix

Table 11.2 shows a sample effects mix cue sheet based on a digital audio system printout of the tracks as labeled in the DAW. Be aware that you can add or change track data in the DAW. For instance, you could replace the library tag number of an FX cue and enter a description such as "motorcycle rev" or "popgun FX." Or you can type in special instructions like "add reverb" or "futz" to clue the mixer on how to treat a particular cue. When you create Foley footsteps cue sheets, include the name of the character. For ADR cues, enter the character's name and first and last few words, e.g., Cop: "You have the right to remain…will be used against you."

**TABLE 11.2**
**SOUND MIX CUE SHEET**

MP_R1_v0709_BG.A-B

| ABG_1.L | ABG_3.L | ABG_5.L | ABG_7.L | ABG_9.L | ABG_11.L | ABG_13.L | ABG_15.L | ABG_17.L | ABG_19.L | BBG_1.L | BBG_3.L |
|---|---|---|---|---|---|---|---|---|---|---|---|
| 1 | 2 | 3 | 4 | 5 | 6 | 7 | 8 | 9 | 10 | 11 | 12 |

**Column 1 — ABG_1.L**
- 9' POP.L ↳10'
- 53' EXT NIGHT AIR SW01_02-] ↳65'
- 300' EXT NIGHT AIR SW01_02-] ↳327'
- 393' EXT HSE AMB SW01_18-] ↳398'

**Column 2 — ABG_3.L**
- 63' THEATER AIR 7007_03-] ↳292'
- 323' OFFICE AIR SW01_08-] ↳356'
- 389' OFFICE AIR SW01_08-] ↳394'
- 445' OFFICE AIR SW01_08-] ↳452'
- 486' OFFICE AIR SW01_08-] ↳494'

**Column 3 — ABG_5.L**
- 63' THEATER AIR 10013_07-] ↳292'
- 323' OFFICE AIR OFFICE AIR-] ↳356'
- 389' OFFICE AIR OFFICE AIR-] ↳394'
- 445' OFFICE AIR OFFICE AIR-] ↳452'
- 486' OFFICE AIR OFFICE AIR-] ↳494'

**Column 4 — ABG_7.L**
- (empty)

**Column 5 — ABG_9.L**
- 291' LOBBY AIR SW01_16-] ↳301'
- 378' HALLWAY AIR SFK048_43-] ↳390'
- 479' HALLWAY AIR SFK048_43-] ↳487'
- 514' HALLWAY AIR SFK048_43-]

**Column 6 — ABG_11.L**
- 291' LOBBY AIR SW01_15-] ↳301'
- 378' HALLWAY AIR SW01_14-] ↳390'
- 479' HALLWAY AIR SW01_14-] ↳487'
- 514' HALLWAY AIR SW01_14-]

**Column 7 — ABG_13.L**
- 355' BATHRM AIR SW01_04-] ↳379'
- 430' BATHRM AIR SW01_04-] ↳446'
- 451' BATHRM AIR SW01_04-] ↳480'
- 492' BATHRM AIR SW01_04-] ↳515'

**Column 8 — ABG_15.L**
- 355' BATH AIR SW01_05-] ↳379'
- 430' BATH AIR SW01_05-] ↳446'
- 451' BATH AIR SW01_05-] ↳480'
- 492' BATH AIR SW01_05-] ↳515'

**Column 9 — ABG_17.L**
- 397' HOUSE AIR SW01_04-] ↳431'

**Column 10 — ABG_19.L**
- 397' HSE RM AIR SW01_05-] ↳431'

**Column 11 — BBG_1.L**
- 9' POP.L ↳10'
- 53' TRA F AMB SW01_19-] ↳65'
- 300' TRA F AMB SW01_19-] ↳327'
- 393' OS A M TRA F SFK052_10-] ↳398'

**Column 12 — BBG_3.L**
- 53' TRA F BYS SFK045_15-] ↳65'
- 300' TRA F BYS SFK045_15-] ↳327'
- 393' DIST TRA F SW01_21-] ↳398'

# Send In the Tracks

To get the cut reels to the mixer, upload the session to a server or send them over on a removable hard drive.

## *Assisting the mixer*

DAWs allow you to mix, fade, and reverb up to 128 tracks. Most mixers don't want sound editors to do any of this work. They have superior equipment that can do it better so they want the raw tracks. But ask them what they want. Most likely they'll politely infer, "You do the editing, I'll do the mixing." If you want to gain more creative control, do what some sound supervisors and directors do: Learn how to mix your own shows.

Normally you want to accommodate the mixers and be present on the stage during the mix. If you can't be there, make sure they've got your work #, cell #, beeper #, assistant's #, bf's #, gf's # … you get the idea. Mix stage rates are high so you need to help the mixers solve problems and make decisions as quickly as possible.

# THE MIX

*"A lot of the editing I do actually happens with the sound editors and the post-production mixer. You can really change the feel of a scene by how you mix things."*
—JOHN SAYLES, writer/director/editor, *Casa de Los Babys*, *Sunshine State*, *Lone Star*

The mix is both a creative and technical process. The goal of the mix is to re-record the edited sounds — dialogue, effects, and music — so that they harmonize and can be heard in a way that supports the show and fulfills the director's intentions. The mix, commonly called the dub, can take from one day to several months, depending on the length and budget of the show. If you have limited funds, prepare your sound reels and cue sheets meticulously and be clear how you want your show to sound. A mix is expensive and advances like a herd of turtles, so you don't want to do anything to slow the process even more.

# What Arrives on the Mix Stage

You.

**When you first go to a mix stage** — and you should attend a mix before doing your own — you may be overwhelmed: The room can be bigger than some movie theaters and house huge mix boards (consoles) with panels of lights and pots extending like a cockpit in front of a screen. At the back of the stage is a long high table for the director, producer(s), client(s), and editors (Picture, Sound, and Music), though typically not all are present at one time. Have a seat at the table — if there's room and it's politic — or plop down in one of the theater seats.

**Observe**. The show plays on the screen for a few seconds on up to a minute or two. The sound track comes to life then urrrh! The sounds die with a gurgle, the picture fades to black — the mix lurches to a halt. A few seconds later the picture and sound revive

**11.f** Mix stage for feature films. *Photo courtesy of Todd-AO/Ascent Media Creative Services.*

themselves and the process starts up again. Then it staggers to a halt again. It's the stop and start nature of the mix which will repeat until the mix is done. Once you've absorbed this rhythm and the visual pictures, try to listen more than look. Become aware of all the sounds. At first there may be only dialogue and few effects but then some music will come in. The sound track is being created in front of your very ears!

Next, focus on what the mixers are doing. Optimally, there are three mixers: a dialogue and ADR mixer, an effects and Foley mixer, and a music mixer. Frequently there are only two so they double up; one handling dialogue and music and the other all the effects, though they may trade Foley and music cues, depending on their placement. The mixers will have cue sheets spread out in front of them. While the picture plays, notice the music mixer raising the pot to bring in the music. Urrrh! Restart.

**Tune in and learn**. The mixer, the sound supervisor, and the director are talking. The director wants the music to come in more gradually. To accomplish this, the music must start earlier. The music editor tells the mixer there's an alternate cue with a longer (slower) start. The mixer spies the alternate on the cue sheet and switches to it. Again the picture runs, the music comes in. Everyone is happy. The picture runs on, advancing into a new area with new cues. More sound is mixed until the director, sound supervisor, or mixer is unhappy and urrrh! The picture and sound stutter to a stop once again.

After awhile you'll get the hang of things. You may find the mix tedious. It is. Progress is made with each restart as the mixers, sound supervisor, and director painstakingly work through the picture, minutes or seconds at a time. Think about how you would mix the show and marvel at the world of sound that's being created and how it affects the film.

# The Pre-Mix

*"When I'm sound editing or sound designing, I'm not listening to all the other elements. It's only in the pre-mix that I start to combine all the elements together… For example, I know what I've done with the water, so I know when to mix in the metal or the glass."*
—CHRISTOPHER BOYES, sound designer on *Titanic*, mixer on *Lord of the Rings* trilogy

The pre-mix, widely referred to as the pre-dub, is a preliminary mix of certain sounds — BG effects and dialogue usually — performed ahead of the mix. Essentially a pre-dub is a mixdown of sounds in preparation for the mix. Feature films are most likely to pre-dub because they usually have so many tracks that the mixers can't play them all at the same time. On other shows, the pre-dub is the initial stage of the mix and is sometimes referred to as a rough mix. The main reasons to do a pre-dub are:

- To set levels and make primary technical decisions.
- To save time during the mix.
- To reserve the more important decisions for the final mix.

The sound supervisor and possibly the director, picture editor[2], and the producer are present at the pre-dub. Definitely the sound editors are at the table, along with their DAWs so if changes are needed they can make them on the spot. Making changes on the dub stage used to be a "no-no" but now they're an everyday, efficient part of the pre-dub and mix. The pre-dub lays the foundation for the mix. At the mix you'll add the music, listen to all the tracks mixed together, and make final decisions about the sound of your sound track.

## What is pre-dubbed

During the pre-dub, dialogue is mixed in dialogue groups, effects in effects groups. Keeping dialogue and effects separate during the pre-dub greases the skids for the final mix where they will be mixed together with the music. They are recorded to separate sessions which the mixers can easily reload and dip into to fix or tweak as needed during the mix. The mixers keep careful records of which sounds are put to what channels so they can be easily located during the mix. The editors update the cue sheets to reflect how cues were treated, e.g., dropped or moved.

### DIALOGUE

All split dialogue tracks are re-recorded. Alternate lines are not recorded; their tracks are kept muted. ADR lines are pre-dubbed and the original production track is held in case the director wants to use it and dump the ADR in the final mix.

### EFFECTS

SFX are pre-dubbed in various groups according to the film's demands (every film is unique). These groups include Foley, BGs, and specific FX for certain characters or entities, e.g., the cell block, the creature of the bog, etc. Effects requiring major manipulation and important decisions are left for the mix.

---

2. On TV series the picture editor is off cutting the next episode; on lower budget shows the picture editor is often let go before the mix so the producer, associate producer, or director oversees the mix.

## MUSIC

Ordinarily music is not pre-dubbed, as it's pre-mixed by the composer and/or music editor and shows up at the final mix. However, on a musical or a music-dominated show, the music is pre-dubbed with the focus on levels and technical details. Instruments, songs sung on screen, and other important numbers are isolated so there's plenty of leeway for final decision making during the mix.

## Pre-dub process

*"It isn't enough for a sound to be merely loud, or high-fidelity, or digital. It needs to remind you of, resonate with, other sounds, places, feelings, in other times."*
—RANDY THOM

The process of re-recording the audio is the same for the pre-dub and the mix. The show is mixed one reel at a time, frequently not in reel order. As the picture advances and rewinds in sync with the audio being mixed, a counter runs at the bottom of the screen, counting in time code or feet and frames. While the show runs, the mixers sit at their mixing boards, ease faders (pots) up and down, pan and expertly corral the sounds to fit the picture. Other audio manipulations include: adding echo, futz, and reverb and reducing

**11.g** Mixing console. *Photo courtesy of Avid.*

noise with noise filters (denoisers) and hum filters. With the new automated mixing boards, the mixers can program a lot of these settings.

The first time or two that the tracks play, the mixers audition them for levels, EQ, etc. Following these adjustments, the show plays and the sounds are mixed and saved in the session. When a section is complete, it's played back for everyone. Any changes are made by punching in, remixing the area, and re-saving the session. Then the section's played back one last time. If everyone's satisfied, it's onward and forward to the next section of the show. Slowly, the show takes on a new life.

## Scheduling

The time required to complete a pre-dub and a mix depends on the budget, amount of sound to be mixed, and the length of the show. On shorter, low budget shows, the pre-mix is part of the mix. Dialogue and background effects are always mixed first. Here's a guide:

| AVERAGE DUB TIMES | | |
|---|---|---|
| **SHOW** | **PRE-DUB** | **MIX** |
| 1 hour show | Part of mix | 1-3 days |
| TV movie | Part of mix | 3-5 days |
| Feature | 2-9 weeks | 1-4 weeks |

## After the pre-dub

Once the last reel is complete, the mixers save the sessions for the final mix, which often takes place on the same stage. Instead of cue sheets, sound editors create pre-dub layout sheets for the final mix which pinpoint the effects' location in the different pre-dub groups.

# THE MIX

*"I felt like I should be wearing a helmet doing the mix [on* Saving Private Ryan*]. The same effect a film that powerful has on an audience, it has on the people that work on it. We took a lot of breaks. You have to go out and have a candy bar, remind yourself that there's a candy machine just down the hallway and that you're not really at Omaha Beach."*

—GARY RYDSTROM, C.A.S., sound designer and mixer, *Finding Nemo, Saving Private Ryan,* and *Jurassic Park*

The mix is the last creative chance to illuminate the film's story, characters, shadows, and theme. It should support and articulate the characters' connections to others and their world as well as their thoughts and feelings. On nonfiction shows the mix should clarify the story and subject and bolster its connection to the audience.

## Who's on stage

The players are the same as at the pre-dub: two or more mixers, the sound designer/supervisor as well as the sound, music, and picture editors and the director, client, and producer. The mixers control the mix, taking direction from the director and the sound designer. The mixers should have viewed the show and should know the kind of sound desired.

It's crucial that everyone be a collaborative team member and have the show's best interests at heart. Frequently the mixer has worked previously with the sound supervisor and/or the director, so a good working relationship is already established. Some directors and sound supervisors learn how to run the mixing boards and actively mix the show. James Cameron not only directed *Avatar* and *Titanic* but also edited these blockbusters (along with two other picture editors) and mixed their sound.

## Mix with an ear to the audience

*"The trick in movie making, and certainly no less in mixing sound for movies, is to focus the attention of the audience. It's very misguided to think that every element has to be in play at all times, because then you just end up with visual and aural noise."*

—RANDY THOM

Just as the writing, shooting, and editing of a show are designed to tell the audience what they need to know when they need to know it, so is the sound. Consequently, throughout the mix you want to keep in mind what clues, what experience, and what information the sound and music convey to your audience at each moment of the show. This can mean concentrating a lot on the surround sound. You can take Paul Ottosson's word on that from his experience designing and mixing sound on *The Hurt Locker*, which took the Oscars for sound editing and sound mixing in 2010. Ottosson explains, "If all the sounds you created came from the front, they're assuming you're watching this movie, so by building the sound all the way around you, I'm putting you directly in the drama, its events, and where it's located."

**11.h** Audio mix suite for TV show, promos, and many other types of shows. *Photo courtesy of AlphaDogs.*

## What happens during the mix

As at the pre-dub, the show plays on the screen, the counter runs, and the mixers ride their boards, eyeing the music cue sheets and sound pre-dub layout sheets. This time around however, they mix the pre-dubbed dialogue and effects tracks together with the music and any dialogue and FX cues that were not mixed before. Again, it's a slow process of manipulating the levels and EQ'ing; blending and balancing the sound in order to create the best sound track.

## 3-D shows

*"… once we were able to finally listen to the mix against the finished 3-D picture it was still an amazing and exciting experience… you just go by what feels right and make sure that in the end, you believe it really happened."*

—STEVE BOEDDEKER, sound designer and supervisor on *Alice in Wonderland 3-D*

On 3-D shows, mixers work to a 2-D picture until the end when the VFX are completed and the 3-D version is finally available. However, due to 5:1 (and now 7:1) surround sound, sound designers and editors have operated on a 3-D plane in essence for many years, moving characters and objects front, left, right, back and around to match the actions on screen. Boeddeker reflects on mixing *Alice in Wonderland 3-D*, "You can really get away with a lot of sound tricks in 3-D…. So as we all were making, editing, and mixing the sound effects we tried to always keep in mind that things will be more extreme in 3-D. The Cheshire cat won't just fly off, he will fly right over your head, and the Red Knights will seem to march right into the theater. So we tried to push the surrounds as much as possible knowing it will be much more believable in 3-D."

## Hitting the finishing line with just the right amount of sound

*"There's a law of diminishing returns in sound editing and mixing. If you start putting in too much stuff then it doesn't sound good anymore, it just sounds like mush."*

—GARY RYDSTROM

On any show, not all the music, FX, and dialogue will make it to the final mix. Some cues will be dropped; others will be altered, advanced, or retarded. The goal is to mix all elements so that the sound track complements and enhances the show at every frame. Certain questions inevitably come up: "Does the ADR work or should we drop certain cues and live with the production track?" "Do we really need music here?" "We need a music cue right here."

Once the mixers have mixed everything, the mix will be played against the final version of the picture for the director, producer, and/or client. There will be notes and changes and finally, approval.

## What the Mix Produces: The DME and Stems

The result of the mix is that all the tracks are mixed down to three groups: dialogue, music, and effects. This three-group mixdown is called the *DME*. The individual parts of the DME are identified as *stems*. Hence, there's a dialogue stem, a music stem, and a sound effects stem. The combined music and effects stems are referred to as the *M & E*. The mixers usually create other stems as well, according to the show's delivery requirements, such as an ADR stem, Foley prop stem, Foley footsteps stem, 5:1 or 7:1 stem, mono stem, stereo stem, and DA-88 stem. DME stems are used for:

- Remixing: It's not uncommon for a section of a show to be remixed.
- Making mono stems from the original stereo mix.
- Creating the TV version of a feature film.

  At a later date, the show will be remixed with alternative ADR lines and production lines to cover words barred from TV.

To create *foreigns* (non-English versions of the show), the dialogue stem serves as a guide track for recording the new language and is muted in the mix. The M & E is remixed with the PFX track and the dubbed foreign language. Also, to get ready for the finishing process (fully discussed in the next two chapters), the mix will be kept as a session and transferred to DAT, DA-88 tape, or OMF. For shows destined for theatrical release, the mixers will create a printmaster which will be put to file or film for projection.

## PART ONE WRAP-UP

Now that your sound is edited and mixed, it's time to marry it to picture and finish your show. This merging is what Part Two — Chapters 12 and 13 — are all about. First you may wish to turn to the two appendices that follow this chapter. Appendix G supplies a blank ADR Cue Sheet and Appendix H the budgeting form for sound, music, and the mix. These are also available under the Free tab of www.joyoffilmediting.com.

# Appendix G

## ADR Cue Sheet

| ADR CUE SHEET | | | SHOW: | | PAGE 1 OF 1 | | | |
|---|---|---|---|---|---|---|---|---|
| **REELS** | | | **COMMENTS** | | **DATE/VERSION** | | | |
| **TIME CODE START** | **CUE** | **CHARACTER** | **DIALOGUE** | | **RECORDED TAKES** | | | |
| | | | | | | | | |
| | | | | | | | | |
| | | | | | | | | |
| | | | | | | | | |
| | | | | | | | | |
| | | | | | | | | |
| | | | | | | | | |
| | | | | | | | | |
| | | | | | | | | |
| | | | | | | | | |
| | | | | | | | | |
| | | | | | | | | |
| | | | | | | | | |
| | | | | | | | | |
| | | | | | | | | |

**KEY**

**NG** No Good          **X** Printed Take          **O** Alternate Take

# Appendix H

## Stage III: Budget for Sound, Music, and the Mix

Now that you're familiar with how sound and music are created, edited, and mixed, you can budget for this stage of postproduction. Also, you can photocopy this form or download it from the Free tab of www.joyoffilmediting.com.

| | BUDGET FOR SOUND, MUSIC, AND THE MIX | | | | | |
|---|---|---|---|---|---|---|
| **ACCT #** | **DESCRIPTION** | **AMOUNT** | **UNITS** | **X** | **RATE** | **TOTAL** |
| **5000** | **SOUND** | | | | | |
| 5001 | Sound supervisor | | week | | | |
| 5002 | Sound editor | | week | | | |
| 5003 | Dialogue editor | | week | | | |
| 5004 | Assistant sound editor | | week | | | |
| 5005 | Narrator | | hour | | | |
| 5006 | Sound spotting session | | hour | | | |
| | | | TOTAL FOR CATEGORY | | | |
| **5100** | **ADR/LOOPING** | | | | | |
| 5101 | ADR stage | | day | | | |
| 5102 | ADR/Recordist | | hour | | | |
| 5103 | Loop group | | allow | | | |
| 5104 | ADR editor | | week | | | |
| | | | TOTAL FOR CATEGORY | | | |
| **5200** | **FOLEY** | | | | | |
| 5201 | Foley stage | | hour | | | |
| 5202 | Foley artist | | hour | | | |
| 5203 | Foley editor | | week | | | |
| | | | TOTAL FOR CATEGORY | | | |
| **5300** | **TRANSFER** | | | | | |
| 5301 | SFX from library | | allow | | | |
| 5302 | Record wildSFX | | day | | | |
| 5303 | Dubs | | allow | | | |
| | | | TOTAL FOR CATEGORY | | | |
| **5400** | **MUSIC** | | | | | |
| 5401 | Composer | | allow | | | |
| 5402 | Music editor | | week | | | |
| 5403 | Assistant music editor | | week | | | |
| 5404 | Music spotting session | | hour | | | |
| | | | TOTAL FOR CATEGORY | | | |

*(continues next page)*

| \multicolumn{6}{c}{**BUDGET FOR SOUND, MUSIC, AND THE MIX**} | | | | | |
|---|---|---|---|---|---|
| **ACCT #** | **DESCRIPTION** | **AMOUNT** | **UNITS** | **X** | **RATE** | **TOTAL** |
| **5500** | **SCORING SESSION** | | | | | |
| 5501 | Conductor | | allow | | | |
| 5502 | Songwriter | | allow | | | |
| 5503 | Lyricist | | allow | | | |
| 5504 | Musicians | | allow | | | |
| 5505 | Contractor | | allow | | | |
| 5506 | Orchestrator | | allow | | | |
| 5507 | Arranger | | allow | | | |
| 5508 | Singer(s) | | allow | | | |
| 5509 | Copyist/proofreader | | allow | | | |
| 5510 | Scoring stage | | day | | | |
| 5511 | Misc. | | allow | | | |
| | | | **TOTAL FOR CATEGORY** | | | |
| **5600** | **MUSIC FEES** | | | | | |
| 5601 | Source MX | | allow | | | |
| 5602 | Stock MX | | allow | | | |
| 5603 | Rights/license fees | | allow | | | |
| 5604 | Original song purchase | | allow | | | |
| | | | **TOTAL FOR CATEGORY** | | | |
| **5700** | **PRE-MIX** | | | | | |
| 5701 | Mixers | | day | | | |
| 5702 | Pre-mix | | allow | | | |
| 5703 | Pre-mix EFX tracks | | allow | | | |
| 5704 | Transfers | | allow | | | |
| 5705 | Stock | | tape | | | |
| 5706 | Dubs | | hour | | | |
| 5707 | Misc. | | allow | | | |
| | | | **TOTAL FOR CATEGORY** | | | |
| **5800** | **MIX** | | | | | |
| 5801 | Mixers | | day | | | |
| 5802 | Pre mix | | allow | | | |
| 5802 | Mix stage | | allow | | | |
| 5803 | M & E | | allow | | | |
| 5804 | Foreign version M & E | | allow | | | |
| 5805 | Printmaster | | allow | | | |
| 5806 | Transfers | | allow | | | |
| 5807 | Stock | | tape | | | |
| 5808 | Dubs | | hour | | | |
| 5809 | Laugher | | hour | | | |
| 5810 | Misc. | | allow | | | |
| | | | **TOTAL FOR CATEGORY** | | | |
| | | | **GRAND TOTAL** | | | |

## PART TWO

# PART TWO

# Finishing and Delivering

## Introduction

Organizing, logging, digitizing, cutting, mixing — you and your project have been through a lot together. Now you're ready to wrap it up — apply the finishing processes and deliver your show for presentation to its audience. You planned for this step from the start when you chose your finishing format in Chapter 1. Chapter 12 guides you through how to complete your project on tape, file, or disk. Chapter 13 presents the parallel process for finishing on film and details the DI process.

Following these closing chapters is Appendix I, a budgeting form corresponding to this last stage of postproduction. After it is a section on how to find that elusive editing job and a list of resources including books, websites, magazines, and organizations to support your quest and keep you up to date on the world of editing.

## CHAPTER 12

# Finishing on Tape, Disk, or the Web

## Overview

Finishing is the post-editing phase during which you go through the final processes to produce your final tape, disk, or file. After this it's show time: Time to put your baby out there for all to see. This chapter concentrates on the online finish, leading you through the preparatory tasks for the online session. It also guides you through color grading and the rest of the finishing procedures that take place after online. The chapter starts by covering the popular alternative to onlining; finishing from your digital editing system. But first, let's talk about something you'll be tending to throughout this phase: titles and credits.

### TITLES AND CREDITS

*"A main title in its best form is like a prologue to a movie. Ideally, it sets you up for the emotional content of the film and gets you excited about it."*

—KYLE COOPER, title designer, *Rango, Tron: Legacy, Ironman,* and *Spider-Man 2*

Titles and credits are lettered graphics that are added to your film or video. Titles include the name of your show and subtitles like "Beijing, 2008" or "Dateline: Omaha." Credits are seen at the head and/or tail of your show, parading its cast, crew, location, and acknowledgments. There are many famous "type geeks" who live and breathe graphics (GFX) and title design. One of them, Kyle Cooper, explains, "Type is like actors to me. It takes on characteristics of its own. When I was younger, I used to pick a word from the dictionary and then try to design it so that I could make the word do what it meant…"

## *Purpose of titles and credits*

*"[Titles] can do very much or very little; but really shine when they live within the story and reflect an important quality driven by your director."*

—SUSAN BRADLEY, title designer, *Wall-E, Up, The Motorcycle Diaries, Ratatouille,* and *An Inconvenient Truth*

Ostensibly, head titles, a.k.a. head credits, provide the names of the principal actors and creators of the film. Many filmmakers believe they shouldn't stand apart from the movie but should blend in and be a part of the story's exposition. However, if the budget allows and the director and designer are savvy, titles can do a whole lot more. A head credit sequence can clue the audience into the film's plot, location, time period, style, characters, and, along with music, help establish its emotional tone or viewpoint. The split screen credits at the start of *127 Hours* (Figure 12.a) give insights into the film's risk-taking hero as he determinedly drives through the night to escape the city and set off on his fateful desert hike.

End credits are usually more utilitarian. Networks routinely cram them to one side of the TV screen to make room for promos, a practice known as "squeeze and tease." But sometimes end credits can be just plain fun and extend the movie, such as those tailing *Ratatouille* or *Spider-Man 2* (Figure 12.b).

**12.a** Head credit from *127 Hours*.

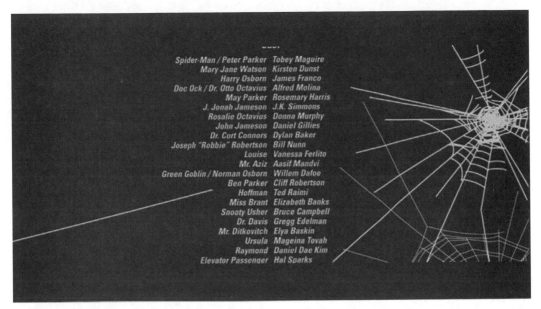

| | |
|---|---|
| Spider-Man / Peter Parker | Tobey Maguire |
| Mary Jane Watson | Kirsten Dunst |
| Harry Osborn | James Franco |
| Doc Ock / Dr. Otto Octavius | Alfred Molina |
| May Parker | Rosemary Harris |
| J. Jonah Jameson | J.K. Simmons |
| Rosalie Octavius | Donna Murphy |
| John Jameson | Daniel Gillies |
| Dr. Curt Connors | Dylan Baker |
| Joseph "Robbie" Robertson | Bill Nunn |
| Louise | Vanessa Ferlito |
| Mr. Aziz | Aasif Mandvi |
| Green Goblin / Norman Osborn | Willem Dafoe |
| Ben Parker | Cliff Robertson |
| Hoffman | Ted Raimi |
| Miss Brant | Elizabeth Banks |
| Snooty Usher | Bruce Campbell |
| Dr. Davis | Gregg Edelman |
| Mr. Ditkovitch | Elya Baskin |
| Ursula | Mageina Tovah |
| Raymond | Daniel Dae Kim |
| Elevator Passenger | Hal Sparks |

**12.b** Tail crawl on *Spider-Man 2*.

## Credit list

The producer provides a list of the credits and is responsible for the accuracy of the list: job titles, spellings, credit order, and professional associations like A.C.E. Whoever puts the credits in the show — editor, online editor, or film lab technician — is responsible for accurately duplicating the list. Typically, the editor lays out head titles and cred-

its temporarily on the digital system before they're placed permanently in the show by the post house or lab. The director (or producer if the show is a TV series) has the final say on the look and placement of titles and credits. The director may be present during the lay out or wait until the editor has fully laid out the head title and end credit sequences before viewing and approving

**12.c** Creating a title on Avid Media Composer®. *Photo courtesy of Chris Senchack.*

them. No matter who creates the credits, the editor is responsible for checking that the producer's list is reproduced exactly.

## Crawls and cards

Most end credits roll (a.k.a. crawl), scrolling name after name with job title after job title, from the bottom of the screen to the top. When a credit pops on the screen and then pops off to be followed by another, it's referred to as a *card*. A show's top players are credited first and have a *single card*, meaning no one else is on their card. Their card may be *up* (on the screen) longer than others. The majority of U.S. films run VIPs' end credits on cards as the action ends and freezes, then fade to black and roll the rest of the credits.

### A long time ago in a galaxy far, far away… How long to keep subtitles up on the screen

To make certain they can be understood, leave subtitles up long enough to be read three times at a moderate pace. Most of the time subtitle text is short: "Somewhere on the eastern front" or "Ten years later." Often the text consists of an interviewee's name and title, e.g., "Professor Henry Louis Gates, Jr." or "Sophia, next-door neighbor." For superior readability, editors habitually place subtitles on the lower third of the screen so they don't block any important action or body features; hence they are often referred to as "lower thirds."

## Placing credits

There is a Hollywood hierarchy of who gets a front credit (at the head of the show) and who gets a back credit (after the end of the show). Editors (except for additional editors) always get a front credit; the assistant and the rest of the post production crew receive a back credit. (On television shows, these credits and their placement vary from network to network.) The director's credit is always the closest to the body of the show which makes it the last credit before the show starts.

From time to time, everyone's credit appears at the back of the show. This is done when the director wants to involve the viewer immediately in the film as Terence Malick did on *The Tree of Life*. With this scheme, the director gets the first credit after the show. Moving the credits to the back means that those who contractually have a head credit, (principal actors, the writer(s), producers, DP, editor, sound designer, costume designer, etc.), have to "sign off" — sign a waiver — about the placement of their credit.

# Creating titles and credits

Titles and credits are designed and built at the post house, a title house, a design company, or a production studio. They can also be created by the editor directly on the digital editing system. The next section describes each scenario for creating credits, starting with the editor.

## *Editor*

Most digital systems incorporate a titling tool with a variety of fonts, colors, drop shadows, transparencies, sizes, and other choices such as 3-D. You can create credits that roll (move vertically), crawl (move horizontally), or appear with any chosen transition and/or keying effect. You can also import credit files, text styles, and fonts from other programs such as Boris Title 3-D, Apple's LiveType or Adobe's Photoshop or After Effects.

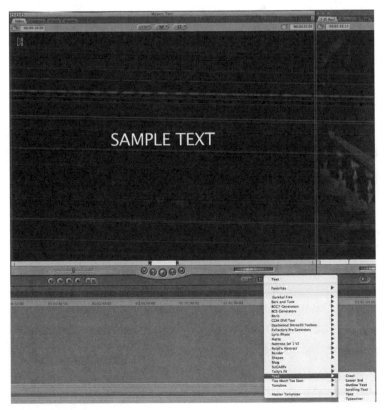

**12.d** Title tool on Final Cut Pro.

Here's the basic procedure for making titles, subtitles, or credits:

---

### CREATING A TILE ON THE DIGITAL EDITING SYSTEM

1. Create the title with the title tool.
   Type it in. Choose font, color, kerning, size, placement, etc.
2. Save the title.
3. Add a new video track on your time line and edit the title into it.
4. Add a transition into and out of the title (a dissolve normally).
5. Render the title as necessary. Since you now have three layers, video, title, and effect, the system may not be able to play all three. Because it's text, the title is usually the most swiftly rendered layer.

---

## BACKGROUNDS

Titles most commonly are set against picture ($$$) or a colored background ($$) or think black as Woody Allen invariably does ($). *Clean titles* are those that are the easiest to read and don't bleed (appear to run into the background). In order to achieve the cleanest titles, bear in mind that:

- White lettering is the cleanest.
- Script takes longer to read as does any font with curlicues or indistinct letters.
- Blue and red lettering are rarely used due to their readability (poor) and bleedability.
- Drop shadows can sometimes enhance readability.

## TITLE PLACEMENT FOR TV

When placing titles in a show, you must be aware of how they and the action in the frame will appear on a 4:3 or 16:9 television screen. This is particularly critical when you're transferring picture from film, computer, or DVD and when your show is finishing on multiple formats with different aspect ratios such as HD or SD. There are two ways to measure how the credits and action will be seen: Safe Title Area and Safe Action Area. All digital finishing systems and many offline systems include graphic overlays, which outline these areas on the frame as shown in Figure 12.e.

Safe title is the area in the center of the TV screen where it's safe to place a title or graphic so that it won't get cut off on the viewer's screen.

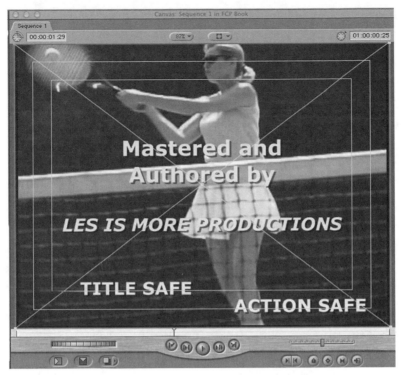

**12.e** Title and action safe overlays on Final Cut Pro. Notice line for title safe: All type is in. Then look at line for action safe: Ball is out of action safe as is top half of tennis player's head; they will not be seen on a TV screen. *Photo courtesy of Chris Senchack.*

Slightly larger than safe title, safe action is where the action should be restricted so that the audience can see all of it. Camera operators and the director should monitor this area during the shoot. Otherwise, your post house will need to resize the frame or pan and scan the scene for viewers to take in the necessary action. If you ignore safe title and action areas, your credits and action will be cut off on the TV screen.

### TIMING TV CREDITS

During offline, your main task is to time the head credits properly and make sure they fit against the picture. To start, ask the post supervisor what the timing requirements are for your show. Television credits typically fade up for a minimum of 15 frames, hold full up on screen for two seconds, and fade out for another 15 frames, for a total of three seconds. This means, ideally, you need a shot that's at least three seconds to run underneath the credit. Since you are responsible for the initial lay-out of credits, you can slip and slide shots so they fit the credits. If not, you'll be forced to run a credit across more than one shot.

## Post house

The post house drops in the titles and credits for television and low budget shows. The online editor receives the titles via OMF, AAF, or XML file from the offline editor and adds them after the show has been onlined and color graded. (More on exactly how the credits are put into the show in the online section of this chapter.)

## Title house

For decades, title houses have produced optical titles and title sequences for film shows. Now they've added computer designed titles and other services such as pan and scanning, film restoration, and website design. In fact, title houses, design companies, and post houses overlap services.

The title designer at the title house creates the entire title sequence with input from the director and helps with footage as needed from the editor. Alternatively, the editor cuts the background footage for the title sequence and the title house designs and marries the titles to it. The spectacular title sequences for *North by Northwest* and *The Pink Panther* showcase what title houses can do.

## Design company

In the 1990s, digital technology brought down the cost of building titles with new and fast compositing, motion graphics, and editing software. A boutique industry of design companies sprang up whose prominent designers created titles as well as commercials, GFX, effects, websites, and corporate content. To craft a title sequence, the graphic designer works with the director to absorb the show's theme and mood and produce a smashing, evocative title. These designers have advanced the art of making titles with *Up in the Air, Thank You for Smoking, Kiss Kiss Bang Bang, Catch Me If You Can,* and the groundbreaking sequence in *Seven.*

## Studio

Some studios, notably Disney and Pixar, control their pictures and brand by having in-house design teams. These teams have designed some notable title sequences in *Toy Story 3, Ratatouille,* and *Wall-E.*

## Tape, File, and Disk Finish

No area is changing more rapidly in postproduction than the final processes for finishing on tape, disk, and file. A prime example: offline and online. The line between the two is ever-blurring, trending toward erasure. As offline systems offer ever more sophisticated audio, color grading, and other finishing tools, editors are completing more shows right on their Adobe Premiere Pro, Avid, or FCP. Still, most TV shows go through the online process at a post house. The upshot? We'll cover how to finish with and without onlining starting with weighing the advantages of each method. In the next chapter we'll discuss the third completion method — the Digital Intermediate (DI) process — which can produce all finishing formats.

### *Advantages and disadvantages to finishing without onlining*

The main advantage to finishing a show yourself on your digital system is dollars: online costs big bucks. There are a few downsides: Online editors, colorists, and other post house professionals are experts in putting out top notch shows that meet network (broadcast) standards; if there's a problem, they stand behind their work. When a show I edited was onlined incorrectly and rejected by the network, the post house re-onlined it at their expense. Another point to consider is that doing the finishing work takes up a lot of the offline editor's time which might be better spent working on the next show, episode, or client project.

Onlining at a post house is a tried and true route for finishing which produces a broadcast quality show master tape or file. Customarily, online rates and dates are locked in during the budget and scheduling phase of preproduction and sometimes adjusted later. Often the post house that performs your online is also responsible for your dailies and may even rent you rooms and your digital editing system. This is a mutually convenient arrangement, especially since it gets you a package deal with lowered online rates and other costs.

### *Conclusion*

When deciding whether to finish by outputting from the digital system or by online at the post house, base the decision on your project's budget, time frame, and delivery requirements as well as on the skills and talents of the editor. Put your best show forward in sound and image: Your work and your audience deserve nothing less.

# Tape, File, and Disk Finish without Online

Before we get going, here's a quick preview of where we're headed. To finish via tape, file or disk, you will create a master tape or file by outputting your locked sequence from the digital system. You will then use this show master to create and/or deliver your final tape, file, or disk for exhibition and/or distribution. So first we will talk about how you create the show master on tape or file. Then we'll focus on how you use it to finish on disk or on file for the Web or intranet.

## *Preparation*

It's all in the preparation! You have been setting up your show all along for final output so getting ready consists of double-checking yourself. You should have mixed down all your audio so it sounds the best. You should have finalized titles and rendered everything on your time line: VFX, titles, clips, GFX, transitions, etc. If your show will be broadcast, you may be required to format it for logos and commercials. While the network allots the amount of time needed for commercials and is responsible for inserting them into your show, you may have to slug for them and logos so read your delivery requirements.

If you edited at a low res, now's the time to link your final sequence to your original hi res tapes, e.g., DVCPRO or HDCAM or files, e.g., P2, RED, or XDCAM. If you didn't preserve the original source tapes or files, alternatively, you can transcode to the best res your system allows. Lastly, on the practical side, check that your tape deck and mixer are working properly and that you've pre-striped a high quality tape if your output requires time code.

## *Color grading, a.k.a. color correcting or color timing*

*"Color changes the story and how you feel about it. So you want to make the color flow from shot to shot and scene to scene."*

—RICH MONTEZ, colorist, Whipping Post Services

Using your system's color grader, work your way through your sequence, scene by scene. You may want to make a few passes through your time line, addressing a different set of corrections with each pass. Color grading could take up a whole other book so we'll just touch on the major aspects. To start, correct any production problems such as where the image exposure is too light, dark, or muddy.

On fiction shows, balance the light and color within each scene so all the shots look like they were shot in the same place and time. On non-fiction shows, adjust the shots within each section so viewers' eyes don't have to do the adjustment work. This scene-to-scene color correcting work is the bulk of the work you'll do. When a bad-looking shot can't be fixed and stands out in a scene, you may be forced to modify all the other shots to match it. Rich Montez says ruefully, "If the color is bad or you have to match to badly lit or colored shots with no room for change, at least it's all bad." This is the worst-case scenario. Mostly you'll be correcting skin tones, fine-tuning color, and sharpening or diffusing light so that shots and scenes look consistent and read the way you want.

As with many VFX, you can use key frames to make changes occur over time and isolate specific areas to change. You can also create moods by de-saturating or intensifying the color for, say, a flashback, flashforward, or fantasy shot or scene. You can warm up scenes or cool them down and employ color filters — blue, red, yellow, sepia, etc. — to support what your film is communicating.

**12.f** Media Composer's color corrector uses key frames to "animate" the grading. *Photo courtesy of Avid.*

Your system's video tools will aid in ensuring your color levels meet video signal standards. There are many scopes but here are the primary ones: the *vectorscope* which measures hue (color) and saturation (amount

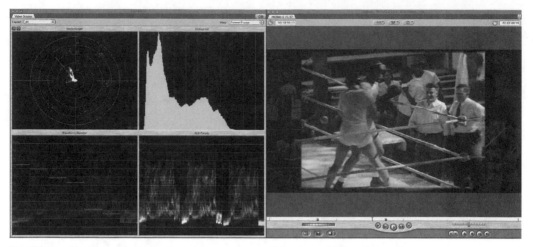

**12.g** FCP's color scopes clockwise from top: vectorscope, histogram, RGB, and waveform.

of color), the *waveform* which reveals color level (brightness and contrast), and the *histogram* which looks at luminance (black and white levels). But the scopes are not enough if your show is destined for broadcast. For broadcast, at a minimum, you must use a calibrated broadcast monitor, which brings us to the thorny topic of broadcast quality.

## Broadcast quality

All material[1] for broadcast must meet the standards set by the FCC (Federal Communications Commission). Network engineers check all programs with scopes to ensure they have proper blanking and color burst (see Glossary for these terms) and meet a host of other specs.

### IMAGE AND SIGNAL

There are no broadcast *image* quality standards, there are only broadcast *signal* quality standards. Consumer format tapes, videos from cell phones and the like do not make the grade. Digital editing system manufacturers often boast that their systems output broadcast quality material. They are referring to the image quality, not the signal quality of the final tape. Don't be misled.

### CONFUSION AND CONCLUSION

You're thinking, but what about the home videos we see of the latest disaster in Texas or Japan? Or of the crimes scenes captured by the surveillance camera that are broadcast regularly? They're clearly not up to

---

1. Presently most networks require tape deliverables (so they can add commercials and other interstitials), though they usually ingest the tapes into their server and broadcast them from a file-based queue. However, as tapeless workflows continue to snowball, networks will be accepting more file deliverables. The future? Files as well as tapes — all broadcast materials — will need to meet standards.

standard. True, but, since they're considered newsworthy, the network engineers retrofit them to meet standards.

So what if you didn't finish via the online route, how do you know if your material will meet standards? First, know the broadcaster's standards, shoot on a professional format, and finish your show to meet them. If you don't, pay a post house to bring the final tape or file up to standard. The phrase "saving it in post" applies here: If you didn't do it right to start, you can fix it later, but you will pay!

## Making the tape or file

Add color bars, leaders, and a 2-pop. Then monitor your show as you output it to tape or file. Afterwards, play back the show to make sure it plays flawlessly down to the last frame: You want to be abso-blumin-lutely certain it's perfect before duplication. One way to check your work is to make a QT or other file of the locked offline cut. You can then drag it to your time line and lock it with your finished, uprezzed show to visually check your show, cut by cut.

# DISK FINISH

To finish your project on disk, there are three routes, depending on what your completed DVD or Blu-ray will contain. First, if your disk will be single sequence — contain only your final sequence — it can be a short process: You create a QT (or other uncompressed file) of your sequence and export it to disk, then burn a lot of copies using your digital system or a disk burner. Second, you can enlist a post house to helm the entire disk authoring, mastering, and production process via online or the DI route. If your disk will have multiple sequences, be divided into chapters, or contain graphics, menus, buttons, etc., you'll need to follow the workflow shown in the Disk Workflow on page 358 and the three steps outlined below.

## Step 1: Compress and encode

You start with your final uncompressed video sequence.[2] It can be SD, 3-D, or HD and should be the best looking and sounding sequence you can make. Make a QT or other uncompressed file of the video. Compress the audio — .wav or .aiff file — to an .AC3 file. The reason for compressing the audio separately is to reserve more space on your disk for high quality video streams and motion menus.

---

2. If you didn't edit hi res, you'll have to upres your show or online it first.

Next, compress the video to an MPEG-2 file (which has frame size of 720x480) if it will be a DVD. For Blu-ray disks you can choose MPEG-2, VC MPEG-4, VC-1, or MVC MPEG-4 (if your show is 3-D). Compress the .AC3 audio file to an MPEG-2. If you have multiple sequences, repeat the compress and encode process for each sequence.

**12.h** Adobe Media Encoder software queues up sequences for encoding. *Photo courtesy of Adobe.*

## SIDES AND LAYERS

Disks have sides and layers of information. You will need to choose what kind of disk you want to make. The most popular choice today is single-sided, single-layer since it holds a feature film. However, with time, the advance of disk players, and content needs, this will likely change. Table 12.1 gives the lowdown on each type.

**TABLE 12.1**
**DISK SIDES AND LAYERS**

| SIDE | LAYER | WHAT DISK HOLDS | GB OF STORAGE | HOURS OF VIDEO |
|------|-------|-----------------|---------------|----------------|
| single | single | A & V for feature including 5.1 sound in three languages. | 4.4 | 2 |
| single | dual | Double what single-sided, single-layer holds. | 8 | 4 |
| double | single | Usually contains TV version on one side and a widescreen version on the other side. | 8.75 | 4.5 |
| double | dual | Holds the most but requires manual flipping to play other side or a dual-side-play mega changer. | 15.9 | 8 |

## Step 2: Author

You can do the authoring yourself using programs such as Adobe's Encore, Apple's DVD Studio Pro, or Avid DVD, or farm it out to a facility and inspect the result. Either way, the process proceeds like this:

1. Import assets, i.e., dropped scenes, cast, crew, and director interviews, etc.
2. Interleave (sector) the disk into chapters, referred to as chapter points.
3. Create titles, subtitles, menus, buttons, and graphics, and color balance the disk.
4. Options: Add games, read-alongs, and branching depending on budget and what kind of experience you want viewers to have.
5. Transcode to make A & V compatible and design the navigation.
6. Test everything: navigation, buttons, menus, etc.

## Step 3: Preview and burn

You (or the facility) make a test disk. If it's acceptable, it becomes the master from which you burn copies. Alternatively, you can create a master image and send it or the master disk to a disk facility to make the copies. Up to 50 copies is termed a duplication process; more than that, a replication process. The facility slaps on labels and the disks are good to go.

## FILE FINISH FOR WEB OR INTRANET

Completing your project for the Web is simple and straightforward:

1. Make a file from your final, uncompressed sequence: it can be HD, 3-D, etc. Put your best file forward!
2. Go to YouTube, Vimeo, or whatever website you'd like to exhibit your video.
3. Log in, check out the site's file formats and requirements, and follow its directions.
4. Fill out the rest of the information: title, description, tags (keywords), etc.
5. Upload!

If you're working at a news station, you will upload your story to the station's server and be prepared to re-edit and re-upload it if there are updates. If your video is destined for your company's intranet, get it to your webmaster on file or disk for uploading. Watch the uploaded video all the way through to make sure it plays correctly. You're done.

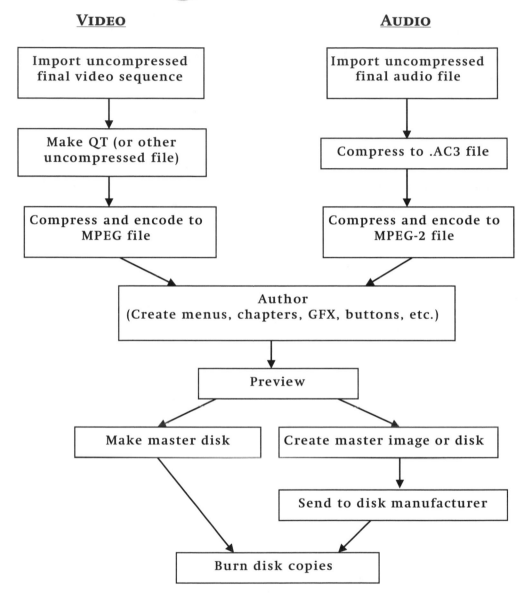

**DISK WORKFLOW**

# ONLINE FINISH

This topic comprises the bulk (and the rest) of this chapter because it involves several processes and is the typical route taken for broadcast projects: commercials, TV series, music videos, etc. There are three distinct phases: 1) Preparing for online; 2) The online session; and 3) The final, post-online finishing processes. We'll start off with a short overview.

# Understanding the Online Process: An Overview

*"Online is a translation of file formats, tape formats, and frame rates to make one delivery format standard for a project."*

—BARRY COHEN, online editor, *JAG, SpongeBob SquarePants,* and *Hey Arnold!*

Offline editing created a final, locked cut with compressed picture images from non-master sources — tapes or files — ingested into the editing system. Online editing reproduces the locked cut from your original, master sources to create a show master. Following the online session, the master is color graded and the sound mix is laid back to it. The show master then becomes the broadcast deliverable and can also be used to make the show's Web or disk version.

## Linear and nonlinear

There are two types of online systems: linear and nonlinear. In a nutshell, nonlinear online editing is a relinking and conforming process; linear editing is an assembling and recording process. They're both reproductive processes that match cut the locked sequence. Here's a brief overview of each.

### OLD STANDARD: LINEAR ONLINE

In the 1960s, when there were only film labs, linear online machines showed up, driving the establishment of post houses. Their influence carries on today with online terms, EDL formats, and post facility operations. Linear systems use an EDL to re-create shows by playing back original source tapes and recording each edit to a new tape. Edit by edit, in a linear fashion, the show master is assembled.

The linear workhorses of past decades — Ampex, CMX[3], GVG[4], and the rest — are being put out to pasture, though a few are still kicking around. Multi-cam shows (primarily sitcoms) and title creation keep some machines employed. Others have been integrated with new equipment to create hybrid systems that are linear in some aspects, nonlinear in others, e.g., they assemble linearly from tape but produce a file and upload it.

### New standard: Nonlinear online

Today's online systems are digital and work off of EDLs or more commonly, AAF, OMF, AFE, MXF, and XML files which replicate the offline final cut's time line and contain all the metadata for VFX, transitions, etc. Avid's Symphony Nitris DX and DS (Digital Suite) systems dominate. The online editor receives a file via server or hard drive with a bin of the show's sequence and metadata, and re-links to the original media.

**12.i** Avid's Symphony Nitris DX online system. *Photo courtesy of Avid.*

## *Staying native*

*"Postproduction is like a train track; there are various stops along the way where you need to transfer to different formats."*

—Barry Cohen

The current wisdom advises everyone to stay on the same system and codec the whole way through, i.e., if you offline on Avid, online on Avid,

---

3.  CBS, Memorex, eXperimental. A groundbreaking, tape-based linear online machine that was the standard from the 1970s–1990s.

4. Grass Valley Group. Northern California company which continues to be renowned for its online editing systems, switchers, and news editing systems.

ditto for FCP and Adobe Premiere Pro. Why? Because systems don't accept other system's files seamlessly. Crossing platforms brings translation problems, causes information to be lost on occasion, and may have the online editor eye-matching shots — a time- and money-consuming process. But of course, lots of folks don't stay native and cross platforms daily. Translation programs such as MetaFuze and Automatic Duck help files cross platforms and the future promises easier file exchanges but still, staying native is preferable. The more file formats and systems there are to traverse, the more complicated and costly everything becomes.

# Preparing for Online

You get ready for online from the first day of dailies as you enter correct time code and reel data into your digital editing system and make certain that your original source tapes or files are properly vaulted or preserved. The essential prep steps are:

1. Prepare the locked cut and notes for the online editor.
2. Create a final tape or file.
3. Ensure the post house has all the source material.
4. Create an accurate list (file) of your sequence and its data.

The rest of this section on preparation explains the first three steps in detail. Step #4 follows in a section of its own titled "Creating the Online File."

## 1. Prepare the cut

### FRAME CODE MODE (FCM)
Select DF or NDF, depending on your show's requirements.

### TRACKS
You should lay out and order all tracks clearly according to the online editor's preference. And don't forget to add a sync pop at the head and tail of your show.

### FORMATTING
Perform any necessary formatting; each network has different requirements. Slug for head or tail credits, teasers, bumpers, a.k.a. recaps, commercials, logos, etc. You may need to fill out a format sheet with the start time and end time for each element (e.g., show segment, title, commercial, etc.) of the show.

**NOTES**

You can place markers at locations on your time line with comments for the online editor such as "remove boom mic," "smooth speed effect," etc. It's wise to send a typed or handwritten note to the online editor with a "heads up" about any issues. The note should contain your contact info and let the editor know that you're available should any questions or problems arise.

## 2. Create chase tape, a.k.a. chase cassette

Frequently the online editor working in a linear bay will set up a tape to chase — run side by side — the online version of your show as it's built to ensure they match. Before you output the locked cut to make the chase tape, inquire whether the editor wants it to be anamorphic or letterboxed. For the online editor in a nonlinear bay you can create a chase file for inserting in the time line and placing over a corner of the picture.

## 3. Ensure post house has source material

Ordinarily your post house shepherds you through the post process from daily tapes or files to delivery tape or file. This means that your online house is the same as your daily transfer house so it has stored all your master source reels. Once you put in a request, the post house un-entombs these reels from the vault and moves them to the online suite.

You will most likely have acquired a lot of non-daily source reels such as stock reels, GFX reels, VFX reels, a main title reel, and your company's logo reel. If you kept any of these or your source files in the cutting room, now is the time to send them over to the post house. Since they are the highest quality, your source reels will now have the starring role during online in assembling your final, onlined show master tape or file.

**LIST OF REELS AND SUPER LOG**

The files or tapes you use to online are referred to as original tapes or files, source tapes or files, master tapes or files, daily reels, or daily masters. Your offline editing system can spit out a list of all the daily tapes needed to online your show. Use this list, if the post house doesn't have its own, for checking materials in and out of the post house. Post houses take reels real seriously; it's no fun for anyone when a reel goes missing. So send the hard and soft copies around so everyone can easily access the list at any time.

Since this list contains reel numbers and no other data, it's worth taking the time to consult your daily logs and compose a super log of reels. Type up the following info about each reel: reel number, time code at the start and end of each reel, the media on the reel (video, audio, or both), and, optionally, a brief description of the reel's contents. The super log helps you and the post house locate material.

Sometimes, despite all your efforts, you'll find yourself on a show where you're aware of problems in the EDL. This happens for a variety of reasons such as your being hired on the show after dailies were input or a time code error on a tape never being resolved. If you know there are problem edits, arm your online editor with an accurate final tape or file of the locked cut and a super log, and plan to be on hand. These steps, together with a dedicated online editor will go a long way toward solving the problems.

### 4. Create an accurate list (file) of your sequence and its data

There are two types of files that you can send to online: 1) An EDL that carries basic time code, edits, and reels data; 2) A project file that contains time line and metadata. Table 12.2 below describes the differences.

**TABLE 12.2**
**EDL VS. PROJECT FILES**

| FILE TYPE | USED PRIMARILY ON | PROCESS | FILE TYPES |
|-----------|-------------------|---------|-----------|
| EDL | Linear tape systems and in DI process | Assembly process: Playback and record, building master tape as you go. | CMX, GVG, Sony |
| Project file | Nonlinear system | Conform process: Re-link to media on drives, then output to master tape or file. | AAF, AFE, MXF, OMF, XML |

We'll go over the ins and outs of EDLs first, then cover project file types.

## Understanding an EDL

Before creating an EDL, it's good to know exactly what you're making and how to decipher it. Each line in an EDL, a.k.a. "the list," is referred to as an edit or an event. Events are numbered sequentially, starting with #1 on the first page of the list. Here are the first few events in a CMX-style EDL:

```
                    TITLE:  The Hunter
FCM: DF

Ev#  R#   Ch Trans   SOURCE IN      OUT        RECORD IN      OUT
001       B  BL     01:01:00;00  01:01:01;15  01:00:00;00  01:00:01;15
002  003  B  D  045 03:15:22;17  03:15:29;17  01:00:00;00  01:00:06;28
003  002  B  C     02:56:09;14  02:56:12;20  01:00:06;28  01:00:10;04
004  002  V  C     02:47:12;16  02:47:16;23  01:00:10;04  01:00:14;11
005  002  A  C     02:47:12;26  02:47:16;23  01:00:10;14  01:00:14;11
006  001  B  C     01:18:24;13  01:18:29;05  01:00:14;11  01:00:19;03
You can add notes like this one before the edit you wish to comment on.
007  003  B  W  060 03:35:12;26  03:35:18;23  01:00:19;03  01:00:25;08
```

## READING THE EDL

There are seven events in the short A-mode list above. Each event is an entry, usually one line, on the list. Working from left to right, the following box explains the eight columns for each event:

### DECIPHERING THE EDL

1. **Ev#** = Event number 1, 2, 3,... last event.
2. **R#** = Reel number. Which source reel the edit comes from.
3. **CH** = Channel. The type of an edit it is:
   A is an *audio-only* edit.
   V is a *video-only* edit.
   B (or AV on some systems) means it's *both audio and video*.
4. **TRANS**: Type of transition going into the edit followed by its duration in frames.
   C = *cut* to the edit.
   D = *dissolve* to the edit.
   W = *wipe* to the edit.
   BL = Black, which is used to make the dissolve, is created from an AX or Aux (auxiliary) channel in the online system.
5 & 6. **SOURCE IN AND OUT**: Source reel time codes for the start and end of the edit.
7 & 8. **RECORD IN AND OUT**: Record time codes in and out.
   This is where the edit falls in the show on your record tape, which is your show master tape. Since the black and coded record tape begins at 1:00:00;00, the first event's Record in time code is 1:00:00;00.

# Creating an EDL

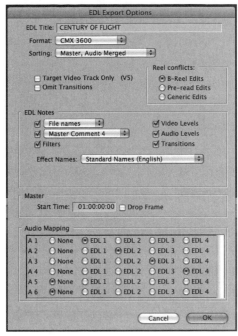

You must have a 30 fps sequence in order to make an EDL. If you have a 24 fps sequence because you've set up your project to finish on film, your system will let you convert it to a 30 fps sequence with a couple of clicks. Label this sequence appropriately, e.g., "30 fps Final Cut for EDL" and use it to make your EDL.

To create an EDL, select your system's EDL tool. Its menu gives you many choices, a.k.a. export options, for configuring your EDL. Listed below are the five main choices.

**12.j** Final Cut Pro's EDL tool.

## 1. List type

Depending on what system your online is being performed, you will make one of three types of lists: CMX (most common), GVG, or Sony. If your online system is not one of these three machines, it will be compatible with one of these list formats. To find out what type of list to generate, ask your post house or post supervisor.

## 2. Assembly mode

Mode defines the order by which your show will be assembled — put together — in a linear online bay. There are five modes: A, B, C, D, and E. Each mode sorts the events on the list in a different order for the online machine to perform the edits.

A-Mode is the default option and the only mode where your show is assembled in linear, sequential order. It is the slowest method but the safest should you have any doubts about the accuracy of your list or need to make changes in duration during online. It is also the easiest list to read and understand since the edits are laid down in order from the beginning of your show to the end so it is perfect for checking your list, which you will want to do before sending it out.

Modes B-E assemble the show in nonlinear, nonsequential order. Because they are faster and therefore more cost effective, these modes are regularly employed, primarily on TV series where the online editor typically works alone. You should online B-E mode only when you are absolutely confident in your list, are onlining on a linear system, and don't plan to make any duration changes during online.

A-mode is invariably the way you send a list in; the online editor can change it to another mode if preferred. It's helpful to understand the modes so when you oversee an online session you'll understand what's going on and can give input if asked about which assembly mode to use so here's some more information.

### A-MODE — *Sequential by record IN time code*

In A-mode, the online editing system reads and records all edits from first to last, requesting source tapes as they are needed. This means that the record tape is built from the beginning of the show to end, from first edit to last; for example, from event #1 starting at 1:00:00:00 to event #300 ending at 1:23:00:00. It also means that your source tapes are loaded into the machine, played back, and unloaded, repeatedly. How so? Well, if Reel 1 is used for events #20-30, then not again until event #150, it's taken down. Other tapes are loaded and their edits played back until Reel 1 is required again. This takes time since each reel must be checked for network specs every time and accounts for why A-mode assembles the slowest.

### B-MODE — *Nonsequential by source reel and record IN time code*

In this assembly method, the events are first arranged in source reel order: Reel 1, Reel 2, Reel 3... Reel 11 and then by Record IN time code order like A-mode. The online system records all edits from the source reel, leaving gaps to be filled later by subsequent reels. B-mode is easiest on the Record reel — the show master reel — because it has to shuttle less than in any other mode.

### C-MODE — *Nonsequential by source reel and source IN time code*

C-mode is the same as B-mode except that the edits play back from each source reel by source reel time code. The events on the EDL are arranged in source reel order: Reel 1, Reel 2, Reel 3... Reel 11 and then by source IN time code, e.g., on Reel 2: 2:01:00:19, 2:03:01:11, 2:03:33:06, etc. Online editors prefer C-mode because it takes the shortest amount of time since the source reels shuttle back and forth the least.

D-MODE — *Same as B-mode except dissolves, wipes, and other effects are performed last.*

E-MODE — *Same as C-mode except dissolves, wipes, and other effects are performed last.*

Both D- and E-modes add a bit of efficiency to B and C modes by performing all the transitional effects together.

## 3. Video choices

You can have the EDL show video filters, transitions, and other effects, as well as video and audio levels.

### B ROLL, *a.k.a. B reel or dub file*

This situation arises on linear systems only. Let's say you've dissolved from a lake at sunset to a lake at sunrise. Both shots are on the same tape reel, say Reel 5. Some tape formats cannot dissolve from the same reel. So to dissolve from Reel 5 to Reel 5, the second lake shot is dubbed off (recorded) to another tape. This tape is referred to as the dub reel, dump reel, B reel, or B roll. The A roll, a.k.a. A reel — the original source reel — has the other shot in the dissolve. It's a timesaver if the online editor can perform all these same reel dissolves to the dub reel at the beginning of the session. To accomplish this, select the appropriate command on your digital editing system's EDL tool.

## 4. Audio choices

There are numerous audio choices available for EDLs. Here are a couple:

### MAPPING CHANNELS

While you can cut many tracks on digital systems, they currently restrict you to 8 (FCP) or 12 (Avid) tracks for exporting to an EDL. EDLs restrict you further, allowing one to four audio channels. This is due to videotape having a maximum of four channels. If you have more audio tracks, you'll have to map the first four to the four EDL channels and make a second EDL to map the extra channels, deactivating the already exported tracks. Video always has only one channel on an online list so you must generate an EDL for each track of video.

### AUDIO- AND VIDEO-ONLY LIST

Select audio-only and no video edits will appear on your list, which is what sound editors usually request. You make video-only lists when only the video will be onlined and the sound married to it afterwards during layback — a common TV workflow. Here are the first five events from an audio-only list, with clip names (another option) included:

```
                          Audio-only EDL

TITLE:    BC 122 SND TC 0806_1
FCM: NON-DROP FRAME
001      AX      AA     C      00:00:21:13  00:00:21:14   00:59:58:00  00:59:58:01
* FROM CLIP NAME:    TONE: 1000 HZ @ -20.0 DB.1
002  82         A      C      07:55:58:26  07:56:10:16   01:00:01:08  01:00:12:28
* FROM CLIP NAME:    1-2 A
003  82         A      C      07:56:04:28  07:56:13:11   01:00:12:28  01:00:21:11
* FROM CLIP NAME:    1-2 A
004  82         A      C      10:16:43:21  10:16:47:25   01:00:21:11  01:00:25:15
* FROM CLIP NAME:    1D-1 A
005  82         A      C      10:16:48:03  10:16:48:26   01:00:25:15  01:00:26:08
```

## 5. Start time

You can enter the time code for the Record reel where you want your first edit (FFOP) to start. Normally you set the record reel to begin at 1:00:00;00. However, if your show is over one hour long, you'll have two reels since most master tapes are one hour maximum in length. You'll probably want to distinguish the reels and enter a start time for the second reel of 2:00:00;00.

# Creating a project file

Here are the file types you can make:

## AAF — Advanced Authoring Format

## OMF — Open Media Framework

OMF and AAF files carry project data such as time line, title, and VFX info as well as metadata. OMF is the older file type, slowly being supplanted by AAF.

## MXF — Media eXchange Format

A close cousin of AAF, MXF has a simpler file format. It can contain video and audio media.

## AFE — Avid File Exchange

An AAF that works with Avid systems exclusively and provides proprietary information for recreating Avid sequences.

### XML — eXtensable Mark-up Language

Final Cut Pro's AFE in essence, Apple's developed this file format for transferring project info between FCPs. Avids and other systems now work with XMLs.

**12.k** Exporting an XML on Final Cut Pro.

### Making the file

Before generating the file, check your time line carefully to be sure that all edits are clean and that there are no unintended jump cuts. (It's easy to overlook 1–2 frame miscuts on digital editing systems.) Label your locked sequence and its bin clearly, e.g., Brooklyn Zombies Ep 44, Locked Final Sequence May 10. Then create a project file for the sequence and export it to a hard drive or upload it to a server for the post house. Figure 12.k depicts exporting an XML on FCP.

## After creating the online file

Whatever type of file you're sending to online, there are three things you should do ahead of the session:

1. Check the list. Make sure everything looks right: time code, reel numbers (no characters cut off), frame code mode, master tape or file start time code, etc. By now you know your show so well that even the list will be familiar.

2. Send a test bin or EDL to the editor before the show locks to make sure your file is readable and there aren't any problems. This helps establish a good relation with the post house and lowers everyone's stress around onlining the show.

3. Send a pull list (list of reels needed for online) over early. This helps, especially on shows where the online editor will be recapturing the media at hi-res.

### Sending the list

Get the final online file to the editor a day ahead of the online session. This gives the editor time to import it into the online system, print it out, inspect it, and get comfortable with it before starting the online session. Having said this, turning the list over early is not always practical, as sometimes you'll complete the final edit at the last minute. Still, do your best to give the file to the online editor ahead of time, even if it's only 30 minutes before the online session starts. This saves time and, if you're attending the session, means you won't be waiting while the online editor does the setup work.

Whew! You're done. Now sit down and watch your show come together in much less time than it took to edit: It's online time!

# THE ONLINE

Normally, an online session is a straightforward reproduction of your offline locked cut: Offline has resolved most if not all of the editing and creative challenges. Depending on the nature of the online and of your job responsibilities, you may or may not attend some or all of the online session. If you go, you are there

**12.1** Post house lobby that pays tribute to the past. *Photo courtesy of AlphaDogs.*

to make certain the show goes together as locked and to help the editor resolve list problems and any other issues that surface. If you don't go, you'll review the show thoroughly afterwards.

Online expenses depend on the tape format, the equipment used, the number of personnel, the number and complexity of VFX the editor must make, and the rate of the online room itself. A low budget room employs the online editor, a couple of tape machines, and you, anticipating and feeding tapes to the editor to keep up the pace. A high priced room — called a bay — is backed up by and wired to the machine room. Here's a little more about each room.

## *Machine room*

This is the behind-the-scenes room which holds racks of tapes, banks of tape machines, supporting devices such as media storage

**12.m** Machine room with VTRs and supporting devices. *Photo courtesy of AlphaDogs.*

drives, and a patch bay of cables for linking machines. More modern facilities have routing rooms in addition, which have few patch cords, are attached to storage area networks (SANs), and can download and upload dailies, etc. They can also send scenes to clients around the world for live color grading sessions, viewing dailies, approving work, and so on: The virtual and global post house is a growing reality.

## Online bay

A typical bay has a long desk with the editing keyboard, often a tablet, a character generator (CG), and other devices the online editor needs to perform her magic.

An upscale bay is plush, adorned with fish tanks, thick rugs, artwork, video games, and the like. A swanky couch, frequently on a platform above the online editor's desk, is reserved for the producer or director, although ordinarily they don't attend the session. When things are going smoothly, the offline editor or assistant takes over the couch to make phone calls or grab a few winks during a late or all-night session. (The rates go down with the sun so many companies schedule overnight onlines.) Since sessions regularly cross meal times, many online houses provide meals. Be prepared to pig out due to stress, boredom, or just because it's there.

**12.n** Post house suite used for onlining as well as offlining with the all-important client couch. *Photo courtesy of AlphaDogs.*

# Online Personnel

There are four people who you will interact with at the post house and/or whose jobs it's important to understand. Let me introduce you.

## Project manager

Usually there's a point person for your project in the client services department of the post house. If your show telecined at the same house, the project manager, working with a scheduler, coordinates your show from the beginning. This is your "go to" person to consult before, during, or after a session with any questions or complaints.

## Tape operator

The tape op lives in the machine room, loading the tapes for your project, taking care that the show master meets all broadcast specs, and keeping the machinery humming along. The editor supervises the tape op or may act as the tape op, depending on the post house and the scope of the particular job.

## Graphic artist

The artist or online editor runs the titling computer which creates and stores the text and font information for your credits and titles. The titling session can occur at the end of the online session or after color grading. In any case, the graphic artist or editor enters the data ahead of time using a machine such as Avid's Deko or Chryon's Lyric.

## Editor

The online editor is many things: editor, VFX creator, technical wizard, and a fresh pair of eyes. While online can be strictly a conforming process, you should always remember that the online editor is not a mere button pusher; being called this pushes their buttons.

**12.0** Deko HD titling machine. *Photo courtesy of Avid.*

For years the job and career path of the online editor has been distinct from that of the offline editor. With the advent of digital technology, the distinctions are hazier: Today's offline editor is more technical and the online editor more creative than in the past. Today, an editor must cut the show, assemble the show master, add credits, effects, adjust the color, and make sure the show master tape or file meets technical standards. No matter how the work is divided, every editor who does a good job makes a contribution and deserves respect.

## THE ONLINE SESSION

*"Online editors have to be able to consume every element that comes our way to converge all elements into one delivery standard for a tape or file out."*
—BARRY COHEN

### Arriving at the session

As the client/supervisor, you should arrive 30 minutes early. Immediately confirm that all the source reels are in the edit bay by checking them against your list together with the tape op. If reels are missing, track them down and get them there, pronto. You don't want to hold up online for any reason. Showing up early means you're ready to meet any problems and it sets a professional tone. And it means you'll have time to grab a bagel and say hi to the fish.

### Supervising the online process

You are the client. You get to call the shots. Literally. The best approach to take is that you're all on the same team — the team that works together to create the best show possible. Don't badger the online editor with unnecessary questions; let them do their work. The time to crack the metaphorical whip is when there's a personnel problem (rare) or you're on deadline and the machines are malfunctioning, causing too much "downtime" (non-productive time). Some downtime is par for the course, but when it compromises your show's schedule or budget, consult with the online editor and call in the project manager. They will move the session to another bay, re-schedule it, or come up with another solution. The online editor is probably struggling hard to move things forward but may not have the clout to change the bay or the schedule.

# Linear online process

Although the linear process is giving way to nonlinear, we'll discuss it in detail as it lays a good foundation for understanding the terms, process, and challenges of the online phase.

## *Terms*

### WORDS THAT DESCRIBE MAKING EDITS

Edits are made, performed, laid down, onlined, assembled, or recorded; these terms all mean the same thing. The process of making the edits is referred to as "building the reel" or "assembling the show."

### AUTO ASSEMBLY

Auto assembly is the most common way shows are onlined. The online editor puts the machine "on auto" and it records each edit in the list automatically, usually in C-mode.

### MANUAL ASSEMBLY

The online editor presses a key to preview the edit (if on a linear system). Once satisfied, the editor presses another key to perform the edit.

### RIPPLING THE LIST

When the duration of an event changes, or an event is deleted or added, the events after it must have their record IN and OUT points shifted. This shifting effectively ripples — corrects and updates — the list. On a linear, tape-based system, the editor initiates the ripple after scrutinizing the list to ensure that no events will be overwritten, deleted, or otherwise altered as a result. On a nonlinear digital system, rippling occurs automatically in the background and is a non-issue.

## SEVEN STEPS OF LINEAR ONLINE PROCESS

1. Online editor imports the EDL into the computer and saves it.

2. Tape operator:

   - Inserts a blank tape into the record machine for assembling the show master.
   - Loads source reels into the playback machines.
   - Checks that playback and record machines are calibrated to meet network technical specs.

3. Editor slates the show master reel and lays down color bars.

   - Slate contains: Show's name, the date, and the reel's label: Edited Master.
   - Slate and the bars are for reel ID purposes only: Viewers will never see them as they are recorded before 1:00:00;00 where your show's first edit will appear.

4. Auto or manual assemble. The online editor decides how to lay down the show and presses a key to start the process. You and the editor watch as each edit is laid down. If there is a problem with an edit, the online editor halts the process, remakes the edit, and updates the list.

5. Any duration changes are made first if you're assembling by B-E mode. With A-mode you make them as they come up. (More about making duration changes in the next section.)

6. Once online is complete, you and the editor view the show master tape and note any problems.

   - The editor fixes problems on the spot or at a later "Fix" session.

7. Editor saves and prints a new EDL of the show as it was actually assembled. Usually this list is close to the EDL you brought in but not a perfect match as a few adjustments have been made such as slating and adding bars and tone. It's important that you and the post house hold on to this new list as it will be used for color correction, making fixes, and by the sound editors.

## Changing edits in online

There's a certain hush to online. You've been working so long and hard, and finally your project is in the bay. You sit and relax for a few in the darkened room, then whammo! The first edit blinks up on the monitors. It's as if you're viewing your show under a huge magnifying glass. You've seen it 50 times already but now you're watching pristine tapes and the show looks beautiful and new again. Sigh. Uh oh. That pan shot includes a few frames of the crew that you never noticed before. All of a sudden previously invisible warts are glaringly apparent...

You should not plan on making any changes in online, especially on linear systems; offline was for experimenting and locking, online is for conforming and creating a final tape version. However, when an excruciatingly bad edit shows up or you or the editor can make an easy fix, you'll want to do what's best for the show. Changes cost time and therefore money.

### DURATION CHANGES — WATCH OUT!

Changes that alter the duration of your show are the most problematic. Why? If you've already mixed your show the sound mix will now be out. Also, if you had to bring your show "to time," i.e., cut it to a specific length as you do with network TV shows, you will need to find another place to adjust the show and bring it back to time.

### ACCEPTABLE CHANGES

If necessary, you can ask the editor to slip or slide a few frames here and there, while maintaining sync of course. Replacing one shot with another, frame for frame, is another acceptable change. Routinely, you slug for a stock shot, insert shot, or other shot for which the master source is unavailable, then "drop the shot in" during online or the fix session a day or two later.

## Adding VFX

Customarily, on a show onlining on a linear tape system, any VFX are created before the online and are part of the show. Simple VFX like dissolves, supers, and wipes are reproduced in online along with the edits. A more complex effect from a special effects house arrives via tape in the cutting room and is cut into the show during offline. It then becomes an event on the EDL and is onlined from a source tape like any other event.

The editor can also create VFX during online. Usually the client is present to supervise and sign off on these special effects. Creating complex VFX can be time-consuming and pricey so plan ahead. For instance, if you're flying in boxes with the hosts of your show in them, have the reels and time code numbers of the shots you intend to use handy. If any new effects will change your show's duration, do them first so the editor can add them to the EDL and ripple it.

### Last word

If things are going swimmingly — and they should since you've done your homework — you may get bored. Check your work email, multitask, even snooze if it's an overnight session (the online editor will wake you if there are any problems), and enjoy ordering in, but always, always keep an eye on the prize — your show!

## Nonlinear online process

**12.p** Nonlinear online bay with editor performing dual duty as tape op. *Photo courtesy of AlphaDogs.*

The nonlinear process, while capable of accomplishing much more complex editing feats in much less time than the linear process, parallels the offline process in certain aspects, so is much more straightforward to describe. Here are the basic steps the online editor takes to onlining on a nonlinear system. The editor:

1. Imports the file (EDL, OMF, AAF, AFE, XML, or MXF) into the computer along with the offline editor's bin with the locked sequence.
2. Uses the pull list to batch capture uncompressed media from tape or file into the online system.

3. Accesses the sequence's time line and the online system's media manager to relink to the media.

4. Reviews the show once it's completely conformed and sends it to the client for review.

The advantages to nonlinear online are huge and all due to the top-of-the-line nature of today's digital systems. They can readily make duration and other changes without re-laying any edits. If the client isn't on site, the editor can easily output the show to server, tape, disk, or file for client review. Shows can lock and unlock as many times as necessary to accommodate last-minute changes before the sound mix occurs. Once the show finally locks, the online editor sends it on for color grading and the final finishing steps before delivery, which neatly brings us to the next section.

# After Online: Finishing the Show

Following online, there are a few more important steps before you deliver the final file, tape, or disk to the network or exhibitor. On TV shows, the post supervisor manages most of these finishing processes while the editor moves on to a new episode. On other shows the editor may be involved in some or all of these processes, so it's important to understand them.

### Protection master, a.k.a. safety master

As finishing processes take place and your show master is played and edited, it's possible for it to become damaged or destroyed, especially on a linear online system. Protection with videotape means making copies of the show at critical junctures. It's well worth the price because if the online master is lunched and there is no protection master, you will have to re-online, probably at your expense. Remember: copies are protection! You protected your original dailies, now protect your onlined show by making a protection master.

### Fix session

Most onlined tapes require a few fixes. The fixes can include correcting edits or dropping in a stock shot, CGI, or other footage. Additionally, there are "dirt fixes." Believe it or not, dirt and hair get caught on your source tapes, usually during production, and passed on to your show master during online. An editor — often the online editor — in a small bay cleans up the shots, sometimes electronically by running the tape through the online house's dirt removal system.

## Color grading

*"The meat and potatoes of what a colorist does is to make stuff cut."*
—RICH MONTEZ, colorist, Whipping Post Services

Color correction takes place in a data color room, often the same as telecine, efficiently making it a dual purpose room. Grading can be quite a creative time as the lighting and look of the film are revisited and fashioned for the final time. The colorist works with the DP and the director (features) or producer or AP (TV) who may be glued to the room for the grading or show up at intervals to inspect and approve it.

Colorists work on cutting-edge systems like Blackmagic's DaVinci Resolve and Autodesk's Lustre. They ingest the show master tape or the conformed sequence along with an EDL and the original media on tape or drive. In addition, the colorist may receive a LUT (the look-up table created for the project during the shoot to maintain its color values) which is essentially a preliminary grading.

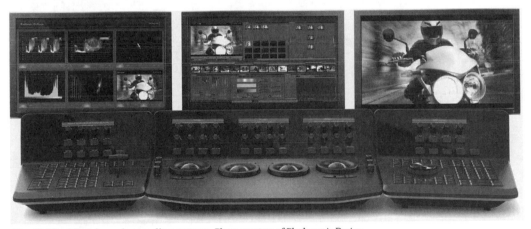

**12.q** DaVinci Resolve color grading system. *Photo courtesy of Blackmagic Design.*

### FILM-TO-TAPE COLOR CORRECTION PROCESS

On a show shot on film that's not going through the DI process, the colorist corrects the negative and any film opticals. Working off a film pull list, the colorist threads up the negative camera rolls to grade the show. The negative, like the tape source reels, is unchanged. In essence, the colorist re-telecines the show, grading each shot for the director or DP's approval.

## STREAMLINED COLOR GRADING

On many shows, chiefly TV series with established "looks" and locations, the colorist performs preliminary color correcting on dailies. This is done to maintain continuity during offline editing and cut down the time required for color grading following online. Shows that used a DIT (data image technician) will also need less grading later and may have the online editor perform the final color corrections.

**12.r** FCP color correction suite at a post house. *Photo courtesy of AlphaDogs.*

## WHAT GETS COLOR CORRECTED?

The colorist corrects image data that is encoded in three channels in either an RGB (red, green, blue) or YUV (luma and chroma) color space. Both color spaces are found in graphic and digital video editing software and used to color grade. RGB, with its higher (4:4:4) uncompressed subsampling rate, produces a higher grade so it is used for grading film. YIQ, a.k.a. Y'CBCR, is the NTSC standard for broadcasting all tapes and files. Since the naked eye picks out differences in brightness better than differences in color, YIQ cannily compresses and discards color data in accordance with viewers' vision.

### SUBSAMPLING

Subsampling defines how this discarding of color data is accomplished and is measured in ratios of luma (brightness) to chroma (color). The number 4 means the data is uncompressed; any number less than 4 means the data's compressed. So 4:2:2, the YUV (PAL) broadcast standard, signifies that the luma data (4) is uncompressed and the two color data channels (2:2) are compressed. 4:4:4, the RGB standard, means nothing is compressed.

So how does this relate to color grading? A colorist can grade a video to be 4:4:4 which is a good goal — you want the highest quality. But it will not be broadcast that way. Also, if the source tape, e.g., DVCPRO50, had a 4:2:2 color sampling, its missing color data cannot be recovered. However it can be improved through grading and upsampling at 4:4:4. Word to the wise: Filming in compressed formats affects color and other image qualities. So shoot in professional formats (no lower than 4:2:2).

### Bit depth

Bit depth is the amount of color data in a digital image and is measured in bpp (bits per pixel). The higher the bit depth, the more color data and tonal range there is for the colorist to work with. The bit depth of your source media is directly related to how your crew originally captured the media during production. Most SD and HD consumer and professional digital video formats capture at 8-bit, e.g., DVCPRO50, DVCPRO-HD, HDCAM, and HDV. The RED and a few other cameras work at 12-bit. (Offline editors work with RED's low res proxy files.) A 16-bit depth is optimum but is a storage hog so currently is prohibitive.

Artifacts such as stairstepping and banding show up with lower bit depths in areas in shots with narrow gradients such as a blue sky. Luckily, color grading systems can up the bit depth to aid the colorist in grading. Future developments will most certainly improve bit depths across all devices.

### CTM, a.k.a. CCM (color timed master or color corrected master)

Color grading produces a new show master tape labeled the CTM. It becomes the new edited master to which titles will be added and the final sound mix will be laid back. The tape op makes a protection master of the CTM if needed.

## VFX

With the CTM and a joystick, trackball, and/or tablet pen in hand, the online editor or another editor performs extra VFX work. This includes compositing VFX layers, removing wires from shots, e.g., where an actor "flew" across the screen, repositioning (repo-ing) shots, and other detailed finishing work.

12.s Post house suite with tablet for GFX and VFX. *Photo courtesy of AlphaDogs.*

## Adding credits and titles

Next, it's time to add titles and credits to the show. A graphic artist or the online editor loads them into a titling machine such as the Chyron and adds them to the CTM. The editor or artist will likely put the titles on an *alpha channel* (which FCP and other offline systems also use). The alpha channel, often referred to as a matte channel because it can combine images, is a separate video channel. It holds the transparency data for displaying the three other color channels, so is employed for titling and laying images over one another.

The editor or graphic artist will also create a *textless version* of the show, if the delivery reqs specify one. The textless consists of the background bed of shots used in the main and end title sequences minus the titles and credits. It's used for inserting different titles and subtitles for international or nontheatrical (TV) release. The editor will tack the textless material onto the tail of the reel where it's also handy should it be needed to re-do the credits. Alternatively, the textless is put to LTO (linear tape — open), a magnetic tape cassette.

## Audio Layback

While all this has been going on at the post house, the sound editors and mixers have been busy creating and mixing the audio. The post house imports the final mix from file or tape and lays it back to the CTM.

## Formatting the show

Your online house will make sure your show master is formatted properly for broadcast. Formatting encompasses: closed captioning, putting in black for commercials to be dropped in at the network, adding bumpers, trailers, creating the textless version, and varispeeding.

### VARISPEEDING

When a TV show is too long or too short, rather than edit it to time, the entire show or part of it can be sped up or slowed down to bring the show to time. Most networks frown on it and presently it cannot be done with HD due to the havoc it wreaks on the moving images, but producers still sneak in varispeeded shows on occasion. One minute per hour, (3.5% rate), is the maximum amount of time you can gain or lose.

It is strongly recommended that you do NOT varispeed your show. Re-edit instead. Or get special dispensation from the network to run long or short. Why? Varispeeding alters the speed that your sound plays, so your original mix is useless should you ever have to reformat the show. Also, if a foreign distributor should wish to add dialogue, music, or effects, they will have a devil of a time matching your new varispeed rate. Foreign distributors routinely forbid varispeeding in their contract so if you do varispeed, you may have to create two versions of the show: normal and varispeed.

## Quality Control (QC)

Once finishing processes are complete, your show master moves to a bay for QC. An editor may run a QT file of the locked cut in a monitor against the show to check that they match and that the onlined show meets network specs. Alternatively, the post facility will *spot QC* the show: wind through it and inspect a few places, especially heads and tails. It's money well spent to have a 100% QC clause in your contract as this makes the post house responsible for the show passing network specs, not you. If your show arrives damaged at the network or a foreign distributor's office, this clause fully protects you.

## *Conversion and storage*

The postproduction supervisor's job has gotten more complicated due to the variety of formats that are often required by the network, exhibitor, and production company. It's not unusual for the post super to manage the completion of three versions of a show: film, HD, and SD tape. The SD and HD versions are broadcast. The film or 24p version is vaulted for archival purposes or used to generate a PAL version. Down conversion is the most common practice: It's easier to go from a higher standard to a lower standard, e.g., from HD tape to SD tape. Increasingly, shows are being archived to LTO because one cartridge can store hundreds of gigabytes.

## *Delivery*

The AP or post supervisor takes charge of the show's delivery. They supervise the shipping and delivery of all elements required by broadcasters and exhibitors as well as the dispatch of materials to the trailer or promo house and to the marketing company. The tape or file delivered to the network for airing is called the air master. Often a protection air master is sent in case there's a problem.

## CHAPTER WRAP-UP

Congratulations! Your project is complete and delivered. On to the next job! Or the intense marketing phase! Or to the backyard and lolling over the paper and the superlative reviews of your show! From here, you can also move on to Chapter 13 and learn about the DI process and how to finish your project on film or to Appendix I to complete your budget for this last phase of postproduction.

# Finishing on Film and via Digital Intermediary

## Overview

The end of a show is a flurry of overlapping activity: sound editors editing, mixers mixing, negative cutter match cutting, and picture crew aiding everyone. This final chapter covers the digital intermediary, a.k.a. digital intermediate (DI) process which the majority of Hollywood features use to finish. We'll chart how DIs are regularly used to finish on tape, file, and disk. But first, we'll steer you through the traditional film negative cutting process and final film workflow: Understanding these lays the foundation for the DI process. The chapter then describes the final sound workflow and wraps with a look at the future of film and how it's intertwined with digital technology. Let's get trekking!

## Film Finish via Negative Cut

How do you get there from here? If your final locked cut is on work print, please go to www.joyoffilmediting.com and look under the Free tab for how to proceed, then return here for related, updated information. If your final locked cut resides on your digital editing system, read on.

To get your show through negative cut and into the cinema, here are the five major steps:

1. *Telecine*

   Colorist scans film to make tape or file dailies, creates database with keycode numbers, camera roll numbers, and other pertinent picture and sound data.

2. *Edit*

   Editor or assistant ingests dailies and imports database file into digital editing system. Editor edits and makes final locked cut.

3. *Make cutlist*

   Editor or assistant generates cutlist of locked cut.

4. *Cut negative*

   Negative cutter match cuts film negative.

5. *Make film prints*

   Film lab makes prints with sound track for theater projection.

As you can see, we're already almost half way there, having completed steps #1 and 2. The next sections will take you the rest of the way through the negative cutting and lab print processes.

# Preparing the Picture for the Negative Cutter

*"There are people who understand film really well, and there are people who understand digital really well, but there aren't a whole lot of people who understand both. You don't have to know everything about film, but knowing as much as you can about the process and what has to happen before you go into the digital editing machine, and then when you come out, is very important."*

—CELIA HAMEL, director of post production, ABC studios

A miscut negative is everyone's worst nightmare. You've worked so hard to come this far, don't blow your show now! Prepare your locked cut properly before handing over your show to the negative cutter.

## General rules

1. Take great care in prepping lists.

   Incorrect information, unless the negative cutter happens to catch it, causes a miscut negative for which there is no undo button.

2. Communicate clearly with the negative cutter.

3. Ensure the negative cutter has the entire negative.

   This is no small feat on shows where there are lots of opticals[1], stock shots, etc., and their negatives are scattered at different facilities.

---

1. Film effects made at an optical house on an optical printer from new negative (as opposed to the OCN).

## *Observe the cutback frame*

The cutback frame is the frame of film an editor leaves so the negative cutter can make a negative splice. To explain: If an editor cuts from Frankie at frame A to Johnny and then back to the same take of Frankie, the editor cannot use frame B — the very next frame — of Frankie. The editor must use frame C or later on Frankie. Why? Because the negative cutter *hot splices* one frame to another by overlapping them on a heated splicer and searing them together with cement glue. Part of frame B is used up with this hot splicing.

Specifically, to cut from Frankie's frame A to Johnny, the neg cutter will actually cut after the first half-frame of Frankie's frame B. The neg cutter overlaps a half-frame of B, cementing it on to the first half-frame of Johnny's shot. The rest of frame B is useless as is the frame before the first frame of Johnny's shot. After Johnny's shot, Frankie's frame C is the first frame that can be used.

### CUTBACK RULE

When editing and re-using any shot, don't cut back to the very next frame. It is the cutback frame that must be left for the negative cutter to cut and splice the negative. To be safe before cutting back:

| 35mm | Allow 2 frames. |
|---|---|
| 16mm | Allow 8 to 10 frames, or 3 frames at a minimum on each side of the edit. |

— Due to its smaller gauge, 1½ 16mm frames are cemented over another to make a hot splice so it's necessary to leave more frames.

Also, when using the end of a shot, don't use the last frame. The flash frame is not a viable cutback frame. Exception: When you're going the DI route, you don't need to worry about cutback frames as the film scanner can reproduce frames.

### BREAKING THE RULE

There are times, usually due to not shooting enough film, that you have to re-use frames. If you do decide to use the cutback frame, you will need to make a dupe negative of that shot for the negative cutter to use. This is a big expense for one frame or a handful of frames so it's rarely done. (How to make a dupe negative will be covered later in the section about making the release print.) In most circumstances you want to be mindful and leave the cutback frame for the negative cutter.

## BE AWARE OF THE CUTBACK FRAME AS YOU EDIT

When you're editing on a digital system, it's easy to forget about the cutback frame. Hip to this, digital film editing systems have a feature to check for cutback frames. Run this check on every reel. To make sure you didn't use the same frame in two different reels, cut all the reels together into one big sequence and run the check on it. If you find that you left in the cutback frame or reused frames and you can't substitute another shot, see Table 13.1 below to find the remedy.

**TABLE 13.1**
**FIXES FOR CUTBACK FRAMES AND FRAME RE-USE**

| TYPE OF SCENE | PROBLEM | SOLUTIONS |
|---|---|---|
| DIALOGUE (or other sync sound scene) | You've cut from Harry to Voldemort, then back to Harry, reusing 3 frames of Harry's shot. | SOUND: Don't touch it.<br>PICTURE: Trim 3 frames (or more) from the tail of Harry's first shot or from the head of his second shot. Then add the same amount to the head or tail of Voldemort's shot. Check for sync and the cutback frame again. |
| ACTION MONTAGE NARRATION (or other non-sync sound scene) | You used 5 frames of the waterfall shot twice. | PICTURE:<br>1. Trim the 5 duplicate frames of picture and sound from one of the shots.<br>2. Or slip *picture only* for the 5 duplicate frames on one of the shots.<br>SOUND: Actually you can slip sound with picture if you wish. However chances are that you've laid the sound in exactly the way you like and you don't want to touch it. |

## *Divide show into projection reels*

Break your show into 10- or 20-minute reels (most common), depending on the negative cutter's preference. These reel durations translate to 1000- or 2000-foot reels in 35mm and 400-foot reels in 16mm which takes 10-minute reels only. Make each reel a sequence and label it accordingly, being careful not to break scenes across reels.

## *Create cutlist for each reel*

This is the critical step that you've been building up to since you imported the database from telecine with the negative keycode and camera data. Here are the steps:

### 1. CHECK DATA

When you make a cutlist — actually you'll make a series of lists as detailed in Step #2 — your digital system accesses the database to generate the data the negative cutter will need to match cut the negative to your final locked cut. As discussed in the "Vital Verifications for Film Finish Shows" section of Chapter 4, you should have verified the data in the database each day after ingesting dailies. If you did not do this, you must do it now.

This is the only way you can be sure of having an error-free negative cut-list and cut negative. At this point you do not have to check every shot you ingested, just the clips which made it into the final locked cut.

## 2. MAKE LISTS

Every digital system that does film projects has a film tool (FilmScribe on Avid and Cinema Tools on FCP) or plug-in for making film cutlists. The tool gives you various cutlist choices regarding film stock, handling dissolves, etc. To best prepare, take a course on film assisting on the digital system you'll be working on. You want to be a knowledgeable interface between the digital cutting room and the film conforming room.

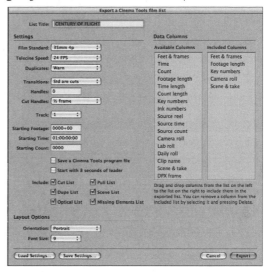

13.a Exporting film lists from FCP's Cinema Tools menu.

Here are the five lists you'll want to make, check, and print out for each locked reel and give to the negative cutter:

1. *Camera roll list*

   This list contains all the camera rolls from dailies, stock footage, opticals, or other reels that you used to cut the reel. It organizes the camera rolls from lowest number to highest. The negative cutter depends on this list to obtain the camera rolls from the vault.

2. *Pull list = Camera roll list + shot and keycode data*

   In addition to the camera roll, this list consists of the clip name and number, start and end key code for each shot, and its length. It's ordered by camera roll and then by ascending key code shots. The negative cutter relies on this list to pull shots (cut them from camera roll) so they're ready to cut and assemble.

3. *Cutlist, a.k.a. assembly list = Pull list in edited sequence order*

   This important list includes the same data as the pull list, arranged from first cut to last cut in the reel. The neg cutter uses the cutlist to match cut the shots and assemble the negative reel. A cutlist shows the cumulative footage from a 0000 00 start in the film synchronizer so that the negative cutter can double check that the right shot is being cut in at the right place. You can generate a 35mm list (A Roll list) or a 16mm list (A/B Roll list). (More about these in the next section on how the negative cutter puts the show together.) To see what this list looks like, study Table 13.2 below.

4. *Optical list = list of lab-made film effects*
   This lists opticals for the negative cutter to oversee to completion. Since this will be the case for the majority of 16mm opticals, on a 16mm show you make an optical pull list in addition. Most 35mm opticals will have already been created and edited into the final cut. They will be included on the cutlist and not the optical list and the negative cutter should have already received their negative. Conversely, on most 16mm shows, the neg cutter is responsible for completing opticals, so you will make an optical pull list in addition to the cutlist.

5. *Dupe list = list of re-used frames for duplication*
   Arranged by key code, this list flags re-used frames that must be duplicated. Always make a dupe list, even if you have already checked for re-used frames and the cutback frame. This list does one of three things: 1) Proves that you have no dupe frames; 2) Lets you know where re-used frames slipped in by mistake so you can fix them; 3) Tells the negative cutter what re-used frames must be duplicated.

**TABLE 13.2**
**SAMPLE CUTLIST WITH KEY CODE**

| List name: Reel 5 Film Cut | 72 cuts | handles = 0 | Page: 1 of 12 |
|---|---|---|---|
| Project: Home Free | 0 dupes | inside/inside | Date: Aug 2, 2012 |
| Assembly List | 0 opticals | total footage: 874+01 | 35mm 24 fps |

| Cut # | Start/end | Length | Key code Start | End | Cam Roll | Sc/Tk |
|---|---|---|---|---|---|---|
| 1. | 0+00 9+14 | 9+15 | KZ 36 7471-3316+11 | 3822+09 | A597 | 48/3 |
| 2. | 9+15 18+14 | 9+00 | KZ 36 7471-3792+07 | 3800+06 | A597 | 48A/1 |
| 3. | 18+15 29+13 | 11+14 | KZ 36 7471-3334+02 | 3545+15 | A597 | 48/3 |
| 4. | 29+14 42+02 | 12+05 | KZ 36 7471-3812+13 | 3824+01 | A597 | 48A/1 |
| 5. | 42+03 47+12 | 5+10 | KZ 36 7471-3454+10 | 3460+04 | A597 | 48/3 |
| 6. | 47+13 51+10 | 3+14 | KZ 36 6331-2463+03 | 2467+00 | A598 | 48C/2 |
| 7. | 51+11 54+12 | 3+02 | KZ 36 7471-3764+11 | 3766+12 | A597 | 48/3 |
| 8. | 54+13 64+09 | 9+13 | KZ 36 7471-4407+09 | 4418+13 | A597 | 48B/2 |

**3. MAKE TAPE(S)**

Make a tape of each locked reel with digitized head leader, sync pops at head and tail, and burnt-in time code and key code. The negative cutter will use this tape to visually match cut the show.

### Summary: What to send to the negative cutter on a negative cutlist show

**1.** All the negative.

**2.** Tapes of locked reels.

**3.** Lists: Camera Roll List, Pull List, Cutlist, Optical List, Dupe List.

# What the Negative Cutter Does

A working knowledge of the negative cut process will help you achieve a perfectly cut negative. To understand the process, keep in mind that negative cutting is also referred to as negative conforming or negative matching as those terms sum up the job. One vital task is to treat the negative with scrupulous care so that no dust, hairs, or scratches get on it. Negative facilities go to great lengths to maintain a "clean room." When handling the negative, the neg cutter wears gloves and keeps the area dirt and dust free. After acquiring all the negative camera rolls and ordering any opticals, the negative cutter cuts each reel of negative in three steps:

## 1. Pulls shots

Using the pull list, the neg cutter removes each shot from its camera roll and cores it (winds it onto a plastic core). The cutter lines up the "pulls" — the cored shots — on a rack.

## 2. Matches locked cut

Next, the negative cutter matches up each negative take with each shot in the show.

**13.b** Cores (2" and 3"). *Photo courtesy of Chris Senchack.*

This visual match is made by lining up the negative against either of the following:

**A)** Work print reel

▸ Negative is placed in the first gang of the synchronizer.

▸ Work print in the second gang.

**B)** Video tape
  ▸ Negative is placed in the first gang of the synchronizer.
  ▸ Videotape runs in tape machine.
  ▸ Film and tape are locked together to run in sync by an electronic synchronizer such as a LokBox.

The neg cutter checks the match cut by verifying that key code and picture correspond. After confirming the match, the negative cutter snips the negative with a small pair of scissors.

**13.c** Match cutting with LokBox which syncs the tape in the deck with the negative film. LokBox and tape deck are below the bench. Neg cutter winds the film through the synchronizer while eyeing the tape in the small monitor. *Photo courtesy of Chris Senchack.*

## 3. *Splices and assembles the reel*

Last, the neg cutter splices the cut negative pieces together to assemble the reel. In fact, the negative cutter hands these pieces to someone else to do the splicing or sends them to the lab where a team assembles the negative reels. Why not splice as you go, as you do when cutting the work print? Read on!

### SPLICING NEGATIVE

With a cement glue (composed mostly of Acetone), and heat using a hot splicer, a.k.a. cement splicer, the neg cutter splices the frames.

### HOT SPLICER

Understanding how the hot splicer works cements your understanding of how frames are lost during negative cutting and why you must leave cutback frames when editing. Here are the steps:

1. The negative cutter scissor-cuts the shots on the A side and the B side of the cut.

   **16mm**
   Shot on A side: Cuts 1½ frames after the cut.
   Shot on B side: Cuts 1½ frames before the cut.

   **35mm**
   Shot on A side: Cuts half-frame (two sprockets) after the cut.
   Shot on B side: Cuts half-frame before the cut.

2. Negative cutter scrapes off the film emulsion on the B side.
   **16mm** Entire 1½ frames scraped.
   **35mm** Half-frame scraped.

**3.** The neg cutter spreads cement glue on the scraped area and brings down the top plate of the hot splicer. This action cuts out the extra half-frame (35mm) or frame and a half (16mm) and presses the frames together on the frame line which hides the splice. With 35mm two sprockets on each

**13.d** Hot splicer with Acetone cement for joining two pieces of negative. *Photo courtesy of Chris Senchack.*

frame are glued together on top of each other. With 16mm one-and-a-half frames are glued together. A heated element in the splicer speeds up the drying of the cement and completion of the splice.

### A ROLL

When 35mm is spliced, the frame line covers up the splice so it is cut in one roll, known as an A roll or single strand.

### A/B ROLL, *a.k.a. double strand, zero cut, or checkerboarding*

Because its frame line is so thin that a negative splice would be noticeable, the lab uses an A/B roll method for assembling a 16mm negative. This method uses two synchronized camera rolls, referred to as A/B rolls. The A roll contains shots 1, 3, 5, etc., and the B roll holds shots 2, 4, 6, etc. Between each shot is black leader for the length of the missing shot, e.g., the A roll would have Shot 1, black leader for the length of shot 2, Shot 3, black leader for the length of shot 4, Shot 5 and so on. The B roll would have the opposite. Once they're completely assembled, the rolls are processed together to make one reel of 16mm positive film.

## Conclusion

Once the negative is matched, cut, and spliced, it's sent on to the lab, which is what the next section is all about.

## GETTING FROM THE SHOOT TO THE THEATER

Here are the steps from beginning to end that it takes to bring picture and sound together to make a final film print ready to project.

# The Picture Process: from Negative Cut to Release Print

Working back and forth between negative (gray arrows) and positive (white arrows and final box), there are seven steps to arrive at a release print:

**1**

**SHOOT NEGATIVE FILM IN THE CAMERA.**

This is the OCN (original camera negative).

**2**

**PROCESS OCN FOR TELECINE OR WORKPRINT TO CREATE FINAL LOCKED CUT.**

From the processed OCN there are two paths to the locked cut.

1) Telecine creates daily tapes or files for ingesting and editing on digital system and producing the final, locked sequence, which is used to make a cutlist for the negative cutter.

2) Classically, a positive work print is printed from the processed OCN. The work print is edited and becomes the final, locked cut.

**3**

**NEGATIVE CUTTER CUTS THE OCN.**

The negative cutter match cuts to a tape and a cutlist or the work print reels. Opticals are completed.

**4**
**MAKE ANSWER PRINT (AP) FROM CUT OCN.**
The AP, a.k.a. the First Trial Print, is a positive, color timed print.
The timer at the lab manipulates the red, green, and blue printer
lights on each shot for optimum exposure and color balance so
that the shot corresponds to the skin tones, lighting, and density
of the other shots in the scene.

An AP of each reel is screened with the director, DP, and timer.
Typically, several APs are made for each reel until the director
and DP approve it.

**5**
**MAKE INTERPOSITIVE (IP) FROM CUT NEGATIVE.**

**6**
**MAKE INTERNEGATIVE (IN), A DUPE NEGATIVE, FROM THE IP.**
Steps #5 and #6 are necessary because the cut negative, with its
cement splices, would deteriorate and self-destruct if used to make
the required number of theatrical prints. The original cut negative
is preserved in the vault while the IN is put into action. The IN is a
spliceless negative that can make from 50-100 release prints. As the
IN deteriorates, another IN is struck from the IP.

**7**
**MAKE CHECK PRINT, THEN RELEASE PRINTS FROM IN.**
The check print is the final trial print made from the IN and is
thoroughly checked before release prints are struck from the IN.

# The Sound Process: From the Shoot to the Theater

Just as the picture goes through various steps to get from shoot to release print, so does the sound. Here are the six steps necessary to bring picture and sound together for the final release print.

**1**
**CREATE AND RECORD SOUND AND MUSIC.**
During production, record sync and wild sound.
During postproduction, record ADR and Foley and obtain SFX from library.
Compose, score, and record music or obtain recordings from MX library.

**2**
**EDIT SOUND AND MUSIC.**
Ingest all sound and music into DAWs and edit.

**3**
**MIX SOUND AND MUSIC.**
Create DME (dialogue, music, & effects) stems and printmaster.

**5**
**MARRY OPTICAL SOUND TRACK TO AP.**
Run each AP reel and listen intently to check the optical sound track.
Have the lab fix any problems. Approve final AP.

**6**
**MAKE RELEASE PRINTS WITH OPTICAL SOUND TRACKS.**
Ship release prints to theaters for projection.

The product of the traditional film and sound process — the optical track on the finished film — is illustrated by a frame of fill in Figure 13.e. This blown-up frame also reveals DD (Dolby Digital) and DTS (Digital Theater Sound) encoding. Since some theaters are equipped for DTS and others for DD, both are encoded on optical and digital sound tracks along with a third system, SDDS (Sony Dynamic Digital Sound). All three hold 5:1 and 7:1 surround sound and compress and encode audio for digital and optical theater projection. DD and DTS are the more prolific and popular systems, with DD dominating. Both are also used for broadcast and on disks and video game consoles. Interestingly, all three standards encode analog audio tracks in case the digital decoding or data fails.

**13.e** Blow-up of optical track: The two tracks on right are the analog track. The dashes on the left are the DTS track. Look closely and you'll see two opposing half moons in the gray area between the sprocket holes. This is the Dolby logo and means that this piece of film is encoded with a DD track. *Photo courtesy of Chris Senchack.*

# Digital Intermediate (DI) Finish

*"Traditional negative cutting for commercial feature films doesn't exist anymore... The job has changed completely! I used to say that my job was similar to how Woody Allen described flying: Hours of boredom interrupted by moments of terror. That's all gone now. Now that Digital Intermediate (DI) is being used by almost everyone, we're taking full lab rolls straight from telecine and sending them to be scanned."*

—Mo HENRY, negative cutter, *The Blind Side, Julie & Julia,* and *The Dark Knight*

Coming of age with the millennium, the DI corrals all images — film, tape, and digital — into a data file, based on the locked cut. The DI process combines parts of traditional film and online processes to produce all desired finishing formats: film, tape, disk and file for projection, Web, home entertainment, regular broadcast, and, increasingly, special event broadcasts such as sports shows. We'll describe the DI process in detail, but first, a few definitions.

## Film scanner

This device scans in OCN as well as positive film and spits them out as digital data. There are two types: film scanners and telecine scanners.

### FILM SCANNERS

These dedicated machines have been in service for years and upgraded for the DI process. They run slow, taking 8 fps for 2K data scans. However, they perform the most accurate, best quality image work at the highest resolutions because they use pin registration which holds each frame in place to expose it. Post houses mostly rely on Arriscan but Cintel's diTTo and other machines are also employed.

**13.f** Arri film scanner. *Photo courtesy of ARRI.*

### TELECINE, A.K.A. DATACINE SCANNERS

Telecine systems are multi-purpose, used at the beginning and end of the postproduction process. While they run faster, performing real time data scans (in part because they don't use pin registration) and scan the film on the fly, they need to be slowed down to produce the best quality images.

## 2K, 4K, 6K, and 8K

These terms represent the amount of data — 2048, 4096, 6144, and 8192 horizontal pixels respectively — that gets scanned from

**13.g** Spirit 4K DataCine film scanner. *Photo courtesy of Digital Film Technology and The New Hat Post facility.*

film negative to file. The more data, the higher the picture quality and the larger the storage requirements. A 2K file contains the minimum amount of data necessary for color grading and other finishing work so it is used for the majority of DI finishing work. 4K scans are also performed and are accelerating with technological advances.

At present, the majority of digital prints are 2K for several reasons. 1) Most cameras shoot at 2K, although a few models (e.g., the RED) can shoot at 4K and that number will only grow. 2) Digital projectors work at 2K, although Sony's committed to 4K projectors. 3) Storage requirements soar with 4K and above so post facilities work at 2K and bump to 4K. Still, a few films, notably *Baraka* at 8K, have used the higher resolutions as have archivists. As the technology advances, the future promises the most amazing images we've seen yet.

## CIN and DPX

These two file formats are used in DI work due to their superior ability to preserve color data and store its associated metadata. DPX (digital picture exchange) files are more prevalent than CINs (Kodak Cineon files). Both are usually referred to by their resolution, e.g., a 2K file, 4K file, etc., rather than their file name.

## DI workstation

This high end system is sometimes called the DI lab due to its multi-tasking abilities: It can edit, color grade, composite VFX, and produce a master file or tape for a film, disk, file, or tape finish. Ideally, a DI workstation should also be able to interface with a film scanner to ingest images and a film recorder to export them. Often, workstations interface with other systems that perform the conforming, VFX, or color-grading steps. Brands include Avid's Nitris DX and Quantel's iQ.

## Film recorder, a.k.a. laser recorder or laser printer

These machines take the completed digital AP file and record it back to

**13.h** Arrilaser film recorder. Negative film reel runs in dust-free magazines and records images from DI file via solid state laser beams. *Photo courtesy of ARRI.*

film frames. They work by scanning images onto negative film frames using three RGB lasers. Since it takes over 0.8 seconds to record each frame, it's a time-consuming process.

# The Digital Intermediate Process

*"The show is a blank canvas; the DI writes the picture. The process has brought about more collaboration between the DP and postproduction than ever before. Together we can create a look for every state of mind of a picture. More and more we get the script and make our recommendations before the budget is set and the show begins to shoot."*

—PETER WARE, COO & Senior VP of Worldwide Production, Stargate Digital Films

The DI process begins by commandeering all the data (files with lists) and media for the images in the final locked cut:

- Lists: cutlist, pull list, EDL, OMF, AAF, AFE, or XML.
- Media
  - Film negative
    - ▸ The OCN may be in one of three states: Completely conformed and assembled, broken into selects (pulled takes with handles), or uncut.
  - Uncompressed tape.

The DI process proceeds in three phases: conform, edit, and master. Figure 13.1 charts the DI workflow; here are the details.

## 1) *Conform*

The DI editor starts by importing the project's list(s): pull list, cutlist, EDL, AAF, OMF, AFE, or XML and highest resolution media into the DI workstation. The media has all been transferred to digital data: OCN scanned via film scanner or datacine machine, uncompressed tapes captured, and files imported. The editor then uses the lists to conform the media to the locked cut and create a DI file — a .DPX most likely or a .CIN. For film this will be a 2K file, or perhaps a 4K file. Alternatively, this conforming stage is offloaded to another system like Autodesk's Smoke so that the main DI task — color grading — can be performed concurrently.

**13.i** With 2K and color grading capability, this Avid Symphony Nitris DS can perform as a DI workstation. *Photo courtesy of AlphaDogs.*

## 2) Edit

*"The DI is the most significant contribution that has happened to image making since I've been a cinematographer...You can do different timings and watch them, and you can flip through different versions of the timings to see which way you want to go."*

—ROGER DEAKINS, ASC[2], *True Grit*, *The Reader*, and *O Brother, Where Art Thou?* (first feature to use DI process) from *Cinematography for Directors* by Jacqueline B. Frost[3]

In DI work, editing stands for image manipulation and the final finishing processes; the locked cut is not re-edited. Editing is the creative phase of the DI process where the DP (or director or producer) sits with the colorist to grade the picture and achieve the precise look they desire. The WYSIWYG[4] principle applies as with each evolving version the DP views their vision anew, exactly how the audience will see it. The colorist may create a LUT (look-up table) with different color grades for each deliverable, e.g., HD video, SD video, disk, film, airline version, etc.

---

2. American Society of Cinematographers.

3. For a great discussion on how DPs feel about the DI (pro and con) and how it's influencing the way they shoot, read Frost's book.

4. What you see is what you get.

This phase can also include titling, resizing frames, compositing VFX, and finalizing opticals as well as panning and scanning the images. Once the DP, director, or producer approves all the edits, the DI is complete.

## 3) *Master*

*"Digital mastering, postproduction and distribution is driving the approach to film production through rapid and exciting changes. Technological breakthroughs are enhancing the creative possibilities of this move towards, what is commonly becoming known as Digital Intermediate."*

—From website of Cintel, manufacturer of film scanners and telecine machines

The completed DI is transferred to make the digital masters (.DPX or .CIN files) for all the different deliverables and then archived. There are four types of masters: film, tape, disk, and file.

### FILM MASTER

The film master becomes a digital AP for digital projection. For film print projection, a film recorder makes an internegative. The DI process eliminates the optical print and interpositive steps of the traditional photochemical lab finish and can produce 35mm, 70mm, and IMAX prints. The printmaster is added to both APs and the Dolby, DTS, and SDDS audio encoded. The digital AP is turned into a DCP (digital cinema package consisting of encrypted files) for projecting and sent to theaters via hard drive, satellite, or the net. From the internegative, release prints are struck, distributed, and projected as usual.

### TAPE MASTER

The DI is transferred to a high quality, uncompressed digital tape such as D5 and the audio mix is laid back to it. There are masters for different formats, e.g., music videos, commercials, broadcast, etc.

### DISK AND FILE MASTER

A master file is created for making disks (one for DVD and one for Blu-ray) and the mix is added to it. Other master files are created for digital broadcast, trailers, and promo material including high- and low-resolution requirements such as print media and Web content.

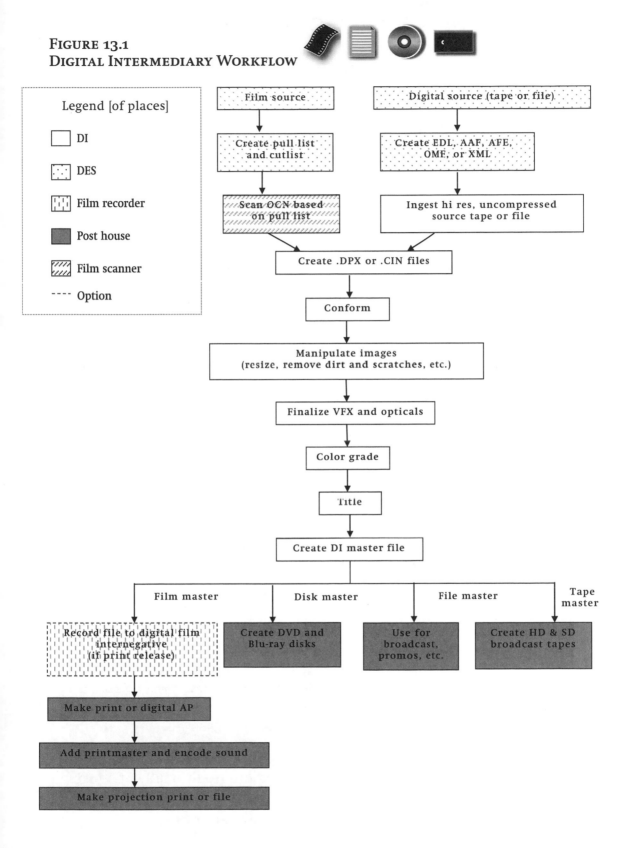

FIGURE 13.1
DIGITAL INTERMEDIARY WORKFLOW

# Digital Cinema, a.k.a. D-Cinema

*"We believe that digital cinema is not a product but a process. We are developing a system that begins with the conversion of film images to high quality digital files that are color graded by the cinematographer. Once the look is locked, we ensure that it is faithfully presented to audiences."*

—ROBERT J. MAYSON, former General Manager and VP of Digital Motion Imaging Digital Systems, Eastman Kodak Company

Currently there are over 16,000 theaters equipped with digital projectors in the United States, 60.5% of which are 3-D. Most of these project 2K files, but 4Ks are on the way with Sony's $315 million deal with AMC to replace all of its movie projectors with 4K projectors by the end of 2012. While North America boasts the most digital screens, with 46.2% worldwide, they are proliferating globally; in 2009 they multiplied 121.8%. So the digital wave shows no signs of cresting and print projection appears likely to be swept away. However... there are few obstacles that are slowing its takeover.

**13.j** Digital projector. The show runs from the DLP (digital light processing) box in the front, illuminated by the xenon lamp in the Christie projector in the back. *Photo courtesy of Texas Instruments Inc.*

Money and technology sum up the hurdles. Film projectors cost $50K and last 30–40 years. For $150,000, screen theater owners can convert to a digital technology they fear will be obsolescent in 5–10 years. On the plus side, digital "prints" don't deteriorate like film prints, cost considerably less, and the piracy worry is lower due to file encryption and the ability for simultaneous universal releases.

## DI process and the future

*"To see its full potential, the Digital Intermediate process will require combining the skill sets of film, video, and information technology professionals."*

—FREDDY GOESKE, VP and Director of Technology for MESoft Partners

Goeske's prediction from 2003 is coming true daily as the DI process makes inroads into all forms of postproduction. Additionally, it's fusing the stages of filmmaking with the embedding of DPs in the postproduction process. The DI allows cinematographers to see their images

— colors, lighting, transitions — and have the colorist swiftly make changes, which is a time-consuming, trial and error, cost-prohibitive process at the film lab. Also, the IT contribution is in play as DPs, directors, and others can screen DI color grading remotely when they're off scouting or shooting their next project. Last, the DI process promises to make it possible for smaller films, which couldn't afford a print release, to have a theatrical run.

The downside of the DI process continues to be cost. This affects archiving, as the cost of storing 4K prints is 1100% higher than that of storing film masters[5]. The upside is that what is true for the digital and computer technology in general is also true for the DI process: As it continues to be developed, the DI process will become faster and cheaper; it has already cornered the feature film market with over 90% of films abandoning the traditional lab route for the DI route. TV shows are jumping on the bandwagon, using tapeless workflows and DIs and other, less well-endowed shows will undoubtedly follow.

## Film and the future

*"Film is still the best possible image data capture medium and the most durable of formats. It will be here for many years to come and will complement alternative image capture technologies and outlive other storage format."*
—From website of Cintel, manufacturer of film scanners and telecine machines

It seems fitting to end this last chapter of the book talking about film since that's where the craft of editing and filmmaking began. Even though the majority of projects are shot on tape, file, or disk and posted digitally these days, film is not dead. In fact, it has a strong pulse for two reasons: 1) Many filmmakers still contend that it possesses the best image quality. 2) Despite all the digital formats and devices, film remains the global format that allows filmmakers from all countries to share their wares and visions.

And speaking of digital technology, forward-thinking production people in post are asking, "What's next?" With Blu-rays overtaking DVDs, three flavors of 24p, 48p on the rise, and loads of different cameras and codecs — the list could go on — they wonder, "What technology will be around long enough for archiving?" Tapeless technology is making giant strides, but so far there are no standards for displaying file-based deliverables and no time-tested archive methods for tapeless or tape footage.

---

5. According to a 2007 study by AMPAS (Academy of Motion Picture Arts and Sciences).

The answers are unknown.

So filmmakers continue to shoot, exhibit, and archive their projects on film and digital media. The posse of formats is still riding off toward the sunset with the landscape of the new day unknown.

## CHAPTER WRAP-UP

Congratulations! Your show is on air, up on the Web, headed toward home entertainment centers, or running in theaters. Now you can watch your credit, er, the show, with a real audience. Or fly to Tahiti with your hard-earned dough. Or take that next job on a better picture with better pay and more creative opportunities!

Following this final chapter is Appendix I with a budget form for this last finishing stage of postproduction. After it is a section on how to find a job in editing and a list of resources you can tap into to learn more and keep your editing knowledge up to date.

# Final Wrap-Up

*"People want everything to get better and not change…and that's of course not possible."*
—Philip Hodgetts, technical guru, software developer, and editor, *The Terence and Philip Show*, March 5, 2011 podcast

So what will the future bring? Change, change, and more change. With more software, workflows, formats, and remote work than ever, the landscape continues to transform in many directions and even dimensions thanks to the re-emergence of 3-D. What's standing fast are the pillars of good editing: engaging storytelling — whether by modern or traditional editing — and clear, emotive communication through image, sound, and music.

And so our trek through thirteen chapters reaches fade-out. I hope this book helps you on your journey through the uncharted terrain of tomorrow. I wish you many splendid editing adventures and collaborations. And may the show you edit always surpass your dailies.

Feel free to keep me posted at www.joyoffilmediting.com.

# Appendix I

## Stage III: Budget for Finishing

Now that you have a handle on the mastering and finishing processes, you can budget for this stage of postproduction. Remember, you can photocopy this form or download it from the Free tab of www.joyoffilmediting.com.

| | BUDGET FOR FINISHING | | | | | |
|---|---|---|---|---|---|---|
| Acct # | Description | Amount | Units | x | Rate | Total |
| 6000 | MAIN TITLES & END CREDITS | | | | | |
| 6001 | Main titles | | allow | | | |
| 6002 | Title artwork | | allow | | | |
| 6003 | Subtitles | | allow | | | |
| 6004 | Other titles & graphics | | allow | | | |
| 6005 | End credits | | allow | | | |
| 6006 | Lab costs | | allow | | | |
| | | | TOTAL FOR CATEGORY | | | |
| 6200 | ONLINE | | | | | |
| 6201 | Session (editor & equip) | | allow | | | |
| 6202 | Media prep | | hour | | | |
| 6203 | Tape stock | | tape | | | |
| 6204 | Dubs | | hour | | | |
| 6205 | CG prep | | hour | | | |
| 6206 | Titling session | | hour | | | |
| 6207 | Color grading | | allow | | | |
| 6208 | Formatted air master | | hour | | | |
| 6209 | Protection master | | hour | | | |
| | | | TOTAL FOR CATEGORY | | | |
| 6400 | DI PROCESS | | | | | |
| 6401 | DI 2K scan | | allow | | | |
| 6402 | DI 4K scan | | allow | | | |
| 6403 | Negative pull selects | | reel | | | |
| 6404 | Printmaster + M&E | | hour | | | |
| 6405 | Dolby digi printmaster | | allow | | | |
| | | | TOTAL FOR CATEGORY | | | |
| 6500 | SOUND FINISH – TAPE/FILE | | | | | |
| 6501 | Laydown | | hour | | | |
| 6502 | Sweetening | | hour | | | |
| 6503 | Layback | | hour | | | |
| 6504 | Dubs | | hour | | | |
| 6505 | Vault charges | | day | | | |
| | | | TOTAL FOR CATEGORY | | | |

| ACCT # | DESCRIPTION | AMOUNT | UNITS | X | RATE | TOTAL |
|--------|-------------|--------|-------|---|------|-------|
| | BUDGET FOR FINISHING | | | | | |
| 6700 | **NEGATIVE CUTTING** | | | | | |
| 6701 | Negative cutter | | allow | | | |
| 6702 | A Roll | | rolls | | | |
| 6703 | B Roll | | rolls | | | |
| 6704 | Final opticals | | allow | | | |
| | | | TOTAL FOR CATEGORY | | | |
| 6800 | **FILM FINISH** | | | | | |
| 6801 | Answer print | | feet | | | |
| 6802 | A Roll | | feet | | | |
| 6803 | B Roll | | feet | | | |
| 6804 | IP | | feet | | | |
| 6805 | IN | | feet | | | |
| 6806 | Check print | | feet | | | |
| 6807 | Release prints | | feet | | | |
| 6808 | Low contrast print (lo-con) | | feet | | | |
| 6809 | Develop & print optical neg | | feet | | | |
| 6810 | Academy leader | | allow | | | |
| 6811 | Misc. lab charges | | allow | | | |
| | | | TOTAL FOR CATEGORY | | | |
| 6900 | **SOUND FINISH — FILM** | | | | | |
| 6901 | Sound optical negative | | allow | | | |
| 6902 | Optical track transfer | | allow | | | |
| 6903 | Dolby sound license | | allow | | | |
| | | | TOTAL FOR CATEGORY | | | |
| | | | GRAND TOTAL | | | |

# Finding an Editing Job

*"Be pleasantly persistent."*
— KATHLEEN Korth, *Fly Girls, Africa's Elephant Kingdom, Eye on the Sparrow*

You can and will find a job. As long as you put your heart and soul, fingertips and shoe leather into it, it will happen. You may find it on the Internet or it may come from the freebie you did months ago or that last phone call that you forced yourself to make. However it transpires, through your initiative, follow-up, and hard work, one day you will find yourself at the right place at the right time.

## Presenting Yourself

Be clear about what job you're pursuing and what you can do. Keep a file or notebook with your stated goal, the contact info of people and companies to call on, and a record of when you emailed, telephoned, and visited them. Get in touch with everyone you know, contact everyone they know, follow every lead, climb every stairway. Every time you call someone and they don't have anything, inquire when you can phone them again. Mark down the date and dial! Persistence pays!

### Follow every path you know and then some

*"Get around. Get on the radar of people who make the shows you like. It doesn't matter if you're technically good: Show them you're in their world."*
—STEVE RASCH, A.C.E., *Important Things with Demetri Martin, Curb Your Enthusiasm, Spin City*

Knock on doors, make cold calls — get out there! Put yourself in the employer's position: What are they looking for? Roam studios, cutting rooms, post houses. Roam with respect and friendliness, don't stalk! Use the excuse that you're dropping off your résumé. Then say, "Oh, if Chris (the person you spoke to on the phone and the one who could hire you) happens to be free, I'd love to say 'hi' and put a name and résumé with a face."

Drop off your résumé instead of emailing, mailing, or faxing it. This way you can check out the place. You never know who you may run into — a helpful stranger or an old friend who's aware of a job. Yours truly got her first Hollywood job as a result of roaming the Twentieth Century Fox lot and approaching someone she'd never met, heard of, or been referred to.

### USERS GROUPS

Many editing systems have users groups that meet monthly. FCP has quarterly Supermeets around the country; Adobe and Avid host big road shows to introduce new products and software versions. These are great places to meet people, learn, and maybe win a raffle! Be prepared with your business card, what you plan to tell and ask people, and network away — everyone else is! No matter how depressed or pessimistic you feel, put yourself out there. You'll be surprised at what you'll learn and whom you'll connect with.

### WEBSITES AND SOCIAL NETWORK SITES

Frequent the net for jobs: CraigsList.org, www.Mandy.com, www.Media-Watch.com and other sites list film jobs. Use Facebook and Twitter to get connected and put the word out. If you've made or participated in a professional video that's on the net, let people know. Create a website for your projects if that will help you and your work stand out.

### CLASSES

Learn the latest version of a system's software, brush up on software you haven't worked on for awhile, or train on a new tool. You will need to do this whether or not you're employed, so take advantage of your downtime. Go out to lunch with your training mates and keep up with them. You never know when someone will respond with a gig for you.

### GUIDES, MAGAZINES, AND DIRECTORIES

There are plenty, available from bookstores and newsstands, in big film towns like Chicago, LA, and NYC which list production companies, post companies, ancillary companies, and shows starting production.

## INFORMATIONAL INTERVIEWS, MENTORS, AND PROFESSIONAL SOCIETIES

To find out more about the type of job you're interested in and how to get it, take someone to lunch or out for coffee who's doing it or done it. Be clear that you're not going to hit them up for a job but simply interview them about their professional life. Before you meet the person (and this goes for any company you're interested in too), find out as much as you can about them via Google and IMDb. It's always a good ice breaker if you loved a project they worked on.

During the interview, ask all your questions: How they got to where they are, what they like and dislike about it, how a person should go about getting a job, etc. Occasionally these interviews lead to a mentor relationship or work. Hooray for you if this happens. But don't expect it: Keep the meeting strictly informational as agreed and leave it to the person you're interviewing to suggest any further steps.

Two more tips: Show up on time and properly dressed for all meet-ups and be interested and upbeat. Continue to seek out people once you get a job. Going out for lunch and coffee is a way to have friends in the biz, make contacts, and set the stage for future work.

Lastly, if there's a program in your area, you may find a mentor who can give you advice. Or there may be a group you can attend or join to get help, e.g., Women in Film offers internships, mentors, and other assistance to its members.

### BULLETIN BOARDS

Every college film department — named something different at every school — will have a board with jobs listed. It doesn't always matter if you're a student at that school or anywhere else. The job may be menial and unpaid but it can lead to experience, knowledge, and future contacts.

## Résumé

Your résumé should feature:

- Projects you've worked on and the positions you've held on them.
- Producers, directors, and editors you've worked for.
- Picture and sound systems you know: FCP, Pro Tools, film, etc.
- Editing-related and Web software: VFX (Boris AE, Maya, etc.), GFX and photo programs (Adobe Photoshop, Dreamweaver), color grading, music composing, DVD authoring, etc.
- Technical and IT skills: SANs (Unity, Cloud, etc.)

- Awards you or a project you've worked on have won or been nominated for.
- Unless you've just graduated and you're a film major, listing your college isn't necessary.

Carry your résumé on your Smartphone so you can blast it immediately. Sometimes the first person to get there gets the job! Be on the alert and act when messages come in.

## It's not what you know, it's who you know

This industry adage is as loathsome as it is ungrammatical. I think both are true: It can be *what* you know and/or *whom* you know. Plus know-how. You can be hired off a résumé by strangers who like your work (it's happened to me) or lose work because they've taken on an unskilled nephew (it's also happened to me).

Director/editor Victoria Rose Sampson puts it directly: "You can have a great résumé but if no one knows you, no one hires you." At first you probably won't know anyone, but the more you work, the more people will want to work with you. Soon you will get jobs from knowing people. Always continue to make new contacts as the old ones frequently change or fade away. If you happen to be a niece or a nephew, a girlfriend or a boyfriend, feel lucky! Everyone has to get in somehow. Just make sure you want the job and are qualified for it. Few people begrudge anyone who does their job and works well with others.

## People to call

*"It's all about meeting people, connections, relationships. You want to work with people and they want to work with you."*

—Adam Coleite, *Legend Quest* (producer), *Fact or Fake*; *Paranormal Files*, *Bleeding Ohio*

These are people who will know about jobs, leads, places to look, or be able to hire you. Keep after them! Here's a list ordered by the most helpful:

- Picture and sound editors, assistant editors, and apprentice editors
- User group contacts
- Heads of postproduction at studios
- Instructors and managers on digital systems or at colleges
- Directors, associate producers, line managers, postproduction supervisors
- Post house personnel

Maintain a mental Rolodex of people so when you run into them again you can speak enthusiastically and intelligently.

# First Job

*"Don't give up. Be open minded. Realize that it's harder to find work than to do the work."*
—BARRY COHEN, online editor, *JAG*, *SpongeBob SquarePants*, *Hey Arnold!*

You're afraid you'll never get started but there are actually some advantages to your position. You are no threat to anyone — you don't know enough to be competition. This means that people will try to help you. People feel good helping someone get a job. And someday you'll pay it forward yourself.

The flip side is that you can be taken advantage of. Many of us have had that job from Hades, mostly because in our eagerness and need to succeed we let someone push us around. I hope this doesn't happen to you. If you do find yourself in a bad situation, evaluate if it's worth staying. If it isn't, get out as gracefully as possible. Chances are the person or place already has a bad rep and leaving won't hurt you. If you do decide to stay, focus on something positive: the credit on your résumé, future contacts, skills learned, getting in the union, or the paycheck.

## Places to contact

*"Show business is… worse than dog-eat-dog. It's dog-doesn't-return-other-dog's-phone-calls…"*
—WOODY ALLEN (as Cliff Stern) from his movie *Crimes and Misdemeanors*

These are places you should be tracking down in alphabetical order:
- Corporations with in-house production and postproduction departments
- Government film agencies
- Networks
- Post houses
- Production companies (independent, large, and small)
- Special effects and title houses
- Studios

## Type of jobs to start with

If you get a job as an apprentice or assistant editor, volunteer to cut anything: scenes, promo, gag reel, teaser, bumper, the director's wedding video, etc. It will not only give you knowledge and confidence but it may be worthy of putting on your reel and résumé as examples of things you've edited. (If your work is not used in the show, do not pretend it was.)

Since digital systems allow infinite versions, experiment and practice cutting as much as you can. Show your work to other assistants, to the editor, to anyone who will give you good feedback. And who knows, you may get to cut part of the show or a director or producer will take a shine to you and hire you for another project. I've seen it happen. At the very least, you'll improve your editing skills and system knowledge.

## Type of project to start on

*"I took every single job I could find. I probably edited 50–60 reels of film hairstylists. I would do anything."*
—Dean Gonzalez, editor, *Green Day: Heart Like a Hand Grenade*, and others

Anything. Just get hired. There are so many types of editing projects: animation, awards shows, commercials, corporate films, documentaries, educational films, features, government films, infomercials, IMAX movies, music concert shows, music videos, promos, PSAs, trailers, and training films. Not to mention television and its many types of programming: cartoons, game shows, MOWs, news, reality shows, series, sitcoms, soaps, and talk shows. Working at a post house, audio or VFX facility or other company that serves postproduction is also a good way to get experience.

Whatever you get hired on, remember: It's editing, it's experience, and it will help you wherever you end up. You never know when having worked on a music video, commercial, or documentary may win you the job on a new drama because the director wants a commercial, documentary, or music video feel. Conversely, your dramatic experience may get you that docu-drama job because the producers want someone with drama experience. Job by job you will build experience and a life in editing.

Most editing jobs are freelance, but there are many staff jobs also. Both can be union or non-union, corporate, documentary, or entertainment. The following table weighs the upside and downside of each.

# Freelance vs. Staff Editing Work

| TYPE OF EDITOR | ADVANTAGES | REALITY |
|---|---|---|
| FREELANCE | • You go from project to project.<br>• You can work in different states and countries.<br>• You choose your projects.<br>• You can take time off when you want.<br>• You usually can command a higher rate than a staffer. | • You never know when you're going to get work and may find it hard to take a vacation.<br>• There are periods with a lot of work and periods with none during which you can collect unemployment.<br>• You are responsible for keeping your skills up, usually.<br>• You go to conventions and join organizations on your own dime. |
| STAFF | • Security: known hours, pay rate, medical benefits, co-workers, and projects.<br>• Your employer pays for training on new equipment and you may have input about it.<br>• Your company may also pay for professional memberships and send you to conventions. | • You can feel stuck in a rut, continually working on the same kind of project.<br>• The pay is steady but can be less than that of a freelancer. |

# Union vs. Non-union

## Non-union jobs

There are union and non-union jobs. In many places, Hollywood included, it's fine to work non-union even when you're in the union. There simply aren't enough union jobs and most people work both. Chances are your first job will be non-union.

## Union jobs

### FEATURES AND TV

Most feature movies and TV shows edited in Hollywood and New York City are union shows. This means you must be a member of the Editor's Guild, Local 700 of the IA[1] to work on them. Local 700 covers New York, Hollywood, and northern California. The union, as its business agents always say, is not a hiring hall so do not expect to get a job through it; few do. The union does protect you as a union employee and signs up new production companies each month.

### NETWORK SHOWS

News, sports, talk shows, game shows, and their promos are produced by the networks and covered by two unions, NABET (National Association of Broadcast Engineers and Technicians), and IBEW (International Brotherhood of Electrical Workers). NABET extends throughout the

---

1. IA is short for IATSE which stands for International Alliance of Theatrical and Stage Employees.

country but many small TV stations are non-union. NABET is not a hiring hall either.

### SHOULD YOU JOIN THE UNION?

This is your decision. If the type of projects you work on are always non-union, you do not have to spend your time, energy, and money getting in. If however, you wish to work on union projects, you will need to get in. Simply put, joining the union increases your job opportunities if you're in an area where there's both union and non-union work.

### GETTING IN THE UNION

Getting in the union is often the old Catch-22: companies won't hire you unless you're in it but you can't get in it unless you're hired. The best strategy? Keep your eye on the goal and keep working. Call the union and find out what the requirements for membership are. Sooner or later a door will present itself — and it may be a back door since the unions have more people than they need. There is no *one* way people get into a union but here are a few:

- Accumulated time on-the-job work experience. This is the most common method.
- The show you're on goes union. This happens when the production company decides to do the right thing or is forced to.
- Special skills: You can work a piece of equipment required for the job that no one on the union availability list can work.
- Contacts and nepotism.

## Last Word

No matter how brilliant, persistent, and likeable you are, your editing career will have twists and turns, slumps and zeniths. Yes, editing, like any career in film, is a roller coaster. One minute you're depressed, hitting the tube and the Haagen Daz (pick your poison), the next minute the phone rings and you're socked in across town for months. Many have given up editing due to the Olympian hours or lack of them and the sometimes less-than-fair treatment. Editing is not for the wimp, space case, or the indifferent. You need stamina and desire to see you through. Keep your passion for your career, loved ones, and pursuit of happiness in balance when following an editing path and you'll be surprised where it leads you.

# Resources

*Gear, Jobs, Software Tips, Training, and More*

Here are some useful select sites, books, and institutions. The list is endless and increases daily but these should get you started. Please refer to the Bibliography for more books, articles, and websites.

## ACADEMIES AND INSTITUTES

Academy of Motion Picture Arts and Sciences, *www.oscars.org*

Academy of Television Arts and Sciences, *www.emmys.com*
> Helms student award, grants, and an internship program and provides member screenings, forums, and topical events throughout the year. Publishes *Emmy Magazine* which has articles on all types of filmmakers in Hollywood as well as on ATAS business and is available free at the website.

AFI (American Film Institute)
> 2021 Western Avenue, Hollywood, CA 90027
> 323/856-7600 www.afionline.org/home.html
> A great place to get cutting room knowledge, a credit, and contacts no matter how much or little experience you have: Most Hollywood professionals have done at least one AFI project. AFI offers a graduate program in editing and holds screenings, classes, and events year round.

## DIGITAL EDITING

www.2-pop.com
> Concentrates on DV editing and offers editors' forums where you can ask all your questions on a multitude of subjects including Avid, Final Cut Pro, and special effects. A commercial site by Creative Planet Communities, a division of United Entertainment Media, which offers same for videographers, cinematographers, etc.

www.adobe.com Home of Adobe and its many digital, Web, print, etc. products.

www.apple.com/finalcutstudio/finalcutpro/ Apple's Final Cut Pro website.

www.avid.com Avid website.

> Tips, tutorials — all things Avid.

www.creativecow.net

> Serving "creative communities of the world," this site has tons of tutorials on making VFX, forums for getting your questions answered, a magazine, calendar of events, and much more. Milk it!

www.digitalcinemasociety.org

> A nonprofit corp headed by a cinematographer with editors and members from all motion picture fields dedicated to "educating and informing the entertainment industry about digital motion picture production, post, delivery, and exhibition."

www.friendsofed.com

> Apress Publishers sponsors this site which contains links to film books, tweets, and other Web resources for professional designers, DV creators and innovators. Every Thursday a selected eBook is available for $10.

www.hershleder.com/avid_information#tips_tutorials

> Find Avid tips and tutorials, and more on this fun site by an experienced editor/producer working in the trenches.

www.lafcpug.org/ Long-running international Final Cut Pro users group.

> Get all your FCP queries answered here.

http://www.larryjordan.biz/

> Based in LA but tapped into Apple, Larry is an FCP guru whose site offers tutorials, training, and articles on FCP and related editing issues, e.g., storage, etc. Sign up for his free newsletter and check back regularly as he's in the forefront of the FCP brigade and announces the good, the bad, and the ugly.

www.lightworksbeta.com/ Lightworks website.

www.media100.com Media 100 website.

www.philiphodgetts.com/

> Editor/programmer/consultant/author Phil is an FCP guru who writes regularly about HD, new media, and all sorts of topical, technical issues and is half of a regular podcast, "The Terence and Philip Show."

http://www.productionhub.com/, Jobs, gear, contest, products, services, and more.

Staten, Greg and Steve Bayes. *The Avid Handbook: Advanced Techniques, Strategies, and Survival Information for Avid Editing Systems, 5th Edition.* Boston, MA: Focal Press 2008.

http://splicehere.wordpress.com/technical-tips-list/
> Avid guru Steve Cohen provides a wealth of tips and info about Avid and savvy comments on Final Cut Pro as well.

www.zerocut.com
> Click on Tech Tips for links to helpful info on film and video from a knowledgeable editor.

## EDITORS ON EDITING

www.artoftheguillotine.com
> Topical site based in Toronto that offers a forum, info, and which aims to establish an online film community for film editors.

www.joyoffilmediting.com
> Author's site where you can buy her books and everything else is free: Award-winning blog, downloads of editing forms, syllabi, and chapters on film editing. Cut-of-the-Month feature shows different types of cuts from docs, films, and TV shows.

LoBrutto, Vincent. *Selected Takes: Film Editors on Editing,* Praeger Paperback, 2001.

*Transitions: Voices on the Craft of Digital Editing,* Division Press, 2003.
> Astute advice authored by 15 current Hollywood editors about the art of editing. Starts with the first cut and covers a multitude of topics including the changing face of editing today, cutting animation, and cutting for television.

Oldham, Gabriella. *First Cut, Conversations with Film Editors*, Berkeley, CA: University of California Press, 1992.

Winters, Ralph. *Some Cutting Remarks,* Scarecrow Press, 2001.

## GETTING A JOB

www.film-connection.com
> International career service that offers courses and helps place aspiring filmmakers. Lots of links to other film sites.

www.mandy.com/
> Find editing jobs worldwide as well as film sales, equipment and vendors.

www.mediajobmarket.com/jobs/index.jsp
> *Hollywood Reporter* magazine's site for job postings. Check the mag, too.

*Pacific Coast Studio Directory*
> A-Z monthly listings for all film services inside Hollywood and around the U.S. A veteran booklet and a poster (hung in many a post house) that has survived the digital age. Now available online at http://visualnet.com/

www.varietymediacareers.com/home/index.cfm?site_id=7307
> *Daily Variety* magazine's site for job postings. Check the mag too.

www.workplacehollywood.org/index.php/200803162/About-Workplace-Hollywood/About-Workplace-Hollywood.html

> …"a nonprofit organization dedicated to training and placing a qualified and diverse workforce in the Entertainment Industry." Not up and running yet but we can all hope…

## GETTING YOUR MOVIE MADE

http://www.dvcreators.net/

> Site advertises itself as a "LinkedIn or Facebook for digital video creators" and seeks to help filmmakers create and connect.

www.fromtheheartproductions.com

> Film grants, workshops, and consultations offered by Carole Dean, a successful filmmaker who thrives on helping low budget and independent filmmakers realize their movies.

*Shaking the Money Tree: How to Get Grants and Donations for Film and Video: 2nd Edition* by Morrie Warshawski.

> A no-fail approach written by a consummate fund-raiser.

## GUILDS, ORGANIZATIONS, AND UNIONS

A.C.E. American Cinema Editors

> An honorary society that also runs a student internship program and has an education wing. www.ace-filmeditors.org

Cinewomen

> A nuts-and-bolts organization located in LA and NY dedicated to helping its members progress in their profession.

IDA — International Documentary Association

> This nonprofit organization supports the doc maker with seminars and a newsletter on funding, filmmaking processes, and holds screenings, an awards ceremony, and events honoring docs and their makers. Membership is open to all and has a sliding scale. www.documentary.org

IFP. Independent Feature Production

> A national organization currently in six cities that supports indies with seminars, knowledge, newsletter, and a place to network. It holds the annual Spirit Awards in LA to honor independent work. These awards have gained in prestige over the years. www.ifp.org

Motion Picture and Videotape Editors Guild

> IATSE Local 700 for the U.S. www.editorsguild.com Site has news, articles, and interviews with top guild editors.

NABET — National Association of Broadcast Employees and Technicians

> Locals in all major cities. 1-800-882-9174, www.nabet.com

WIF — Women in Film.
> A worldwide, nonprofit organization of professional filmmakers which runs a mentoring program, funds scholarships and productions, holds seminars and award shows to recognize women's accomplishments. www.wif.org

## HISTORY AND THEORY

*The Cutting Edge: The Story of Cinema Editing.*
> A 2004 documentary produced by A.C.E. and UCLA. Definitive movie on how films are edited and how editing and the role of the editor has evolved since the beginning of film, told by Academy Award-winning editors and directors Spielberg, Lucas, Scorsese, Tarantino, and other Hollywood luminaries.

O'Steen, Bobbie. *The Invisible Cut: How Editors Make Movie Magic.* Studio City, CA: Michael Wiese Productions 2009.

Mast, Gerald. *A Short History of the Movies, Tenth Edition*, Essex: UK, Pearson Longman, 2007.

Pearlman, Karen. *Cutting Rhythms: Shaping the Film Edit,* Boston, MA: Focal Press 2009.
> Dr. Pearlman turned her dissertation into a book which provides a thoughtful analysis of editing and what goes on inside editors' heads as they cut.

## INTERNET WEBSITES FOR MOVIES

www.imdb.com/ Internet Movie Database.
> Commercial site that catalogs movies and filmmakers and contains a movie glossary. Use it to look up potential employers for their film bio (not always up to date).

## MUSIC EDITING

www.filmmusicmag.com/
> Self-billed as the "professional voice of music in film and television," this site is chock full of articles on the current issues, players, and events in the world of film music.

www.filmmusic.net/
> Looking for film music work? Go here.

## ONLINE DICTIONARIES AND GLOSSARIES

www.alphadictionary.com/directory/Specialty_Dictionaries/Film/
> Compendium of cinema dictionaries.

www.dvdrhelp.com/glossary
> Excellent dissection of digital video terms.

www.grassvalleygroup.com/docs/Miscellaneous/Dictionary/
DictionaryB2_A.html GVG's glossary of video, digital, effect, and engineering terms

www.jamesarnett.com/sections.html
> Guidebook for guerilla filmmakers. On the set and need to know something quick? Look it up here. For instance, select "Crossing the Line" and you can click on eight different pairs of angles to get a quick, animated illustration of which angles cross the line and which don't.

http://motion.kodak.com/US/en/motion/Education/index.htm
> Link to Kodak's online glossary and education content.

www.tech-notes.tv/Glossary/Title%20&%20Index.htm/
> Glossary of broadcast terms.

## PRACTICE OF EDITING

Chandler, Gael. *Film Editing: Great Cuts Every Filmmaker and Movie Lover Must Know.* Studio City, CA: Michael Wiese Productions, 2009.

http://www.editorslounge.com/
> A roving series of panels on current events in the editing world that take place periodically in the Hollywood area and annually before and during NAB, hosted by Terence Curren and his team at AlphaDogs Post in Burbank, CA.

www.moviemaker.com/
> Contemporary e-zine and print-zine on the art of movie making focused on direction, acting, producing, distributing, writing, editing, and shooting.

www.studentfilmmakers.com/
> Just what the name suggests: Offers forums and resources for students and subscriptions to their magazine.

## SOUND EDITING

www.filmsound.org
> Top-notch site about how to design, edit, and mix sound by the lions of the industry. Includes topical articles on sound clichés, history, and just plain sound advice. Includes links to books on the subject and an extensive list of sound libraries for downloading and obtaining on CD and offers free SFX.

http://filmsound.studienet.org/
> Has current, authoritative articles about sound and the history of sound and includes a bibliography, glossary, and links to sound effects libraries.

LoBrutto, Vincent. *Sound-On-Film, Interviews with Creators of Film Sound.* Westport, CT: Greenwood Publishing Group, Incorporated, 1995.

www.marblehead.net/Foley/jack.html
> Learn about the art of Foley and its inventor.

Sound effects for free: www.stonewashed.net/sfx.html and www.part-nersinrhyme.com

Sound effects for fee: www.sounddogs.com

Helpful digital audio and a few video links from audio practitioners: www.soundwithmotion.com/links.htm

http://woodyssoundadvice.com/
> Worthwhile advice from Woody Woodhull, sound recorder/designer/mixer, president of Allied Post Audio in Santa Monica, CA.

## TRAINING ON PICTURE AND SOUND DIGITAL EDITING TOOLS

The Film Connection www.film-connection.com/
> Nationwide.

Future Media Concepts www.fmctraining.com/
> Boston, NYC, Philadelphia, and Washington, D.C. Authorized training on tons of products.

Maine Media Film workshops http://www.mainemedia.edu/workshops/

Moviola Digital www.moviola.com/ LA and NY.

Online college www.cybercollege.com
> Covers a range of subjects from the technical to the historical about film and television.

Video Symphony, Hollywood, CA www.videosymphony.com
> Full-scale, nationally accredited post production career school that attracts both beginners and professionals from around the world.

Weynand training http://weynand.com/
> Tips, blogs, info, and training on FCP. LA based but advertises trainings in Austin, Boise, and Raleigh.

# Glossary

**¼".** Magnetic tape, ¼" wide, used to record sound on stage or on location on a Nagra or other sound recorder until the digital age.

**¾".** Common term for ¾" wide U-matic videotape format.

**1:1.** See **dupe or work track**.

**1080i.** Common HD broadcast format defined by the 1080 interlaced scan lines visible to the viewer.

**180 degree rule.** See **crossing the line**.

**24 track.** See **multitrack**.

**24b.** 24 bits of audio. Bits — bit depth — measure the number of bits you have to capture audio.

**24p.** Progressive scan digital tape that runs at 24 fps.

**2K.** 2048 horizontal pixels: Quality and amount of data resulting from scanning film negative to a file. A 2K file is the minimum amount of data necessary for color correction, title, image manipulation and other finishing work. 4K uses 4096 horizontal pixels, 6K uses 8192, and so on. See also **digital intermediary**.

**2-pop.** See **head pop**.

**3 perf.** Three perforations per 35mm film frame as opposed to the normal 4 perfs. The image area is the same but 3 perf uses less film stock: 1000' plays in 14 minutes instead of 10. Since 3 perf cuts down on film stock and re-loads on the set and thereby saves money, it is frequently used for shooting TV in Hollywood. Post production software can handle 3 perf but three different pull-down sequences must be noted and checked.

**3-D effect.** Blending layers of shots together on an X, Y, Z axis into one shot so that it appears to have three dimensions: height, width, and depth.

**4:4:4.** The ratio of the luminance sampling frequency (4 or the first number) to the two different color sampling frequencies (4 in this case) employed during the capturing or rendering of media. Other ratios are: 4:2:2, 4:2:2:4, and 4:4:4:4; the latter two add a key channel. Ratios with 2s are compressed; without are uncompressed.

**480.** SD broadcast format defined by the 480 scan lines visible to the viewer.

**5.1.** Sound configured with five channels: left, right, and center in the front plus left and right surrounds. The "1" is for the LFE (low frequency effects) channel.

**7:1.** Same as 5:1 with the addition of left rear and right rear surrounds. See also **Dolby digital.**

**720p.** Common HD broadcast format defined by the 720 progressive scan lines visible to the viewer.

**A roll.** Assembling the film negative in one roll as is typically done with 35mm. Also called single strand.

**A side.** Outgoing shot or left side of the cut.

**A.C.E.** American Cinema Editors. An honorary society of editors who are voted into membership based on their professional achievements, dedication to the education of others, and commitment to the craft of editing. A.C.E. always follows their members' names on screen. A.C.E. hosts its own annual editing awards ceremony where winners receive the Eddie Award. In addition, A.C.E. runs an editing internship program.

**A/B reel.** Two videotapes that are used to create a transition effect such as a dissolve, fade, or wipe. State-of-the-art digital editing machines do not require A/B rolls as the effects can be done simultaneously in real time or by rendering.

**A/B roll.** Two synced rolls of negative that are checkerboarded to produce effects and the final release 16mm print.

**AAF.** Advanced authoring format. A file format used to exchange project data and metadata between picture, sound, and online editors.

**AC-3.** See **Dolby digital.**

**Academy leader.** Piece of film or tape or a digital clip attached to the head or tail of a show for the purpose of maintaining sync between picture and sound. See also **head leader, tail leader,** and **sync pop.**

**action match.** Matching the action (movement or motion) of characters or objects in one shot to the action in the next shot where the action continues or completes.

**address track.** LTC track on analog tape that's narrow and designed to hold time code. See also **LTC.**

**Adobe Premiere Pro.** Digital editing system manufactured by Adobe Systems.

**ADR.** Automated dialogue replacement. The process by which a line of dialogue is recorded and re-spoken by an actor in sync (hopefully) with the picture to replace the original sync production line. Also referred to as looping or EPS (electronic post sync).

**AES.** Audio Engineering Society. A U.S. organization which recommends standards and practices for technical audio issues.

**AFE.** Avid file exchange. An AAF that works with Avid systems exclusively and provides proprietary information for re-creating Avid sequences.

**AIFF or AIF.** Audio interchange file format. A PCM audio format created by Apple which allows files to be altered readily to meet projects' standards while maintaining fidelity. It can also be used as a storage format. See also **PCM**.

**air master.** Show tape that is broadcast.

**ALE.** Avid Log Exchange. What an Avid converts the telecine log file into. The ALE file becomes part of the film database that the cutlist program will access to make the film cutlist for the negative cutter.

**aliasing.** An artifact that occurs while reproducing digital video or audio.

**alpha channel.** Separate video channel consisting of the transparency data for displaying the three other color channels. Often used for titling or overlaying or combining other images. One of the four channels (or components) of information that is contained in each pixel of an image. This channel defines the transparency of each pixel, allowing portions of the foreground image to reveal or block the background image.

**ambience.** Wordless, background sound recorded on location. Often called *presence*.

**A-mode.** Method in which online assembly events are numbered in sequential order by Record IN time code.

**AMPAS.** Academy of Motion Picture Arts and Sciences. "The Academy" hands out the annual Oscar awards, holds screenings throughout the year to honor U.S. filmmakers, and generally promotes the recognition and preservation of motion pictures.

**amplitude.** Measured in decibels (dB), amplitude is the loudness (strength or amount) of a signal.

**analog.** An electrical signal that varies continuously as it records. Analog takes the original data and converts the video and audio information into a varying voltage or magnetic field.

**analog audio recorder.** Analog audio recording device such as reel-to-reel recorder and cassette deck.

**answer print, a.k.a. AP.** The first color timed trial print that is made from the cut negative and screened with the director, DP, and timer or colorist. Typically several APs are made for each reel until the director and/or DP are satisfied and give their approval.

**Arrilaser.** A type of laser film recorder. See also **laser film recorder.**

**artifacts.** Unwanted effects or distortions on a digital tape, file, or disk not found in the original (digital or analog) video or audio.

**ASCAP.** American Society of Composers, Authors, and Publishers. A prominent performing rights organization of which there are many. Composers and publishers affiliate with one of these organizations which collect and pay out royalties when music they represent is exhibited in a movie theater or aired on a television show.

**aspect ratio.** The width to height ratio of a frame of film or video linked to the size of the screen it will run on.

**ATSC.** Advanced Television Systems Committee. U.S. board that sets standards for digital TV broadcast.

**audio delay.** A split edit where video starts first and audio second. See also **split edit.**

**audio time code.** See **LTC**.

**authoring tools.** Tools for the non-programmer for creating interactive applications such as DVDs.

**authoring.** Creating a document for the Web or a DVD.

**auto assembly.** Online method by which a tape-based machine initiates and records each edit in the list automatically while the editor monitors the result. The opposite of manual assembly.

**Automatic Duck.** Software (and name of the company that produces it) that aids in translating sequences and files between systems, e.g., After Effects, Avid, FCP, and Pro Tools.

**AVCHD**. Advanced video coding high definition. File-based format for recording and playing back HD tapes and disks.

**AVI.** Audio video interleaved. Microsoft's multimedia file format similar to MPEG and Apple's QuickTime, which interleaves (stores in alternate segments) and compresses audio and video.

**Avid.** Professional digital editing system.

**B neg.** See **uncircled takes**.

**back porch.** The TV signal located between the back end of horizontal sync and the back end of corresponding blanking.

**balance.** During the mix, ensuring that all the elements — dialogue, SFX, and music — blend and can be heard.

**bandwidth.** The rate at which digital data passes through a cable, channel, disk, drive, or network, measured in bps (bits per second) or Mbps (Megabits per second).

**banner.** Useful, temporary graphic that functions as a placeholder (timed or untimed) until the final material can be dropped in, e.g., stock shot missing, scene missing, insert commercial here, etc.

**bars and tone.** Video and audio references for setting up consistent video and audio levels.

**base side.** Shiny side of picture or sound film that consists of a thin plastic backing.

**basey.** See **tubby.**

**beep.** See **sync pop**.

**bit.** Binary digit. (b) A bit defines two states or levels such as on or off, black or white, etc.

**bit depth.** Amount of color data in a digital image.

**black burst generator.** Electronic device that generates a reference signal — a black burst — which records as pure black on videotape and is used for timing by colorists, tape operators, and editors.

**black out.** When a shot cuts to black.

**blanking** (noun and verb). The short period between video fields when the picture is not being scanned and its information is blanked (blacked out). The creating of the blanking in the videotape by a sync generator.

**blue screen.** Same as green screen except that a blue screen is used. See green screen.

**BMI.** Broadcast Music Incorporated. A prominent performing rights organization of which there are many, including ASCAP. See also **ASCAP.**

**B-mode.** Method in which online assembly events are numbered in nonsequential order by Source reel and then Record IN time code.

**bps.** Bits per second. The rate of data transfer in a communication system. Used to measure bandwidth, modem speed, and other data rates in communication lines.

**B roll.** Modern term for second unit footage or background, filler footage. Term originated with 16mm where it denotes the negative camera rolls are edited and slugged on two different reels — A and B rolls — by the negative cutter for printing.

**B side.** Incoming shot or right side of the cut.

**bumper.** Five second re-cap of what just happened on a television show intended to hold the viewers' interest until after the commercial when the next segment airs.

**BWF.** Broadcast wave format. Latest standard PCM-type audio file format used in professional audio recording and broadcasting which contains time code for smooth syncing with filmed film or video images. See also **PCM.**

**byte (B).** A unit of data that equals 8 bits. The amount of memory space required to store one character, such as a letter or number, on a computer.

**C.A.S.** Cinema Audio Society. Honorary professional organization of mixers which hosts educational meetings throughout the year and an annual awards banquet. C.A.S. follows a member's credit on screen.

**canned music.** See **source music.**

**capture.** Input footage from a digital tape into a digital editing system.

**CCIR 601.** Analog SD video broadcast sampling standard that is now called ITU-R BT.601. See also **ITU-R BT.601.**

**CCD.** Charge-coupled device. An image sensor device used in a telecine film-scanning machine like the Spirit DataCine. The machine moves the film continuously over a line array of three CCDs to scan the image and produce a video signal. The CCD operates by splitting the film image into the three primary colors: red, green, and blue. Three CCDs are employed — one for each color — to convert the images into electrical impulses which are then turned into a video signal and recorded onto videotape or broadcast.

**CCM.** Color-corrected master. See also **CTM**.

**cel side.** See **base side**.

**cement splicer.** See **hot splicer**.

**CG.** See **character generator**.

**CGI.** Computer generated imagery. Digital effects created on computers, encompassing an ever-growing array of visual possibilities, both moving and static, animated and live action.

**change list.** List of changes to a reel made during a recut for conforming a film reel to the digital cut, a sound reel to a film reel, or updating the negative cutter.

**character generator.** The CG, a.k.a. the "black box," is a small computer designed to generate text for broadcast or for adding credits and titles to a master tape.

**check print.** Made from the dupe negative and similar to the AP, the check print is the final trial print which is run and checked thoroughly for any problems before release prints are struck.

**checkerboard.** Split dialogue tracks by alternating dialogue lines and sound fill. Also used to describe A/B rolling. See **A/B roll.**

**choker.** ECU of a person's face where the neck is not visible or barely visible.

**chroma.** See **chrominance**.

**chroma-key.** A type of composite effect with a chroma background layer and a foreground layer which contains the image or subject. The background layer is keyed out and the subject, such as a weather forecaster, appears to be interacting with a second video layer such as a weather map. While any color can be used for the background, blue and green have proven to be the most keyable so lately chroma-keying is referred to as blue screen or green screen.

**chrominance.** The part of the color video signal that holds the color data. Video picture information contains two components: luminance (brightness and contrast) and chrominance (hue and saturation).

**Chyron.** A brand name that has become synonymous with character generator. See also **character generator.**

**CIN.** File extension for a Kodak Cineon file which is used in DI work and akin to DPX. See also **DPX**.

**Cinema Tools.** FCP program for film projects that allows you to create a cutlist for a film finish.

**circled takes.** On a film show, takes the director called out to be printed by the lab.

**click track.** Based on frames and half-frames of 35mm, this is a track of beats and a tempo that is recorded onto a digital recorder, multitrack, MIDI sequencer, or other recorder. A click track is used to synchronize performers, e.g., dancers on the set during the shoot or musicians playing during the scoring session.

**clip.** Video: A shot ingested on a digital system. Audio: Distort or overmodulate an audio signal.

**close-up.** (CU) A shot framed close, usually on the face and neck of a person.

**Cloud.** Computing network system which allows editors to pull media from servers anywhere in the world, clone it, and start cutting, color grading, etc.

**C-mode.** Method in which online assembly events are numbered in nonsequential order by Source reel and then Source IN time code.

**CMX.** CBS, Memorex, eXperimental. A groundbreaking, tape-based linear online machine that was the standard from the 1970s to the 1990s. The brand also created some nonlinear offline and online systems.

**CMX EDL.** An EDL format. See also **EDL**.

**code** (verb). Video: Represent a video signal level as a number. Film: Add ink code.

**color balance.** Adjusting primary colors in a camera or other electronic device using white as a balance. In postproduction, the part of color grading in which the intensity of a color is desaturated (decreased) by adding white. For example, skin tones are routinely balanced (matched) in scenes. See also **saturation**.

**codec.** Compressor/decompressor or encode/decode. A two-step process used in video editing, video-conferencing, and streaming media applications which 1) compresses huge multimedia files into smaller files so they can fit on a DVD, CD-ROM, or other media and then 2) decompresses them to their original file size so they can be played back on a computer. Codecs can also encode and decode video signals.

**color burst.** Reference located near the end of horizontal blanking that tells the monitor what hue to make the color information found in the video signal

**color grading, a.k.a. color correcting.** Changing or improving the color of a film, file, or tape image to be consistent with the desired look of the scene or project.

**colorist.** Telecine operator who syncs, transfers, and color grades film, file, or tape images.

**component video.** A video signal that separates RGB and luminance signals in order to display picture information. Component video can be analog or digital; either way it delivers a picture superior to composite video.

**composite video** A video signal that combines RGB and luminance signals in order to display picture information. The signal contains horizontal, vertical, and color synchronizing data. Composite video is analog only and inferior to component video.

**composite.** Create a shot by merging two or more separate images or shots.

**conform.** Reproduce the locked cut on the original film negative or master show tape.

**consolidate.** Make new clips (data files and media) of the edits in a sequence on a digital editing system.

**continuity.** Maintaining the physical relationships, performance, action, and narrative flow of the filmed scene from cut to cut (or during filming, from shot to shot).

**continuity sheet.** List of a show's scenes in editing order accompanied by a phrase or sentence describing what happens in each scene and its duration.

**contractor.** Person who contracts musicians for a scoring session. The contractor makes sure that the musicians' hours are correctly accounted and paid for and is a resourceful liaison between the musicians' union and film companies.

**count down leader.** See **Academy leader.**

**coverage.** Angles shot in addition to the master shot: close-ups, medium shots, over-the-shoulder shots, etc.

**cross cutting.** Editing two (or more) dependent lines of action together — characters, settings, or subjects — that interact directly and are aware of each other.

**crossconversion.** Transfer from one format of HD to another, e.g., 720p to 1080i.

**crossing the line.** Ignoring the invisible line in every camera setup that bisects the scene horizontally at 180°. Crossing the line results in two angles that when cut together appear to make people or objects jump out of position.

**CRT film recorder.** See **EBR.**

**CRT.** Cathode Ray Tube. A special type of vacuum tube, the CRT does for the computer monitor display what the picture tube does for the television display: It renders the images by causing an electron beam to strike a phosphorescent surface.

**CRT.** Cathode Ray Tube. An electronic type of vacuum tube that creates the picture in a TV and helps create it in a computer monitor.

**CTM.** Color timed master. Master tape of color-corrected show created after online by the colorist.

**cut negative.** The original negative cut to match the locked film cut: From the cut negative, positive prints are made for movie theaters.

**cut point.** See **edit point**.

**cut.** (noun) 1) An edit 2) A series of edits 3) A completed edit or re —edit of a show. (verb) The joining together of two different shots or two parts of the same shot.

**cutaway.** (CA) Any shot that will be used to cut away from the main action in the master shot.

**cutting on action.** See action match.

**cutlist.** A list composed of the camera rolls, start and end key codes, and length of each cut in a film reel that is made by the digital editing system or the negative cutter. Often referred to as the assembly list, the cutlist is used by the negative cutter to assemble the shots that will be spliced together on the negative reel.

**DaVinci.** A popular color grading and telecine machine.

**DA-88.** Digital Audio 8mm. An 8-track deck used in picture and sound editing and on the mix stage to bring in audio from DA-88 cassettes.

**DA-98.** Latest version of DA-88. See **DA-88**.

**dailies.** Footage, normally shot the previous day, that arrives daily in the cutting room from the production crew.

**DAT.** Digital audio tape. DAT uses two channels to record sound on location or on the sound stage.

**DAW.** Digital audio workstation. Computer used to record, edit, and mix sound and music.

**DBS.** Direct broadcast satellite.

**DCP.** Digital cinema package. The deliverable for digital projection.

**de-Bayer.** Convert Bayer pattern color filter array footage, such as that produced by a RED camera, to a full RGB image. Process required in order to view or finish with full resolution color footage.

**Decibel (dB).** Logarithmic unit used to measure the intensity of a sound in relation to a reference level such as 0 dB.

**defrag.** See **fragmented**.

**degausser.** Tool that demagnetizes sound heads and erases audio from mag film or tape.

**de-interlace.** Turn two interlaced video fields into a single *frame*. Used when the video runs at a different frame rate than it was created in or to remove interlacing artifacts when making a still frame. See also **interlace**.

**delayed edit.** A video term for overlap. See also **split edit**.

**deliverable.** Materials contractually required by a distributor or network to exhibit a show such as a master tape, release print, sound elements, timing sheets, music cue sheets, and list of screen credits.

**demosaic.** See **de-Bayer**.

**DES.** Dolby-Encoded Stereo. A noise-reduction system that reproduces stereo optical tracks in movie theaters. See also **Dolby digital**.

**development.** Phase of a project where the director, producers, casting director, principal talent (actors) are hired and the script is set. Development follows greenlighting and precedes the preproduction phase.

**DF.** See **drop frame**.

**DI.** See **digital intermediate**.

**diegetic.** Description for sounds that sync to an onscreen source, e.g., a book being slammed shut.

**digital audio recorder.** Digital audio device used to record ADR, Foley, dialogue, music, the final mix, etc., that holds 8 to 48 tracks (depending on the machine). The machine records to a digital medium such as hard disk, DAT, DC, or DVD.

**digital cinema.** Developing technology that compresses and encrypts the film or digital tape master onto a medium (e.g., data file, DVD, 24p tape, optical disk, or portable hard drive) for exhibiting in a theater via satellite and/or a digital projector.

**digital editing system.** A computer used to edit digital audio and video input from files, film, or tape. Called by many compound names including digital system/editor/workstation or NLE.

**digital film.** Film master that is used to make release prints which contains footage created digitally such as digital effects or CGI. The digital footage is transferred to negative, cut, and processed along with the footage shot on film and digital tape to make the digital film.

**digital intermediate, a.k.a. digital intermediary and DI.** Scanning process that brings together all source formats — film, file, and tape — to create a digital master of the locked cut for the final finishing processes which will produce the show master on film, file, and/or tape.

**digital.** A digital signal that has limited variation within a small set of numerical variables. Digital records audio, video, and data as files composed of binary numbers (zeroes and ones) that can be read by a computer.

**digitize.** Input footage from an analog tape into a digital editing system.

**dirt fixes.** Cleaning out dirt and hair that get caught on the show master tape via a fix session or removing them electronically by running the tape through the online house's dirt-removal system.

**dissolve.** A transitional effect where the first (outgoing) shot disappears as the second (incoming) shot appears.

**distribution.** Phase of a project during which it's marketed and contracts are signed for exhibition in theaters or for home viewing on DVD, TV, etc. Distribution follows the postproduction phase of a project and precedes the exhibition phase.

**DIT.** Digital Imaging Technician. Data wrangler who works with the cinematographer during production to get the best digital images possible by monitoring exposure and making certain camera settings such as codec and time code are correct, creating LUTs, and ensuring that the shot images and their data are correctly transferred to the production drive, and more. New position, where lab meets camera, which originated with the digital age and continues to be developed and defined.

**DME.** Dialogue, Music, and Effects. The three stems that form the mixdown of the final sound mix and are used to make the final sound track or Printmaster.

**D-mode.** Method in which online assembly events are numbered in nonsequential order by Source reel and then Record IN time code where all effects are performed last.

**DNLE.** Digital Nonlinear Editing system. See also **Digital Editing System.**

**Dolby digital.** Audio compression technology for film prints, TV broadcast (SD and HD), disks, and video game consoles developed by Dolby Laboratories. Originally called AC-3 due to its being based on Dolby's Audio Compression 3 format. Dolby digital has various flavors such as Dolby Digital Surround Ex which includes 5:1 and 7:1 sound for theaters.

**Dolby Digital.** Developed by Dolby Laboratories in 1977 to accompany *Star Wars,* Dolby Digital (DD) sound is a high-end noise reduction and surround sound system that combines multiple channel LCRS audio in an encoded signal for recording, projecting, and broadcasting. See also **LCRS.**

**dongle.** Small hardware plug-in device that tells a computer to activate certain software. It allows a customer to buy a digital system and only pay for the software they need.

**double perf.** 16mm or other lower gauge film with sprocket holes on both sides.

**double strand.** See **A/B roll.**

**double system.** Production method where audio and video are recorded on two different formats, e.g., film and file, and require syncing before they can be edited.

**downrez, a.k.a. down convert.** Convert from a higher resolution to a lower resolution, e.g., going from HD to SD or capturing footage in the digital editing system at a lower res than that at which it was shot.

**DP.** Director of photography, i.e., the cinematographer.

**DPX.** Digital picture exchange. Standard file format used in DI and VFX work due to its ability to preserve the color data of scanned film negative and store the metadata associated with it.

**drop frame.** Method of numbering and accounting for NTSC videotape frames that doesn't count (drops) certain frames in order to be time accurate.

**drop out.** Loss of video or audio on an analog tape during playback.

**DSLR.** Digital single lens reflex. Type of still camera that records HD video to computer disk. Starting to be used to shoot segments and entire shows due to its sharp, film-like images.

**DTS.** Digital Theater System. Digital sound encoded on film, tape, and DVD and direct competition to Dolby Digital (DD). Since some theaters run DTS sound and some run DD, sound tracks are encoded with both digital tracks.

**DTV.** Digital broadcast TV.

**dub.** 1) Copy or re-record audio and/or video. 2) The mix. See also **mix.**

**dupe.** Duplicate work print reels printed up by the film lab, usually for the sound editors when they edit on film. Also known as a dirty dupe, black and white, or 1:1.

**duration.** Length of a shot or edit on a digital or video editing system.

**DV.** Digital Video. Stores video, audio, and other information in digital form.

**dynamics.** Relationship between low and high volume on sound tracks, which if mixed correctly, will differentiate between soft and loud sounds, contain organic high points and low points, and be uncompressed.

**EBR.** Electron beam recorder. A popular tape-to-film transfer finishing machine in use since the '70s that scans digital images to film by breaking each video frame into three separate RGB images and exposing each image to three stripes of black-and-white negative. The three exposed negatives are then step-printed together to create a color negative. Also referred to as a CRT film recorder.

**EBU.** European Broadcasting Union. Paraphrasing its website: the EBU is an organization of broadcasters which provides a full range of operational, commercial, technical, legal, and strategic services for its union members.

**edge code.** See **ink code**.

**edge numbers.** See **key code**.

**edit point.** Frame that you mark and decide to edit in.

**edit.** (noun) A portion of a shot put into a show.

**editorial.** See **postproduction**.

**editor's cut.** See **first cut**.

**EDL.** Edit Decision List. The "list," as it's often referred to, contains the reel number and time code numbers for each edit in the final offline cut. An EDL recreates the offline cut and is used by the online editor to conform the show.

**EDTV.** Enhanced-definition television or extended-definition television. A Consumer Electronics Association term for certain DTV formats and devices, EDTV is superior to SDTV and inferior to HDTV. See also **HD** and **SD**.

**EFX.** A sound effect or a special visual effect, depending on the context.

**electronic slate.** See **smart slate**.

**element.** See **unit**.

**E-mode.** Method in which online assembly events are numbered in nonsequential order by Source reel and then Source IN time code where all effects are performed last.

**emulsion side.** Dull side of picture or sound film that contains the actual image or magnetic sound.

**EOR.** End of reel.

**EPS.** Electronic post sync. Another term for ADR. See also **ADR.**

**EQ.** Equalize. Adjust the volume level of individual frequencies of a sound in order to change its tone, e.g., EQ'ing dialogue so that ADR lines match the production track.

**equalize** See **EQ.**

**equalizer.** An adjustable audio filter, measured in decibels (dB) that lowers or boosts frequency and alters amplitude.

**essence media.** Bits and bytes that represent the digital video and audio. Also called essence data.

**essence.** As opposed to metadata, the video, audio, graphics, animation, and text in a digitally edited piece.

**event.** An edit in an EDL.

**exhibition**. Final phase of a project where it's projected in a theater, broadcast or downloaded to a television, or streamed or downloaded on a computer and viewed by its audience. Exhibition follows the distribution phase.

**export.** Send a file out of a digital editing system.

**exposition sequence.** Series of shots or scenes at the beginning of a film that set its time, place, situation, characters, tone, and/or theme.

**extreme close-up.** (ECU) A shot framed so tight that if it's on a person's face you just see the eyes.

**eyeline.** A character's line of vision — the direction their eyes are looking.

**fade in.** A dissolve *to* a filmed shot from black, sometimes white, and, once in a great while, yellow, blue, or another color.

**fade out.** A dissolve *from* a filmed shot to black, sometimes white, and, once in a great while, yellow, blue, or another color.

**FCC.** Federal Communications Commission. Independent government agency that regulates interstate and international communications by radio, television, wire, satellite, and cable in the United States.

**FCM.** Frame Code Mode. Notation on a digital editing system's EDL that reports that the list is either DF (Drop Frame) or NDF (Non Drop Frame).

**FCP.** Final Cut Pro. See **Final Cut Pro.**

**FFOA.** First frame of action. First frame of a film or video after the leader which is often black as the picture fades in. Same as FFOP.

**FFOP.** First frame of picture. Same as FFOA.

**field.** Half of a video frame. A videotape frame is composed of two fields.

**file-based workflow.** See **tapeless workflow**.

**fill leader.** See **fill**.

**fill.** Recycled movie film used to fill in the gaps and keep sync on sound reels where there is no sound or a portion has been removed temporarily. A film term that is also applied to digital editing where tracks and shots have electronic fill.

**film lab.** Facility that produces the final film reels that are projected in the theaters. The lab also creates the final special effects on film. Labs used to hum with the bustle of producing film dailies and the final prints for movie theaters. But the digital age and its need for dailies on digital tape, not film, (and, coming soon, digital projection) has put this era in the past. Many film labs have teamed with post production facilities to stay alive.

**film recorder.** Machine that transfers digital images to exposed film, most often a color timed internegative. There are two types of machines: the EBR and laser film recorder.

**film scanner.** Device that inputs OCN and outputs digital data which is used in the digital intermediate process or for digital VFX.

**Film Scribe.** Avid program for film projects that allows you to create a cutlist for a film finish.

**filter.** A type of equalizing device that eliminates selected frequencies from a signal. For example, a high-pass filter removes low frequencies and allows high frequencies to pass. A low-pass filter would do the reverse.

**Final Cut Pro.** A prosumer and professional digital editing system made by Apple, Inc.

**FireWire.** Apple's name for its IEEE 1394 interface, available as cable, wireless, fiber optic, and coaxial connectors. FireWire, widely used in cutting rooms, is a user-friendly, inexpensive cable that allows for real-time data transfer from digital professional, prosumer, and consumer products, (camcorders, DV tapes, DVDs, etc.) to personal computers and digital picture- and sound-editing systems.

**firmware.** Combines fixed computer instructions and data to internally control an electronic device such as a TV remote controller or DVD-ROM drive.

**first cut.**, a.k.a. the editor's cut, is the first cut of the show put together by the editor.

**fit-to-fill.** Fitting a video shot into a certain time slot by changing its speed. The editor tells the computer the length of the video and the audio shots and it calculates the speed change and puts in the video.

**fix session.** Post house session scheduled after the online editing to correct edits, add missing shots, and make dirt fixes.

**flashback.** Shot, sequence of shots, or scene which transports the story into the past.

**flash card.** See **memory card**.

**flashforward.** Shot, sequence of shots, or scene which transports the story into the future.

**flash frame.** Clear, white frame at the end of the take where light entered the film camera when it stopped between takes.

**flatbed.** Film editing machine on which reels run flat (horizontally).

**flex file.** Log file sent by telecine with film data for inputting into a digital system and finishing a project on film.

**flip.** An effect where the frame is turned upside down vertically, e.g., if you flop the shot of a person standing on their head, they will now stand on their feet.

**flop, a.k.a. mirror.** Picture: An effect where the picture is turned horizontally 180° so that an object on the left side of the frame is now on the right. Sound: Turning the film track 180° so it is silent when played.

**Foley.** Sound effects recorded in sync with specific actions on the screen. Foley is recorded by a Foley artist (a.k.a. Foley walker or Foley dancer) on a Foley stage as the picture runs on the screen.

**Fostex.** Digital audio recorder used to capture sound on set and location.

**fps.** Frames per second. Rate at which frames move. Nominally film runs at 24 fps and tape at 30 fps in the United States.

**Frankenbite.** Frankenstein + sound bite. New line pieced together from pieces of several lines and put in interviewee's mouth. Coined by reality TV editors who struggle hard to tease out the truth and continuity of the story from hours of footage.

**free and clear.** Music in the public domain that does not have a copyright nor require a fee.

**freeze frame**, a.k.a. **freeze** or **still frame.** Effect where the action holds (freezes) for as many frames as desired.

**frequency.** Measured in hertz (Hz), frequency is the number of waves (cycles) that reach or pass a point in one second.

**front porch.** The horizontal sync signal located between the front edge of the blanking pulse and the front edge of sync on a videotape.

**FS.** 1) False Start by camera noted on camera log. 2) Full shot. See also **full shot.**

**full shot.** (FS) A shot framed to include the whole person, animal, or object being shot.

**fullcoat.** Film sound track where the entire surface is covered with brown, magnetic particles. 16mm track is always fullcoat. 35mm fullcoat is used to record mixed sound tracks.

**fully filled.** Contractually required by foreign distributors, fully filled music and effects tracks are those which contain all the effects as originally mixed.

**FX.** Special effect. Also written F/X or referred to as VFX.

**gag reel.** Comic reel made of a show's outtakes and crew tomfoolery shown at the end-of the-season or wrap party. Sound effects, music, and narration are often added.

**gain control.** Audio potentiometer that raises or lowers the record, mix, or playback signal strength.

**gain.** The increase or decrease in strength of an electrical signal measured in decibels or number-of-times of magnification. Mixers constantly "ride the gain" to ensure a consistent audio level from show start to finish.

**garbage matte.** A rough matte created when keying green screens to remove garbage (undesirable elements such as wires or models) or retain parts of images, e.g., light spills that the green screen might wipe out.

**GB.** See **gigabyte**.

**generation loss.** Loss of picture and sound quality which occurs each time an analog tape is dubbed to another tape.

**genlock.** Locking one device to another via an internal signal generator to achieve synchronization.

**gigabyte.** GB. 1024 megabytes or 1 billion bytes. A unit of measurement used to measure computer file sizes, data storage, and memory.

**glitch.** Distortion of video or audio on an analog tape during playback.

**GOP.** Group of pictures (frames). In video coding, how intra- and inter-frames are ordered and arranged.

**GPI.** General purpose interface. An interface that allows the computer to control specific functions on a variety of remote devices. Used extensively on switchers and online machines. Usually means a serial connection (RS232 or RS422) between computers.

**grade.** Color time a film or tape. See also **color correct** and **timing**.

**gray scale.** The 7 to 10 shades of gray which form a test pattern that corresponds to the brightness range that a television system can reproduce. Used by cinematographers, film and video technicians.

**greenlight.** To formally approve a project and acquire its financing. Once it's greenlit, a.k.a. greenlighted, a project moves into the development phase.

**green screen.** Special effect created by shooting a subject in front of a green (or blue) screen. Shot 1, a live action shot, is the background. Shot 2, the green screen shot, contains the subject (talent) and is the foreground. When the two shots are composited (merged), the green screen washes out and the subject appears to react to what's happening in the background, e.g., a farmer reacting to a giant spider. See also **chroma-key**.

**guide track.** See **work track**.

**GVG.** Grass Valley Group. Northern California company renowned for its online editing systems, switchers, and news editing systems.

**GVX.** Graphics file.

**handle.** Extra frames at the head or tail of a shot that allow for fades, dissolves, and other effects. When consolidating on a digital editing system, handles can be created so edits can be slightly adjusted.

**hard effects.** SFX created to match specific screen actions such as car-bys, glass breaks, door closes, etc.

**HD.** High Definition, a.k.a. Hi Def. High resolution television standard which uses 16:9 aspect ratio and is superior to SD (Standard Definition) due to its use of more scan lines and one or two million pixels per frame, roughly five times more than SD. See also **SD**.

**HDMI.** High-definition multimedia interface. Compact interface that transmits uncompressed digital A & V data. HDMI also connects digital A/V sources such as DVD and Blu-ray disk players, PCs, etc., to compatible digital audio devices, computer monitors, video projectors, and digital televisions.

**HDSLR.** High definition digital single-lens reflex. See **DSLR**.

**head.** Start of shot, cut, tape, time line, or reel.

**head leader.** Piece of film or tape or a digital clip attached to the beginning of show for the purpose of maintaining sync between picture and sound. Head leader counts down from 8 to 2 (or 12 to 2) and is always followed by the FFOP.

**head pop.** A sync pop placed on the audio head leader aligned with the #2 picture frame to serve as a sync reference during screenings, sound editing, and sound mixing. Commonly called a 2-pop. See also **sync pop.**

**hiss.** Unwanted high frequency sounds attenuated through EQ'ing

**horizontal blanking.** Similar to the outer edges of a piece of film, horizontal blanking determines the width of the video image. It also carries information about the front porch, back porch, horizontal sync, and color burst. It is the period of time when the scanning beam repositions horizontally from one end of a line of picture information to the start of the next. See also **blanking.**

**hot splicer.** Heated splicer that's used by the negative cutter to scrape, cut, and glue film negative frames together. Also called a cement splicer.

**hot.** Loud. The VU meter is in the red.

**hue.** Color of a video image or signal.

**Hz.** Hertz. Standard unit for measuring frequency of a wave. One Hz equals one cycle per second (cps).

**IA.** See **IATSE.**

**IATSE.** International Alliance of Theatrical Stage Employees and Moving Picture Technicians. The umbrella union for picture and sound editors, cinematographers, and all below-the-line crafts. Within the IA, locals are divided by craft. The Editors' Guild is Local 700 and includes all picture and sound editors, assistants and apprentices, as well as sound mixers and has taken in projectionists, story analysts, TDs, and videotape operators in recent years.

**IEEE 1394.** A high-speed digital interface standard created and developed by Apple Inc. that FireWire employs.

**import.** Copy a file into a digital editing system.

**in point.** Starting edit point.

**ingest.** New term for intake of media from a tape or live feed.

**ink code.** Code added to the edge of a film work print reel and its corresponding sound reel to give them a sync reference. Also referred to as Acmade code or edge code.

**input, a.k.a. ingest.** Copy media along with data into a digital system.

**insert edit.** In digital editing, a term for putting a clip into a sequence so that the edits to the right of it get pushed down the time line and time is added to the sequence for the amount of the clip's duration.

**insert shot.** Shot of some small but significant detail in a scene shot during post-production on an insert stage or picked up on the set. Term used interchangeably with cutaway. Technically, an insert is filmed during the production phase.

**inset.** Effect where a reduced shot is placed on another shot, typically to highlight a detail of the main shot.

**intercut.** Taking two sequential scenes and cutting between them so that the scenes advance and complete together. Intercut scenes are either parallel action or cross cut scenes.

**interlace.** Type of videotape scanning that scans Field 1 (odd numbered lines) and then Field 2 (even-numbered lines). As opposed to progressive scanning. Also referred to as interleave scanning.

**interleave.** 1) A segmenting method for arranging data on a DVD, for instance, to achieve more efficient storage. Like data types are stored close to each other (e.g., audio, video, or text) which when retrieved by the device will be put back in correct order. 2) A videotape term referring to the way video fields are scanned, a.k.a. interlace. See also **interlace**.

**interlock projector.** A film projector that syncs (interlocks) a picture reel with a sound reel for a screening while the film is being edited. A regular projector runs a single reel because release prints are double system (sound and picture are on both on the reel).

**intermediate.** Negative film print made from negative originals used in the preparation of a positive master from which release prints can be struck as well as tape masters, DVDs, and digital cinema releases. An intermediate is also used as a recording film on laser recorders and CRT film recorders.

**internegative.** The IN is a spliceless dupe negative made from the interpositive which is used to make release prints.

**interpositive.** An IP is a positive print on negative stock which is made from the cut negative and used to make opticals and reprints. It is part of the release print-making process and sports an orange background with colors that are the reverse of the negative: white is black, red is green, etc.

**invisible editing.** Editing that is so smooth that viewers become engrossed in the movie and don't notice the individual cuts.

**IP.** See **interpositive**.

**ITU-R BT.601.** International Telecommunications Union, the UN committee governing communication. The BT stands for Broadcast Television. The standard sampling standard for SD analog waveforms being converted into digital data. See also **CCIR 601**.

**jam sync.** Reproducing time code from one device, tape, file, or other recording format to another by using a time code generator, reader, or synchronizer to match (jam) the time code.

**JPEG** Joint Photographers Expert Group. A standard form of lossy (reduced) data compression which compresses and decompresses video and audio into digital images. JPEG compression is designed and applied to still images like scanners, Web video, and desktop publications. A motion JPEG (M-JPEG) is used to compress shots for nonlinear editing.

**jump cut.** A cut where objects or characters appear to jump because the shots are too similar. Technically, this is due to the camera angles of the two shots being less than 30° apart.

**junior.** A four-plate KEM. **See also KEM.**

**Kbps.** Kilobits per second. Used to measure modem speed. See also **bps.**

**KEM roll.** Reel of picture or track wound on a core for editing on a KEM.

**KEM.** Flatbed film editing machine.

**kerning.** Space between letters of text that can be adjusted when titling or adding credits to a show on a CG or on a digital editing system.

**key code.** Sequential numbers embedded in the edge of the film stock at regular intervals during manufacturing that are visible on the negative and work print.

**key shot.** See **matte shot**.

**key.** Cutting an electronic hole (think of a keyhole) in a picture so another image or text can be seen. A key is a composite effect consisting of the background which contains the hole and the key element which fills the hole.

**Keykode.** Eastman Kodak's bar code version of key code placed on the film in addition to and duplicating the key code.

**keylink.** A telecine log file. See also **flex file**.

**keyLog.** A telecine log file. See also **flex file**.

**kilobyte.** kB. 1,024 bytes. A unit of measurement used to measure computer file sizes, data storage, and memory.

**Kinescope**. Transferring video to film by filming the videotape as it plays on a monitor.

**L cut.** See **split edit**.

**laser film recorder.** Latest tape-to-film transfer finishing machine that works by scanning digital images onto negative film frames using three RGB lasers. Also referred to as a laser recorder or a laser printer.

**latency.** The time between a request for data and the start of the data transmittal; a waiting period, in essence. The term is applied to networks, disks, channels, and communication between devices. Low latency means a short waiting period.

**latent edge numbers.** See **key code**.

**lay in.** Put in music or sound from first frame to last to see how it fits against cue time and the picture. When the music lays in perfectly, no adjustments are necessary.

**layback.** Transfer of the completed sound mix onto the videotape show master.

**laydown** (noun or verb). Record or transfer audio, black, picture, time code, etc., from one tape or medium to another tape or medium.

**LCRS.** Left-center-right-surround speaker channels in a movie theater. During the premix and mix, the mixers assign tracks to LCRS speaker channels.

**leading.** Space between lines of text that can be adjusted when titling or adding credits to a show on a CG or a digital editing system.

**level.** Video: Brightness and contrast of the color. Audio: Amount of signal strength.

**LFOA.** Last frame of action. Last frame of picture or sound on a film reel which is the final frame to be included when measuring reel length. The LFOA is noted on mix sheets and in the notes for each reel sent to the negative cutter. Same as LFOP.

**LFOP.** Last frame of picture. See **LFOA**.

**Lightworks.** Professional digital editing system.

**limiter.** An analog circuit in an audio recorder that automatically adjusts volume to prevent clipping when a digital or analog signal surpasses a preset level.

**line cut.** Tape of the switches from one camera angle to the other, which were called out by the multiple cam director as the show was shot.

**linear editing.** Making or recording each edit sequentially from the beginning of the show to the end of the show.

**lined script.** Pages of script shot each day and marked by script supervisor with vertical lines indicating where each take starts and ends.

**locked cut.** The final edited version of the cut created by the editor in the cutting room.

**lo-con.** Low contrast positive film stock made from OCN, dupe neg, or interneg that's printed and timed brighter in the lab, then telecined to make a video master.

**logger.** 1) Person who enters (logs) info about tape (description, take number, time code, etc.) so editor and other post personnel can locate footage. 2) Person who marks transcripts so editor and other post personnel can locate footage.

**LokBox.** Essentially an electronic synchronizer, the LokBox locks (syncs) a video-tape machine with a film synchronizer so that the negative cutter can cut the negative. Used on shows that have been edited digitally and have no work print, the LokBox runs forwards and backwards and has also been used to cut sound on film.

**long form.** TV show that is feature length, such as a variety show, MOW, or mini-series.

**long shot.** (LS) A shot framed long that focuses on the action from a distance.

**loop group.** A group of professional actors who perform walla and wild lines to simulate members of a crowd and are recorded on an ADR stage. Also called loopers.

**loop.** Another word for ADR. To "loop" an actor means to replace their dialogue.

**looper.** A member of a loop group. See also **loop group**.

**looping.** ADR. See also **loop** and **ADR**.

**lossless.** Scheme of file compression which retains all the data in the image so that when it's decompressed the data can be completely reconstructed. For example, a GIF (Graphics Interchange File) used on the Web is lossless as are spreadsheets, text files, and MPEG files. Opposite of lossy.

**lossy.** Scheme of data compression which reduces the amount of data in the image so that when it's decompressed some of the original data is lost. Commonly used for video and sound image files such as JPEGs and MPEGs where users won't notice the image loss. Opposite of lossless.

**LTC.** Longitudinal Time Code. Analog time code that can be read when the tape is moving and that is laid down lengthwise (longitudinally) during or after production to an audio track.

**LTO.** Linear Tape-Open. Magnetic tape storage technology used for archiving since it can hold hundreds of GB on a single cartridge.

**luma.** See **luminance**.

**luminance.** Noncolor portion of a video image or signal that holds the black and white data (brightness and contrast).

**LUT.** Look-up table. A software chart used on set and at the post house to maintain images' color values during shooting and finishing.

**Maya.** Autodesk's 3-D animation, modeling, simulation, and compositing software used by CG artists.

**M & E.** Music and Effects. The music and effects resulting from the final sound mix which are used on the sound track of foreign (non-English version) movies.

**Machinima.** Genre of filmmaking which combines 3-D game technology with animation to produce cost and time-efficient animated films. Once characters and backgrounds are created, they can be shot real time and scenes composited real time within a 3-D virtual environment.

**mag.** Magnetic coated film stock used for recording, editing, playing, and mixing sound.

**master shot.** Shot that encompasses all the action in a scene from beginning to end. Although a master routinely starts framed close on a small object and can zoom and pan as needed to capture the action, it mostly stays wide to frame all the action.

**match cut.** 1) Picture editing: A continuity cut where the majority of the elements are duplicated (matched) from the last frame of the first (outgoing) shot to the first frame of the second (incoming) shot. The elements to match are: screen direction, eyeline, camera angle and framing, props, sound (wording, volume, or pacing), weather, wardrobe, hair, makeup, lighting, color, and action. 2) Negative cutting: Term for conforming the negative cut to the locked positive work print or tape, cut for cut. Match cut is generalized to other situations such as cutting in a film reprint or reproducing any section of a project (e.g., title, effect, or scene) cut for cut.

**matte shot.** Cutting a hole in a shot and placing (matting or keying) another shot in that hole.

**MB.** See **megabyte.**

**Mbps.** Megabits per second. Used to measure bandwidth. See also **bps**.

**Media 100.** Professional digital editing system.

**Media Cleaner Pro.** Terran Interactive's suite of industry standard compression software used for encoding and compressing files for the Web, DVDs, etc.

**media.** A digital term for video and/or audio.

**medium close-up.** (MCU) Between a CU and an MS, a MCU is shot from the shoulders up through the top of the person's head.

**medium shot.** (MS) A shot framed from the waist or chest up through the top of the person's head.

**megabyte.** MB. 1,024 kilobytes or 1 million bytes. A unit of measurement used to measure computer files sizes, data storage, and memory.

**memory card.** Re-recordable electronic flash memory data storage device used in cameras and editing systems as well as laptops, phones, MP3 players, and video game consoles for storing digital contents.

**metadata.** Summarized as the "data about data," metadata is the background information that identifies the condition, content, and other qualities of data. In film and video this means time code, blanking, frame rate, aspect ratio, sync, color burst information and descriptive data about clips, such as the location of their media and effects layers.

**MHz.** Megahertz. One million Hz or cps (cycles per second).

**MIDI.** Musical instrument digital interface. Protocol for the types of control signals that one electronic musical device sends to another. In less technical terms, midi is a plug-in which enables a musician's computer to communicate with a host of devices such as MIDI sound modules (samplers, synthesizers, etc.) and to send and receive time code.

**MIDI controller.** Keyboard, drum kit, guitar, piano, or other electronic musical device that generates MIDI messages to adjust individual controls like pan or gain on devices in the MIDI network.

**mismatch.** A cut in which continuity is lost due to a difference between elements such as action, eyeline, camera framing, camera position, prop, wardrobe, or makeup. See **match cut:** picture editing.

**mix.** Recording session where all the dialogue, ADR, sound effects, Foley, and music are blended together and recorded to make the final, composited sound track.

**mix.** The blending of a show's sound and music to produce a final sound track.

**mixdown.** (noun or verb) Bringing together a number of recorded audio tracks by recording them onto fewer tracks en route to making the final mixed sound track.

**mixer.** Person or equipment that does the mixing.

**mode.** Order by which a show is assembled in online. Each of the five modes (A, B, C, D, and E) sorts the events on the list in a different order for the machine to perform the edits.

**modem.** Modulate-Demodulate. A device that connects computers to each other for transmitting data via a telephone line or a cable network. Widely used for sending and receiving email, downloading files, and exploring the Web. The term originated with phone modems where the modem modulates (converts) the computer's digital data into analog signals to be transmitted over the telephone line and then demodulates (reconverts) the signals back into digital signals to be received by the computer. Modem speed is measured in bps (bits per second).

**mono sound.** Where one track is recorded by a nonstereo mic and the same track is played to each speaker. As opposed to stereo sound.

**montage.** A succinct, self-contained sequence of images inserted to convey facts, feelings, or thoughts that usually functions as a transition in time or place.

**morph.** A special effect where one object or image transforms into another, e.g., a man turns into a monster.

**MOS.** Without sound; no sound was recorded on the shot. Legend has it that the term originated from an early Hollywood director, a German immigrant, who would call for a shot "mit out sound."

**Moviola.** Upright film editing machine.

**MOW.** Movie of the Week. A feature-length show created for television.

**MPAA.** Motion Picture Academy of Arts. The board that rates a feature film, bestowing a G, PG, PG-13, R, NC-17, or X rating.

**MPEG.** Motion Picture Editors Guild. See also **IATSE.**

**MPEG.** Motion Picture Experts Group. It works to standardize compression formats in the files that are named after them. There are many types of MPEG and more on the way. Those in most current use are: MPEG-1, the standard for VCD; MPEG-2, the standard for DVD authoring, SVCD, and HDTV broadcast; MP3, the audio version used for downloads from the Web; and MPEG-4, the current standard for multimedia applications.

**M.P.S.E.** Motion Picture Sound Editors is a professional organization of sound editors, like A.C.E., that hosts the annual Golden Reel Awards to honor sound editors.

**MP3.** MPEG-1 or MPEG-2 + Audio Layer 3. Digital audio encoding and storage format that uses lossy compression to transfer and play back MX and SFX on digital audio players.

**multitrack.** Device used in ADR, Foley, and other sound recording situations which records 8 to 48 tracks (depending on the machine) on 2" digital or analog tape. Often referred to as "the 24-track" since the commonly used machine has 24 tracks.

**MXF.** Media eXchange Format. A close cousin of AAF, MXF has a simpler file format. It can contain video and audio media. See also **AAF.**

**NABET.** National Association of Broadcast Engineers and Technicians, union for television networks which includes editors.

**NAT.** Natural sound recorded by a news crew on the field tape which may be sync or wild sound.

**natural pause.** Animation term. Three to four frames added to the dialogue track where a speaker would pause naturally, usually before and after every line and at spots the director calls for during a line.

**NDF.** See **non-drop frame**.

**needle drop, a.k.a. canned music.** Background music — often source and a song — that requires a license fee to use in a show. Term dates to the days of vinyl when each drop of the record player's needle required a separate fee. See **source music.**

**negative continuity.** A list of every edit in the film, which is written by the negative cutter, editor, or assistant editor, on a show that cuts and finishes on film. It includes the shot number, slate, length, and start and end key code.

**negative cutter.** Person who cuts the negative.

**negative.** Film that is shot in the camera and developed by the lab where the colors are opposite their true hues.

**NLE.** Nonlinear Editing System. See also **Digital Editing System.**

**nondiegetic.** Description for asynchronous sounds that do not have a visible source and play in the background, e.g., a river babbling.

**non-drop frame.** Method of numbering and of accounting for NTSC videotape frames that counts each frame in order to be data accurate.

**nonlinear editing.** Making or recording each edit in nonsequential order.

**NTSC.** National Television Standards Committee. U.S. videotape standard with 525 video scan lines which runs on a 60-hertz AC power cycle at 30 fps and has a frame size of 720 x 480. Also used in the rest of North America and Central America as well as Japan and environs, South Korea, the Netherlands, and parts of South America.

**Nuendo.** Music editing software used in DAW for editing and sequencing.

**OCN.** Original Camera Negative.

**ODB.** Offline Editing Database. What Lightworks converts the telecine log file into. The ODB file becomes part of the film database that the cutlist program will access to make the film cutlist for the negative cutter. Equivalent to an Avid ALE file.

**offline editing.** Making all the creative editing decisions and locking the show.

**OMF.** Open media framework. A file format which can contain media used to exchange project data and metadata between picture, sound, and online editors.

**one-lite daily.** The daily work print that the lab processes using the same printer light setting to time (develop the color for) all reels.

**one-liner.** Script supervisor's sheet that contains a one-line summary of each take of dailies.

**online editing.** Reproducing the locked cut from an EDL using the best quality tapes.

**on the fly.** Cutting between shots while they're running without starting, stopping, or marking them first.

**optical printer.** Optical house machine that combines a projector and a camera to shoot an IP on negative raw stock and create the optical. It's being overtaken by CGI and other digital effects machines.

**optical.** A special effect made at an optical house on an optical printer from new film negative.

**out point.** Ending edit point.

**output.** Put out material —a show, sequence, or shot — from a digital system to a tape. Outputting is also called printing or playing out (to tape).

**over the shoulder.** O/S or OTS. A shot from the waist or chest up that includes the shoulder of one character while focusing on the other character.

**overhead.** OH. Often filmed from a crane, an overhead shot looks down on the scene from above.

**overlap.** A cut where picture and sound cut in at different times so that one overlaps (extends beyond) the other.

**overwrite edit.** In digital editing, a term for putting a clip into a sequence edit so that edits to the right of it are replaced for the duration of the clip.

**P2.** Short for Professional Plug-in, Panasonic's professional DV format that stores media in GB on a solid-state flash memory card.

**PA.** Production assistant.

**package.** A precut news story of timely human interest.

**PAL.** Phase Alternating Line. Videotape standard used in the United Kingdom and most of Europe, China, and parts of Africa and South America. It has 625 video scan lines and runs on a 50-hertz AC power cycle at 25 fps with a frame size of 720 x 576.

**pan.** Short for panorama. (noun and verb). Cinematography term: Shot where camera moves horizontally left to right or vice versa. Sound term: The left-right position of a sound on a mixer or other sound device or piece of software. Panning directs the sound to the right, left, or center speaker channel.

**paper cut.** Outline that provides the initial plan of attack for editing a documentary or other nonscripted piece.

**parallel action.** Editing two (or more) independent lines of action together — characters, settings, or subjects — that do not interact directly and are unaware of each other.

**PB.** Petabyte. 1,000 terabytes. Postproduction facility require PBs of storage.

**PCM.** Pulse-code modulation. Standard digital audio recording protocol that creates different uncompressed audio file formats for play back on computers and standard devices such as CDs, Blu-ray disks, DVDs, etc.

**PFD.** Professional Disc. Sony's optical disc format for recording SD and HD in its XDCAM professional video devices.

**pick-up master.** A new master shot that is "picked up" (continued) from a slight bit before where an incomplete master left off.

**picture editor.** Editor who puts the show together initially.

**picture fill.** See **slug**.

**pitching audio.** How high or low the audio sounds. Pitch is the main way the audience distinguishes sounds.

**pix.** Picture.

**pixel.** Pix element. Smallest unit or sample of a digital image on a screen. It holds data such as black-and-white, color, and gray scale information.

**playback.** Running a recorded video or audio tape from a tape deck, camera, or other device. Commonly done for the purpose of reviewing material or recording it to another device. Raw or cut footage is frequently played back as a reference for actors or other performers so they can be photographed in sync with the action, e.g., green screen, animation, music.

**playback machine.** Online tape deck that plays back the source tapes which are referred to as the playback tapes.

**playback music.** Music recorded for the sole purpose of being played (back) on the set on each musical take. It enables the actors and actresses to maintain sync with the music while singing and/or dancing.

**point-of-view shot** (POV) A variation of a reverse shot, a POV shot corresponds exactly to where a character is looking; it is *what* they're seeing.

**pop.** See **sync pop**.

**postproduction.** Final creation phase of a show during which all editing and finishing work take place. Also referred to as editing, editorial, or post. Postproduction is followed by the distribution and exhibition phases of the movie.

**postproduction house.** Facility where the final cut of a show is reproduced in the digital format contractually required for airing on television or screening in theaters. Post houses also produce digital dailies and perform a myriad of other post production tasks. Frequently, they rent cutting rooms and screening rooms and provide free meals in an attempt to take care of their editing clients every need.

**post viz.** Temp VFX that use the source footage.

**pot.** Potentiometer. A resistor device controlled by a slider or knob used to change the EQ, gain, pitch, tone, pan, etc. during the mix.

**POV** See **point-of-view shot**.

**preditor.** Producer/editor.

**pre-dub.** See **pre-mix.**

**pre-lay.** Transfer the edited tracks to tape before the pre-mix or mix.

**premastering.** Creating a disk image for a DVD; part of the authoring process.

**pre-mix.** Preliminary mix of certain sounds — background effects and dialogue usually — ahead of the mix. Also called the pre-dub or rough mix.

**preproduction.** Preparatory phase of a show during which the script and financing are finalized, talent (actors) and crew hired, locations and schedules locked, and sets, wardrobe, props, etc. created. Preproduction follows the development phase and precedes the production phase.

**presence.** See **ambience.**

**previsualization, a.k.a. previs or previz.** Determining camera moves, lighting, etc., ahead of production. Often done on animation shows, heavy duty VFX shows, and those requiring playback or other pre-shot and/or cut scenes for use during the shoot.

**printmaster.** Final product of the sound mix for a show destined for theatrical release. A film printmaster is recorded to an optical sound negative to make an optical sound track for projecting in commercial theaters.

**production.** Phase of a show during which the filming takes place on set or location. Also referred to as the "shooting" phase, "the shoot," or "principal photography." Production follows the preproduction phase and precedes the postproduction phase.

**production track.** Original sync audio recorded at the time of filming.

**progressive video streaming.** Method of Web streaming that requires downloading the video to view it.

**progressive.** Type of videotape scanning that scans Field 1 and Field 2 at the same time. As opposed to interlace. See also **interlace.**

**protection master.** Dub of show master recorded after online to be used in case the master is damaged. The final sound track is laid back to the protection master so there are two copies of the final show.

**Pro Tools.** Popular sound editing and recording tool (DAW) manufactured by Avid Technologies, Inc. that runs on a Mac OS.

**proxy.** Low res file that links to higher res file (2K, 4K, etc.) and contains all its data.

**PSA.** Public service announcement.

**pulldown sequence.** Succession of film frames that are transferred to tape timecode fields during telecine.

**pull list.** A list of camera rolls and start and end key code for each edit in the final locked reel. The pull list is used by the negative cutter to pull (acquire from the vault) the camera rolls in preparation for match cutting the negative.

**pull up.** (noun or verb) Slip, slide, or trim an edit so that it starts sooner. Opposite of a push down.

**pull-in frame.** Frame used in telecine to start the pulldown sequence, typically the "A" frame.

**punch in.** Fix a particular section of a mixed track and leave the surrounding areas alone.

**push down.** (noun or verb) Slip, slide, or trim an edit so that it so that it starts later. Opposite of a pull up.

**quad split, a.k.a. q split.** Locking four (or more) cameras on a screen (via software channel or hardware box) so that they play simultaneously and can be intercut easily, e.g., "on the fly." See also **on the fly**.

**QuickTime.** Apple's multimedia file format that's become a standard for the integration of full-motion video and digitized sound into application programs.

**R3-D.** Red camera file.

**RAID.** Random Array of Independent Disks. When media is lost or destroyed on one disk, Raid technology allows for it to be regenerated on another so that a show can continue to be edited or broadcast.

**raking shot.** A tight form of a two-shot (or other shot) usually, that is filmed from the side and favors one character.

**random access.** Ability to locate any frame anywhere at any time on a digital system.

**raw stock.** Film or tape that has nothing shot or recorded on it.

**real time.** Responding immediately without delay in real, clock time as the event or process happens without dropping frames, e.g., creating visual effects, animating images, broadcasting live video, etc.

**real time effect.** A video or audio effect on a digital system for which the creation time equals the time taken to select it and put it in a sequence. As opposed to a rendered effect, which takes time to make and for which new media is created.

**real time video streaming.** Method of Web streaming where the video is viewed online from a streaming video server.

**record machine.** Tape deck or other device that records the footage being played back by the playback device. An online term originally, where source tapes playback edits to create the record tape which will become the edit master.

**rectangular pixel.** See **non-square pixel**.

**remaster.** Make a new master, usually in a different format or medium.

**render.** Create new media in order to play back a digital video effect or image.

**render farm.** A roomful of computers networked to render complex CGI and other VFX.

**re-recording engineer.** See **mixer**.

**resolution.** The clarity of an image on a screen based on different measurements according to format. Analog format measures resolution by the ratio of horizontal resolution lines to scan lines; digital uses pixels; and film goes by number of line pairs per millimeter.

**reverse.** 1) An angle shot from the exact opposite angle of the master shot action.
2) A cut to the opposite (reverse) angle. The cut can be from the *front* of a character to *behind* the character (or vice versa) or *from* a character (or characters) *to* the character (or characters) they're facing

**reverse telecine.** Removing the extra pulldown frames from 24p video that the digital editing system automatically added when ingesting it into a 30 fps project. Done so that you can edit at 23.98 fps or 24 fps. Achieved automatically during ingest by hardware or by using digital system's software tool.

**RGB.** Red, green, blue. The three primary colors of light which can be mixed to produce all the other colors and which are used in processing component and composite video or printing film. When generating video on a computer screen, RGB are displayed as separate analog or digital signals of red, green and blue dots. RGB are produced by the CRT which employs three electron guns to beam each color at the screen.

**rippling the list.** The shifting of events in an EDL on a linear system caused when the duration of an edit is changed, or an event is added or deleted. This shifting effectively ripples — corrects and updates — the events on the list that follow the change.

**Rock 'n' roll.** Swiftly fix or finish a section of the mix and move on.

**room tone.** RT. Interior ambience. See also **ambience.**

**rotoscope.** Create animation imagery or mattes frame-by-frame via tracing or otherwise referencing live footage, to create new images or repair images.

**rough cut., a.k.a. first cut or editor's cut.** The first cut of a show put together by the editor. In the past, the first cut was considered rough because it lacked visual effects, music and sound effects, and additional dialogue tracks due to the limitations of the Moviola and KEM film-editing machines. With digital editing equipment, an unlimited amount of sound and video tracks are available and first cuts are becoming more and more sophisticated, though lacking all the final ingredients of the final show. Editors have never considered their work "rough" as they have always worked hard to finesse character, story, action, and dialogue. Many editors prefer the term "first cut" or "editor's cut."

**RS-232.** A standard, unbalanced interconnection scheme for serial data communications designed for short distances of up to 30 yards.

**RS-422.** A standard, balanced interconnection scheme for serial data communications used for control links in production and postproduction areas for VTRs, digital editing machines, and other equipment.

**RT.** See **real time effect, room tone,** or **running time.**

**rubber numbers.** See **ink code**.

**running time.** The duration (length) of a scene, section, or an entire show.

**rushes.** See **dailies**.

**safe action.** The area where it is safe to extend the action so that it's visible on a television monitor.

**safe title.** The area where it is safe to place titles so they do not get cut off on a television monitor.

**safety master.** See **protection master**.

**sampling rate.** Rate at which an audio signal is sampled (read) during recording.

**SAN.** Storage area network. Networked storage devices that, as used in postproduction, allow editors to share and access data and media files quickly and efficiently with other editors including sound editors and the post house.

**saturation.** Amount of color in a video image or signal.

**scoring.** Session where musicians play composer's score, cue by cue, while a tape of the show runs on a screen. The music is recorded and then edited into the show.

**scratch track.** Temporary voice-over track — laid into a cut for editing and timing purposes — that will be replaced with the voice of the hired narrator.

**screen direction.** The direction where a character or object enters or exits a shot.

**scribe.** A small, metallic pencil-like tool with a replaceable steel point for inscribing missing key code numbers on the edge work print for the negative cutter.

**script notes.** Page opposite the lined script page that contains camera info and other notes.

**scrub.** Run sound back and forth to locate an exact right frame for marking or editing in.

**SD.** Standard definition. Television resolution that meets standards including a 4:3 aspect ratio but is lower quality than HD (High Definition) due to employing fewer scan lines and pixels per frame. See also **HD**.

**SD.** Secure Digital. Memory card format widely used in DV cameras and many handheld electronic devices.

**SDDS.** Sony Dynamic Digital Sound. Sony's version of stereo, surround 5.1 sound for movie theaters which can be decoded into four, six, or eight channels and played back on a host of audio systems. Direct competition to DTS.

**SDI.** Serial Digital Interface. Transmittal of digital data in serial (time sequential) form. Commonly used to refer to television broadcast signals.

**SDII.** Sound Designer II. Standard Macintosh audio file format created by Apple.

**SDDS.** Sony Dynamic Digital Sound. An audio encoding system that competes with DD and DTS. See also **Dolby Digital**.

**SDTV.** Standard Definition TV format defined by its 525 or 625 scan lines, 4:3 aspect ratio, and analog sound.

**seamless editing.** See **invisible editing**.

**SECAM.** Sequential Color and Memory. Videotape standard used in France, Poland, Russia, most of Asia, and parts of Africa. It has 625 video scan lines, runs on a 50-hertz AC power cycle, and runs at 25 fps with a frame size of 720 x 576.

**sequence.** Term used for a cut of an edited scene, show, or part of a show by many digital editing systems.

**sequencer.** Software program used for creating music that records and plays back both audio and midi.

**session.** Created by the sound editor working on a digital audio system, a session consists of the cut tracks and is where the editor works. A session can be a scene, reel, or an entire show depending on how the editor sets it up.

**SFX.** Sound effect(s). Also used to mean special effects. To avoid confusion, this book uses SFX for sound effects and VFX for special effects.

**shooting ratio.** The amount of footage shot compared to the amount of footage used in the final cut. 20:1 is average for a high budget feature film. 6:1 is a good ratio to shoot for — er, figure on — for a low budget film or video.

**short cut.** A cut that has a brief duration — less than two seconds.

**short form.** TV show that is an hour or less such as a cartoon, comedy, or dramatic series, or a music video.

**shot.** Picture: Camera start to camera stop. Sound: Sound recorder start to stop.

**show master.** Final tape of a show, ready for broadcast. Referred to by many other names including the edit master, broadcast tape, final tape, show tape, and tape master.

**showrunner.** Credited as executive producer, the person — usually a writer — on a TV series who oversees each episode from idea to completion and is responsible for its creative vision and path as well as presenting it to the network.

**signal.** Audio term for the electricity that flows through a mic — cabled or wireless — to a media storage device such as a disk, drive, or tape.

**simo.** Dub that is made simultaneously with the original tape recording.

**single perf.** Sprocket holes on one side only. Found on 16mm-gauge film and smaller.

**single strand.** See **A roll.**

**single system.** Production method where audio and video are recorded on the same format: film, tape, file, or disk.

**skip frame.** An effect where alternate frames are printed so the film looks speeded up or pixilated, e.g., printing every other frame or every third frame.

**slave.** Control of one device such as a smart slate, tape deck, or a digital editing system by another for the purpose of dubbing, jam syncing time code, playing a show to air, etc.

**slide.** Change an edit's position in a cut by moving it up or down. Sliding an edit changes it externally, making it occur sooner or later in the cut, and causing the edits on either side of it to grow and shrink in duration by equal amounts. Sliding does not change the duration of the edit or the cut.

**slip.** Adjust an edit by changing where it starts and stops. Slipping changes the edit internally but does not change its duration.

**slo mo.** Effect where the pace of the action is decreased from what occurred in reality in front of the camera. This retardation is accomplished during editing or, more traditionally, during filming by overcranking — running the film through the camera at a faster rate than it will be played back. Opposite of speed up.

**slug.** Film term: Picture fill, composed of clear leader, that is used to fill in and keep sync in the picture reel where shots have been cut out (KEM rolls) or are missing, removed, or to be inserted (cut picture reels). Evolved digital meaning: Black fill readily available on the digital system for inserting in the time line.

**smart slate.** Electronic clap stick that generates time code which is jam synced to the Nagra (or other audio recorder). It displays time code on a red LED and greatly speeds up syncing.

**smash cut.** Variation on a short cut. An unexpected, lightning-quick cut designed to deliberately jar the audience by zapping the action from one place/object/person/image to another.

**SMPTE leader.** See **academy leader**.

**SMPTE time code.** Analog time code.

**SMPTE.** Society of Motion Picture and Television Engineers. An international technological society which invented time code in 1967 and which recommends — and often effectively sets — the standards that manufacturers worldwide use for time code and for many other tape, film, and telecommunication applications.

**sneakernet.** As applied to postproduction, this term means transferring media physically by external drive, tape, etc., from one computer to another.

**soft cut.** Short dissolve of one to four frames.

**soft effects.** Non-sync SFX that don't need to match on-screen action, e.g., background sounds like water lapping, scene ambience, birds chirping, etc.

**SOT.** Reporter's voice Sync on Tape. News editing term for sync sound.

**sound editor.** Editor who labors to perfect the show's sound.

**sound fill.** See **fill**.

**source music.** Music that has a clear, visual source onscreen such as a radio, album, or piano. Source music often plays in the background and is usually purchased, but can be composed.

**SPDIF.** Sony Philips Digital Interface. A standard digital-to-digital audio transfer file format utilized by digital video and audio editing machines, DAT machines, and other digital equipment.

**special effects house.** Facility where effects are created and finalized.

**speed up.** Effect where the pace of the action is increased from what occurred in reality in front of the camera. This acceleration is accomplished during editing or, more traditionally, during filming by undercranking — running the film through the camera at a slower rate than it will be played back. Opposite of slo mo.

**split edit.** A video editing term for overlap. In a split edit the audio and video edit do not start at the same time; either video or audio is delayed. Also called an L cut or a delayed edit.

**split screen.** Dividing the screen into two or more parts with different shots in each division.

**spotting session.** Meeting where the director views the completed show with the Sound Designer and Music Composer (in separate sessions) to map out the sound and music work to be done on the show.

**square pixel.** 1:1 pixel aspect ratio found on all computer screens and most computer-generated graphics. Must be compensated for when importing graphics to DV and running on TV because they use non-square pixels which display the graphics differently. See **non-square pixel**.

**non-square pixel, a.k.a. rectangular pixel.** Non-1:1 pixel aspect ratio used in DV and on all TV screens.

**stem, a.k.a. split tracks** or **splits.** Individual parts of the final mix: there's a dialogue stem, a music stem, and a sound effects stem. See also **DME.**

**stereo sound.** Identical tracks that are separated and played to different speaker channels, usually left and right. LCRS is a sophisticated form of stereo audio and is the standard. Created by recording two tracks at the same time with a stereo mic. As opposed to mono sound.

**still frame.** See freeze frame.

**still store.** Device that stores a frame from each take of a scene used in telecine, color correcting, and building effects.

**stinger.** A music cue that runs only a few seconds.

**stock shot.** Shot used to establish a location that is independent of the show and can be used on other episodes or shows. Stock houses provide stock shots or they can be obtained during the shoot. Examples: the Walton's barn, the NYPD Blue police station, the Indy 500 racetrack.

**straight cut.** When picture and sound are cut at the same frame as opposed to an overlap where picture and sound are cut at different times.

**streamer.** A diagonal line put on a tape or film to cue music for an orchestra at a scoring session or to cue a line for an actor in an ADR session.

**streaming.** A continuous, one-way transmission of data, usually audio or video, over a data network, typically the Web or a company's intranet. Most frequently associated with playing audio or video as it's downloaded from the Web (as opposed to storing it in a file on the computer before playing it). A fast computer and connection are required to view streaming media smoothly. Streaming may be in real time as from a live broadcast event or have a delay of a few seconds. Web browser plug-ins make streaming possible by decompressing and playing the Web file.

**stripe.** Add time code to a tape.

**subliminal cut.** A cut consisting of a few frames which zip by so fast that the viewer is only subliminally (subconsciously) aware of them.

**sub dub.** See **mixdown**.

**submaster.** See **protection master**.

**superimposition.** A "super" is an effect where two shots (or more) are held on top of each other full screen.

**SVCD.** Super Video Compact Disk. An upgraded VCD in most aspects which uses MPEG-2. See also **VCD**.

**sweetening.** Adding extra audio elements to an effect to make it work.

**switcher.** Machine used in broadcast, live tapings, and postproduction that allows the operator to select video and audio sources and make transitional effects between them.

**sync (shortened from synchronize).** Align recorded picture and sound so they play together as originally shot and can be edited.

**sync block.** The heavy metal body of a film synchronizer.

**sync pop.** A 1,000-Hz beep tone placed on the audio head and tail leader to keep sync during screenings, sound editing, and sound mixing.

**synthesizer, a.k.a. synth.** An electronic instrument that produces an endless variety of sounds and music that may imitate instruments or create new sounds. There are hard (hardware) synths that plug in to DAWs (ProTools almost universally) and soft (software) synths that export the composer's MIDI file into the DAW.

**tail leader.** Piece of film or tape or a digital clip attached to the end of a show for the purpose of maintaining sync between picture and sound. Tail leader runs for a few seconds after LFOP. See also **tail pop.**

**tail pop.** A sync pop that appears on the audio track two seconds into the tail leader, often corresponding to a flash frame or a frame with the word "End" printed on it. See also **sync pop.**

**take.** A shot that starts (or ends) with a camera slate (clapstick).

**tapeless workflow, a.k.a. file-based workflow.** Filmmaking process where dailies are imported from a video camera that shot on card, disk, file, or film, edited on a digital system, and exported as a file.

**TB.** See **terabyte**.

**TBC.** See **Time Base Corrector**.

**TCP/IP.** The standard protocol suite for data communications and the Internet, e.g., IP addresses.

**TCR.** See **time code reader**.

**TD.** Technical Director. Upon getting the director's command over the headset, the TD switches the videotape from angle to angle on sitcoms, sports events, and major talk shows.

**telecine operator.** See **colorist**.

**telecine.** Transfer of film to tape.

**temp dub.** A temp mix.

**terabyte.** TB. 1,024 gigabytes or 1 trillion bytes. A unit of measurement used to measure computer file sizes, data storage, and memory.

**textless.** A background bed of shots — the credit material — without the credits, used to redo credits or to make foreign or other versions of the show.

**TIFF.** Tag Image File Format. A widely used photo and graphic image file.

**Tiger.** Apple's SAN. See also **SAN**.

**tilt.** Shot where camera moves vertically up and down or down and up.

**time base corrector.** A TBC is an essential electronic device inside a videotape machine that corrects timing errors in the video signal and regulates the signal's video and chroma level, hue, and setup during playback.

**time-code generator.** Electronic machine that adds (creates, syncs, or records) time code to a tape.

**time-code reader.** A stand-alone device or one that's part of a playback machine or a time code generator that reads LTC and VITC time code frame accurately.

**time-code slate.** See **smart slate**.

**time code.** Code based on clock time which is recorded on each frame of a video or audio tape.

**time line.** Graphic representation of a cut on a digital editing system. A horizontal bar graph of a cut which reads left to right, starting with the first edit and ending with the last.

**timer.** Film lab person who times a film print.

**timing.** Setting the red, yellow, and blue printer lights and adjusting the degree of lightness or darkness on each shot or reel. Also used referred to as grading. During the digital intermediate process, grading, timing, and color correcting are used interchangeably to mean the same thing.

**TOD.** Time of Day. Time code that runs continuously and in sync with clock time.

**tracking, videotape:** Adjusting the position of a tape head during playback to produce the strongest signal.

**tracking, music:** When the music editor is responsible for finding, arranging, and editing the music in a scene or a show. Frequently a temp dub is tracked for any show or project that cannot afford original music.

**tracking shot, a.k.a. dolly shot.** Shot where camera follows the action (often a character) while mounted on a dolly that is pushed along a set of temporary tracks laid down on the ground.

**transcode.** Convert from one digital format to another.

**transfer.** Recording picture or sound from one medium or format to another for viewing or editing.

**transition effect.** Effect, such as a dissolve or wipe, which moves the action from one cut to another.

**trim (verb):** Shortening a scene by removing footage. **(noun):** Piece of film (picture or sound) cut out of the show.

**trim bin.** Metal bin with bracket and pins for holding trims on shows that are editing on an upright Moviola.

**trim box.** Labeled box for storing Moviola rolls and KEM rolls on racks for editing.

**trim tab.** A thick piece of paper inserted into a Moviola roll that gives its scene and take number along with a short description of the scene and its start and end ink code.

**TRT.** Total running time of a reel or show.

**TS.** Tail slate. Slate after the action is completed at the end of the take.

**tubby.** Overpowering, low frequency sounds attenuated through EQ'ing.

**two-shot.** A shot with two characters' faces that is usually framed medium.

**uncircled takes.** On a film show, takes shot but not circled for printing. Also known as B neg, these takes may be printed — as desired or required — during editing.

**unit.** An edited reel of mag track. For every film picture reel there are many sound units. Also called an element. A term used when sound is edited on film.

**Unity.** Avid's SAN. See also **SAN**.

**Universal master.** Videotape format from which all distribution formats can be derived.

**upcut.** Cut off a line at the head or tail so that part of it is missing.

**uprez, a.k.a. upconvert.** Convert from a lower resolution to a higher resolution, e.g., from SD to HD.

**UPS.** Uninterruptible power supply. A UPS prevents electrical power surges, drops, or outages from damaging or destroying the digital editing system.

**varispeed.** Altering the rate at which a TV show runs by speeding it up (usually) or slowing it down to fit its prescribed time slot.

**VCD.** Video Compact Disk. A CD-ROM standard that plays up to 80 minutes of full motion video and audio at near-VHS quality, which was introduced in 1993, three years before the DVD was introduced. Was widely used in Asia and plays on Asian-made CD and DVD equipment. VCD uses MPEG-1 for compression and is easier to produce than a DVD. It is professionally produced for corporate projects since it plays on a PC but not for the consumer market in the U.S. due to its inferiority to DVD and its incompatibility with most U.S. CD and DVD players.

**vertical blanking.** Similar to the film frame line that divides one frame of film from another, vertical blanking defines sequential units of videotape picture information. It also encapsulates time code, sync pulses, the ability to record test patterns, and closed-captioning info. It occurs when the scanning beam moves from the bottom of one video field to the top of the next field. See also **blanking**.

**VFX.** Visual Effects. Digital effects created or completed during postproduction such as blue screen, composites, key frames, etc.

**visible time code.** Longitudinal time code (see also **LTC**) burnt in (superimposed) over video so that the image and time code can be seen together.

**VITC.** Vertical Interval Time Code. Time code that's encoded on the "video frame line" (the vertical interval between video frames of the video signal) as a series of black and white pulses during production. Can be read during pause mode and can encode other info such as reel number and film key code. It requires special decks to decode it so it can be read and must be regenerated with each dub as it deteriorates.

**volume.** See **gain.**

**VOT.** Reporter's Voice on Tape. News editing term for voice over.

**VTR.** Videotape recorder. Tape deck (analog or digital) that records video and audio.

**VU.** Volume unit for both analog and digital signals.

**VU meter.** Calibrates audio to ensure consistent levels throughout a show by displaying the dB (decibel) level of the audio during mixing or recording.

**walla.** Non-sync background conversation made up of indistinguishable words voiced by actors.

**WAV** or **WAVE.** Standard PCM-type audio file format created by Microsoft. See also **PCM**.

**white out.** Effect where a shot cuts or dissolves to white. Often involves organic elements such as a light, a camera flashbulb, or steam.

**wide shot.** (WS) A shot framed wide that encompasses much if not all of the action.

**wild line.** Nonsync sound-only line of dialogue spoken by an actor.

**wild sound.** See **wild track**.

**wild track.** WT. Sound effect that is recorded nonsync, i.e., without picture.

**window burn.** See **visible time code**.

**window dub.** See **visible time code**.

**window size.** Aspect ratio of video for Web. See also **aspect ratio.**

**wipe.** A transitional effect where the incoming shot replaces the outgoing shot by appearing to wipe (erase) it from the screen.

**worldizing**. Aligning audio elements — usually ADR or Foley — to match a character's environment by placing them in a live room "world" to make them sound more real.

**work print.** Positive print struck from the developed OCN and printed by the lab so that the colors are true but not fully timed. Used to view, edit, and project film.

**work track.** Sound reel that the sound editor works with. A dupe of the production track, it's also referred to as the 1:1 (one to one) or guide track.

**WT.** See **wild track**.

**WYSIWYG**. Acronym for What You See Is What You Get. Pronounced "wizzy wig," this expression is used to describe a myriad of works-in-progress. It's applicable to color correcting, the creation of titles or effects, and to any situation where a draft allows you to see what the final product will look like.

**XDCAM.** Sony's product line that records to disk or SxS flash memory cards and integrates into tapeless and tape-based workflows.

**XML.** eXtensable Mark-up Language. A simple, adaptable text format developed for Web page information exchange and electronic publishing used to exchange project info within digital editing systems, notably FCP.

**Xsan.** FCP's SAN. See also **SAN**.

**YUV, a.k.a. YIQ and Y'CBCR**. Three-channel color space that encodes luma and chroma data and is the NTSC standard for broadcasting all tapes and files.

# Bibliography

Aesthetics issue, March/April, 2000, *The Motion Picture Editors Guild Newsletter.*

Almo, Laura, "Navigating the Changing Waters: A Panel of TV Editors Discuss the State of Their Craft," Vol. 30, No. 6, Sept/Oct 2009, *Editors Guild Magazine.*

Amyes, Tim. *Audio Post Production in Video and Film.* Boston: MA. Focal Press, 1998.

Art House Movies, Independent Films website, "Post Production Sound," 2002. *www.arthousemovies.com/arthousemovies_post_production_sound.htm*

Avid Community Blog. http://community.avid.com/blogs/buzz/archive/2010/03/05/alice-in-wonderland-s-jc-bond-answers-questions-from-the-industry-about-what-it-was-like-to-edit-tim-burton-s-3d-spin-on-the-classic-tale.aspx

Beacham, Frank, "A Field Guide to TV News Editing," September 2, 2010, *TV News Check.*

Browne, Steven. *Video Editing, A Postproduction Primer, Fourth Edition.* Boston, MA: Focal Press, 2002.

Bullock, Tom (Film Guy). *Film Editing Nutz and Boltz, Sound Editing Nutz and Boltz* (one volume), Emeryville, CA: Metro International, Inc., 1994.

Burder, John. *16mm Film Cutting.* Boston, MA: Focal Press, 1997.

"Carol Littleton: In Praise of *Greed*," December 3, 1999, Editors Net website, *www.uemedia.com/CPC/editorsnet/index.shtml.*

Case, Dominic. *Film Technology in Post Production.* Oxford, UK: Focal Press, 1997.

Castellucci, Cecil and Cristina Clapp, "Interview with Nina Gilberti, Editor, *Wasteland*," October 21, 1999. Editors Net, www.uemedia.com/CPC/editorsnet/index.shtml.

Cercel, Elif, Interview with John Sayles, Writer/Director/Editor, *Limbo*," June 4, 1999.

Chunky, Thunder "Interview: Pixar, titles and type with Susan Bradley," Feb 19, 2008, www.thunderchunky.co.uk/articles/pixar-titles-and-type-with-susan-bradley

Dashwood, Tim. "A Beginner's Guide to Shooting Stereoscopic 3D." http://www.dvinfo.net/article/acquisition/a-beginners-guide-to-shooting-stereoscopic-3d.html, May 1st, 2010.

Editors Net www.uemedia.com/CPC/editorsnet/index.shtml.

Cercel, Elif, "Interview with Mary Pat Plottner, First Assistant Editor, *The Phantom Menace*," May 19, 1999. Editors Net www.uemedia.com/CPC/editorsnet/index .shtml.

Cercel, Elif and Trevor Anthony, "Interview with Lee Unkrich, Editor, *A Bug's Life*," December 29, 1998, *Motion Picture Editor's Guild Newsletter*.

Clark, Barbara and Susan J. Spohr. *Post Production for TV and Film: Managing the Process*, Boston, MA: Focal Press, 2002.

Clark, Jim and John H. Myers, *The Dream Repairman: Adventures in Film Editing*, Crockett, TX: LandMarc Press, 2010.

"Conrad Gonzalez Edits *The Sopranos*," January 10, 2000. Avid Universe, www.uemedia .com/CPC/editorsnet/index.shtml

Coleman, Lori Jane & Diana Friedberg, *Make the Cut: A Guide to Becoming a Successful Assistant Editor in Film and TV*, Boston, MA: Focal Press, 2010.

Cooke, Christopher, "Action Cut!" Winter 2000 article in *American Cinema Editor Magazine*.

"Creative Challenges in Television Part 1," November/December 2001, *The Motion Picture Editors Guild Magazine Vol. 22, No. 5*.

Crittenden, Roger. *Film and Video Editing*. London, UK: Chapman and Hall, 1995.

Cutting, James, DeLong, Jordan, and Nothelfer, Christine, "Attention and the Evolution of Hollywood Film," February 5, 2010, *Psychological Science Online*.

Dancyger, Ken. *The Technique of Film and Video Editing, History, Theory, and Practice, Fifth Edition*. Boston, MA: Focal Press, 2011.

———, *The Technique of Film and Video Editing, History, Theory, and Practice, Third Edition*. Boston, MA: Focal Press, 2002.

Dmytryk, Edward. *On Film Editing, An Introduction to the Art of Film Construction*. Boston, MA: Focal Press, 1990.

Essman, Scott, "Controlled Chaos: Music Editing on 'Any Given Sunday' A Conversation with Bill Abbott," Vol. 21, No. 1 - Jan/Feb 2000, *The Motion Picture Editors Guild Newsletter*.

Film Sound website, *www.filmsound.org/randythom/contact.html*, Thom, Randy, "Designing a Movie for Sound," 1999 & 1998.

Frazer, Bryant. "Editing for 3D on *Alice in Wonderland*." http://www.studiodaily.com/ filmandvideo/currentissue/Editing-for-3D-on-Alice-in-Wonderland, February 25, 2010.

Frost, Jacqueline B. *Cinematography for Directors*, Studio City, CA: Michael Wiese Productions, 2009.

Geffner, David, "First Things First, on the Art of Film Titles," Fall 1997, *Filmmaker Magazine*.

Gilchrist, Garrett, Mar/Apr 2009: Vol. 30, No. 2, "'Monsters' Mash-Up: Joyce Arrastia and Eric Dapkewicz Pioneer 3-D Editing in Animation," *Editors Guild Magazine*.

Goldman, Michael, "Boxing Pamela: Editor Martin Goes the Distance on 'The Fighter' and Scores a TKO," Vol. 32, No. 1, Jan/Feb 2011, *The Editors Guild Magazine.*

Hand, Randall, "Post Production Changes explored at Alpha Dog's Pre-NAB Editor's Lounge," April 8, 2011, VizWorld, www.vizworld.com/.

Harris, Brooks, "Advanced Authoring Format and Media Exchange Format," Vol. 24, No. 3 - May/June 2003, *The Editors Guild Magazine.*

Hawkins, Erik, "Cartoon Cutups: Music Editing for TV Animation," June 1, 2000, *Electronic Musician.*

Henry, Mo, "Negative Cutting in the Age of Digital Intermediates" Vol. 1, April 2010, *The AMIA Tech Review.*

www.hitfix.com/blogs/awards-campaign-2009/posts/wes-anderson-talks-black-swan -with-oscar-nominee-andy-weisblum, "Wes Anderson talks 'Black Swan' with Oscar nominee Andy Weisblum: An interesting conversation into the process of the editor" by Gregory Ellwood.

Hollyn, Norman. *The Film Editing Room Handbook, How to Tame the Chaos of the Cutting Room, Fourth Edition.* Berkeley, CA: Peachpit Press 2010.

Igel, Rachel, "Let It Cook: An Interview with Terry Williams and Danny Greene," The Motion Picture Editors Guild Directory of Members 1996–1997, LA: CA; The Motion Picture Editors Guild, IATSE Local 776, 1997.

"Interview with Christopher Boyes, Sound Designer, Titanic," Editors Net, 1997. www.uemedia.com/CPC/editorsnet/index.shtml.

"Interview with Dane Davis, Sound Designer, The Matrix," 1999. Editors Net, www .uemedia.com/CPC/editorsnet/index.shtml.

"Interview with Gary Rydstrom, Sound Designer, *The Haunting,*" August 5, 1999. Editors Net, www.uemedia.com/CPC/editorsnet/index.shtml.

"Interview with Gary Rydstrom, Sound Designer, *Saving Private Ryan,*" 1998. Editors Net, www.uemedia.com/CPC/editorsnet/index.shtml.

Isaza, Miguel, "*Alice in Wonderland*: Exclusive Interview With Sound Designer Supervisor Steve Boeddeker," March 18, 2010, http://designingsound.org/2010/03/alice -in-wonderland-exclusive-interview-with-sound-designersupervisor-steve-boeddeker.

———, "The Sound Design of Avatar," Dec 28, 2009, http://designingsound.org/ 2009/12/the-sound-design-of-avatar/

Johnson, Tom, "Making Contact," Sept 1997. Original URL *http://prostudio.com/studio-sound/sept97/pp_contact.html*

Joplin, Ben, "Spotlight on Oscar Nominee Gwen Yates Whittle '79," March 3, 2010, http:// www.buffaloseminary.org/uploaded/News_Images/Whittle_interview_tahoma.pdf

Kaufman, Debra, "Soundbender: The Aural Adventures of Randy Thom," Vol. 31, No. 4, July-Aug 2010, *Editors Guild Magazine.*

———, "Video Spawned the Editing Star: What Hath MTV Wrought?" Vol. 27, No. 3, May-June 2006, *Editors Guild Magazine.*

Kerner, Marvin M. *The Art of the Sound Effects Editor.* Boston: MA. Focal Press, 1990.

Kiderra, Inga, "Scoring Points," Winter 2000, *USC Trojan Family Magazine.*

Koppl, Rudy, "The Hurt Locker: Blurring the Lines between Sound and Score," 2009, Music from the Movies Media, The Beek Blog, www.musicfromthemovies.com.

Kunkes, Michael, "Avid Enters the Third Dimension: Stereoscopic Capability and Native XDCAM Support in Media Composer 3.5 Release." https://www.editors-guild.com/FromTheGuild.cfm?FromTheGuildid=56, 03/19/2009.

————, Jan/Feb 2010: Vol 31, No. 1, "Dream Capturers: James Cameron's Brave New World of Filmmaking" and "Editing on Another Planet: John Refoua and Stephen Rivkin," *Editors Guild Magazine.*

Lahr, John, "Becoming the Hulk," June 30, 2003, *New Yorker Magazine.*

Lauten, Erin K., "Editing Tragedy: An Interview with Susan Perla, CBS News," November 6, 2001. Editors Net, www.uemedia.com/CPC/editorsnet/index.shtml.

————, "Richard Marks, A.C.E. and Larry Jordan on Editing *Riding in Cars with Boys*," Editors Net www.uemedia.com/CPC/editorsnet/index.shtml, October 25, 2001.

Lissak, Keith, "The Guild Shines at CSUN," Jan/Feb 1999, *The Motion Picture Editors Guild Newsletter.*

LoBrutto, Vincent, *Selected Takes, Film Editors on Editing.* Westport, CT: Greenwood Publishing Group, Incorporated, 1991.

————, *Sound-On-Film, Interviews with Creators of Film Sound.* Westport, CT: Greenwood Publishing Group, Incorporated, 1995.

Lodge, Guy, "Tech Support Interview: The Crafts of *The Hurt Locker*," www.incontention.com/2010/01/07/tech-support-the-crafts-of-the-hurt-locker/

Lustig, Milton, *Music Editing for Motion Pictures*, Fern Park: FL, Hastings House Publishers, 1980.

Matarazzo, Richard, "The Film Titling Industry, Silent Films....Saul Bass....Kyle Cooper....and beyond....," 2003.

May, Julia, "The Art Of Film Title Design Throughout Cinema History," Oct. 4th, 2010, *Smashing Magazine.*

Millar, Gavin and Karel Reisz, *Technique of Film Editing, Second Edition.* Boston, MA: Focal Press, 1995.

Monksfield, Stuart and Lindenkreuz, Morris, "Bones Dailies Open Post Production Framework White Paper, Notes V1.2," DFT Digital Film Technology, 2009.

Monohan, James, "The Art of Cutting Commercials: An Interview With Owen Plotkin," March 20, 2000. Editors Net www.uemedia.com/CPC/editorsnet/index .shtml.

Motion Picture Editors Guild, "What Directors and Others Say About Editors," *Vol. 1, No. 1* - June 1997, *The Motion Picture Editors Guild Special Issue Newsletter.*

Mott, Robert L., *Sound Effect: Radio, TV, and Film.* Boston: MA. Focal Press, 1990.

Murch, Walter, "A Digital Cinema of the Mind? Could Be," May 2, 1999, *New York Times.*

———, *In the Blink of An Eye, A Perspective on Film Editing, Second Edition,* LA, CA: Silman-James Press, 2001.

———, "Stretching Sound to Help the Mind See," October 1, 2000, *New York Times.*

Ohanian, Thomas A., *Digital Non Linear Editing: Editing Film and Video on the Desktop, Second Edition.* Boston, MA: Focal Press, 1998.

———, "Universal Mastering and Resolution coexistence," www.postproduction-buyersguide.com/PDF/Bones Dailies White Paper.pdf

Oldham, Gabriella, *First Cut, Conversations with Film Editors,* Berkeley, CA: University of California Press, 1992.

Optus net website, Matthew Tucker, "Editing and Painting," 1998, copyright, *http://members.optusnet.com.au/~matthewt/Editpaint.htm*

O'Steen, Bobbie, *The Invisible Cut: How Editors Make Movie Magic.* Studio City, CA: Michael Wiese Productions, 2009.

Parisi, Paula, "The Talented Mr. Murch," December 22, 1999. In Editors Net www.uemedia.com/CPC/editorsnet/index.shtml

Peters, Oliver, "Hot Fuzz: Police Raids & Color Grades," May 22, 2007, *Videography.*

———, "The Network for 'The Social Network' — Developing the Post Workflow on David Fincher's New Feature," September 29, 2010 *Videography.*

Reesman, Bryan, "Lisa Gerrard: The Color of Sound," February 1, 2003, *Mix Magazine.*

Rosenblum, Ralph and Robert Karen, *When the Shooting Stops...the Cutting Begins,* 1979, reprinted 1989, NY, NY: Da Capo Press, 1989.

Rowe, Robin, "Bride Stripped Bare: Jonathan Lucas Unveils His Editing Secrets on 'Corpse Bride,' the First Stop-Motion Animation Feature," Vol. 27, No. 3, May-June 2006, *Editors Guild Magazine.*

———, "Remote. Control. Sonoma. Editor Kirk Demorest is a Telecommuter," Vol. 30, No. 3, May-June 2009, *Editors Guild Magazine.*

Ryan, Liz, "Ten Best Careers," May 29, 2011, Bloomberg Businessweek.

Shaw, Steve, "Digital Intermediate: A Real World Guide to the DI Process," white paper for Light Illusion Revision Nov 14, 2009.

Simon, Deke. *Film and Video Budgets,* Studio City, CA: Michael Wiese Productions, 2010.

Skweres, Mary Ann, "The Editor as Storyteller: Reality Shows Stretch the Cutters' Role, July 2004, *Below the Line.*

———, "Swietlik's Saga: How Editing *Inconvenient Truth* Led to *Sicko,*" June 8, 2008, hwww.btlnews.com/

Smith, Howard E. and Paula Parisi, "An Interview with Golden Eddie Winner James Cameron," February 25, 2000, *Motion Picture Editor's Guild Newsletter.*

Sonnenschein, David, *Sound Design: The Expressive Power of Music, Voice, and Sound Effects in Cinema,* Studio City, CA: Michael Wiese Productions, 2001.

Thom, Randy, "More Confessions Of A Sound Designer (A Sound Fails In The Forest Where Nobody Hears It), 1995, http://www.filmsound.org/randythom/confess2.html

Thompson, Roy, *Grammar of the Edit*, Boston: MA. Focal Press, 1993.

Tomlinson, Holman, *Sound for Film and Television*. Boston: MA. Focal Press, 2001.

Truffaut, Francois, *Hitchcock*, NY, NY: Simon and Schuster, 1966.

Twenty4's website, J. Counts, "Just the Beginning: The Art of Film Titles," 2001. *www.twenty4.co.uk/on-line/index.htm*

Van Beeck, Toon, "Dying Industries" Special Report March 2011, www.ibisworld. com

Viers, Ric, *The Sound Effects Bible: How to Create and Record Hollywood Style Sound Effects*, Studio City, CA: Michael Wiese Productions, 2008.

Winter, Jessica, "The Lost Art of Editing," August 13, 2006, *The Boston Globe*.

Woodhall, Woody, *Audio production and Postproduction*, Sudbury, MA: Jones & Bartlett Learning, 2010.

———, "Interview: Charles Martin Inouye, a.k.a. Chuck Martin — Music Editor," February 27, 2009, http://www.blogcatalog.com/blogs/woodys-sound-advice.

———, "Interview: Jeff Toyne — Composer," October 23, 2009, http://www.blogcatalog.com/blogs/woodys-sound-advice.

# Index

16:9, 41–43, 51, 348 *See also* aspect ratio

16mm, 12, 25, 27, 41, 88, 173, 254, 261; and neg cut, 387–388, 390, 392–393

180° rule *See* crossing the line

24 fps, 25, 35, 36, 41, 107, 109, 113, 115, 129, 131, 365 *See also* frame rate

24p, 12, 25, 27, 31, 40, 41, 128, 135, 384, 408

2-pop, 254–255, 355 *See also* sync pop

3:2 pulldown, 109, 131–135

30 fps, 35–37, 41, 113, 115, 129, 131, 225, 365 *See also* frame rate

35mm, 12, 19, 20, 25, 27, 41, 88, 254, 261, 308, 402; in daily database, 107–108; and neg cut, 387–388, 390, 392–393

3-D, 27, 111, 113, 173, 347, 404, 407; disk finish, 355–357; editing, 9, 176, 180–182, 195; and sound, 282, 336; VFX, 55, 235–236; and workflow, 65, 72

4:3, 41–42, 348 *See also* aspect ratio

5:1 sound, 51, 291, 336–337, 356, 397

60i, 25, 36, 40, 41

7:1 sound, 291, 336–337, 356, 397

A frame, 132–133

A roll, 367; in negative cutting, 390, 393, 409

AAF, 312–314, 316, 350, 360, 363, 368, 377; and DI, 400, 403

A/B roll, 393

action, 114, 145, 147, 155, 158, 165; and aspect ratio, 346, 348–349; editing action scenes, 161–162, 168, 169, 172–180; match cutting on, 150–152; parallel, 177–179; shooting, 7–8; and sound and music, 282, 284, 286, 288, 297, 209, 315

Adobe Premiere Pro, 47, 58, 60, 69, 122, 226, 351, 361; transcript program, 92, 118–119 *See also* digital editing systems

ADR, 268, 287, 289, 295, 297, 319; cue sheet, 321, 338; cueing (prepping), 299, 321, 328; editing, 284, 299, 316–318, 320–324; and looping, 291–292, 323; and mix, 327, 331, 332, 336, 337; and post schedule, 80, 82;

purpose of, 320–321; recording, 290, 292, 322–323; and sound workflow, 301

AFE, 360, 363, 368, 369, 377; and DI, 400, 403

ambience, 13, 16, 89, 258, 287, 297; in dialogue editing, 284, 313, 318–320, 324

A-mode, 364–366, 357

analog, 53, 294, 295; tape, 25, 30–31, 34, 49–50, 323; track, 395, 397

angles, 181, and editing, 146, 163, 166, 168, 170, 177, 184; mismatched, 156–157; multi-cam, 200, 202; shooting cuttable, 7–10

animation, 169, 207, 208, 217; 3-D, 197, 235, 266; and digital system, 31, 51, 111, 112; editing, 193–197

AP (answer print), 82, 83, 93, 395–396, 399, 402, 409; and workflows, 73–74, 301, 305, 403

AP (associate producer), 24, 45, 64, 77, 82, 113, 379, 384

archiving, 51, 55, 99, 105, 250–251, 384; and DI, 402, 405; future of, 405–406; news, 102, 103, 213–214

aspect ratio, 32, 41–43, 250, 266, 348

assemble edit, 95, 97, 98, 265

audience, xviii, 4, 6, 8–10, 13, 42, 52, 69, 215, 250; 3-D, 176; and color grading, 253, 401; and credits and titles, 344, 355; documentary, 142, 208, 260; and editors, 143, 146–149, 155, 159, 162–163, 167, 168, 185, 197, 207, 218, 244; sitcom, 199–203; screenings and preview, 255, 258, 265, 266, 272; and sound, music, and mix, 190, 281, 282, 284, 285, 288, 292, 294, 308, 334, 335; and viewing format, 22, 23, 27

audio, 31, 111–113, 116, 294, 300, 312, 314; equipment, 68, 72, 123, 290, 292, 294, 295; files, 286, 313–314, 358; level, 96–97, 120, 258, 263, 264, 291, 295, 367; and online, 364, 367, 368, 383; terms, 16, 17, 19, 20, 289–295; for theater projection, 397, 402 *See also* digital editing system and sound

Avid, xvii, 46, 52, 58–61, 92, 98, 118, 122, 181, 226, 360, 411; codec, 111; files, 109, 313, 368;

and film, 109, 134, 266, 389; ingesting, 69, 70; tracks, 272, 367

B-mode, 365–367
B Neg, 68, 278
B roll, 104, 114, 125, 126, 174; in online 367; in negative cutting, 393, 409
backing up, 51, 53–55, 109, 128, 238, 246–248, 250, 271
batch capture, 106, 106, 377 *See also* digitize and ingest
bars and tone, 96–97, 375 *See also* color bars
beats, in editing, 158, 159, 173–174, 187, 199; music, 190, 216, 244, 308; in sound editing, 287–288
bin, 122, 125–128, 253, 271; and online, 360, 369; VFX, 238
broadcast, 359, 384, 397; and DI, 398, 402, 403; and offline system, 52, 120, 253, 352; and post house, 83, 351, 383; quality tape, 351, 354–355; standards, 39, 41–42, 372, 380–381
budget, 11, 24, 62, 66, 69, 79, 80, 84, 137; dailies, 138; editing, 178; finishing, 351, 357, 400, 408–409; sound, music, and mix, 68, 112, 286, 302, 339–340

C-mode, 365–367
camera report, 88–89
camera roll, 5, 127, 379; and daily tapes, 34, 88, 90; film, 19–21, 119, 123, 129, 132; and ingest, 117–118; and neg cut, 266, 389–391, 393; and telecine, 43, 44; and VFX, 240
capture, *See* batch capture and digitize
CG, *See* character generator
CGI, 81, 180, 235, 236, 278, 378
change list, 273–274, 326
character generator, 80, 371, 408
cheating shots, 161–162, 181, 217, 220
cinematographer, *See* DP (director of photography)
click track, 286, 308
clip, 32, 48, 92, 235, 254, 257, 263; editing, 49, 52, 213, 223–234, 244–246; film, 129–131, 133–135, 274, 389; ingesting, 107, 110, 112, 118, 121; organizing, 50, 122, 125–127, 200, 219; re-linking, 33, 247; storage, 70, 113; sub clipping, 126, 127; syncing, 122–123; trimming, 241–244
codec, xvii, 111–112, 120, 207, 250, 312, 360, 405
coding, 21–22, *See also* ink code, key code, and time code
color bars, 96–97, 106, 265, 355, 375
color grade, 18, 30, 43–45; and DI, 399–401, 403–405; on offline system, 253–254, 351–354; at post house, 379–381; and post schedule, 80, 82; and workflow, 67–71, 73, 74

colorist, 18, and color grading, 44–45, 379–381; and DI, 45, 401, 405; and film finish, 43, 72, 74, 386; and telecine, 43–45, 90, 109
comedy, 26, 169; editing, 159, 164, 170, 171, 177, 186, 197–204; multi-cam, 200–202; single cam, 202–204
communication, 5, 77–78, 92
composer, 82, 191, 257, 285–287, 298, 303–305, 339; composing process, 302, 306–308, 324, 333; creating dubs for, 32, 68, 95, 265, 268, 314; and scoring, 308–311
consolidate, 249
continuity, 145–147, 150, 152–153, 156, 168, 175, 220; in color grading, 45, 380; sheet, 261–263, 266, 276–277, 314; shooting for, 7 *See also* match cut and mismatch
coverage, 6, 93–95, 142, 174, 217
credits, 55, 82, 183, 344–350, 361, 372–373, 382, 408 *See also* titling
cross cutting, 177–179
crossing the line, 8–10, 168, 156–157, 167, 181
CTM, 380–381
cue, 289, 299, 311; ADR, 321–323, 338; dialogue, 318, 320; and mix, 331–332, 334, 336; music, 286, 297, 298, 303–305, 307–309, 324–325; sheet, 289, 301, 326–332; sound, 315–317
cut (noun) 17, 115, 125; final cut, 51, 52, 115, 218, 268, 274, 316, 390; first cut, 68, 76, 218, 228, 234, 241, 252–253, 268–269; fine and rough cut, 144, 226, 247, 252; motivating a cut, 143, 148, 180, 256; paper cut, 92, 105, 142, 173, 208, 266, 268, 307; and post schedule, 80–81; prepping for screening, 69, 91, 246, 252–266; screening, 20, 54, 68, 69, 266–271; straight cut, 162–163, 241, 244–245, 261, 320 *See also* locked cut, negative cut, and sequence
cut (verb) *See* edit
cut point, 15, 145, 155, 224, 238
cutaway, 10, 95; editing in, 144, 155, 156, 160, 174, 189, 208, 215, 232
cutback frame, 387–388, 390, 392
cutting patterns, 164–171
cutting room, 4–6, 23, 29, 99, 234; and dailies, 35, 36, 43, 44, 78, 84, 85, 91, 101, 102, 114, 123; digital, 29, 30, 45–58, 62, 81, 389; and editing, 90, 187, 201, 215, 270; screening in, 263; setting up, 65, 74–77; terms 14–21; and VFX, 241, 362; and workflows, 67, 71–73
cutlist, 20–21, 51, 72, 83, 115, 119, 129, 240, 265, 273; and DI, 400, 403; creating, 266; and neg cutting, 386, 388–392, 394; verifying data for, 129, 130, 135; and workflow, 73, 74

D-mode, 365, 367
dailies, 16, 44–45, 49, 77, 128, 200, 407; film, 19–20, 43, 109, 129–135, 371; ingesting, 97, 119–122; prep for ingest, 112–119;

organizing after ingest, 122–128; reports, 84–91; screening and viewing, 52, 78, 263; and workflow, 66–69, 71–73

database 51, 127, 240; creating, 106, 107, 118, 119, 386, 388; film data, 129–133, 266; log, 106–109; sound data, 135

DAW, 289–290, 312, 327; in music editing, 303, 305, 306, 310, 324; in sound editing, 68, 283, 295, 296, 299, 301, 314, 316–317, 321, 328 *See also* Pro Tools

delivery requirements, 24, 115, 260, 320, 337, 351, 352, 382, 384; and workflow, 69–71

DI, 30, 43, 48, 50, 80, 83; and film, 21, 72–74, 115, 237, 266, 273, 387; finishing by, 397–400; process, 400–403

dialogue editing, 6, 284, 317–320, 323, 327; in animation, 196; scenes, 185–186

digital audio workstation, *See* DAW

digital cinema, 402, 404

digital editing system, 21, 32, 35, 49–50, 248–249, 312; choosing, 62–63; common systems, 58–61; data entry on, 117–119; editing on, 46, 49, 162–164, 189, 223–235; and features, 34, 49–58; finishing project on, 347, 351; history, 15; ingesting on, 43, 110–112, 119–121; organizing dailies on, 122, 125–127; prepping dailies on, 66, 92, 97, 106; prepping neg cut on, 385, 388–391; prepping for online on, 361–363, 365–369; saving on, 246–248, 250–251; and screenings, 263–264; setting up project on, 13–116; syncing on, 122–124; terms, 45–48; trimming on, 241–245; verifying film data on, 129 135; and VFX, 234–235, 237–239, 245; and workflows, 67–74, 403 *See also* database and media management

digital intermediate, *See* DI

digital video tape, *See* DV

digitize, 25, 49–50, 110, 119, 122, 133, 135, 391 *See also* ingest

director, xi, xv, 4, 45, 80–82, 188; and ADR, 322–323; and color grading, 44–45, 82, 279, 402, 405; and dailies, 68, 78, 92; and dialogue editing, 318–320; and editing, 29, 75, 92, 183, 184, 187, 189, 196, 216; and editor, 29, 142, 147, 149, 175, 179, 180, 186, 204, 207, 215, 218; and finishing, 357, 371, 395; and mix, 329–332, 334–335, 337; and music editing, 285, 287, 297, 298, 303, 306, 309; and recutting, 267–269, 271–273, 275; and screening, 81, 125, 255, 263, 265, 267–269; and shooting, 5–6, 10, 41, 44, 88, 91, 93, 113, 349; and sound editing, 255, 258, 283, 287, 289, 295–296, 298, 316, 318, 319; and titling, 344–346, 350

disk finish, 23–25, 27, 80, 83, 351, 352, 355–357; and workflows, 71, 301, 305, 358

DIT, 44, 68, 69, 380; report, 89, 91

DME, 337, 396

documentary, 23, 105, 262; editing, 185, 189, 190, 208–210, 234, 260; starting to edit, 142–143

Dolby, 397, 402, 408, 409

double system, 17–18, 24; and workflow, 66, 67, 72

downrez, 48, 90; and workflow, 66, 67

DP, 4, 41, 287, 346, 395; and color grading, 44, 45, 68, 82, 379; and DI, 400–402, 404, 405

drop frame, 37–39, 361, 364

dub (copy), 18, 31, 51, 138, 240; cuts, 265, 268; dailies, 117–119; prepping tapes for; 95–99; and time code, 32–34, 119; and workflows, 66, 68, 69, 72

dub (mix sound), *See* mix

DV, 11, 25, 27, 30, 31, 40, 47, 381, 402; and digital system, 49, 50, 60, 111; and time code, 33, 35

DVD, *See* disk finish

E-mode, 365, 367

edit decision list, *See* EDL

editing, xviii; 3-D, 9, 176, 180–2, 195; action scenes, 172–180; budget, 287; and character arc, 185–188; comedy, 159, 164, 170, 171, 177, 186, 197–204; commercials, promos, and PSAs; 204–205; corporate videos, 207; cross cutting, 177–179; cutting patterns, 164–171; dialogue scenes, 185–186; on digital system, 49, 223–235; documentary, 185, 189, 190, 208–210, 234, 260; finding a job, 410–417; getting started, 142–146; music, 184, 190–191, 255, 257–259, 324–325; narration, 159, 160, 167, 170, 188–12–189, 208, 268; native editing, 70, 11, 112, 135, 360–361; news, 23, 59, 103, 105, 123, 250, 256, 357, 360; non-destructive, 46; organizing dailies for, 122–128; reasons to cut, 146–149; recutting, 81, 126, 144, 173, 188, 245, 255, 246, 260, 261, 263, 326; terms, 14–21; *See also* digital editing system, invisible editing, match cutting, offline and online editing, linear, nonlinear, rhythm, TV editing, trimming, and VFX

editor, xi, xv, 53, 61, 77, 193, 287, 289, 400; and actor, 161, 187–188; and director, 29, 142, 147, 149, 175, 179, 180, 186, 204, 207, 215, 218, 269–273, 345; offline editor, 29, 330; online editor, 29–30, 313, 345, 350, 359–363, 365–367, 369–382; picture editor, 11, 16, 24, 92, 149, 152, 169–171, 247, 256, 269; VFX, 48, 77, 180, 240; and workflow, 65, 68, 69, 72 *See also* ADR, dialogue, Foley, music editor, and sound editor

Editors Guild, 252, 414, 417, 421

editor's prayer, 140

EDL, 363–364; and 24p, 135; and color grading, 379; creating, 240, 363, 365–368; and DI, 83,

400, 403; and online, 359, 363, 369, 375–377; and sound editing, 301, 313, 316

effects, *See* SFX (sound effects) and VFX (visual effects)

export, 36, 48, 49, 51, 74, 265, 355, 367; EDL, 365, 369; film lists, 389, 399

eyeline, 8, 150, 154, 168

film finish, 23–25, 27, 74, 80, 82, 83, 351, 352; and workflows, 71, 301, 305

fill, *See* slug

film, 4, 10, 148; continuity sheet, 262, 277; daily reports, 85–90; festival, 23, 24, 27, 260, 302; future of, 405–406; history of editing on, 14–15, 422; measuring, 22–23; and digital editing system, 46, 49, 50, 57–58; opticals, 73, 80, 82, 237, 379, 386, 389–391, 394; screening on, 265–266; terms, 19–21 *See also* 24 fps, sync, and telecine

film finish, 27, 39, 43, 80, 83, 312, 409; database, 108–109; via DI, 397–404; formats, 23–25; via negative cut, 385–397; setting up project on digital system for, 113, 115, 116; verifying data for, 117–119, 129–135; and workflows, 72–74, 112, 301, 305, 394–396

film lab, *See* lab

film leader, *See* leader

film look, 11–12, 41

film negative, 19–22, 73–74, 90

film recorder, 399–400, 402, 403

film scanner, 44, 387, 398–400, 403

final cut, 51, 52, 115, 218, 268, 274, 316, 390

Final Cut Pro, xvii, xxiii, 36, 65, 69, 111, 411; and dailies, 106, 122, 126–128; description, 51, 58–61; files, 313, 361, 365, 369; and film, 109, 134–135, 266, 389; finishing on, 351, 354, 380; operating, 92, 98, 116, 241, 246, 250; outputting tracks from, 260, 264, 367; titling on, 347, 349, 382 *See also* digital editing systems

finding an editing job, 410–417, 420–421

finishing format, 62, 348; choosing, 22–25, 27 *See also* disk, file, film, and tape finish

FireWire, 47, 66, 110, 263, 438

flash frame, 255, 387, 438

Foley, 80, 82, 290, 292, 297, 339; creating, 287, 300, 321; editing, 284, 299, 316, 317, 320, 327, 328; mixing, 331–332, 337; in sound workflow, 301, 396

formats, 17, 47, 72, 110–112, 137, 173, 211, 263; and aspect ratio, 41–41; audio, 108, 300, 302; and DI, 48, 397–399, 402; file, 109, 357, 368–369; future of, 405–406; and offline system, 45, 69, 70, 115, 225–226, 250, 260; and online, 359, 365, 367, 370, 384; shooting, 23–25, 84, 354–355, 381; tape, 31, 37, 40, 260 *See also* finishing format

formatting, 81, 83, 352, 361, 383

fps, *See* frame rate

frame rate, 25, 32, 35–37, 40, 225, 236, 240, 250, 257, 312, 359

frame re-use, 387–388, 390

frame size, 40, 312, 356

FX, *See* SFX (sound effects) or VFX (visual effects)

glossary of terms, 425–462

green screen, 29, 166, 168, 217, 278; creating, 237–239

handles, 196, 249, 314, 390

history, of editing tools and terms, 14–15, 327; of montage, 182–183

HD, 30, 49, 383, 384; and 24p, 41, 107; aspect ratio, 41–42; camera, 10–11; frame size and scanning, 40; in multi-cam, 200; in news cutting, 211, 213; and project setup, 113, 115; tape formats, 25, 27, 225, 348, 381; and transcoding, 47–48, 83, 117, 272; and workflow, 65, 68, 10, 111, 403

high definition, *See* HD

IATSE, *See* Editors Guild

import, 25, 47–51, 92, 119, 226, 253, 347; database, 131, 386; and DI, 400; and disk authoring, 357, 358; and online, 375, 377; project files, 313–314; and sound and music editing, 256, 316, 324, 383; VFX, 68, 235

ink code, 20, 22, 117, 119, 132, 138; and change list; 273, 274

ingest, 24, 25, 46–48, 76, 92, 128, 249, 379; dailies, 49–50, 78, 91, 119, 121, 122, 125; on film finish show, 39, 134, 266, 386, 394, 396; and lost media, 33, 247; prepping dailies for, 97, 101, 103, 105–107, 110–118; and workflows, 66–73, 305, 403

input, *See* ingest

IP, *See* interpositive

insert edit, on time line, 229–231; on tape, 97, 98, 265

internegative, 395, 402, 403, 409

interpositive, 395, 402, 409

invisible editing, 150, 152, 156, 163; and traditional style editing, 166, 168–170

jobs (finding), 410–417

jump cut, xv, 152, 156–157, 168, 170, 183, 189, 205, 220, 369

key code, 20–22, 32, 90, 109, 117–119, 127, 240; and change list; 273, 274; and cutlist, 266, 273; and neg cutting, 386, 388–392; in verifying film data, 129–130, 132–134

lab, 4, 17, 50, 52, 345, 409; and dailies, 5, 20, 85, 88, 90; and DI, 402, 405; and neg cut process, 19, 44, 72–74, 83, 266, 386, 390, 392, 393, 395–97; report, 90, 91 labeling, 19, 99, 101, 107, 200, 238, 246, 250, 375, 381; bins, 125, 126; cuts (sequences), 54, 224, 225, 365, 369, 388; shots, 52, 85, 92–95, 99, 106, 107, 257; sound reels for mix, 326, 327; tracks, 225, 319, 327, 328

laugh track, 203

layback, 18, 67, 71, 83, 294, 301, 368, 383, 408

leader, 97, 254, 255, 265, 312, 355, 391, 393, 409

letterbox, 42–43, 362 See also aspect ratio

level, 120, 367; audio, 96, 97, 258, 263, 264, 291, 294, 295, 319, 332, 333, 336; video, 53, 353, 354

Lightworks, 58, 59, 134, 209

linear, 15, 59, 168, 205; editing, 28–29, 46; online, 359–360, 362, 363, 365–367, 374–377

locked cut, 17, 80–82, 111, 220, 249, 275; and DI, 48, 397, 400–401; getting to lock, 196, 271, 274; and neg cut, 20–21, 385–386, 388–389, 391, 394; and online, 352, 355, 359, 361–363, 369, 370, 376, 377, 383; and sound and music editing, 191, 258, 273, 283, 316, 301, 306, 311, 326; unlocking, 275, 336, 378; and workflow, 50, 68–74

log, 5, 51, 102, 105, 106, 142, 362, 363; database, 106–110, 117, 119; production, 14, 84, 85

logging, 49, 128; dailies, 34, 101–105, 107, 113, 219; shots, 50, 101, 107; transcript, 219, 268

loop, 291–292, 321, 323, 324, 339; group, 287, 292, 323, 339 See also ADR

LTO, 251, 382, 384, 445

LUT, 44, 69, 379, 401

master, 18, 19, 359, 381; air, 379, 383–384; CTM, 381; and DI, 399, 402–403, 405, 408; in disk finish, 357, 358; file, 71, 103, 105, 294, 351–352, 369; film, 402–403; log, 102; and online, 362–364, 366, 368–369, 373, 375–376; protection, 378, 408; tape, 30, 83, 96, 103, 294, 351–352; and workflows, 67, 69, 71, 73, 301, 305 See also printmaster

master shot, 93, 95, 122; 3-D, 180; editing, 144–146, 149, 165, 171; shooting, 6, 7, 202–203

match cutting, 3-D, 353; in color grading, 353; in editing, xv, 8, 93, 150–152, 157, 166, 168, 201, 219, 244; in online, 359, 361, 362, 383; in negative cutting, 21, 115, 388, 389, 391–394; in sound editing, 291, 309, 317–319, 322, 324 See also continuity and mismatch

M & E, 320, 337, 340

measuring, 21–22, 32, 226; sequences, 246, 260–262

media, 46, 53, 54, 99, 112, 247, 263, 316, 406; and color grading, 379, 381; corrupt; 98; and DI, 83, 400; file, 48, 50, 110, 117, 312, 313, 367, 368, 377; ingesting, 50, 117, 119, 120, 237; management, 50, 55, 56, 121, 213, 249–250, 378; and online, 80, 363; re-linking, 77, 247, 250, 316, 360, 363; reusable, 24, 128,

247; sharing, 48, 58, 69–70, 371; source, 30, 35, 37, 117, 213, 381; storage, 48–50, 113, 251, 263, 294, 370; and time code, 33, 34; and workflows, 69, 72, 112

memory card, 23–25, 27, 32, 46

MIDI, 306–307

mismatch, xv, 7, 153–157, 161, 164, 166, 168, 219, 253, 270 See also continuity and match cutting

mix, 19, 203, 273, 287, 330–331, 334–337; on offline system, 54, 246, 256, 258–260, 264, 267, 272; music, 257, 286, 297, 303, 305, 309–310; and post schedule, 80, 82, 83; prepping for, 311, 317–320, 326–330; terms, 289–295; and workflow, 67–74, 301 See also pre-mix, temp mix, and sweetening

mixdown, 30, 292, 324, 337

mixer (audio tool), 53, 116, 120, 289–290

mixer (rerecording engineer), 12, 19, 218, 220, 272, 281–283, 292, 330–337

monitor, 49, 97, 200, 266, 383, 392; 16:9, 41–42, 51; graphics, 52; NTSC, 52, 354

mono audio, 272, 292, 337

montage, 168, 182–185, 190, 191, 208, 231, 288, 388

MOS, 5, 89, 123, 130, 170

Moviola, 14, 21, 247, 271

MTV, 104, editing style, 14, 166–171 See also music video

multi-cam, 80, 122, 218, 360; comedy, 104, 200–203 See also music video

music, 29, 68–69, 82, 116, 170, 247; acquiring, 302–305; beats, 287–289, cueing, 298; department, 285–286; designing, 295, 298; and digital system, 49, 51, 54, 225, 231, 244; editing, 184, 190–191, 255, 257–259, 324–325, 422; power of, 284–285; prep for editing, 311–314, 324; and story, 168, 286–287; terms, 289–295; tools, 314–315; workflow, 305

music editor, 286–287, 289–290, 298–299, 302–304, 324–325; and mix, 314, 331, 333; and scoring, 309–310

music supervisor, 77, 218, 285–286, 298, 308, 324

music video, 26, 75, 80, 173, 268, 359, 402; editing, 215–216, 257; labeling, 104

MXF, 360, 363, 368, 377

narration, 68, 278; and dialogue editor, 317–318; editing, 159, 160, 167, 170, 188–12–189, 208, 268; editing on digital system, 231–234, 243, 244; recording, 53, 256; tracks, 225, 259, 312

native editing, 70, 11, 112, 135, 360–361

negative, 19–20, 22, 250; and color grading, 379; and DI, 398–400; internegative, 401–403; and telecine, 19, 90, 109, 119, 129, 129–130, 132–134, 138, 386; and VFX, 237; and workflow, 50, 72, 73

negative cutter, 21, 74, 83, 391–393
negative cutting, 21, 80, 83, 391–395, 408–409; and lab, 44, 90, 237, 266; prepping for, 109–110, 115, 129–135, 138, 273, 386–391
network (TV), 71, 82, 294, 346; broadcast standards, 351, 352, 354–355, 366, 383; delivering to, 70, 83, 378, 384; formatting for, 361, 383, 384; ratings, 275; timing specs, 260–261, 376; viewing cuts, 82, 265, 272, 274
news editing, 23, 59, 103, 105, 123, 250, 256, 357, 360; process, 210–245
NLE, See nonlinear
non-drop frame, 37–39, 129, 130, 361, 368
nonlinear, 15, 59, 168; editing, 28–29, 45, 46, 54; online, 359–360, 362, 363, 374, 377–378; See also digital editing system
NTSC, 35–37, 39–40, 380; monitor, 52, 135, 354

offline, 17, 112; budget; 348, 362; and color grading, 380, 381; and credits, 349, 350, 382; cut, 47, 82, 313, 355, 359, 360, 370; editing, 29–30, 215, 351, 373, 376, 377; tapes, 39, 97, 98, 103; and VFX, 376
OCN, See negative
OMF, 220, 312–314, 316, 324, 337, 350, 360, 363, 368, 377; and DI, 400, 403
online, 29–30, 39; editor, 29, 33, 39, 97, 98, 351; files, 102–103, 109, 313, 363–369; post online session; 350, 378–384; prepping for, 361–370; process, 359–361; schedule and budget, 80–82, 278, 408; session, 370–378; and sound, 256–257; and workflows, 67, 69–71, 301, 305
optical, 350, 409; disk, 24, 66; and DI, 402, 403; film, 73, 80, 82, 237, 379, 386, 389–391, 394; track, 74, 396–397
organizing, 5, 180, 246; cutting room, 75; dailies, 58, 125–128, 246; for editing, 173, 195; logs and reports, 91, 105; media, 113–114, 249–250 See also logging
output, 98, 112, 351, 378; data, 130, 363; to tape, 48, 255, 260, 264–265, 352, 355, 362; and workflows, 68–69, 71
overlap, 144, 155, 162–164, 177, 258, 287; performing on digital system, 244–245

P2 card, 25, 46, 48, 211, 352 See also memory card
pacing, See rhythm
PAL, 36–37, 39
paper cut, 92, 105, 142, 173, 208, 266, 268, 307
parallel action, 177–179
PFX track, 320, 337
picture editor, See editor
playback, 31; music, 215, 304, 305, 325; in online, 363, 375; on set; 29, 215
point-of-view, See POV
post house, 17, 31, 35, 37, 62, 96–97, 266; choosing, 52; and color grading, 252, 253,

379–381; and DI, 398, 403; labeling and logging dailies, 102, 103, 105, 109; online, 112, 351, 359–363, 365, 369–378; post online, 355, 378, 383–384; and storage, 48, 98, 114; syncing, 18, 66; and telecine, 17, 44, 90; and titles and credits, 345, 347, 349, 350, 382; and VFX, 81, 82, 215, 235, 240–241; and workflows, 50, 66–75, 71–74, 83, 301, 305
postproduction, xxiii–xxiv, 4, 35, 195, 218, 249, 351, 360; schedule, 79–84, 137, 217, 270; shooting for, 5–14 See also editing, post house, and workflow
POV, xi, 8, 93, 150, 236, 286
pre-stripe, 31, 33, 95–98, 118, 265, 352
preproduction, xxiii, 4, 12, 180, 195, 207, 283, 306, 351
preview, 80, 82, 272, 278; prep, 72, 74, 81 See also screening
pre-mix, 80, 315, 331–334, 340; music, 310, 333
printmaster, 21, 73–74, 337, 340, 396, 402, 403, 408
Pro Tools, 46, 68, 289–290, 307, 313–314, 316, 325, 327 See also digital audio editing system See also DAW
production, xxiii, 4, 28, 194, 207, 219, 378, 381, 405; shooting right for postproduction, 5–14; and workflows, 301, 396
production track, 259, 291; and ADR, 320, 324, 336; and dialogue editing, 258, 284, 293, 319, 332; in sound and music editing, 300, 311–312
project, 4, 37, 113, 137, 143, 171, 267; checklist 26–27; and digital system, 36, 62, 99, 113–117, 125, 219, 247, 250; files, 263, 313, 363, 368–369; finishing, 351, 359, 379; formats, 22–25, 41; future, 405–406; and workflow, 65–66, 69, 74, 301
projection, 21, 74, 255, 337, 386, 388, 396–398, 402–404; 3-D, 181; 402; aspect ratio, 41
protection tape, 378, 408
pull-in frame, 132–134
pull list, 369, 377, 379, 389–391; and DI, 400, 403

rating (movies and TV shows), 275
reaction shot, 171, 187, 231; in action scene, 175, 179; cheating, 161; in comedy, 197–198, 204; impact, 159–160, 163–165
reality shows, 114, 173, 219–220
re-cutting, 81, 126, 144, 173, 188, 245, 255, 246, 260, 261, 263, 326; process, 211, 220, 226, 228, 267–271, 273
RED camera, 47, 66, 111–112, 353, 381, 399
release print, 73–74, 83, 394–396, 402
reports, 84–91
resolution, 40, 47, 53, 70, 101, 110, 120, 133, 399, 400, 402 See also downrez and uprez
resources, 418–424

rhythm and pacing, 6, 157–159, 187, 214, 287; in comedy, 197, 202; research, 169; of scenes, 173, 174, 176, 186, 194, 214; of shots, 7, 154

room tone, *See* ambience

rough cut, 144, 247, 252–253

safe action and title area, 148–149

SAN, 48, 69–70, 138, 371

saving, *See* backing up

scanning, and DI, 48, 237, 399, 400, 402; equipment, 44, 387, 398–399; interlace and progressive, 39–40, film, 18, 41, 43, 386; and workflows, 72–74, 403

schedule, postproduction, 79–84, 137, 217, 270; shooting, 5; VFX, 240

scoring session, 80, 82, 308–311

SD, 25, 27, 35, 49, 355, 384; aspect ratio, 41–42; color grading, 381, 401; and digital editing system, 113, 213, 225; frame size and scanning, 40; transcoding, 47–49; and workflow, 70, 403

screen credit, *See* credits

screen direction, 8, 150, 154–156

screening, 79, 91, 196, 220, 271, room, 17, 76, 263, 295; a cut, 54, 81, 266–269, dailies, 78, 138; on disk, 265; on film, 20, 265–266, prepping a cut for, 252–263; on tape, 263–265; and workflow, 67–69, 72, 74 *See also* preview

script, 4, 91, 261, 266; and DI, 400; and editing, 142, 144, 169, 173, 179, 184, 212–213, 219, 223, 261, 268, 283; and estimating cut footage, 114; import programs, 92, 118–119; and lined cut, 91, 200, 217, 218; and music and sound editing, 283, 285, 306; reports, 85–87; supervisor, 4, 5, 7, 77, 78, 84, 88; and VFX, 240

SECAM, 36–37, 39

sequence (digital), 48, 52, 55, 125; 3:2 pulldown, 109, 131–135; editing, 54, 129, 179, 188, 223–232; exporting, 36, 369; labeling, 224–225, 250, 369; organizing, 125–127; outputting, 98, 264–265, 352; saving, 245–246, 271; trimming, 241–244; *See also* cut

SFX, 116, 170, 173, 272, 293, 294, 332, 396; 3-D, 336; acquiring, 13, 256, 299–301, 424; and digital system, 225, 225, 231, 245, 247, 249, 257; editing, 315–317; prepping for screening, 255–256; and sound design, 282, 287–288, 295–298; tracks, 259, 320, 326; types, 297; *See also* mix

single system, 17–18, 24; and workflow, 66, 67

slate, 16, 25, 88, 200; shooting, 5–6, 14, 66; smart, 44, 123; tape master, 375; types, 44, 89, 123–124

sliding, 241–245, 270, 349, 376

slipping, 124, 241–245, 270, 316, 349, 376, 388

slug, 174, 189, 241, 253, 261; and online, 265, 352, 361, 376; news editing, 103

smart slate, 44, 123

SMPTE, 34–35, 254

sound, 13, 82, 170; dailies, 120, 123–124, 134–135; department, 285–286; and digital system, 46, 49–51, 53–55, 98, 110, 116–119, 123, 258, 312; Dolby, 397, 402, 408, 409; mismatches, 153, 155; recording, 5, 12–13, 16–18, 24, 36, 96–97; reports, 89–90, 108–109, 130; and screening, 247, 255–260; terms, 16, 17, 19, 20, 289–295; tools, 257, 259, 272, 314–315; wild, 13, 16, 89, 256, 257, 313; workflow, 66–74, 301, 358 *See also* audio, mix, syncing, telecine, and track

sound design, 82, 295–298; beats, 287–289; spotting, 295, 299; and story, 286–287

sound designer, 257, 282–283, 287, 299, 315; and mix, 334–336; and pre-mix, 331–332

sound editing, 315–324; acquiring sound for, 299–301; power of silence, 287–288; prep for, 311–314; resources, 423–424; *See also* ADR, dialogue editing, and Foley

sound editor, 12, 13, 16, 183, 281, 283, 287, 294, 316; and mix, 330, 332, 334; and picture editor, 115–116, 135, 272, 312–313, 326, 367, 375; and prep for mix, 289, 318, 326–329; and workflows, 67, 68, 71, 73, 301 *See also* SFX

sound effects, *See* SFX

sound mix, *See* mix

sound mixer, *See* mixer

soundtrack, 19, 69, 82, 168, 256, 284, 287; mixing final, 330–332, 336, 396 *See also* tracks

source tape, 18, 33, 376, 381, 403

split screen, 167–168, 170, 171, 206, 220, 344

split tracks, 318–319

spotting, 80, 82, 339; dialogue, 320, 323; music, 298–299, 307, 309; sound, 295–299

standard definition, *See* SD

stereo, 294, 328, 337

stock shot, 27, 105, 114, 249, 253, 278; and digital editing system, 76, 125, 247; and online, 378; and neg cut, 386, 389; slugging for, 241, 262; and storage, 114, 249

storage, 46, 50, 249, 356, 370, 384, 399; 3-D, 381; format, 250, 405; and ingest, 105, 110, 112–114, 133, 135 *See also* SAN

storyboard, 127, 137, 180, 204, 216, 240; animation, 194–196

streamer, 309, 322

surround sound, 51, 291, 336–337, 356, 397

sweetening, 19, 203, 294, 322, 408

sync, 17, 78, 138, 211, 254, 266; and ADR, 289, 322–324; and double system, 18, 36; equipment, 34, 53; film dailies, 20, 43, 44, 130; and Foley, 300, 317; maintaining during editing, 161, 184, 189, 231, 233–234, 241, 243, 255, 258, 388; methods, 122–124; and mix, 302, 333; multi-cam, 200–201, 211; non-sync audio, 13, 90, 255, 257, 292, 297, 323, 388; and playback, 29, 304; software programs, 92, 118; in sound editing, 290, 293, 297, 312, 316, 396; and workflows, 66–67, 69, 72–73

sync pop, 254–255, 312, 326–328, 361, 391

tape, 18, 23, 25, 27, 31, 35; blacking, 53, 95, 97, 98, 364; pre-striping, 31, 33, 95–98, 118, 265, 352; terms, 28–29

tape finish, 23–25, 27, 74, 80, 82, 83, 351, 352, 357; and workflows, 71, 301, 305

tapeless finish, See file finish

telecine, 17, 19, 39, 43–45, 51, 108, 112, 138, 372; 24p, 41, 135; and color grading, 379–380, 386; database, 51, 106, 108, 109, 118, 129, 266; and DI, 45, 397, 398; and film data, 119, 129–135, 388; in film workflow, 112, 394; letterboxing, 43; report, 90; reverse, 135; and syncing, 122, 130

television, See TV

temp mix, 256, 272, 300, 313; and music, 191, 301, 303, 305, 306; and workflows, 67–68, 71–73

time code, 23, 32–39, 43, 90, 95–96, 352; burnt in, 34, 43, 119; coding and measuring, 22, 97, 98; and dailies, 76, 89, 90, 103, 105, 117, 118, 120; in editing, 127, 224; in logging database, 106–107, 109, 127; and neg cut, 72, 109, 119, 129–130, 132–134, 266, 391; in online, 68, 377; and online prep, 361, 363–364, 366, 368, 369; and output to tape, 265, 312; and mix, 328, 333; signal standards, 35–37; SMPTE, 34–35; in sound and music editing, 68, 116, 135, 257, 296, 306, 314, 317, 321, 327, 338; syncing with, 44, 123, 200

titling, 80, 82, 313, 344–350, 402, 408; in offline, 55, 253, 265; at post house, 350, 360, 362, 372, 381–382; safe title area, 148–149; and workflows, 68, 69, 71, 73, 357, 403

track (audio), 116, 220, 289, 326, 367; analog, 395, 397; cleaning and prep for screening, 253–257, 260, 272–273; click, 286, 308; editing, 163, 201, 273; laugh, 203; laying out, 259, 361; music, 273, 286, 303, 308–310; on offline system, 54, 122–124, 225, 231–234, 241, 244, 246, 247; optical, 396–397; recording, 13, 90; scratch, 189, 195, 256; soundtrack, 19, 69, 82, 168, 256, 284, 287; wild, 13, 16, 89, 256, 257, 313 See also sound

track (video), 225, 229, 231–233, 241–242, 244, 253, 348; and VFX, 238–239, 245, 247

trailer, 205–206, 234, 384

transcode, 47, 69, 83

transcript, 91–92, 138, 208, 219, 266, 268; software programs, 92, 118–119

trimming, 52, 60, 233, 241–245, 249, 270

TV, 22, 26, 27, 250, 359, 378–380, 383; credits, 183, 344–346, 348–351, 382; final approval, 268, 274; format, 23; dailies, 102–104, 107, 108, 118; ratings, 275; schedules, 80–82, 270; standards, 36, 37, 39 See also aspect ratio, HD, and SD

TV editing, 15, 169, 175, 190, 202, 217, 247; cartoons, 194–196; continuity, 261, 262; reality, 114, 173, 219–220; soap opera, 218; sound, 283, 291, 294, 300, 321, 328, 332, 337; systems, 59–60; timings, 260, 376; and workflows, 65, 66, 68–70, 367–368, 405 See also MTV

union, 212, 252, 414–417, 421

uprez, 30, 48, 83; and workflow, 67, 68, 70–72

UPS, 53, 58, 76

user groups, 11, 61, 223, 248, 411, 413

varispeed, 168, 236, 258, 383

VFX, 4, 17, 32, 49, 54, 76, 105, 110, 114, 125, 247, 249, 253, 263; and 3-D, 336; creating, 49, 55, 57, 62, 80, 180, 195, 217, 226, 234, 235, 241, 245; editor, 48, 77, 180, 240; and DI, 83, 399, 402, 403; files, 313, 368; and online, 352, 360, 362, 370, 372, 376, 377, 381, 382; rendering, 54, 55; and workflow, 4, 67–71 See also green screen and split screen

visual effects. See VFX

VO, See narration

volume, See level

walla, 321, 323

wild line, 90, 256, 284, 297, 313, 321, 323

wild track, 13, 16, 89, 256, 257, 313

workflow, 4, 61, 65–66, 194, 207, 368, 405; on digital editing system, 49–50; DI, 400–403; disk, 358; file (tapeless), 61, 69–71, 102, 111–112, 117, 354; film, 72–74, 112; music, 305; neg cut, 394–395; sound, 301, 395; tape, 66–69, 111

work print, 20, 22, 90

XML, 350, 360, 363, 369, 377; and DI, 400, 403

YouTube, xvii, 32, 70, 112, 168, 197, 357, 472

# About the Author

It all started in a small drive-in theater in Santa Rosa, California, to paraphrase anchor Ted Baxter from *The Mary Tyler Moore Show*. The author got a job as a cashier at Star Vue Motor Movies but was more interested in the projection booth. There she learned base and emulsion, cement and tape splicing, and other 35mm fundamentals. Eventually her union brothers and the town's theater managers were persuaded to let her in the union. This meant she got to run *Rocky, Star Wars,* and *Saturday Night Fever* for months and take location assignments doing grip, electrician, and craft service work. Much film through projectors and two BAs later, she headed for Hollywood and began slipping through studio gates.

Her first job was as an assistant at a small sound recording studio where she transferred 500 tiger growls from ¼" to 35mm on her starting day. It was a good place to meet editors and led to her first assistant editor job in what she dubbed the "syncing pool" on the television show *That's Incredible.* (She's still friends with several other pool members, some of whom helped on this book.) From there it was a whirlwind of jobs and trips to the unemployment office.

Gael Chandler has edited comedies, dramas, documentaries, features, corporate videos, and promos and cut on every type of medium: film, tape, and digital. Nominated twice for a CableACE award for editing a comedy series, she is a member of the Editors Peer Group of the Television Academy of Arts and Sciences and annually judges the Emmy and College TV awards.

She has taught editing at Loyola Marymount University and California State universities at Los Angeles, Long Beach, and Northridge and trained hundreds of professionals, professors, independent filmmakers, and students to operate digital editing equipment.

The author's second book, *Film Editing: Great Cuts Every Filmmaker and Movie Lover Must Know,* which debuted in October 2009, illuminates the types of cuts editors make and how these cuts advance the story and affect the audience. She blogs regularly on a bevy of editing subjects at her website www.joyoffilmediting.com, which won *MovieMaker* magazine's "Best 50 Filmmaker Blogs" award. She has also written a handful of feature screenplays, one of which is optioned and another of which won the Scriptwriters Networks' Producers Outreach Program contest and may yet be coming to a theater near you. The writing has made her a better editor and vice versa.

Chandler has walked the halls of Hollywood, both dark and cluttered with film reels and bright and glittering with Emmys, Clios, and Oscars. She is dedicated to passing on her experience to all who seek to open cutting room doors or understand editing. She continues to live and thrive now back in northern California.

You can contact her at:

www.joyoffilmediting.com or at info@joyoffilmediting.com

GREAT CUTS EVERY FILMMAKER AND MOVIE LOVER MUST KNOW

# FILM EDITING
## GREAT CUTS EVERY FILMMAKER AND MOVIE LOVER MUST KNOW

### GAEL CHANDLER

*Film Editing: Great Cuts Every Filmmaker and Movie Lover Must Know* makes the invisible art of editing visible by using nearly 600 frames from popular, recent films. The frames, accompanied by brisk descriptions, make it perfectly suited for quick study readers who like to 'gaze' rather than 'graze' and don't want to read a book. Written by an editor and the author of *Cut by Cut: Editing Your Film or Video*, it shows how editors can make or break a movie.

This one-of-a-kind book is your 'must have' cheat sheet to learning to make great cuts. Great for filmmakers, students or anyone who wants to see how the editor makes us believe. YouTubers, prepare yourselves to add juice to your creations.

"*Those of us in the movie business often say that if we notice something, that means we didn't do a good job. Our job as filmmakers, is to do what we do as seamlessly as possible. Gael Chandler takes a microscope to those seams to show the subtleties and techniques used by seasoned professionals, using words and pictures that an average movie-goer or up-and-coming filmmaker can appreciate and experiment with. This dissection, together with quotes of working directors and editors, make* Film Editing *a practical and aesthetic addition to any film buff, film student, or filmmaker's arsenal.* "

> — Victoria Rose Sampson, writer, director, film and sound editor; MPSE Award for Best Sound Editing: *Pirates of the Caribbean: Curse of the Black Pearl*, *Speed*, *Romancing the Stone*, *The River;* Grand prize winner for writing and directing, Harley-Davidson commercial contest short film, *Her Need for Speed*

"*A comprehensive and easy-to-read description of the techniques editors use to seamlessly tell stories. The use of film frames clearly illustrates the editing concepts. A must-read for any film student, or anyone just interested in the art of editing.*"

> — Nancy Morrison, A.C.E., editor, *Desperate Housewives*, *Starter Wife*, *Malcolm in the Middle*

GAEL CHANDLER has edited comedies, dramas, documentaries, features, corporate videos, and promos and cut on every type of medium: film, tape, and digital. Nominated twice for a Cable ACE award for editing a comedy series, she is a member of the Editors Peer Group of the Television Academy of Arts and Sciences and annually judges the Emmy and College TV awards.

**$34.95 · 208 PAGES · ORDER NUMBER 129RLS · ISBN: 9781932907629**